ADVERTISING
CAMPAIGN STRATEGY

A Guide to Marketing Communication Plans

A D V E R T I S I N G
CAMPAIGN STRATEGY

A Guide to Marketing Communication Plans

Donald Parente
Middle Tennessee State University

Bruce Vanden Bergh
Michigan State University

Arnold Barban
University of Alabama

James Marra
Temple University

The Dryden Press
Harcourt Brace College Publishers

Fort Worth   Philadelphia   San Diego   New York   Orlando   Austin   San Antonio
Toronto   Montreal   London   Sydney   Tokyo

Acquisitions Editor	Jim Lizotte
Associate Editor	R. Paul Stewart
Project Editor	Sandy Walton
Production Manager	Carlyn Hauser
Art Director	Jeanette Barber
Arts & Literary Rights Editor	Elizabeth Banks/Cindy Robinson
Electronic Publishing Coordinator	Ellie Moore

Copy Editor	Janet Willen
Proofreader	Kay Kaylor
Indexer	Sonsie Conroy
Text Type	10/12 Trump Mediaeval

Address for Editorial Correspondence
The Dryden Press, 301 Commerce Street, Suite 3700, Fort Worth, TX 76102

Address for Orders
The Dryden Press, 6277 Sea Harbor Drive, Orlando, FL 32887
1-800-782-4479, or 1-800-433-0001 (in Florida)

ISBN: 0-03-012898-6

Library of Congress Catalog Number: 95-68010

Printed in the United States of America

5 6 7 8 9 0 1 2 3 4   016   9 8 7 6 5 4 3 2 1

The Dryden Press
Harcourt Brace College Publishers

THE DRYDEN PRESS SERIES IN MARKETING

Avila, Williams, Ingram,
and LaForge
The Professional Selling Workbook

Bateson
*Managing Services Marketing:
Text and Readings*
Third Edition

Blackwell, Blackwell, and Talarzyk
*Contemporary Cases in
Consumer Behavior*
Fourth Edition

Boone and Kurtz
Contemporary Marketing^{Plus}
Eighth Edition

Churchill
Basic Marketing Research
Third Edition

Churchill
*Marketing Research:
Methodological Foundations*
Sixth Edition

Czinkota and Ronkainen
Global Marketing

Czinkota and Ronkainen
International Marketing
Fourth Edition

Czinkota and Ronkainen
*International Marketing Strategy:
Environmental Assessment and
Entry Strategies*

Dickson
Marketing Management

Engel, Blackwell, and Miniard
Consumer Behavior
Eighth Edition

Futrell
Sales Management
Fourth Edition

Grover
*Theory & Simulation of Market-
Focused Management*

Ghosh
Retail Management
Second Edition

Hassan and Blackwell
*Global Marketing: Managerial
Dimensions and Cases*

Hutt and Speh
*Business Marketing Management:
A Strategic View of Industrial and
Organizational Markets*
Fifth Edition

Ingram and LaForge
*Sales Management: Analysis and
Decision Making*
Second Edition

Lewison
*Marketing Management:
An Overview*

Lindgren and Shimp
*Marketing: An Interactive
Learning System*

Krugman, Reid, Dunn, and Barban
*Advertising: Its Role in
Modern Marketing*
Eighth Edition

Oberhaus, Ratliffe, and Stauble
*Professional Selling:
A Relationship Process*
Second Edition

Parente, Vanden Bergh, Barban,
and Marra
*Advertising Campaign Strategy:
A Guide to Marketing
Communication Plans*

Rachman
Marketing Today
Third Edition

Rosenbloom
Marketing Channels:
A Management View
Fifth Edition

Schaffer
Applying Marketing Principles
Software

Schellinck and Maddox
Marketing Research:
A Computer-Assisted Approach

Schnaars
MICROSIM
Marketing simulation available for
IBM PC and Apple

Schuster and Copeland
Global Negotiations: Planning for
Sales and Negotiations

Shimp
Promotion Management and
Marketing Communications
Third Edition

Talarzyk
Cases and Exercises in Marketing

Terpstra and Sarathy
International Marketing
Sixth Edition

Weitz and Wensley
Readings in Strategic Marketing
Analysis, Planning, and
Implementation

Zikmund
Exploring Marketing Research
Fifth Edition

Harcourt Brace College
Outline Series

Peterson
Principles of Marketing

Preface

These are challenging times in the field of advertising. Change is everywhere. Along with change comes opportunity. Students can capitalize on these opportunities, but they need to understand the new marketing environment, as well as be prepared to adapt to new situations with progressive changes. This book is designed as a resource manual on how to prepare a marketing communication campaign. We hope that it will be a valuable addition to the library of every marketing and advertising student.

Today, manufacturers and retailers alike are changing and expanding the way they use and view advertising. Many of these changes are the result of new ideas and technology, such as relationship marketing and interactive media. Much of these changes, however, reflect the significantly increased emphasis placed on concepts that have been around for many years. It has always been unwise to plan an advertising campaign separate from the other promotional elements in a marketing mix. Nonetheless, some companies in the past did just that.

Today, smart companies start with the premise that they are planning a marketing communication campaign—not an advertising campaign. This assumption not only helps companies avoid any overreliance on advertising, it also helps them proactively consider other promotional options as part of a unified selling strategy. Far too often, communication tools, such as sales promotion, direct marketing, and public relations, are merely combined with an advertising program rather than integrated together to produce a seamless selling effort.

A lot of emphasis in this book was directed toward strategy, because it encourages planners to consider the interrelationships among the various elements in a campaign. These relationships are what make a campaign more effective than a collection or a series of ads and promotions. After using this book, which is a comprehensive approach to campaign strategy, students should be able to think through the strategy, develop it, and, finally, implement it.

The concept of strategy implies a plan that is undertaken for a competitive advantage. Certainly, many of the students who use this book will feel very competitive about the campaigns they produce, and that is how it should be. Today's business world can be brutally competitive. To help students compete, we provide extensive coverage of analytical tools, including various tests and procedures to develop and evaluate the campaign. In addition, this book contains in-depth coverage on setting objectives as a prerequisite condition to developing strategy. We devote a full chapter to the core elements of marketing communication strategy. As a result, particular types of strategy, such as relationship marketing, are derivatives of a core strategic element, such as managing brand equity. With a solid understanding of the key elements that make up a strategy, students can stretch their imagination to develop unique strategies and tactics that are, as is sometimes said in the business, "on target and on strategy."

In the second half of the book, we detail how to execute the overall strategy with message, media, and related marketing communications strategies. The final two chapters cover, in detail, the various aspects of presenting the strategy and executions to the client.

Our challenge as educators is to provide conceptual information in a form that is both useable and practical. To accomplish this task, we included numerous examples of the tests, techniques, principles,and procedures that are used in marketing communication, as well as a number of checklists and tips appropriate for a specific area. We recognize there are many ways to achieve a desired end. We know that as situations change, it may be appropriate to also change the approach or the organization. For example, in the chapter on creative strategy, we present eight different approaches for developing a creative plan.

HIGHLIGHTS OF *ADVERTISING CAMPAIGN STRATEGY*

Chapter 1

This chapter introduces the reader to the purpose and scope of the book. After some discussion of the new marketing environment, we present some of the core concepts that should be part of the mindset of students as they prepare for the campaign, including market segmentation, the marketing concept, the communication concept, integrated marketing communications, and a campaign concept. We also present the essential elements in a strategic plan and explain how they relate to a marketing communication campaign. To close the chapter, we present a general outline for the campaign.

Chapters 2 and 3

These chapters cover what many people refer to as the situation analysis. Chapter 2 begins with a discussion of how to get ready for the campaign. This chapter focuses on analyzing the company and the consumer. It includes a comprehensive discussion on sources of information, including their availability in a typical university library; an extensive discussion of syndicated research sources; and a broad coverage of the tests and techniques that can be used to complete the analyses. Chapter 3 essentially is a continuation of Chapter 2 but focuses on the market, product, and competitive analyses. Both

Chapters 2 and 3 provide the principles and tools to make a thorough situation analysis.

Chapter 4

This chapter is basically about setting objectives. We emphasize that setting objectives should evolve logically out of the research foundation. Critical to our discussion of objectives is the importance of brand equity, which we also discuss in greater detail in the next chapter. To lay a foundation for setting objectives, we discuss the nature of problems and opportunities, and how to uncover them. Most of this chapter focuses on setting objectives, including the decision on how to segment the market. To discuss objectives, we follow the principles associated with the management-by-objectives (MBO) philosophy.

Chapter 5

This chapter focuses on the development of marketing communication strategy. We look at four interrelated elements: the management of brand equity, the marketing communication expenditure, the positioning of messages, and the targeting and delivery of messages. We devote most of this chapter to an extensive discussion of brand equity. We cover the communication expenditure only briefly, taking the position that this variable is not something students usually can change. We rely on the next three chapters to cover the positioning and targeting aspects of strategy in greater detail.

Chapter 6

This chapter focuses on the creation of the message, emphasizing the importance of developing the creative plan out of the research foundation. We present eight examples of different approaches to doing a creative plan, including the elements that are similar in each plan. We discuss the creative process in depth, including how to generate ideas, followed by a discussion of the principles that are frequently important parts of a creative plan.

Chapter 7

This chapter covers media strategy and planning. Like previous chapters, it emphasizes the importance of planning media within the context of the research foundation and the marketing background. We cover the importance of setting the media objectives considering key concepts, such as reach, frequency, continuity, gross impressions, and gross rating points. The second half of the chapter amply discusses the value of matching the various kinds of audience profiles with media choices. This chapter closes with a discussion of establishing the media mix, including a discussion of tactical executions, the importance of weighting, and contingencies.

Chapter 8

From an organizational point of view, we considered merging this chapter with the previous one on media, calling it integrated marketing communications. It obviously would have been too long, so we separated advertising media from other types of marketing communication using Chapter 8 to cover sales promotion, public relations, and direct marketing. We know that most advertising students do not get in-depth exposure to these areas, especially sales promotion and direct marketing, so we provided an extensive discussion of the techniques and tools common to the trade.

Chapter 9

Evaluating the effectiveness of the campaign is the focus of this chapter. We present a comprehensive view of the many tests and techniques that are used to measure a campaign's effectiveness, briefly covering many of the commercial research companies that are involved in this type of testing. Unlike many of the chapters in other books on this topic, this chapter is organized correspondent to when the need for a particular type of research would arise in a campaign. First, we discuss concept testing, then move to in-depth discussions of copy testing, concurrent testing, and posttesting. This chapter was written with the assistance of Michael P. Kalasunas, Director of Research and Planning, J. Walter Thompson.

Chapter 10

This chapter covers the task of putting a plans book together, largely focusing on interpreting and presenting the material covered in the previous chapters. For additional insight, we use many of the ideas and advice of various educators around the country who either teach an advertising campaigns' course or work with the AAF competition.

Chapter 11

This chapter focuses on putting together the presentation. This presentation is a comprehensive approach to the most taxing of areas. We are especially appreciative of having Tom Duncan and Sandra Moriarity's outstanding book *How to Create and Deliver Winning Advertising Presentations* as a model. This chapter also includes an extensive discussion of the special problems associated with the National Student Advertising Competition sponsored by the AAF. For this last section, we borrowed heavily from the advice of AAF competition veterans.

The Dryden Press will provide complimentary supplements or supplement packages to those adopters qualified under our adoption policy. Please contact your sales representative to learn how you may qualify. If as an adopter or potential user you receive supplements you do not need, please return them to your sales representative or send them to:

Attn: Returns Department
Troy Warehouse
465 South Lincoln Drive
Troy, MO 63379

ACKNOWLEDGMENTS

This book is the result of the collective efforts of many people, including our family and colleagues. We would especially like to acknowledge the warm and friendly people at The Dryden Press: Lyn Hastert Maize, the acquisition editor who signed this book—now, editorial director; Paul Stewart, the development editor, whose warm, reassuring voice provided positive motivating reinforcement; Janet Willen, the copy editor who often helped redirect, if not challenge our thinking; Jeanette Barber, Carlyn Hauser, Ellie Moore, and Sandy Walton, members of the production team, who helped keep this project on track; and Lisé Johnson, our product manager, who helped direct our marketing effort.

We would also like to acknowledge Michael Robinson, the director of research at Tatham Euro RSCG, for his help with providing ideas and descriptions of research techniques in Chapter 2. We also owe special thanks to Michael P. Kalasunas, the director of research at J. Walter Thompson in Chicago. He provided many ideas for Chapters 2 and 3, while reviewing and writing part of Chapter 9.

We would also like to thank the many educators who provided us with advice, often sharing with us their own particular approach to doing a campaign. Leonard Reid, University of Georgia, thoroughly reviewed Chapters 2 and 3, while providing numerous suggestions for improvement. Edd Applegate, Middle Tennessee State University, read parts of several chapters and offered much valuable insight. Sharon Parente provided important professional assistance in the section on using the library. A number of faculty shared with us their views on how to write a plans book: Louise Gainey, University of Miami; Roger Lavery, University of Oregon; Howard Cogan, Ithaca College; Tommy Smith, University of Southern Mississippi; Carolyn Stringer, Western Kentucky University; and Jim Gilmore, Michigan State University.

Thanks also to Howard Cogan, Ithaca College; John Murphy, University of Texas; Jim Terhune, University of Florida; and Jon Wardrip, University of South Carolina, for their help and insight on preparing a presentation for the AAF advertising competition.

We also received a great deal of assistance from the following practitioners:

Jack Phifer	Leo Burnett Co.
Carol Fletcher	Leo Burnett Co.
Rishad Tobaccowala	Leo Burnett Co.
Josh McQueen	Leo Burnett Co.
Lisa Lager	Leo Burnett Co.
Bill Hull	Hull Marketing Research
Karen Randolph	Foote Cone Belding
Mike Horn	DDB Needham
Susan Sedler	Sunow
Ralph Blessing	Helene Curtis
Roy Bergold	McDonald's Corporation
Elizabeth MacAdams	McDonald's Corporation
John Blair	Quaker Oats
Barb Marusarz	Quaker Oats
Scott Hughes	Quaker Oats
Ted Duff	Nielsen Media Research
Dan Sarullo	Nielsen North America

Meredeth Spector	Nielsen North America
Dan Evarrs	Burke Marketing Research
Lou Schultz	Lintas Marketing Communications

SPECIAL ACKNOWLEDGMENTS TO THE COAUTHORS

I began this book over 10 years ago, but discontinued it mainly because of the difficulty in convincing a publisher of the adequacy of the book's market potential. I am indebted to Arnold Barban for his help and encouragement in getting me to proceed with this project. In addition to writing part of this book, he was especially helpful with ideas, having a strong sense of the way things ought to be organized.

My other coauthors also deserve special thanks for their contributions over and above that to which they are entitled because of the chapters they have written. Bruce Vanden Bergh was especially helpful as he voluntarily assumed the role of account planner on this project, providing ideas, information, inspiration, and feedback. Our thinking was always especially close. As former classmates, we remain amazed at how accurate and conceptually sound our advertising professors were, even though over 20 years has passed since we first heard their words. The teachings of Nugent Wedding, S. Watson Dunne, and Arnold Barban echo throughout this book. We remain grateful.

Jim Marra, our creative specialist, was especially helpful in providing a perspective different from that of the other authors. He often challenged the way we were proceeding, and the book, especially my material, is better because of his input.

Don Parente

Brief Contents

Contents

Advertising from a Marketing Communications Perspective

The communication revolution is here. The field of advertising is in a state of flux as new technology and new media all promise to change the way people conduct business. Corporations that tightened their belts through layoffs and other staff reductions in the early part of this decade later decided that their smaller operations were the right size. As they reexamined, restructured, and reengineered the way they do business, companies learned to operate leaner, and some would say, meaner. But the people in the forefront of this new era understand that the changes are more a function of new attitudes and new ways to look at advertising than a result of new hardware, emerging technology, or new media. Yet for many people in advertising, the business and its purpose are fundamentally the same as they were a decade ago. This book strives not only to provide a transition between new and older ways of thinking but also to indicate where a traditional approach is still valid.

Over the years, advertising practitioners have referred to advertising as a problem-solving business. Typically, the problem involves selling a product, but it can also encompass a service or an idea. Very often these problems are solved through an advertising campaign. In the mid-1990s, advertisers have become increasingly aware that they have a whole range of promotional tools from which they can choose, anything from advertising and public relations to sales promotion, infomercials, and event marketing. The authors have titled this book *Advertising Campaign Strategy* more out of a sense of tradition than as a reflection of the view that advertising can or should be prepared apart from other types of marketing communication.

Advertising is a business. Practitioners are keenly aware of this fact; their customers, clients, and business associates seldom let them forget it. Intellectually, students and people starting out in advertising are aware that advertising is a business, but their lack of work experience sometimes causes them to lose sight of this fact. Some may even think of advertising as an art— a kind of applied art. Professionals understand that there is an art to using advertising creatively, but it is still a business, an important tool of marketing. It is one of the activities that facilitate the exchange of goods between the producer and consumer, or user. This book, and particularly this chapter, looks at how advertising interrelates with other aspects of marketing, including other elements in a promotion or communications mix. The challenge to the student of advertising is to reconcile the differences between any new advertising practices or thinking and the principles and procedures that have proven effective over a period of years.

THE NEW MARKETING ENVIRONMENT

One of the better ways to use advertising to solve problems is to understand the relationship of advertising to other activities in a marketing program. As many authors have noted, to sell a product effectively, it must be the *right product*, at the *right price*, at the *right place*, and with the *right promotion*. Each element must harmonize with each other one. To be effective in the 21st century, a marketer must continually reevaluate the concept of rightness to ensure that the marketing mix is sensitive to a continuously and rapidly changing marketplace.

THE RIGHT PRODUCT

Coming up with the right product has become increasingly more complicated in recent years. At a time when different product and size introductions are on the rise, retailers are trying streamline operations to get a better grasp on the profitability of everything they sell to improve the bottom line. Scanner data systems allow managers to assess the movement of every product variation, or stock keeping unit (SKU), in a store. But getting the right product to the store requires an understanding of how consumers and the marketplace are changing.

Traditionally, marketing-oriented companies either asked consumers what they wanted or made an inference from their behavior. Today, when researchers ask consumers what they want, consumers often don't know. Products in many generic categories have become sufficiently advanced or sophisticated that they do at least a fair job of satisfying consumers' needs or wants. Because it is often easier for consumers to focus on what they feel they lack rather than on what they want, researchers usually get more information if they ask consumers about their gripes or complaints. So researchers are focusing less on consumers' needs and wants and more on their problems.

As consumers are getting more sophisticated, they seem to be making more decisions on the basis of microissues. Ten or fifteen years ago, car manufacturers seemed ambivalent about where consumers set cups, glasses, or cans in an automobile. Today this feature often receives prominent attention in automobile ads, whether the car is inexpensive or pricey. To get a better fix on the right product, researchers and developers focus hard on consumers' problems, no matter how small or seemingly insignificant. Many consumers do not even perceive they have a problem. When this happens, researchers often find it fruitful to shift the focus to consumers' interests. Failure to uncover interests worth promoting usually leads advertisers to build psychological value into a product. They usually develop this value by building a brand image or personality for the product, although increasingly advertisers seem willing to promote their products simply by trying to get consumers to *like* their advertising.

THE RIGHT PRICE

Increasingly, the right price seems to mean the right lower price. The success of Wal-Mart, Home Depot, Toys "R" Us, and other mass-merchandise retailers continues to exert downward pressure on prices as value-conscious consumers patronize low-price retailers in ever-increasing numbers. Brand-name manufacturers are no longer able to dictate to retailers suggested retail prices. For example, Eastman Kodak suggested a "minimum advertised price" (MAP) on its premium-priced Royal Gold film and backed it with dealer rebates for all vendors who held the line on the MAP. The idea was to build a generous margin into the price of each roll of film and thus encourage retailers to do more in-store promotions of Kodak film. However, Wal-Mart disregarded the MAP, gave up the dealer rebate, and priced the product lower than the suggested retail price.[1]

Philip Morris, the consumer products giant, tacitly acknowledged in the spring of 1993 that the consumer trend toward craving lower prices was here to stay. On what some observers refer to as Marlboro Friday, Philip Morris put a 40-cent-per-pack price cut on its full-price brands of cigarettes. The response on Wall Street was a drop in the share prices of many consumer product companies, from Procter & Gamble and Sara Lee to Coca-Cola and General Mills. Traders seemed to be saying that if Philip Morris could not maintain its price margins with Marlboro, perhaps the number-one brand in the world, then other consumer product companies would also be vulnerable.

THE RIGHT PLACE

A revolution in the marketplace has also affected the way marketers view the strategies of place—the right place. An aggressively competitive marketplace has led many companies to get the product to the consumer in ways that would not have been considered in earlier times. McDonald's, long a staunch advocate of the freestanding store, has been experimenting with placing restaurants in gas stations, convenience stores, and other nontraditional locations. Consumer product companies are also steadily losing control over key decisions within the channel of distribution to the giant retailers. Wal-Mart is legendary for exacting stringent requirements on its suppliers regarding inventory control and shelf facings.

Many companies are also opting to market their products directly to consumers. With the increasing ease and widespread use of computers in business, many companies are amassing sizable databases that enable them to target narrowly defined consumers with a minimum of waste.

Although the Sears general merchandise catalog is dead, the success of specialty merchandise catalogers, such as Lands' End, L. L. Bean, and Victoria's Secret, suggests there will be even more material in the mailboxes of the future. Now that the success of home shopping networks is well established, the prospect of the information superhighway, 500 channels, and interactive shopping promises to ensure that changes in the distribution system will continue in a dramatic fashion.

THE RIGHT PROMOTION

Coming up with the *right promotion* in the new marketing environment is likely to pose many more questions than we can now answer. The marketplace is changing so quickly that by the time this book is published there will likely be new questions and new answers. Some industry analysts attribute the changes in the advertising business to the splintering of the mass media into narrower interest segments. On the surface, much of this effect is the result of developments in the creation of new databases, the growing use of ZIP Code target marketing, and the analysis of product movement using special scanners in retail stores. Simultaneously, there is a proliferating array of new media delivery options. The dizzying activity taking place within the media appears to be driving many of the changes in advertising.

A different viewpoint is that the changes in the advertising business are more a reflection of a powerful but natural evolution of the marketplace as it becomes increasingly sophisticated. Building brand equity has become more difficult as products in many generic categories approach parity and consumers change their priorities about the importance of various products in their lives. Companies cope with this difficulty in numerous ways. To reach narrower consumer segments, advertisers experiment with new media delivery systems. But the motivation to use these options may be more a function of the need to fine-tune the message to the specific needs or wants of the consumer than it is to reach the target efficiently. For example, some of the ZIP Code marketing systems, such as PRIZM and ClusterPLUS, allow a marketer to zero in on the geographic location of its prime prospects with a minimum of waste, but they also enable an advertiser to custom tailor the message to the target market's values and lifestyles.

A countervailing force in the marketplace may be occurring as advertisers size up the differentiating characteristics of their products and conclude that there may not be enough opportunity to promote the product on the basis of benefits. Increasingly, consumers perceive that there are no significant differences among products in many categories, and, because of active or hectic lifestyles, it might not matter much if there were. As a result, advertisers often opt for an entertainment approach that focuses on image, attitude—or simply entertainment.

In late 1992, Coca-Cola jarred the advertising business by announcing that it would use the Hollywood-based Creative Artists Agency (CAA) to create the bulk of its television commercials. This news left its long-time advertising agency, McCann-Erickson, unclear about its future role. Michael Ovitz, chairman of CAA and one of the most powerful people in the field of entertainment, had easy access to some of the more renowned directors in Hollywood, and many in the advertising community wondered if Coca-Cola would set an example for other major advertisers to focus more on entertainment and less on selling its product. CAA created numerous spots often without copy, jingle, or any unifying theme other than the tagline "Always Coca-Cola."

Advertising Age commissioned two separate studies to gauge the effectiveness of the campaign. The first study[2] attempted to measure "likeability" and the second one, "persuasibility."[3] Not surprisingly, the campaign scored high on likeability, especially a computer-generated spot featuring polar bears, and ranked below average on persuasibility. Was this an effective campaign? It's hard to measure. Large consumer-goods companies like Coca-Cola are able to contact consumers with various messages or imagery at numerous times through traditional media advertising as well as through packaging and signage. Because of this continual contact, it is extremely difficult to isolate and measure the true effects of the campaign on sales. One could, however, argue the campaign's effectiveness based on whether likeability is a more- or less-important goal than persuasibility. An assessment of the campaign's effectiveness then might well depend on a number of factors other than the survey results: the relative importance of likeability versus persuasibility, whether persuasibility is any better at generating sales than likeability, and, finally, whether one can measure sensitively the difference between the two concepts. Because of the prominence of Coca-Cola's advertising in the media and the attention it has received in the trade press, this campaign sent mixed signals to advertising practitioners and educators.

One position, which might be called the David Ogilvy school of advertising after the legendary advertising great, is that there are factors that make some campaigns succeed and others fail. Advertising educators often favor this approach because it acknowledges that there are a lot of principles and guidelines to sound advertising. Another approach to advertising is loosely associated with the West Coast. It features a lot of unconventional, highly creative approaches and techniques, often dramatizing a relationship between people and the product. Success with this approach is more a function of talent or inherent creativity than with what one might read about advertising techniques in a book.

There have been many successful examples of both approaches throughout the history of advertising. The big question today has to do with whether advertising needs to be more entertaining, creative, and different to break through a seemingly ever-increasing number of multimedia messages, or whether the principles and techniques that have evolved over the years are still effective. To answer some of these questions, it might be helpful to examine some of the principles that are in wide practice.

THE MARKETING CONCEPT

After World War II, many firms adopted what became widely known as the **marketing concept.** Basically, this is a philosophy of how to do business. The marketing concept provides decision makers with a framework for the planning and development of strategies for the right product, price, place, and promotion. Of all the principles associated with this philosophy, **consumer orientation** is the most important. Implementing this principle can range from a simple orientation to a focus on catering to the needs, wants, and problems of specific market segments, or it can mean organizing the entire marketing effort to appeal to a single market segment, or niche.

CONSUMER ORIENTATION

Consumer orientation emphasizes the importance of planning all marketing activities to satisfy the needs, wants, and problems of consumers. The notion that planning should start with the consumer evolved as the marketplace began to change after World War II. Before the war, firms in the United States were production oriented. The population was rapidly expanding, and the Great Depression had left many Americans hungry for products. The demand for goods exceeded the supply, and the main concerns of business were to produce products quickly, efficiently, and inexpensively. Because of the burgeoning consumer demand, products generally sold well. During the war, much of industry shifted from the production of consumer goods to wartime materiel, artificially suppressing consumer demand. Nevertheless, because of the tremendous demands of war, industry expanded considerably along with increases in technology. Following the war, American firms realized that they had the capacity and the technology to produce more than consumers would demand. The result was rugged, aggressive marketing competition.

The firms that competed best were those that catered to the specific needs and wants of consumers. Production became less important to a firm as product development increased in importance. At first, the idea was simply to give consumers what they wanted rather than what the engineers, designers, chemists, or chefs had in mind when they developed a product. This new orientation produced results, but it became apparent that a firm could not quite satisfy all potential consumers with one or two products—nor did it have to in order to make a profit. Product diversification increased as firms vied with one another to satisfy the growing sophistication of the consumers' needs and wants.

MARKET SEGMENTATION

Increasingly through the 1970s, many firms realized that in order to satisfy the growing sophistication of consumers' needs and wants, they had to compete through product diversification. Market segmentation, aimed at specific segments of the overall market, became widespread as firms developed, priced, distributed, and promoted a heterogeneous variety of products to heterogeneous groups of consumers (that is, groups that differ from one another on the basis of some common characteristic such as age, income, or ethnicity). This segmentation happened in many industries, such as shampoo, cigarettes, beer, coffee, and, at a much later date, automobiles. Firms realized they would be more competitive by dividing up the overall market for the generic product into smaller markets, or segments, often targeting each segment with its own separate brand. Each of these markets represented relatively homogeneous groups whose members were similar on the basis of a characteristic, like age, income, or lifestyle, and often also had the same selective tastes and preferences. Leckenby and Wedding, experts in the field of advertising management, have noted that companies appeal to these segments by developing or modifying products to harmonize more satisfactorily with these special tastes. The combination of increased brand competition, the increasing risks associated with new product introductions, the pressures of more complex market segmentation, and increasingly involved channels of distribution caused these firms to reevaluate their marketing philosophy.[4]

Other firms understood that segmenting the market was not simply a better way to compete, it was the *only* way they could compete. Increasingly, companies began to target smaller and narrower segments of the broad market, often by creating a database consisting of current and prospective customers. Direct marketing techniques could then be used efficiently and effectively to reach a fairly narrow target audience.

At the retail level, stores have for many years offered a fairly narrow product line, especially clothing stores such as For Petites Only, 7–8–9, and Lane Bryant, which cater to a certain-size woman. In the 1980s and the 1990s, this kind of segmented selling would be increasingly referred to as **niche** marketing.

NICHE MARKETING

Niche marketing usually means more than merely segmenting the market. Niche marketers typically offer *only* products within a narrow range, but within that range they will offer a fairly deep selection. Sometimes they will compete against a more broadly based company, such as a department store, on the basis of quality, as Victoria's Secret does, and other times they will compete on the basis of price, as Office Depot does.

Many of the new breed of retailers, such as Toys "R" Us, are able to compete on the basis of price, quality, and selection. As a broad-based retailer, Interstate Department Stores nearly went bankrupt. When it decided to focus its concentration on the toys business with which it had been successful, it changed its name to Toys "R" Us and became a multibillion dollar company. These **category killers,** as they are sometimes called, are enjoying spectacular growth and will likely branch out into other areas in the future.

Bed Bath & Beyond is a relatively new specialty retailer offering domestic goods such as housewares and linens in the home furnishings market. The stores are all superstores, with each retail outlet averaging more than 35,000 square feet. Department stores and small retailers like Linens N'Things and the Pottery Barn are its main competition. Its products are a cut above those of mass merchandisers like Wal-Mart and Kmart in terms of selection and the look of the store, but they are usually cheaper in price than those of a department store. By focusing on "Everyday Low Prices" (EDLP), the company has enjoyed tremendous success, nearly doubling its sales between 1992 and 1994.[5]

FIGURE 1–1   THE MARKETING CONCEPT ERA

1950s	1960s	1970s	1980s	1990s
Consumer Orientation		Market Segmentation		Niche Marketing

Figure 1–1 provides a rough approximation of the development of the marketing concept over the last 50 years. There are, of course, wide differences in the way companies within an industry apply the marketing concept, and, similarly, there are great differences among industries. For example, the cigarette industry applied the principles of market segmentation much earlier than the beer industry. It seems inevitable that companies in general will be forced by market pressures to apply marketing concept principles, but it does not mean they will end up as niche marketers. In fact, the opposite may be the case. As niche marketers become more successful, they will likely broaden their product line. Already this seems to be happening with Bed Bath & Beyond, Toys "R" Us, and Office Depot.

MARKETING INTEGRATION

To effectively implement a consumer orientation, market segmentation, or niche marketing strategy, a firm following the marketing concept will coordinate decisions within the major areas of a firm, such as production and finance, with those of marketing. All activities then become part of a total system to produce so-called want-satisfying products and services. In the process, marketing decisions usually take precedence over those of finance or production. Within marketing, product planning precedes decisions on pricing and distribution for the determination of product policy. The marketing concept philosophy encourages executives in and out of marketing to integrate their decisions and activities for the achievement of common goals. Decisions about product quality, pricing, and distribution are often beyond the authority of advertising planners even though decisions made in nonadvertising areas have a direct influence on the effectiveness of an advertising campaign. Many firms recognize this relationship and involve advertising specialists in marketing decisions at the planning stage.

OTHER EMPHASES

The basic principle of the marketing concept is that a firm should marshal its activities toward the production of products or services that satisfy the existing needs and wants of consumers. Rather than emphasizing its own resources as its first priority, instead a company will establish giving consumers what they want as its top priority, or as Ford Motor Company likes to say, "Job One." Ford concluded that what consumers want most in a car is quality, and, in the slogan "Quality is Job One," they are telling consumers that it is their highest priority. In this kind of environment, certain other philosophies, or ways of doing business, become common.

Firms tend to be **research-oriented.** Product development evolves out of consumer research. The needs, wants, and problems of the consumer are ascertained through an objective evaluation of factual data and scientific forecasts. Focus groups, one-on-one interviews, attitude and opinion surveys, lifestyle and ethnographic studies, product-usage observation, sales analyses, consumer complaint feedback, and test marketing are but some of the ways a research-oriented firm gets information about the consumer. In contrast, new product ideas in many firms come from the president or the research-and-development staff, and they are often intuitive and frequently reflect the views of manufacturing or engineering.

In fields that are driven by technology, it often makes more sense to allow the technical people to lead the way because consumers may not be sufficiently sophisticated to know what kind of features are possible in a new product line. In this kind of environment, the focus is less on satisfying needs and wants and more on exceeding needs and wants. Computers, telecommunications, consumer electronics, and automobiles are some examples of product categories where in recent years technical people are producing innovations faster than consumers can articulate that they want them.

Another of the principles associated with the marketing concept is the policy that activities should be **planned.** With the growing sophistication and competitive nature of the marketplace, firms need to anticipate problems and forecast demand. Planned activities are one way to help meet the exigencies of the marketplace. A marketing campaign is the execution of a marketing plan. It is frequently developed by a marketing director and his or her staff, but an advertising agency may assist in its preparation. Plans provide direction for all those involved in the marketing effort. It is common for marketing plans to be written. In advertising , the larger agencies deem it almost mandatory in the planning of an advertising campaign.

The advertising firm Batten, Barton, Durstine and Osborn Worldwide Inc. (BBDO) gives the following reasons a written plan is necessary:[6]

1. It encourages clear and logical thinking.
2. It demonstrates a management approach to advertising by relating media, copy, and art to marketing facts and goals.
3. A written plan offers a factual basis for advertising direction, execution, performance, and appropriation.
4. It provides a complete guide in writing for everyone working on the account, as well as a ready source of information for new personnel joining the client or BBDO.
5. It registers what needs to be done for future improvement and provides an annual benchmark of accomplishment.

6. A plan informs BBDO top management of an account's goals and progress.
7. It serves as a policy document for client advertising management to use, as needed, with other departments, corporate management, directors.
8. It promotes understanding of, and agreement on, objectives and tactics among both client and BBDO organizations.

THE COMMUNICATION CONCEPT

Unlike the marketing concept, there has not been widespread discussion of the communication concept in the literature. Yet like the marketing concept, the communication concept suggests that all planning begin with consumers, and, therefore, greater discussion of this concept could be helpful in the development of an advertising campaign. Communication requires the originator of the message to encode information, whether words or pictures, in terms of the consumers' needs, wants, interests, or problems. To do this task, the message creator has to have a solid understanding of the social and psychological makeup of the target market. In other words, a writer has to understand what makes consumers tick so that he or she can better relate to them—the audience.

Failure to interpret a message in terms of consumers' needs, wants, interests, or problems may mean the advertisement fails to communicate. Either consumers will ignore the ad, or they may simply feel that the message is not meaningful. Moreover, because of hectic consumer lifestyles and the vast number of messages consumers are exposed to every day, a message may communicate well enough, but it may be forgotten unless it is attached to a distinctive advertising property. Motel 6 and Red Roof Inns both offer budget-priced rooms. Part of what makes Motel 6 sound economical is its name—some people still remember when it had rooms priced at six dollars per night. Red Roof Inns gets across its message in a memorable way with a simple slogan: "Sleep Cheap."

The above proposition seems fairly straightforward and sensible. Yet it appears that many ads are developed more from the perspective of the advertiser than from that of the consumer. When this happens, the advertising tends to focus more on the qualities of the product that the advertiser thinks is important, but not, unfortunately, on what the potential consumer thinks is important when considering buying the product.

A related and potentially more serious problem occurs when advertising is created without focusing on consumers' needs, wants, and problems but is created instead to look or sound good. Sometimes this is called creativity for technique's sake. An advertisement can be very entertaining, but it may not help sell the product. Every year after awards such as the Addys and the Clios have been given out to the "best" ads, people in the industry will talk about how the *best* ads did not win. In fact, advertisers often indulge in a sardonic humor contest trying to predict the first award-winning agency that will lose the account for which they had won the award.

Along with a focus on consumers' needs, wants, and problems, the communication concept implies an understanding of what communication can or cannot accomplish. Specifically, communication affects the way people think, believe, or feel. By itself, it seldom is enough to sell the product. Communication, especially advertising, needs to operate in harmony with the other elements in the marketing mix. It is crucial that the strategist understands precisely the role advertising should assume to influence consumer behavior. Because advertising is a form of persuasive communication, its role is often best defined in terms of communication criteria such as awareness, comprehension, attitude, and image that have the ability to stimulate consumer purchasing behavior.

For example, when Gillette was ready to introduce its revolutionary Sensor razor, it knew that its advertising would have to do more than tell consumers that it was a better razor; it would have to explain to consumers that the razor was better because the blade was mounted on flexible springs that would float along the contours of a person's skin. The approach was so successful that the Gillette Sensor is the number-one nondisposable razor in the world. Gillette learned from its experience in introducing double-edged razor blades in 1971 that sometimes you have to get consumers to understand how something works before they will believe a product claim. Before double-edged razors came along, it is doubtful that many consumers ever gave much thought to the idea of using more than one blade at a time. Gillette worked hard to get consumers to understand why double-edged razors provide a closer shave. Even today, most readers of this book will be able to complete the following sentence Gillette first put in an ad well over 20 years ago: "The Gillette Trac II gives you a closer shave, because the first blade lifts each hair, and the..." (If you said "the second blade cuts it off at the skin line," you are right.)

Of course, deciding on an appropriate role for advertising is no easy decision. The advertising planner has to project what the effects of each possible strategy would be on consumers' behavior. Would establishing or increasing brand awareness lead to greater sales, for example? Would it be more effective to reinforce or change the attitude of the consumers? Should advertising try to improve or intensify the image of the product?

It is easier to establish awareness than it is to change consumers' attitudes or get consumers to understand how a product operates. Moreover, there are no guarantees that if these tasks are achieved, they will result in increased sales. Not surprisingly, many advertisers opt for the conceptually simpler tasks of increasing awareness or working with a brand's image. With those approaches, however, advertisers run the risk that the copywriter or art director will get misguided and focus more on the creativity or the technique in the advertisement and less on what would be an appropriate selling message.

INTEGRATED MARKETING COMMUNICATION

The idea that a firm should coordinate, or integrate, all of its communication or promotional activities has been around for well over two decades. What is different in the 1990s is that firms understand better that to compete in an increasingly sophisticated marketplace, the messages they disseminate must blend together to achieve interrelated objectives. In the past, companies were often content to let an advertising agency take care of the advertising, a public relations agency handle the PR, and their own marketing department manage the sales promotion program. Very often the advertising would go off in one direction, the public relations program in another, and the sales promotion in still another area. Although the efforts might produce interrelated results, a marketer might question whether this is the most efficient and effective way to operate. The integrated concept embodies the idea that all parties involved in a campaign blend their efforts into producing seamless marketing communication.

Propelling the new emphasis on integrated marketing communications are marketers who understand that the old ways of doing business will no longer work. Today's marketplace has become increasingly sophisticated. Although academicians have discussed integrating and coordinating elements of the marketing and promotions mixes since at least the 1960s, especially by using what was then referred to as a "systems approach," it has been only relatively recently that the concept has caught on.[7]

As the physical distinctions among brands in many categories become negligible, the role of advertising in creating a psychological difference has become more important, but not necessarily more prominent. Advertising is likely to remain a valuable promotional tool well into the next century, especially in building brand equity, but other types of communication, such as sales promotion, direct marketing, and, perhaps, public relations, will probably become even more important. Increasingly, the strategy for many large advertisers is to surround consumers with as many points of contact as is economical. This generally means nontraditional media and related marketing communications will likely become more important.

Because of the tremendous increase in communication technologies, a marketer needs to be flexible to revise strategy and tactics to meet the changing situations in the environment. It is often more efficient and quicker for all of a firm's messages to come from one organization. It is also likely to be more effective and result in messages that are compatible with each other. Typically, there is better communication within an organization than between organizations.

Locating the sources of all of a company's communication within the same organization will likely become more important as firms speak to consumers with an increasing number of voices. As firms apply the lessons of market segmentation, they target smaller parts of the overall market. The research industry is now able to narrowly define market segments through database marketing. Largely gone are the days when a company could rely on a single selling message transmitted through the mass media to a broad base of people. Richard B. Fizdale, chairman of the advertising agency Leo Burnett Co. Inc., says that "the mass market is dead."[8] Using the mass media has always been easier than targeting relatively smaller segments of the overall market, but it has also been wasteful to talk to millions of people who had no particular interest in the product.

For some people, the concept of integrated marketing communication sounds better as theory than it works in practice. Locating the sources of a firm's message in one marketing communication company will only make the operation more efficient and effective if each specialized area of that group works harmoniously with each other and avoids the political infighting that sometimes occurs as each unit vies for a piece of the promotional budget. Ad agencies, especially the big ones, are also at a disadvantage in terms of cost-effectiveness. Advertisers can often outsource promotional work to suppliers who operate with a lower overhead, particularly in terms of real estate. Other advertisers find that they can maintain direct control over promotional elements, such as direct marketing, sales promotion, and packaging, by locating these specializations within the company and at a lower cost.

Regardless of the source of each promotional element, the effect of all activities should be *synergistic,* that is, each individual or unit's activity should be coordinated so that the combined effect of all contributions is greater than the sum of its parts. A **marketing communication campaign** can be very broadly defined as *the performance and integration of all promotional activities into a program designed to achieve interrelated goals.* In Chapter 8 we'll provide a definition that is more comprehensive and specific.

THE ADVERTISING CAMPAIGN CONCEPT

The key to successful advertising is planned advertising. One of the better ways to plan promotional activities is through a campaign that relates all activities to one another. Advertisements that are interrelated have greater retentive value than a series of different one-shot ads. Consumers remember advertising longer when each advertisement helps support or reinforce the others. Although an advertising campaign could and should be used for almost all situations that call for advertising, there may be situations where it is better to release an unrelated ad as elements within a situation change. Although even in this kind of situation, one can probably plan for changing situations.

There are both highly visible and unseen aspects to an advertising campaign. To the average consumer, an advertising campaign is simply a series of advertisements that look or sound alike. To the student or the practitioner, a campaign may involve all the activities that help produce advertisements designed to achieve interrelated goals, such as consumer surveys, brainstorming, or media analysis. This broader concept of an **advertising campaign** could be defined as *a series of advertisements, and the activities that help produce them, which are designed to achieve interrelated goals.*

This definition works in situations where the advertiser relies exclusively on advertising. However, in many cases the advertiser will broaden its promotional focus to include other types of marketing communication, such as sales promotion, publicity, and direct marketing. A broader focus requires more than a new definition; it also requires a new way of looking at a campaign. Therefore, it may be more accurate to think of an advertising campaign as a marketing communication campaign even though it relies exclusively on advertising as its promotional tool. It is likely that the label *advertising campaign* will stick. Whether you think of it as a marketing communication campaign or the more common advertising campaign, the definition above specifies what it does, but it does not tell what an *effective* campaign is or does.

CHARACTERISTICS OF AN ADVERTISING CAMPAIGN

The written form of the advertising plan is usually called either the *campaign plans book* or, simply, the *plans book*. Planning is the process by which one establishes the objectives, strategy, and tactics. The main quality that distinguishes a campaign from merely a collection of ideas and advertisements is unity. Upon seeing or hearing an ad from a unified campaign, people can tell that it belongs to a family of other ads that have preceded it. To unify a series of ads, there should be some element that weaves a thread of continuity throughout the campaign that ties all the ads together. To be effective, campaigns should be strategic in nature, thereby recognizing that campaigns take place over a period of time and should be adjusted and modified to take into consideration the changing situation.

CAMPAIGN CONTINUITY

In a sense, all advertisements for the same product are interrelated inasmuch as they generally try to achieve the same ultimate objective—sell the product. What separates a campaign from a collection of ads is the degree to which each execution is connected. In a campaign, the general plan is to put something in each ad that leaves a similar impression with consumers so that they feel one ad is a continuation of the others. These elements can be something observable (or physical) or something one thinks about (or psychological).

Physical Continuity

Advertisements that look and sound alike help keep creative work on target. Roman and Maas, formerly of Ogilvy & Mather Worldwide, note that an "agency doesn't have to consider, and test, dozens of new ideas every time a new advertisement needs to be produced."[9] Consumers pick up on new advertisements and remember them longer when a common element ties together all the advertisements in a campaign.

Slogans, taglines, and **trade characters** are devices that add continuity to a company's advertising. For example, United Airlines introduced the tagline "Fly the Friendly Skies" in an ad in 1965. By 1966, the tagline was extended to subsequent ads as an umbrella theme to emphasize United's friendly service as well as an overall friendly flying experience. The tagline was originally inspired by a radar device put in the nose of United airplanes to alert the pilot to the presence of "unfriendly skies." A slogan or tagline may be used for a single campaign, or it may endure for many years. In 1994, United adapted the

EXHIBIT 1–1   LEO BURNETT TRADE CHARACTERS

Account or Product	Year of Arrival	Character
Green Giant	1935	Jolly Green Giant
	1973	Little Green Sprout
Pillsbury	1965	Pillsbury Doughboy
Frosted Flakes	1952	Tony the Tiger
Marlboro	1955	Marlboro Man
9-Lives	1969	Morris the Cat
Maytag	1967	Lonely Repairman
Starkist	1961	Charlie the Tuna
Froot Loops	1963	Toucan Sam
Keebler	1968	Keebler Elves
U.S. Department of Transportation	1985	Vince and Larry (the crash test dummies)
7 UP	1988	Spot

tagline to "Come Fly *our* Friendly Skies" following the buyout of the airline by its employees.

Like a good slogan or tagline, an effective trade character can last for years. The Leo Burnett agency has been as successful as anyone in the business in developing trade characters for its clients. The characters have been animated like Tony the Tiger, the Pillsbury Doughboy, and the Keebler Elves, and they have been live-action like Maytag's Lonely Repairman and Morris the Cat. Exhibit 1–1 is a list of some of the trade characters developed by the company.[10]

The opening line in a commercial can also be used as a continuity device. For many years, the opening line "Do you know me?" clearly identified a commercial as one for American Express. **Distinctive sounds** are additional ways to add a unifying element to a campaign. The sounds of a bass drum followed by the gentle marching of a pink bunny signal to consumers the presence of an Energizer commercial.

Psychological Continuity

Advertisements may look and sound alike, but, unless they are psychologically similar or consistent, they are not likely to function as a campaign. Advertisers strive to unify the way people think about their advertising by developing a consistent theme, image, tone, or attitude in their ads. Each of these constructs is similar to each other in that they affect the way people think or feel about an ad. Although a campaign may not have a consistent theme, image, attitude, and tone in every ad, the campaign will present a more cohesive message if they do.

The unifying element in most campaigns is the **theme,** or the overall idea underlying the advertisement. The theme can be expressed in different ways. It often is stated most clearly by a slogan, which is one reason slogans are repeated so frequently. Slogans also add physical continuity because they usually appear in print or in a graphic.

When Virginia Slims cigarettes were introduced in 1968, the women's movement was in its infancy. Philip Morris used the slogan "You've Come a Long Way Baby" to develop the theme that the modern female smoker should have a cigarette that recognized her unique style and attitude. The idea of being "liberated" was a popular one for women in the late '60s-early '70s (at least in the media), and the cigarette's slogan was a way for Virginia Slims to tie the product into an important part of many women's attitudes. By 1985, the brand's share of the cigarette market was about double that of all other women's cigarette brands combined. By the 1990s, the old appeals were losing their relevancy, and the theme in many ads for Virginia Slims stressed the importance of "being yourself"—because, for many women, there really is no other choice.

Knowledgeable advertisers know that a product's **image** can have a significant effect on sales. Campaigns can establish, reinforce, and intensify images or replace them with new ones. Perhaps, the most successful image campaign of all time has been that of the Marlboro Man, which exemplifies each of these actions. Prior to 1955, when the Marlboro Man was introduced, filter-tip cigarettes were largely smoked by women. Male smokers, however, easily outnumbered female smokers. Recognizing the greater market potential in appealing to men, Leo Burnett, president of the company that bears his name, decided to *replace* the earlier, more feminine image with one that would appeal to men by introducing what he called "The Marlboro Man," a rugged, self-assured individual. This mental picture *established* the brand as one with which men could feel comfortable.

In 1955, the Leo Burnett Co. *reinforced* this image by giving the Marlboro Man a tattoo, thereby distinguishing him from competitors. In 1967, the company *intensified* this image by introducing to its television commercials music from *The Magnificent Seven,* a movie about gunslingers that was very popular with men at that time. From this point on, the music influenced the character and quality, or **tone,** of all subsequent commercials. By 1975, Marlboro had become the number-one cigarette brand in the United States, and the Marlboro Man living in Marlboro Country set the tone and direction for all subsequent advertising. In the mid-1990s, Marlboro is easily the best-selling cigarette in the world. For many people, especially those in emerging nations, the Marlboro brand is a symbol of Western or American culture.

Campaigns with **attitude** tend to be judgmental, whereas image campaigns usually focus on an idea or concept of a product, person, or institution. People from certain schools, some companies, even various parts of the country often have similar attitudes. We frequently notice that some people simply have an attitude. Campaigns, too, can sometimes be described as having an attitude. The question for the marketing strategist becomes, Does the consumer agree or identify with the situation or not? The number-one animal in the world with an attitude is the common cat. Unlike dogs, they assume no guilt for house-training mistakes, they won't try to make you feel better when you're down, and they won't get excited if you throw them a crumb. In fact, if you throw them good food, they are just as likely to turn up their noses and walk away as they are with bad food. They're fussy, finicky eaters. Many cat owners both admire and love their cats for their independent ways.

In 1969, 9-Lives, a division of Starkist Foods, adopted a strategy using a trade character named Morris to show that 9-Lives has the cat food even finicky cats can't resist. Morris quickly became famous costarring with Burt Reynolds in the movie *Shamus,* appearing on numerous TV shows such as *Lifestyles of the Rich and Famous* and *Good Morning America,* and even visiting backstage the Chicago and Boston casts of the show *Cats.* In the 1980s, *Young Miss* magazine readers regularly put Morris on their list of Most Admired Celebrities, finishing ahead of Bill Cosby, Dudley Moore, Ronald Reagan, Prince Charles, and Pope John Paul II. Eventually, 9-Lives got around to putting a picture of Morris on the product packaging. Within four months of his appearance, the company's share of market in two cat-food categories doubled. Such can be the power of a trade character.

Many advertising launches start out as cohesive, coherent campaigns, but, somewhere in development, the advertising loses its focus because of weak leadership, poor planning, or executional problems. Inadequate execution can result from a variety of problems, such as lack of talent, deficient work habits, personality problems, or insufficient motivation. Problems with leadership or planning often stem from the wrong kind of orientation. The best campaigns are strategically oriented.

STRATEGIC ORIENTATION

If creative ideas are the heart and soul of a campaign, then strategy is the brain. Strategy provides the direction for all those involved in the campaign to follow. It also provides the framework within which they should operate. Strategy implies that all members of an organization work as a team toward common goals. Strategic plans result from team members who can anticipate the future and who are able to develop the ideas, operations, and procedures to achieve the organization's goals. A major problem with many strategic plans is that they simply take too long to develop, especially when they are put together by a committee. As part of the strategic-planning process, companies need to build into their operations a strict time schedule and a way of limiting discussion of the items in a plan, or they run the risk of what is sometimes called *paralysis by analysis.* Ten years ago, it was common for firms to talk about contingency plans to describe the course of action a company would implement if the situation changed. Today, markets change so quickly and frequently that one can be sure the situation will change and in ways that are often difficult to anticipate. Therefore, it is imperative that firms integrate into their strategic plans some options that will provide sufficient flexibility so firms can respond to changing situations in a timely manner.

Not having a contingency plan can prove costly to a company, as AT&T discovered. In the spring of 1991, MCI instituted its highly successful Friends and Family long-distance calling plan. Within two years, MCI signed up an additional 10 million customers.[11] Initially, AT&T did not respond to the campaign. Eventually, it developed a campaign disparaging MCI's campaign, and in the spring of 1993 it launched a $50 million campaign aimed at luring back customers who had defected to MCI.[12] For the most part it was too late.

A CORPORATE STRATEGIC PLAN

There are a number of elements that are common to strategic plans, although different disciplines may call them by different names. The management consultants Patrick Below, George Morrissey, and Betty Acomb have taken an in-depth look at strategic planning, and their concept of a strategic plan has the following seven elements:[13]

- ☐ Organization mission
- ☐ Strategic analysis
- ☐ Long-term objectives
- ☐ Strategy
- ☐ Integrated programs
- ☐ Financial projections
- ☐ Executive summary

These elements should be an integral part of all campaigns. In an advertising or marketing communication plan, they will likely appear in various sections of a plans book. Listed below is a description of each of these elements, with an explanation of how they might be handled in an advertising plan:

1. **Organization Mission.** An organization mission statement embodies what the organization is concerned with and, perhaps, the purpose of its existence. It is the logical starting point of a strategic plan. In advertising plans, the purpose is to solve marketing and communication problems and to take advantage of opportunities. Naturally, these plans generally take into consideration what companies are concerned with, but the advertising campaign version of a mission typically focuses more on the company's key problems and opportunities. This type of discussion is typically found in a section titled "Situation Analysis."

   In some markets the problems may not be easily or readily solved, and the company may be better advised to veer off in a new direction to capitalize on different opportunities. In the 1980s, IBM concentrated on solving the problems associated with its mainframe computer business. As a result, it failed to appreciate fully the market potential of the personal computer and lost its preeminent position in the computer business to other companies that were quicker and more adept at capitalizing on new opportunities.

2. **Strategic Analysis.** This part of a strategic plan provides its research foundation. In an advertising plan, the strategic analysis identifies the *critical* issues that will be addressed by the advertising and marketing communication strategy, and it is normally covered in the situation analysis. The situation analysis usually consists of an analysis of background information on the company, consumer, market, product, and competition.

3. **Long-Term Objectives.** Goals, or objectives, are statements about what each unit involved in the campaign would like to accomplish. A corporation's strategic plans tend to be written more for the organization as a whole than for the marketing function, and so they tend to be broad based and to reflect what the company wants to accomplish over an extended period of time. In contrast, marketing and advertising goals are typically written for no more than a year and are specific. As the marketplace becomes increasingly dynamic, complex, and fast changing in the 21st century, it is likely that objectives, whether short-term or long-term, will be set for periods shorter than one year.

4. **Strategy.** The critical element in any conceptual understanding of strategy is the importance placed on the *interrelationship*, or *interconnectedness*, of all the activities planned to achieve a goal. Strategists understand the linkages among actions and between actions and a reaction, or, as is sometimes the case in advertising, between an action and no response. This linkage is what differentiates a strategy from simply a list of ideas or actions. Moreover, a strategist understands that actions, reactions, and responses take place over a period of time. Like a master chess player, a marketing strategist has to forecast each move and countermove in the marketplace. In an advertising plan, there might be marketing, advertising, creative, and media strategies, as well as various strategies associated with other types of marketing communication.

5. **Integrated Programs.** This aspect of a strategic plan details the cross-functional actions required to implement the strategy and achieve the objectives. In an advertising campaign, these actions are often referred to as tactics or executions, and they usually appear in major sections pertaining to the media, creative, or sales promotion strategy. The emphasis on *integrated programs* underscores the team concept in which each program or activity is designed to work harmoniously with other units in the company.

6. **Financial Projections.** Financial projections typically involve the financial expectations and the measures used to evaluate the company's performance. In advertising and marketing communication plans, the projections are covered in a number of different ways and places. The actual expenses are normally handled in a section of the plans book dealing with the budget. The sales projections are normally covered under marketing objectives. Profit projections typically are not covered in marketing plans. Measures to

assess the financial projections of a marketing communication program may appear if an advertiser prepares the plan. If the plan is prepared by an agency, it is typically omitted. Since around the mid-1980s, agencies have become decreasingly involved in measuring the effectiveness of advertising programs. That function has largely gone over to the advertiser or to outside research firms. Some agency people are glad to see this responsibility taken over by their clients. As one agency vice-president told two of the authors, "It was sort of like grading your own paper."

7. **Executive Summary.** Although many corporations' strategic plans have an executive summary or overview at the beginning, many advertising plans summarize at the end of major sections, such as the situation analysis, the creative strategy, or the media strategy.

A CAMPAIGN OUTLINE

There are many different ways to outline a campaign, especially if it is for a marketing communication plan. Essentially, a plan serves as a guide for those who work on the campaign and as a proposal for those who have to approve it. As a proposal, there are often a number of different approaches to get someone to approve spending what is usually a substantial sum of money. (Generally, it is a good idea to consider any expenditure substantial.)

At the J. Walter Thompson (JWT) agnecy, planning begins with the answers to five basic questions:

☐ Where are we?
☐ Why are we there?
☐ Where could we be?
☐ How could we get there?
☐ Are we getting there?

When the agency gets the answer to the last question, the process starts all over again. At JWT, employees refer to the process as a planning cycle

---

EXHIBIT 1–2   TWO APPROACHES TO PLANNING A CAMPAIGN

J. Walter Thompson Asks	A Typical Advertising Class Response
Where are we?	Develop a situation analysis.
Why are we there?	Identify problems.
Where could we be?	Identify opportunities.
How could we get there?	Develop message, media, and marketing communication strategy, and tactics.
Are we getting there?	Develop a plan to measure or track the effectiveness of the campaign.

EXHIBIT 1–3   AN OUTLINE FOR A MARKETING COMMUNICATION PLAN

I. **Introduction or Overview**
II. **Situation Analysis**
 A. Company analysis
 B. Consumer analysis
 C. Market analysis
 D. Product analysis
 E. Competitive analysis
 F. Problems and opportunities (optional)
III. **The Target Market Profile**
IV. **Objectives**
 A. Marketing
 B. Communication
 C. Advertising
V. **Marketing Communication Strategy**
 A. Advertising Strategy
  1. Creative or message strategy
   a) objectives
   b) strategy
   c) tactics or executions (often put at the end of the plan)
  2. Media strategy
   a) objectives
   b) strategy
   c) tactics or vehicles
   d) cost estimates
   e) continuity schedule
 B. Sales Promotion
  1. Objectives
  2. Strategy
  3. Tactics or executions
 C. Public Relations
  1. Objectives
  2. Strategy
  3. Tactics or examples
 D. Direct Marketing
  1. Objectives
  2. Strategy
  3. Tactics or examples
 E. Other (Such as Event Marketing, Infomercials)
  1. Objectives
  2. Strategy
  3. Tactics or examples
VI. **Communication Assessment Measures (Optional)**
VII. **Budget**
VIII. **Summary**

because the process is ongoing. There is a beginning but no real end to the way they plan for an account.

In academic circles, the above questions receive a fair amount of attention, but they usually get labeled differently. Exhibit 1–2 shows how these basic questions tend to be handled in an advertising campaigns class.

Listed in Exhibit 1–3 is the type of outline someone would prepare before undertaking a campaign. This plan lists the steps a company would take in developing a marketing communication campaign. Not all organizations would pursue every step. For example, some companies might not have a direct marketing or public relations plan. These steps will be described in greater detail in the following chapters.

ENDNOTES

[1]Gerry Khermouch, "Kodak, Wal-Mart Price Stand-off Is a Royal Rumble," *Brandweek* 35 (April 18, 1994): 6.

[2]Adrienne Ward Fawcett, "CAA Ads Make Big Splash with Youth, Women," *Advertising Age* 64 (April 12, 1993): 1.

[3]Adrienne Ward Fawcett, "CAA's Coke Ads Fall Flat on Persuasion," *Advertising Age* 64 (May 10, 1993): 4.

[4]Material in this section has been abstracted from John D. Leckenby and C. Nugent Wedding, *Advertising Management: Criteria, Analysis, and Decision Making* (Columbus, Ohio: Grid, 1982), chapter 1.

[5]Ellen Neuborne, "Bed Bath & Beyond's Lucrative Niche," *USA Today* (July 6, 1994), sec. B, 3.

[6]*The Advertising Plan at BBDO, A Handbook for Account Managers* (New York: Batten, Barton, Durstine & Osborn, Inc., undated).

[7]Donald P. Robin and Clyde E. Harris, Jr., "An Integrated Approach for Applying Marketing Strategy," *Business Ideas and Facts* (Winter 1973): 35–40.

[8]Quoted in Don E. Schultz, Stanley I. Tannenbaum, and Robert F. Lauterborn, *Integrated Marketing Communications* (Lincolnwood, Ill.: NTC Books, 1992), p. xi.

[9]Kenneth Roman and Jane Maas, *How to Advertise* (New York: St. Martin's Press, 1976): 67.

[10]The information on the trade characters discussed in this section as well as information on United Airlines and Virginia Slims is abstracted from unpublished, undated, and unnumbered material on enduring campaigns from Leo Burnett Company, Inc.

[11]Kate Fitzgerald, "AT&T Aims to Reverse MCI's Charge," *Advertising Age* 64 (July 12, 1993): 15.

[12]Terry Lefton, "AT&T Intros 'i' Series Discounts," *Brandweek* 34 (February 22, 1993): 5.

[13]Patrick J. Below, George L. Morrissey, and Betty L. Acomb, *The Executive Guide to Strategic Planning* (San Francisco: Jossey-Bass, 1987), 9–10.

The Research Foundation I: Understanding Clients and Consumers

The place to start in preparing for a campaign is at a desk with a pad of paper and pencil, a computer, or a typewriter. Whatever tools you choose, the important point is to begin by asking yourself some questions: What kind of information will you need? Where will you get the information? What do you know about how a campaign fits together? Many beginners go to a library or head off to a store to observe the product in the marketplace. Not only is this an inefficient way to proceed, but it can also be counterproductive. More about this point will be discussed later.

Professionals are sensitive about how they manage their time. When they search for information, usually they know exactly what they are looking for—even though they might not actually find it. General or undefined searches take up unnecessary time that could be better spent on other assignments. Practitioners seldom have the luxury of extra time.

DEVELOPING A RESEARCH PLAN

You need the pad of paper or other tools for use in preparing an outline that will help you organize your time as you pursue your research. This plan will enable you to understand both the information you need and how to get it. As you accumulate information, you should be well on your way to building a research foundation. Professionals usually have their own way of working, but if you are a beginner or a student, consider using the following topics as a start in preparing a rough outline:

- ☐ Where to begin in the search for information
- ☐ How to separate the search into sections
- ☐ How to get the information
- ☐ How to process the information

The Start of the Search

Despite this commonsense approach, most professionals can start anywhere. Their experience gives them the kind of judgment that allows them to process information in any order without biasing the information or ideas that follow. With beginners, though, first impressions are often lasting impressions. In the classroom, it is not uncommon to hear students generate creative ideas only minutes after receiving a copywriting assignment and well before they have completed any analysis of background information. Despite being cautioned by the instructor to defer their ideas until they complete a copy platform or brief, the same ideas frequently show up in the finished ads. Not surprisingly, the ideas are often off target and off strategy.

At the Batten, Barton, Durstine & Osborn Worldwide Inc. (BBDO) advertising agency, it has long been the practice to defer the search for product information until after the prime prospects and their problems have been determined. BBDO's concern is that eager staffers too often immerse themselves in product information before they get a good focus on the consumers' needs and wants. By talking first to the designers, engineers, or chemists, the staff runs the risk of assuming that the reasons the R&D people developed the product are the same reasons the consumers buy the product. Although companies hope their motives are the same, quite frequently they are not. For example, several years ago students in an advertising campaigns class did an advertising campaign for Rold Gold pretzels. Very early in the campaign process, the students discovered that pretzels could be differentiated from other snacks on the basis of a health claim—pretzels had far fewer calories and almost no fat compared to other snacks. The students based their message strategy on this finding despite later research that suggested consumers were unlikely to base their purchase decision on the amount of calories or fat in pretzels. If the students had deferred their product research until after they had conducted their consumer research, they might have opted for a message strategy that stressed fun instead of health.

The basic principle of the marketing concept is that all planning should begin with consumers. So an argument could be made that the consumer analysis ought to precede the analysis of the company. However, it is usually more efficient to focus first on the company's problems and opportunities, because a firm simply may not want to proceed in certain directions, regardless of what consumers might want.

Separating the Search into Sections

The goal of the search is to provide information that will enable an analysis of the entire situation. This analysis of background information is usually referred to as a *situation analysis;* it is the research foundation that will provide the basis for the campaign objectives, strategy, and tactics that will follow. At this stage, it is usually a good idea to divide the search into separate areas to ensure that nothing is overlooked. Much of the information you uncover in one area will apply in others, but it's unlikely that any will be overlooked. This kind of organization will help you get most of the information on the first go-around rather than having to go back and fill in missing pieces of information to complete the analysis. You'll find that much of the information you uncover will apply in more than one area.

We suggest you begin your search in the following areas:

☐ Company analysis
☐ Consumer analysis

After you've completed some research on the company, you will probably begin your investigation into consumers. As you'll learn later, you'll then be looking into these areas simultaneously. After your initial research on the company and consumers, the order in which you search for information on other areas is not very important. Nor should it be necessary to complete the company and consumer analyses before you begin to search for information in the areas listed below:

☐ Market analysis
☐ Product analysis
☐ Competitive analysis

Gathering the Information

Information on the company's mission, finances, products, and other matters usually comes from primary sources, such as company executives and staff, and secondary sources, such as magazine articles. You should follow the easiest path and start your research with secondary sources. Secondary research can provide some hard facts about the company and can also be helpful in developing questions to pursue in your later primary research. You may be able to anticipate some of your needs for primary research quite early, and, if so, you should start developing a plan as early as you can.

There are a lot of ways and places to get information. To get the research foundation off on the right footing, it helps if the information is from an objective source. You will probably be tempted to check out the company in the marketplace through either observation or interviews. Although these techniques have value, they may be biased. Similarly, you will want to talk to consumers, but it is better to hold off until you can objectively determine the current users of the product. Typically, this means you will start your active search for information in the library.

Processing the Information

Adopting a Competitive Attitude

Getting the information is only half the task. You must also rework your findings so people who will be working on the campaign can put it to the best possible use. The marketplace is very competitive. Copywriters work hard to develop big ideas, approaches that stand out from the competition. Media planners look for unique or special opportunities to deliver selling messages. Buyers look for the most efficient way to send the messages. Researchers need to be every bit as competitive as creative and media personnel to find the right kind of information that can be used most effectively.

How much information is enough? It is not enough until you can provide campaign planners with better information than the competition is getting. In many mature product categories, sales increases come primarily from the competition's market share. Researchers should strive to provide planners with an edge by providing information that is both comprehensive and insightful.

Analysis versus Description

Comprehensive analyses usually take time, effort, and money. Not all companies (or students) have the resources of their rivals. Therefore, it is worth reemphasizing the importance of efficiently searching for information. Searches that are general often waste time; they tend to be more descriptive than analytical. Descriptive information usually tells people what they already know or could easily find out. An analyst breaks down the background information into components, examining the nature and function of each topic to be analyzed and the interrelationships among sections, as you'll see later. Beginners should think like an analyst. For example, as you look for information on the company, you should have a clear understanding of the function of the company analysis and how this analysis interrelates with the consumer, market, product, and competitive analyses. We will cover these ideas shortly.

The problem with a descriptive analysis is that it usually only tells the obvious. We refer to this treatment as putting the information *in sight*. Even when an analysis is especially comprehensive, most adequate researchers will eventually discover the information. Descriptive information puts the burden of finding value or meaning on the reader (assuming it is a report). The key to doing good research is to interpret the information that is in sight, to provide *insight*. Researchers only gain insight when they clearly understand the inner nature of the object being analyzed. For example, it is not enough to identify the prime prospects and the competition. It is also important to determine why consumers buy the brands they do. This usually requires the researcher to probe beyond what is obvious.

Consider why consumers clip coupons, shop at superstores, or drive miles out of their way to use a gas station that has the lowest price. The obvious reason would be to save money. In the case of Home Depot, it might also be to have access to a wide variety of merchandise. These may be the most important reasons, but there may be more obscure and profound reasons. For many homemakers and do-it-yourselfers, saving money is less important for economic reasons than because of how it makes the saver feel. For some consumers, clipping coupons may be less about saving money and more about reinforcing their self-image of being a thrifty homemaker. Similarly, for many do-it-yourselfers, doing home projects is as much about testing one's abilities as it is about saving money. For these people, shopping at Home Depot may help to reinforce an image that the consumer is a smart person.

These suppositions are merely hypotheses. But if you are developing a campaign for Home Depot or a similar advertiser, they might be worth pursuing. The obvious reasons why consumers buy a product, such as price, quality, or availability, are often the things companies can do very little to change. If the company does not have a clear price or quality advantage, then the company may be lost about how to strategically direct its promotion. Often it is the obscure or secondary reasons consumers buy a product that offer the more creative and effective ways to sell a product.

Viewed objectively, a Saturn automobile does not look significantly different from many other cars. But it is clear that Saturn has tapped into a special consumer motive for buying. In the summer of 1994, 40,000 Saturn owners came to the semirural area around the small town of Springhill, Tennessee, to attend a Saturn homecoming celebration.[1] Was it possible in the short span of a couple of years that Saturn had achieved the kind of cult status that has been true for cars like Jaguar, Porsche, Thunderbird, or even Mustang? Probably not. What the Saturn owners bought is the Saturn experience. The company correctly identified that many consumers simply wanted, as its slogan said, "a different kind of car" from "a different kind of company," even if the difference came primarily in the form of a change in attitude.

THE SITUATION ANALYSIS

The situation analysis consists of the background information that will be used to develop the campaign. The information should be *organized, structured, detailed,* and *focused.* Typically, the information is typed up, put into a document, and then used to develop strategy and tactics. In the business world, this document, or report, is usually put into a loose-leaf binder, signifying that the analysis is ongoing and is subject to continual change. Enlightened companies view analyses as part of a research system, instead of the result of a research project. In a class project, the situation analysis is simply the beginning section of a more comprehensive plans book.

ORGANIZATION

There is more than one way to organize a campaign. We recommend organizing the outline along simple lines. We delineate campaigns by using sections that cover broad topics like the company, consumer, market, product, and competition. By using broad topics, you can include within a section any analysis that makes sense for the particular situation.

STRUCTURE

The situation analysis should be structured so that it is clear that the company's problems and opportunities are uppermost in the minds of the people who are doing the analysis. Although you could make a case to do the consumer analysis first, company representatives usually feel more comfortable if the company is first.

For each of the sections in the company's situation analysis, you should assume an *inside-outside* perspective. With an inside perspective, you should strive to understand the company's problems from its point of view. However, sometimes company executives are too close to the situation to have an objective viewpoint. Therefore, viewing the company's situation from an outside perspective may provide different and valuable information. Similarly, as the analyst, you will want to understand, if not empathize from an inside perspective with, how consumers think and feel. If you only view things from the consumers' perspective, however, you may not get an accurate picture of why they buy or do not buy a product. There are few subjects about which people are less objective than themselves.

Consider consumers who drink Samuel Adams beer. If you ask them why they choose their particular brand, they likely will give you some paraphrase of the answer "Because I like it." If you probe further, they may tell you specifically why their beer is superior to other brands, especially the drinkers of Samuel Adams, the best-selling microbrewed beer. However, in the beer business there is a common saying, "People don't so much drink a brand's beer, as they drink its advertising." This implies that people consume a certain brand of beer more for psychological reasons than physical ones. If so, then the key task of a researcher often involves moving beyond obvious reasons to uncover motives that are more deeply seated. In the case of Samuel Adams, you would want to know how much of the brand's popularity is due to taste and how much of it is a reflection of the various images consumers have of the brand. In some instances, an inside approach of trying to think like the consumer works, and, in other cases, taking a more detached approach, or an outside perspective, will provide a more objective and accurate answer. We suggest in each analysis you take both an inside and an outside approach.

DETAIL

The purpose of the situation analysis is to provide a research foundation that can be used to develop strategy and tactics. Because tactics are detailed executions of the overall strategy, it is important to provide creative and media personnel with sufficient detail to fully exploit their opportunities as well as to keep their work on target and within the strategy. It is not usually enough to learn that consumers value low prices, fast service, and quality food when they choose a fast-food restaurant. This information does not provide enough useful detail. Research questions should be posed to elicit specific information—how low a price, how fast the service—preferably in quantitative terms. If this information is difficult to obtain, then the questions might be stated to provide information of a relative or comparative nature, such as Company A has higher-quality food than Company B.

FOCUS

It is important that the detail in the situation analysis focus on identifying problems and opportunities. Detail without focus is merely padding, or information without a meaningful significance. For example, the history of the company is an important part of the company analysis, but only insofar as it sheds light on the firm's current problems and opportunities. When and how the company was founded is relevent only if it helps to explain recent or current problems, and if it helps make clear why the company can take advantage of an opportunity. Problems and opportunities form the basis for setting objectives. All analyses should focus on identifying the particular aspect of the situation that could either prevent the company from achieving objectives or enable it to exploit a marketing advantage. These aspects are the company's problems and opportunities and will be discussed in greater detail later.

THE COMPANY ANALYSIS

The company analysis should consist of some basic ideas about what the company is concerned with and what it stands for. The focus in the analysis should be on the company's major problems and opportunities. Whether you are working for the company directly, are with its agency, or are doing this project as a class assignment, it is imperative that you operate on the same wavelength as the company. To help you formulate the kind of questions you will ask in your research, try to imagine you are in a marketing staff meeting to review the past year and to make preliminary plans for the upcoming one. What problems would be discussed? What opportunities will the staff talk about? A good company analysis provides a benchmark to keep you from going off on a tangent, pursuing opportunities the company will never consider.

SALES AND PROFITS: A GOOD PLACE TO START

Generally, the problems and opportunities discussed in this type of meeting focus on money, either in the form of sales or profits. Usually money problems are symptomatic of more fundamental problems, especially if you look at sales (or profits) over a period of years. Trend analysis often uncovers problems that barely show up in a static time frame. A company can have an off year for many reasons. If sales problems persist for more than a couple of years, it usually points to a weakness in any or all of three categories: the company itself, the industry, or the overall economy. If you start with the money and ask enough questions, the more deeply rooted problems usually emerge. Exhibit 2–1 shows how you can use an extended line of questions to uncover a company's fundamental problems and to evaluate whether they can become opportunities.

As the decade of the eighties opened, things were not well at General Motors. Foreign imports had made steady inroads in the automobile industry,

---

EXHIBIT 2–1   GENERAL MOTORS: PROBLEMS AND OPPORTUNITY ANALYSIS

Question	Answer
What is the basic problem?	Declining sales, eroding share of market, weak profits.
Why?	Consumers increasingly prefer imported cars, especially Japanese.
Why?	Japanese cars have a higher quality image.
Would consumers buy more GM cars if the quality improved?	Not significantly in the short run.
Why?	The problem is as much perceptual as it is real.
Would it help with the image if GM built a completely new car in a newly formed division?	Only if consumers could be convinced the car was made completely different from the old GM ways by a new kind of company.

---

and GM was having difficulty competing, especially against the Japanese automobile manufacturers.[2] Exhibit 2–1 is a view of how General Motors might have determined its opportunity to develop the Saturn automobile.

Of course, this line of questioning is simplistic. It merely demonstrates the value of extending a line of questioning to uncover hidden problems and opportunities. In an actual discussion, the participants would need more information both to pose the questions and to answer them. To ask and answer questions intelligently, your research should include information that is internal and external to the firm.

Internal Information

Essentially, internal information comes from within the firm, although the company may not be forthcoming with the information you need. In some instances, it must be inferred from outside sources. Consider asking the following questions:

☐ What is the company's mission?
☐ How ambitious is the company?
☐ How much risk is it willing to incur?
☐ What is the state of the company's financial, technological, and managerial resources?
☐ What are the sales trends over the past several years? How about profits?
☐ Has the company's share of market been going up or down?

External Information

External information covers the factors or forces outside the firm that influence its problems and opportunities. Consider asking the following questions:

☐ What has been the sales trend in the industry over the past several years?
☐ What is the general economic climate?
☐ Are there any social, cultural, or political conditions detrimental to the future of the company?

At this point, the analysis should not be in depth, or you would run the risk that the company's perception of its problems and opportunities would bias the way you look at the consumer. To fully evaluate the company's problems and opportunities, you need to complete the situation analysis by examining the consumer, market, product, and competition.

STARTING THE LIBRARY SEARCH

A good place for the research to start is with a general literature search on the company. You will be looking primarily for articles on the company, but information on the industry or a generic category can also be useful. In most cases, a background search covering the last four or five years should give you a good feel for the problems the company or industry is facing. After you have acquired and digested general information, the next step is to focus on specific information about the company. The most informative articles usually come from trade publications, newspapers, and popular periodicals. The articles are likely to be indexed in either print or electronic format.

USING THE LIBRARY

Libraries are repositories of vast amounts of information. Exposure to this information is usually obtained from one of the following access points: a reference librarian, an electronic data search, or a print-based index. A reference librarian is usually the most convenient place to start, but experienced users will probably skip this step and go directly to an electronic data search. Today, most libraries provide these computerized services. They are often quicker, more specific, and more comprehensive than a print index, and they usually offer the researcher the ability to download the information to disk or to obtain a printed copy. Still, there may be some sources of information that are easier and cheaper to search in a print-based format, and some resources may not be available on the electronic service offered by the library. Basically, electronic searches are offered in two formats: on-line and CD-ROM.

On-line

Most academic libraries provide on-line connections to hundreds of databases stored on magnetic tape in remote locations housed by the vendors offering the service. These on-line vendors provide immediate access to numerous databases, including trade publications, newspapers, directories, government documents, academic journals, and other indexes. Numerous vendors offer on-line services such as Dialog, Wilsonline, Mead Data Central (LEXIS/NEXIS), and the Dow Jones Retrieval Service. Check with a librarian to see which services the library can access. Some of the on-line services are expensive, but many libraries are bypassing the high cost of on-line searches by offering users, especially students, the opportunity to purchase a small number of searches for a nominal fee from FirstSearch (OCLC).

CD-ROM

Most academic libraries subscribe to a variety of databases on CD-ROM. These letters stand for compact disk read only memory. These disks look like the CDs used for music, and they contain vast amounts of information. Typically, CD-ROM databases are searched at a microcomputer by the user. Most databases on CD-ROM are updated less frequently that on-line services.

RESOURCES

The most comprehensive and detailed information on a company's structure and finances is in sources from financial investment information services, such as Moody's Investors Service and Standard & Poor's. Occasionally, there may be books on a specific company, but the information in them will likely be dated. A vast amount of information is available in indexes, but much of it will be of limited value in doing a company analysis. Students, in particular, will have to piece together a composite picture from multiple sources, because it is unlikely that any one source will provide enough information to do a thorough company analysis that is relevant for a marketing communication campaign. Some of the more widely available sources of information are listed below:

Comprehensive Investment Services

Moody's Manuals The *Moody's Manuals* series consists of eight volumes that provide financial and operating information on over 30,000 publicly traded domestic and international companies plus 20,000 municipal and government bodies. The manuals of special interest to advertising students are the *Industrial Manual*, which provides in-depth descriptions of top U.S. industrial companies, the *OTC Industrial Manual*, which provides coverage of approximately 2,700 NASDAQ and OTC companies, and the *OTC Unlisted Manual*, which provides information on approximately 2,000 emerging companies. Each manual is published annually with weekly and biweekly news reports serving as updates. Entries typically include a company history, a business description, a list of subsidiaries, and up to seven years of financial statement information. The manuals are available in print, on-line, and on CD-ROM.

Standard & Poor's Corporation Records S&P's records are similar in content to *Moody's Manuals* and provide financial information on 11,000 publicly held U.S. corporations in six alphabetically arranged loose-leaf volumes. The company entries are updated annually on a rotating basis. The service is kept up-to-date with the *Daily News Service* published each business day of the year. *Corporation Records* are available in print, on-line, and on CD-ROM.

Valueline Investment Survey This widely consulted loose-leaf investment service provides in-depth evaluative reports on approximately 2,000 companies representing more than 40 industries. Each company is profiled in a one-page summary, which is updated quarterly on a rotating basis. The entries include a 10- to 15-year statistical history plus a narrative statement addressing recent developments and future prospects. This source is available in print, on-line, and on CD-ROM.

Disclosure The Disclosure database contains detailed financial and management information on more than 12,000 public corporations. The data are taken from annual and periodic reports filed with the U.S. Securities and Exchange Commission. This database is only available on-line and on CD-ROM.

Indexes

ABI/Inform This valuable source indexes articles appearing in over 800 management, marketing, and business journals, including articles on advertising. Each citation includes a 150-word summary of the article. ABI/Inform index is available only on-line or on CD-ROM and contains information from 1971 to the present.

Predicasts F & S Index United States This is another valuable source that indexes the contents of trade journals, U.S. government documents, newspapers, and special reports for current information on products, industries, and companies. Companion indexes include *Predicasts F & S Index International* and *Predicasts F & S Index of Corporate Change.* This index is available in print, on-line, and on CD-ROM.

LEXIS/NEXIS System The LEXIS/NEXIS system provides indexed access to a large collection of databases accessible through its service. The Nexis collection of databases offers the full text of newspaper, wire-service, magazine, and newsletter stories. Of particular interest to advertising students is the NEXIS Advertising and Public Relations Library of databases. The LEXIS collection of databases consists primarily of legal information.

Business Periodicals Index (BPI) This well-known index provides author and subject access to approximately 345 English-language business magazines from 1958 to the present. The BPI is available in print, on CD-ROM, and on-line. The entries do not include summaries, making it more difficult to gauge the relevance of cited articles.

Directories

Million Dollar Directory: Leading Public and Private Companies This five-volume set, published by Dun & Bradstreet, provides brief entries for approximately 160,000 U.S. public and private companies worth $500,000 or more. The information includes the SIC (Standard Industrial Classification) code and estimated sales. The *Million Dollar Directory* is available in print, on CD-ROM, on-line, and on magnetic tape.

Encyclopedia of Associations This comprehensive three-volume directory provides detailed information on over 22,000 American organizations and international organizations with North American ties. At least 4,000 of the entries are trade and industry associations. This directory includes the organization name, address, and telephone number, and the name of a chief contact person you can call on for more information.

Brands and Their Companies **and** ***Companies and Their Brands*** This four-volume set (two volumes for each) matches, by brand and by company, over 230,000 brand names with the 43,000 companies that make or import them.

Miscellaneous

Company Reports Many academic libraries have a collection of annual company reports or other periodic reports or both filed with the SEC in paper copy or on microfiche or CD-ROM. Many services, such as Moody's, Standard & Poor's, and Disclosure, contain excerpts from these reports as well.

Government Documents and the Internet Much government data pertaining to companies and industries are now available on CD-ROM and on-line through the Internet. Check for the extremely detailed economic censuses (for example, the Census of Manufacturers, the Census of Retail Trade, the Census of Service Industries, and the Census of Wholesale Trade) to be released on CD-ROM in addition to or in place of the print versions. The economic censuses are valuable in particular for providing information of interest to marketers. They are organized by state, county, Metropolitan Statistical Area, city, census tracts, and blocks.

Government data of interest to business researchers are also beginning to become accessible on the Internet. Of particular note at this time is the Internet Edgar Dissemination project, which can be accessed by Gopher by typing:

gopher://town.hall.org

For access by World Wide Web, type:

http://www.town.hall.org/edgar/edgar.html

For access by Anonymous ftp, type:

ftp.town.hall.org

When accessing Edgar by ftp you should log in as Anonymous and then supply your E-Mail address as the password. This service provides on-line public access to 1994 10Q, 10K, and other SEC filings. Although now in its infancy, this site should contain data on over 15,000 companies by the end of 1995 when all publicly traded companies will be required to file electronically.[3] Also of note is the National Trade Data Bank (NTDB), which has recently been made accessible on the Internet by the Department of Commerce. Publications now available include *Market Research Reports* and the *U.S. Industrial Outlook.* Access to the NTDB is available through www by typing:

http://www.stat-usa.gov/BEN/Services/ntdbhome.html

For access through Anonymous ftp, type:

ftp.stat-usa.gov

Internet access is generally free to students through a university account.

MOVING FORWARD IN THE ANALYSIS

After you get a good feel for the company's situation, it's time to begin the consumer analysis. Later, as you begin to understand the consumer, you may want to complete the company analysis by observing or interviewing company personnel and getting sales data from within the company. It may seem awkward or contrived to begin the company analysis, move on to the consumer analysis, and then come back to complete the company analysis. Keep in mind that doing research is every bit as much an art as it is a science. The idea is to discover information in such a way that you remain as objective as possible. One way to maintain your objectivity is to select your sources carefully. It can often color your thinking to hear what company personnel have to say.

CONSUMER ANALYSIS

The distinguishing feature of successful advertising is a persuasive, memorable message. The message can be spoken, printed, or simply implied. The key to developing these kinds of messages is not so much to understand words and ideas but to understand people. Leo Burnett, like many advertising greats, intuitively knew how to talk to the average person. He was often described as a man of average appearance and voice, who could instantly grasp the "inherent drama," as Burnett would put it, in a product and relate it to consumers in a way that neither talked up or down to people. Today, as the 21st century approaches, the marketing task is far more complex and competitive than it was as little as ten to fifteen years ago. More than ever, marketing and advertising people need to understand consumers. A good consumer analysis boils down to about four general questions:

- ☐ **Who are the consumers?** What characteristics do they have in common?
- ☐ **What motivates them to buy?** How do they think, feel, or behave?
- ☐ **What do they look for in a product?** What are their needs, wants, problems, and interests?
- ☐ **How do they look at life?** What are their values? How do they go about their daily routine? How does the product fit into their lives? How are they influenced by others?

Who Are the Consumers?

The prime prospects for most products are usually the people who have consumed the product in the past. Although this is not an ironclad rule, it is a guideline that most companies follow. Even though one market segment may be comparable to another in terms of demographic and psychographic characteristics, there may be other factors that influence product usage that are difficult to pinpoint. The simplest way to predict future usage is to look at product usage data. The best place to fish is not necessarily where the fish are but where the fish are "biting" (feeding).

For example, more hot dogs are sold per capita in the city of Chicago than in any other major metropolitan city in the United States. Hot dogs have long been part of the culture in Chicago and have been big sellers there for more than 40 years. The hot dog of choice is a kosher-style, all-beef product, and it is usually sold in a small building specializing in take-out service. The most popular brand is Vienna. Over the past twenty years, entrepreneurs have taken this concept to cities as diverse as Atlanta, St. Louis, Denver, Nashville, and Panama City, Florida. Although these businesses survive, they seldom thrive as they do in Chicago. Why? Because these cities are not Chicago. Apparently, the hot dog does not have sufficient want-satisfying qualities to have anything more than limited appeal. In Chicago, people go out of their way to eat hot dogs.

Product Usage

Although you may be able to get information on product usage from trade publications, the information will likely be more comprehensive and objective if you consult either *Simmons Media and Markets*, published by the Simmons Market Research Bureau (SMRB), or *Mediamark Research Inc (MRI)*. Simmons and MRI, as they are often called, are the two major syndicated research sources of product-usage information. Each of these services reports on the usage of brands, products, and services in approximately 800 categories. Usage is typically cross-referenced according to various demographic characteristics, including gender, age, education, occupation, geographic location, race, income, and marital status. Figure 2–1 is an example of data that might be found in Simmons or MRI.

To understand the consumer, it helps to look at current users. The goal of the analysis is to describe the consumers on the basis of characteristics they have in common. These characteristics can then be used to define or delineate a market segment. A market segment then becomes the *target audience*, or *target market*, if it is the segment to which the advertising is to be directed. The targeting decision is a key element of the campaign strategy and should be deferred until all the individual analyses have been completed. Users are typically described according to the following characteristics:

☐ Demographic criteria
☐ Psychographic criteria

FIGURE 2-1 BOUGHT REGULAR COLA DRINKS IN LAST 7 DAYS (ADULTS)

```
0043                    REGULAR COLA DRINKS (CARBONATED, NOT DIET): ALL USERS, USERS IN LAST 7 DAYS AND KINDS          0043
P 15                                              (ADULTS)                                                             P 15
```

	TOTAL U.S. '000	ALL USERS A '000	B % DOWN	C % ACROSS	D INDX	HEAVY USERS EIGHT OR MORE A '000	B % DOWN	C % ACROSS	D INDX	BOTTLED A '000	B % DOWN	C % ACROSS	D INDX	CANNED A '000	B % DOWN	C % ACROSS	D INDX
TOTAL ADULTS	187747	116443	100.0	62.0	100	40781	100.0	21.7	100	67416	100.0	35.9	100	83598	100.0	44.5	100
MALES	90070	60171	51.7	66.8	108	22123	54.2	24.6	113	34737	51.5	38.6	107	43353	51.9	48.1	108
FEMALES	97676	56272	48.3	57.6	93	18657	45.8	19.1	88	32679	48.5	33.5	93	40245	48.1	41.2	93
PRINCIPAL SHOPPERS	115901	69226	59.5	59.7	96	23395	57.4	20.2	93	39402	58.4	34.0	95	49071	58.7	42.3	95
18 - 24	23951	18155	15.6	75.8	122	8512	20.9	35.5	164	11911	17.7	49.7	138	14019	16.8	58.5	131
25 - 34	41492	29727	25.5	71.6	116	11919	29.2	28.7	132	17962	26.6	43.3	121	21883	26.2	52.7	118
35 - 44	40678	26728	23.0	65.7	106	9554	23.4	23.5	108	16428	24.4	40.4	112	18996	22.7	46.7	105
45 - 54	29045	17131	14.7	59.0	95	5731	14.1	19.7	91	8981	13.3	30.9	86	12518	15.0	43.1	97
55 - 64	21263	11058	9.5	52.0	84	2371	5.8	11.1	51	5428	8.1	25.5	71	7514	9.0	35.3	79
65 OR OLDER	31318	13645	11.7	43.6	70	2694	6.6	8.6	40	6706	9.9	21.4	60	8668	10.4	27.7	62
18 - 34	65443	47882	41.1	73.2	118	20431	50.1	31.2	144	29872	44.3	45.6	127	35902	42.9	54.9	123
18 - 49	122143	84416	72.5	69.1	111	33517	82.2	27.4	126	51286	76.1	42.0	117	62349	74.6	51.0	115
25 - 54	111215	73586	63.2	66.2	107	27204	66.7	24.5	113	43371	64.3	39.0	109	53397	63.9	48.0	108
35 - 49	56701	36535	31.4	64.4	104	13086	32.1	23.1	106	21414	31.8	37.8	105	26447	31.6	46.6	105
50 OR OLDER	65603	32027	27.5	48.8	79	7264	17.8	11.1	51	16130	23.9	24.6	68	21249	25.4	32.4	73
GRADUATED COLLEGE	37353	20997	18.0	56.2	91	5164	12.7	13.8	64	11761	17.4	31.5	88	16319	19.5	43.7	98
ATTENDED COLLEGE	39301	24312	20.9	61.9	100	8947	21.9	22.8	105	13863	20.6	35.3	98	18121	21.7	46.1	104
GRADUATED HIGH SCHOOL	73139	47354	40.7	64.7	104	17169	42.1	23.5	108	27770	41.2	38.0	106	33414	40.0	45.7	103
DID NOT GRADUATE HIGH SCHOOL	37954	23781	20.4	62.7	101	9501	23.3	25.0	115	14022	20.8	36.9	103	15745	18.8	41.5	93
EMPLOYED MALES	62041	43938	37.7	70.8	114	16694	40.9	26.9	124	25568	37.9	41.2	115	32343	38.7	52.1	117
EMPLOYED FEMALES	53100	32042	27.5	60.3	97	10400	25.5	19.6	90	18635	27.6	35.1	98	23781	28.4	44.8	101
EMPLOYED FULL-TIME	99735	65910	56.6	66.1	107	23879	58.6	23.9	110	38595	57.2	38.7	108	48109	57.5	48.2	108
EMPLOYED PART-TIME	15406	10070	8.6	65.4	105	3215	7.9	20.9	96	5608	8.3	36.4	101	8014	9.6	52.0	117
NOT EMPLOYED	72606	40463	34.7	55.7	90	13687	33.6	18.9	87	23214	34.4	32.0	89	27475	32.9	37.8	85
PROFESSIONAL/MANAGER	32308	19356	16.6	59.9	97	5791	14.2	17.9	83	10591	15.7	32.8	91	15012	18.0	46.5	104
TECHNICAL/CLERICAL/SALES	35568	22906	19.7	64.4	104	7950	19.5	22.4	103	13055	19.4	36.7	102	17074	20.4	48.0	108
PRECISION/CRAFT	12562	9015	7.7	71.8	116	3657	9.0	29.1	134	5323	7.9	42.4	118	6186	7.4	49.2	111
OTHER EMPLOYED	34704	24704	21.2	71.2	115	9696	23.8	27.9	129	15234	22.6	43.9	122	17851	21.4	51.4	116
SINGLE	41125	29519	25.4	71.8	116	12812	31.4	31.2	143	18503	27.4	45.0	125	22342	26.7	54.3	122
MARRIED	111354	67368	57.9	60.5	98	21385	52.4	19.2	88	37604	55.8	33.8	94	48005	57.4	43.1	97
DIVORCED/SEPARATED/WIDOWED	35268	19557	16.8	55.5	89	6584	16.1	18.7	86	11310	16.8	32.1	89	13251	15.9	37.6	84
PARENTS	61860	42323	36.3	68.4	110	16427	40.3	26.6	122	25844	38.3	41.8	116	33536	37.5	50.7	114
WHITE	159985	97505	83.7	60.9	98	33970	83.3	21.2	98	55538	82.4	34.7	97	71125	85.1	44.5	100
BLACK	21570	15176	13.0	70.4	113	5586	13.7	25.9	119	9854	14.6	45.7	127	9686	11.6	44.9	101
OTHER	6191	3762	3.2	60.8	98	1225	3.0	19.8	91	2024	3.0	32.7	91	2787	3.3	45.0	101
NORTHEAST-CENSUS	38611	23171	19.9	60.0	97	8350	20.5	21.6	100	15472	22.9	40.1	112	15009	18.0	38.9	87
MIDWEST	45021	26792	23.0	59.5	96	9091	22.3	20.2	93	13895	20.6	30.9	86	21277	25.5	47.3	106
SOUTH	65246	43358	37.2	66.5	107	16342	40.1	25.0	115	26598	39.5	40.8	114	29272	35.0	44.9	101
WEST	38869	23122	19.9	59.5	96	6997	17.2	18.0	83	11452	17.0	29.5	82	18040	21.6	46.4	104
COUNTY SIZE A	76945	46795	40.2	60.8	9R	16271	39.9	21.1	97	26823	39.8	34.9	97	33522	40.1	43.6	98
COUNTY SIZE B	55516	34703	29.8	62.5	101	12337	30.3	22.2	102	20574	30.5	37.1	103	25050	30.0	45.1	101
COUNTY SIZE C	27293	16861	14.5	61.8	100	5989	14.7	21.9	101	9002	13.4	33.0	92	12522	15.0	45.9	103
COUNTY SIZE D	27993	18084	15.5	64.6	104	6184	15.2	22.1	102	11017	16.3	39.4	110	12503	15.0	44.7	100

METRO CENTRAL CITY
METRO SUBURBAN
NON METRO

TOP 5 ADI'S
TOP 10 ADI'S
TOP 20 ADI'S

HSHLD. INC. $75,000 OR MORE
$60,000 OR MORE
$50,000 OR MORE
$40,000 OR MORE
$30,000 OR MORE
$30,000 - $39,999
$20,000 - $29,999
$10,000 - $19,999
UNDER $10,000

HOUSEHOLD OF 1 PERSON
2 PEOPLE
3 OR 4 PEOPLE
5 OR MORE PEOPLE

NO CHILD IN HSHLD
CHILD(REN) UNDER 2 YEARS
2 - 5 YEARS
6 - 11 YEARS
12 - 17 YEARS

RESIDENCE OWNED
VALUE: $70,000 OR MORE
VALUE: UNDER $70,000
RESIDENCE RENTED

DAILY NEWSPAPERS
NET ONE DAY REACH
READ ONLY ONE
READ TWO OR MORE
WEEKEND/SUNDAY NEWSPAPERS
NET ONE DAY REACH
READ ONLY ONE
READ TWO OR MORE

How to read columns A, B, C, and D:

A. This column contains the number of adults who can be described by the user category at the top of the column who fall into the demographic segment at the left. (e.g., there are 18,155,000 users 18–24 years old.)

B. This column contains the percentage of the *user category* that falls into the demographic segment on the *left*. (e.g., 15.6% of all users are 18–24 years old.)

C. This column contains the percentage of the demographic segment on the left that falls into the user category at the top. (e.g., 75.8% of all 18- to 24-year-olds are users.)

D. The index number in this column compares how the demographic segment to the left uses the product to the average usage for all adults. The index number for average usage is 100, and any number above or below 100 indicates above or below average usage. (e.g., 18- to 24-year-olds use the product 22% more than average users.)

Source: © 1994 Simmons Market Research Bureau, Inc. All rights reserved.

☐ Degree of product or brand usage

☐ Degree of brand loyalty

Demographic Criteria Demographic criteria describe the consumer in terms of variables such as age, gender, income, geographic location, marital status, education, race, and family life cycle. These criteria are easily the most widely used form for describing or defining the target market. This information is relatively easy to measure, and a number of research sources, such as Simmons and MRI, publish it.

Although the value of using demographic criteria to segment the market is obvious for some products, for others it may not provide enough discriminatory power to distinguish between prime prospects and only fair ones. For example, two groups may be comparable in terms of age, sex, education, and income, but they may not have the same propensity to buy ski equipment because they differ in ways that demographic criteria are not able to suggest. To better understand consumers, an analyst will often examine the psychological makeup and the lifestyles of consumers to gain insight into other factors that can affect their predisposition to buy. However, when it comes to buying media, planners will usually revert to demographic criteria.

Psychographic Criteria Psychographic criteria include information that is both psychological in nature, such as personality, motivation, and attitude, and sociological in nature, such as lifestyles, activities, and the way people go about their daily routines. Although demographic criteria are relatively easy to measure, psychographic characteristics are not. The data are not likely to be as reliable or valid as demographic information because of the greater difficulty in defining and measuring psychological and sociological constructs. It is usually much easier to measure whether someone is male or female and a high school graduate than it is to measure whether someone is affectionate and liberal and how often he or she eats out. As a result, much of the psychographic information used in advertising is customized to fit specific needs of the advertiser. We will discuss two sources of information in this section: (1) Simmons, which is widely available but of limited value, and (2) the VALS 2 system, which is widely used but not likely to be available in libraries.

Simmons presents some psychographic information cross-referenced to demographic criteria and media exposure. This information is based on a respondent's self-concept and is collected by personal interview. Basically, interviewers ask consumers to rate themselves with respect to a group of adjectives according to a five-point scale. Each of the adjectives, such as affectionate, broad-minded, and egocentric, is then cross-referenced with demographic variables, such as age, income, and geographical location. The psychographic categories are also cross-referenced with product usage data, but this information does not appear in the printed volumes, which, unfortunately, is what most universities have. This information is provided on CD-ROM, which is the way most advertisers and agencies access thin data. The categories (four to a page) are as follows:

AFFECTIONATE	AMICABLE	AWKWARD	BRAVE
BROAD-MINDED	CREATIVE	DOMINATING	EFFICIENT
EGOCENTRIC	FRANK	FUNNY	INTELLIGENT
KIND	REFINED	RESERVED	SELF-ASSURED
SOCIABLE	STUBBORN	TENSE	TRUSTWORTHY

To use this information, an analyst first has to determine the demographic makeup of the product users and then use the above descriptors to help define the market segment.

VALS 2, named for values and lifestyles, is a psychographic system developed by SRI International to segment the market and predict consumer behavior. According to VALS 2, consumers are motivated to pursue and acquire products, services, and experiences that provide satisfaction and give shape, substance, and character to their identities. They are guided by one of three powerful self-orientations:

principle oriented—these consumers are guided in their choices by abstract, idealized criteria, rather than by feelings, events, or desire for approval and opinions of others.

status oriented—these consumers look for products and services that demonstrate the consumers' success to their peers.

action oriented—these consumers are guided by a desire for social or physical activity, variety, and risk taking.[4]

The VALS 2 system also suggests that consumers' behavior is influenced by the *resources* they are able to draw on, such as income, education, energy level, and self-confidence. VALS 2 is able to further define eight segments of consumers with different attitudes, distinctive behavior, and decision-making patterns.[5] Figure 2–2 presents the VALS 2 typology.[6]

Other sources of psychographic information are also available, especially on lifestyle. Most of these sources, such as Claritas, Inc., and SRDS, use the information in coordination with data on specific markets, as will be discussed in Chapter 3 under market analysis. If these sources of information are not available, the researcher will have to collect the information using primary research techniques. We will discuss some of these techniques later in this chapter.

Degree of Product Usage Another useful way to think of consumers is according to the amount of a product they use. The standard way to classify usage is to categorize consumers into *heavy, medium,* and *light* users. Both Simmons and MRI report their data on product usage in this manner. Although it may seem obvious that an advertiser would want to target heavy users, this is not an appropriate strategy for all marketers. Aiming at heavy users usually puts a company into direct competition with the market leader. In some categories, such as candy bars or appliances, advertisers can aim at heavy users, and even if they sell much less than the brand leader, they still can carve out a

FIGURE 2–2   **THE VALS 2 NETWORK**

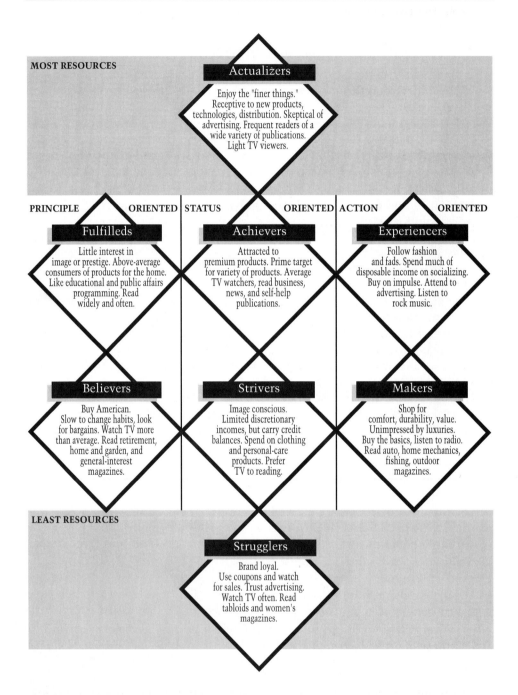

MOST RESOURCES

Actualizers

Enjoy the "finer things."
Receptive to new products,
technologies, distribution. Skeptical of
advertising. Frequent readers of a
wide variety of publications.
Light TV viewers.

PRINCIPLE   ORIENTED   STATUS   ORIENTED   ACTION   ORIENTED

Fulfilleds

Little interest in
image or prestige. Above-average
consumers of products for the home.
Like educational and public affairs
programming. Read
widely and often.

Achievers

Attracted to
premium products. Prime target
for variety of products. Average
TV watchers, read business,
news, and self-help
publications.

Experiencers

Follow fashion
and fads. Spend much of
disposable income on socializing.
Buy on impulse. Attend to
advertising. Listen to
rock music.

Believers

Buy American.
Slow to change habits, look
for bargains. Watch TV more
than average. Read retirement,
home and garden, and
general-interest
magazines.

Strivers

Image conscious.
Limited discretionary
incomes, but carry credit
balances. Spend on clothing
and personal-care
products. Prefer
TV to reading.

Makers

Shop for
comfort, durability, value.
Unimpressed by luxuries.
Buy the basics, listen to radio.
Read auto, home mechanics,
fishing, outdoor
magazines.

LEAST RESOURCES

Strugglers

Brand loyal.
Use coupons and watch
for sales. Trust advertising.
Watch TV often. Read
tabloids and women's
magazines.

Source: *American Demographics*, July 94, p. 3. © 1994 VALS 2, SRI International, Menlo Park, CA.

satisfactory share of the market. In other categories, such as cigarettes, going after the heavy user will pit the company directly up against Marlboro and Winston, the two top brands of cigarettes in the United States. In the case of Marlboro, one of the two or three most powerful brand names in the world regardless of the product category, the competition is especially formidable. When new brands are introduced in the cigarette industry, they usually target the message strategy to the medium and light users. On the other hand, if you have the marketing muscle of McDonald's, you can do as they do and target the super heavy users (SHUs).

Degree of Brand Loyalty It is usually helpful to get some feel for the amount of brand loyalty in a product category. It is widely believed that during the 1980s, consumers became much more value conscious. One study reported that the percentage of customers who would remain with their brand in the face of competitive price deals changed from 80 percent to 60 percent during this period.[7] The amount of brand loyalty displayed by consumers can have a strong influence on both advertising strategy and tactics. Knowing the amount of brand loyalty in the market can help determine whether the brand's core equities are eroding. If so, then the planners have to decide whether to take steps to shore up a brand's equity (to be discussed in Chapter 4) or rely on various pricing and sales promotion tactics.

The most powerful type of brand loyalty measures are behavioral. Both Nielsen North America and Information Resources, Inc. (IRI), measure the extent to which households buy the same brand in two successive time periods. Customers are then divided up into new and loyal customers. New customers are further classified according to whether they purchased on a deal or not.[8]

If the analyst does not have access to scanner data, then an alternative approach is to collect information on consumer buying styles either through primary or secondary research. One method developed by Leo Burnett is to categorize consumers into four different patterns of brand loyalty and buying strategies:

1. *Long loyals* are committed to one brand regardless of price or any other factor. These numbers are declining and are seen mostly when the purchase is "highly involving." Top-of-the-line cosmetics are a good example.
2. *Rotators* show regular patterns of shifting between preferred brands motivated by variety rather than price.
3. *Dealer sensitives* show a pattern of shifting between preferred brands determined by availability of special offers or incentives.
4. *Price sensitives* follow a decision rule to purchase the cheapest option regardless of brand.[9]

Simmons reports information on buying style based on the consumer's self-concept in the following categories:

BRAND LOYAL	CAUTIOUS	CONFORMISTS	ECOLOGISTS
ECONOMY-MINDED	EXPERIMENTERS	IMPULSIVES	AD BELIEVERS
PLANNERS	STYLE-CONSCIOUS		

As stated earlier, the printed volumes do not contain the above information cross-referenced according to product usage. This information is available only on CD-ROM.

WHEN AND HOW OFTEN DO CONSUMERS BUY?

A common premise in advertising is to advertise in line with existing trends of consumer behavior. Two trends that are especially important to media planners are

☐ How often consumers buy the product (that is, the purchase cycle)
☐ When consumers buy the product (that is, the seasonality)

Media planners use information on how often consumers buy, and when they buy, to help them schedule advertising impressions. The most accurate source of information on the purchase cycle and the seasonality of consumer purchases usually comes from Nielsen's or IRI's product-usage audit. An analyst can also find some information from trade articles and industry associations.

What Motivates Consumers to Buy?

After you identify the current users, it can be helpful to understand what motivates them to spend their money one place and not another. To understand the consumers' motivations, you must first understand what factors influence them. Advertisers are always trying to figure out why consumers behave the way they do. Over the years, numerous models have been developed to explain the consumer buying process. These models typically explain the process from a consumer's first exposure to an ad to the actual purchase of the product. These models are explained in most consumer behavior texts, usually under the subheading of *learning hierarchy*, and they are widely available in libraries. You may want to consult them.

Trade articles about consumers can provide some insight into what motivates people to buy a product. Other secondary research is unlikely to be of much help. Primary research will probably be your best source of information. We will discuss some of the techniques later in this section, but first you need to determine what questions to pursue.

One way to organize your understanding of buyer behavior is to examine what consumers think and feel about a product and how they use it. This exercise should help you organize the kind of information you need to understand why consumers will or will not buy a product. Exhibit 2–2 presents

---

EXHIBIT 2–2   RESEARCH QUESTIONS TO CONSIDER

How consumers think about the product

1. To what extent are they aware of the product, especially the brand name?
2. Do they know about the brand's special features, ingredients, or hidden qualities?
3. Do they understand how the product or brand works?
4. Do they understand the brand's superior qualities?

How consumers feel about the product

1. What is their attitude toward the product category?
2. What is their attitude toward the specific brand?
3. To what extent do they like or desire the product or brand?
4. Do consumers trust the brand to deliver the promised benefits?
5. Do consumers have a preference for this brand?
6. What image or personality do consumers associate with the product or brand?

How consumers use the product

1. How do consumers use the product?
2. Where do consumers use the product?
3. When do consumers use the product?
4. Why do consumers use the product?
5. Are there alternative uses for the product?
6. Under what conditions would the consumer use more of the product?

---

some of the questions you should consider pursuing in your secondary or primary research.

The information obtained from these questions will then be used to help determine the campaign problems and opportunities. These in turn will provide the foundation for setting objectives after all the analyses are completed.

What Consumers Expect in a Product

In the course of doing consumer interviews, there is often a subtle shift in the focus from how consumers think or feel about a product to what they would like the product to do for them. Some consumers are able to identify right away how they expect to benefit from using a product, but usually it takes them awhile. If they do not make this shift, you should lead them in this direction, whether you are using a structured questionnaire or conducting an in-depth interview. If you can pinpoint how consumers expect to benefit from a product, then the most direct and effective way to advertise is simply to interpret the want-satisfying qualities of the product in terms of the needs or wants of the consumer.

Although it may have been easy to determine the consumers' needs and wants in the 1950s and 1960s, it is a lot harder in the 1990s. Today consumers expect more from a product because products are generally much better than they used to be. Consumers may not be perfectly satisfied with a product, but it does not necessarily follow that they can articulate exactly what they are looking for in a product. It takes some skill to get consumers to reveal enough information to provide insight into why they might buy a product. Consumers typically buy products for the following reasons:

☐ They satisfy needs or wants.
☐ They help solve problems.
☐ They simply arouse curiosity or interest.

Consumers may also buy a product because they like the values or lifestyle depicted in the advertising. However, this insight is more likely to result from an analyst's inference about consumers' values and lifestyles than from consumers' explanations of why they buy a product. Consumers may say they are buying the product because of the ads, after interviewers show consumers the advertising, but they don't usually offer that information before.

Needs and Wants The difference between a need and a want is generally a matter of perspective. Consumers often confuse this difference. A young boy going to a basketball camp may feel he "needs" a pair of Air Jordan shoes to fit in; a young girl may feel she does not need to eat food for similar reasons. Most people would not agree with the boy or the girl. To a researcher, the difference between a want and a need may be a semantic distinction with no practical implications.

Problems Generally, people's needs and wants are fairly well satisfied with most products. This makes it more difficult to get information from consumers. Even when people are not satisfied with the results of using a product, they may not be aware of what they want in its place. However, if you ask consumers if they have any gripes about or problems with using the product, the information they reveal can provide just enough insight upon which you can base an advertising campaign or make product improvements. For example, consumer research for Gillette uncovered the useful information that when women cut themselves shaving, they blame themselves. Perhaps, not surprisingly, when men cut themselves, they blame the blade or the razor.

Consumer researchers have to be careful when designing questions that they move beyond simple questions that ask people what they need or want in a product. In the case of companies like Gillette, if researchers ask women what they want in a razor, it is very likely that the women would not know what to tell them. However, Gillette researchers know that women have problems shaving, so in their consumer research they questioned women about how they use their razors.

Researchers found that women usually shave their legs in a shower, whereas men mostly shave in front of a sink. The researchers also knew that when men use a razor, the head of the razor is on top, and the stem is on the bottom. Conversely, when women are in the shower, the stem of the razor is usually on top, and the head of the razor is usually facing down. As a result, the underside of the razor catches the water streaming down from the shower head, and women commonly complain the razor slips from their hands, especially if their hands are soapy.

Gillette used this information to redesign the Sensor razor expressly for women. Instead of a thin stem, the housing holding the razor was made to fit the palm of a woman's hand. A special rubbery grip, which Gillette obtained from its Parker Pen subsidiary, was attached to the housing. Because Gillette relied heavily on consumer research to develop the product, its print ads are laden with copy reflecting how the Sensor for Women addresses women's problems.[10]

How Consumers Look at Life

Although a substantial amount of information on consumer values and lifestyles is available from syndicated sources, it may not be specific enough to fit the given campaign. Also, the sources are not widely available in libraries. A number of primary research techniques that can be used to get the above information will be discussed shortly. One of these techniques, based on observation, is widely used in advertising and goes by the name *ethnography*. This type of qualitative research is especially helpful in focusing on those aspects of consumers' lifestyles that directly affect the way consumers use a product.

Ethnography

The literal meaning of *ethnography* refers to the description and classification of various cultures and racial groups. In advertising, it refers more to the observation of consumers as they go about their daily routines. Many of the techniques are borrowed from anthropology. Researchers try to put themselves in the place of consumers by getting as close to them as they can and trying to simulate an actual purchase decision for a particular product. To learn about consumers' lifestyles and how they use a product, an interviewer goes to a consumer's environment and observes behavior patterns and asks questions. As part of the observational process, the interviewer takes photographs.

In research for a food product, for example, an interviewer would ask the consumer questions to reveal his or her eating philosophy and management. Is the family health oriented, and to what extent do the family members make trade-offs between foods that are good for them and food that simply tastes good? How does the family rationalize their choices? How much of a family's food intake is consumed on the run, and how much is part of a regular sit-down meal? How much does the family eat out?

The interviewer may also visit a supermarket with a consumer to see the decision process up close and personal. This process provides the research effort a better understanding of the dynamics and trade-offs consumers make when shopping for a particular product. If an advertiser wants to know what consumers think of a certain restaurant chain, the researcher not only goes to the restaurant to observe consumers but also goes to one of the restaurants with a consumer. This way the researcher can experience firsthand the problems, irritants, and satisfactions from the consumer's point of view. The researcher hopes to gain insight by looking for clues and relationships. The idea is to think like a consumer but interpret like an analyst.

Tatham Euro RSCG, a major advertising agency in Chicago, used ethnographic research, see Exhibit 2–3, to learn about how consumers make decisions about frozen entrées. The company learned that consumers have both rational and emotional needs. Consumers classify brands in either a rational category that would include food that is good for you or an emotional category that would include food that simply tastes good. Consumers perceive all the nutritional brands, like Healthy Choice, Lean Cuisine, and Weight Watchers, as nutritional frozen food. Because these products satisfy rational needs, there was little emotional loyalty to any one brand.

Tatham found that consumers "taste bud" shop rather than "brand shop" for frozen entrées when they stand in front of the frozen food case. They pick the individual items they know taste good and meet their personal nutritional needs. The challenge for the agency and the advertiser was, first, to interrupt this kind of switching behavior and then to try to secure more loyalty toward their brand through more emotional-based communications that were more relevant to their needs and differentiated their product from the others.[11]

Other Qualitative Research Techniques

In addition to ethnography, there are a number of techniques that can be used to gain insights on consumers. In many ways, the research that is done to develop campaigns is more of an art than it is a science. It is common to hear advertising people refer to their research as soft. Technically, this could mean that there were no control groups in an experiment, no systematic manipulation of variables, or that the sample was not randomly selected. Usually, it simply means that the analysis is more qualitative than quantitative. The main purpose of qualitative research is to develop insights into how to talk to consumers. Among the heaviest users of qualitative research are agency account planners.

The Account Planning Revolution By the early 1980s, a number of U.S. agencies, notably Chiat/Day, adopted a system many British ad agencies were using to manage the flow of information used to develop marketing campaigns. This system is called *account planning*.[12] The account planner's main function is to develop and manage the flow of information using traditional and nontraditional research to uncover special consumer insights that could provide the basis for a message strategy. Account planners work directly with the copywriters and art directors, often sharing responsibility for the creative ideas, instead of apart as traditional researchers have often done. Historically, copywriters have had an aversion to researchers bearing numbers. This attitude, in part, led some agencies, such as Foote, Cone & Belding Communications, to replace their researchers with account planners. Although account planners use all kinds of information, much of the research effort they manage is qualitative, including ethnographic studies, one-on-ones, focus groups, and projective tests, which are described later in this chapter. The more

EXHIBIT 2–3	A DAY IN THE LIFE OF AN ETHNOGRAPHER
9:00 A.M.	The researcher arrives at the home of a consumer to discuss food. The appointment has been set up by a firm that specializes in recruiting people to participate in consumer research.
9:05 A.M.	After exchanging pleasantries, the interviewer engages the consumer in a discussion of the family's eating philosophy and the way she (or he) manages the cooking and the availability of food for the family. The interviewer asks about the role other members of the household play in shopping and cooking.
9:15 A.M.	The interviewer asks to see the consumer's cookbooks and any special recipes. A photograph is taken of the books.
9:25 A.M.	The interviewer asks to look in the consumer's pantry and cupboards, carefully noting snack items, national brands, and the proportion of canned to soft-packaged goods. The interviewer photographs the products.
9:35 A.M.	The interviewer asks to look in the refrigerator, noting the amount of fresh food, the leftovers, and the prominence of national brands. More photos are taken.
9:45 A.M.	The interviewer checks the freezer and inquires about the length of time items have been in there. The proportion of entrées to single-item packages including desserts is noted. More photos are taken.
9:55 A.M.	The interviewer takes photos of the kitchen, especially of gadgets and other labor-saving devices. The interviewer asks to go shopping with the consumer and gives her $50.
10:10 A.M.	They arrive at the supermarket, get a cart, and walk down the aisles. The interviewer makes special note of the consumer's interest in fresh produce, bakery items, canned goods, meat, nonfood items, and frozen food. The interviewer observes the consumer's interest in price shopping and the relative importance of store brands to nationally advertised items.
10:40 A.M.	Prior to getting in the checkout lane, the interviewer takes a photograph of the cart. While in the checkout lane, the interviewer asks the consumer to explain the purchase decisions.
10: 45 A.M.	The interviewer says good-bye and prepares to go to the next meeting. Later, back in the office, the consumer's statements will be compared to the photographs and the interviewer's notes.

traditional quantitative research, such as surveys, observation, consumer panels, and experiments, is likely to be done by the advertiser or by a research firm that it hires.

THE ROLE OF QUALITATIVE RESEARCH

The key to successful qualitative research is to understand both the purpose and limitations of the various techniques. Qualitative research is usually conducted to develop the campaign strategy. It is especially useful in gaining insight into consumers. However, this type of research should not be viewed as a substitute for more rigorous and systematic studies because of the limited size and representativeness of the typical sample and the difficulty and subjectivity in coding lengthy conversation. Qualitative studies can be useful in providing ideas and in evaluating concepts, ads, and campaigns, but they may not be as reliable or valid as a more traditional quantitative study.

Asking Questions

The key to a good interview is to know how and when to ask questions. A good interviewer looks for insight into how a consumer thinks, feels, and acts. The most meaningful information is not usually on the surface. An interviewer should use sensitivity and judgment to ferret out the best pieces of information. Interviewers tend to get better with experience; by paying attention to the tips outlined in Exhibit 2–4, beginners should do fine.

One of the main advantages of qualitative research is that it provides an opportunity to uncover consumers' underlying thoughts and feelings, including attitudes, prejudices, biases, and motivations. Although it helps to have an experienced interviewer conduct the research, beginners can use a simple technique, called *laddering*, to link up a product's attributes, or qualities, with the values consumers place on using a particular product.

Laddering   This technique is a type of questioning used with depth interviews. An interviewer asks a series of questions that are designed to trace the relationship between a product's attributes and the value consumers get out of using the product. The technique is based on means-end theory, which loosely means that consumers use products as the means to achieve various ends. These ends get defined in terms of consumer values.[13] Most consumers respond to a question about why they use a product or what they look for in a product with an answer that focuses on the product's qualities, or attributes. This answer is a relatively basic, or lower, form of knowledge. However, consumers do not buy products for their attributes as much as for what they can do for them—how they make them feel. If advertisers can uncover consumers' feelings or how they get value out of using a product, they can use this information to develop a message strategy based on emotions rather than simple product characteristics.

The technique is called laddering because the interviewer keeps asking questions that gradually reveal the relationship between a product's attributes and the value they provide to a consumer. Because an attribute tends to be a physical property and a value is psychological in nature, the interviewer moves from a lower form of knowledge to a higher form. In a sense, the interviewer is moving up the ladder of knowledge about the product.

Conceptually, the element linking an attribute to a value is a *consequence.* As a result of using a product with certain attributes, consumers usually experience an effect, or a consequence. Consumers then interpret this effect in terms of what it means to them (that is, its *value*). These concepts can be further refined. An attribute can be something tangible, or physical, such as flavors, colors, sizes, nutritional ingredients, calories, shapes, and horsepower, or it can be something largely intangible, or psychological, such as *sexy*

EXHIBIT 2–4   TEN TIPS TO A PRODUCTIVE INTERVIEW

---

1. **Be yourself.** It is important to make the consumers feel as comfortable as you can. If they sense you are acting in a way that is very different from your normal personality, it could make them feel uneasy. So be yourself—your warm, friendly, serious self.

2. **Briefly tell the consumer about the interview.** Consumers are naturally curious, if not suspicious. Keep the information general but informative. Tell them you are developing an advertising campaign and want their opinions on the product or category.

3. **Tape record the interview.** Don't take notes. Consumers will tend to forget about the tape recorder. However, if they see you feverishly taking notes, they may slow down to let you catch up. They may also feel self-conscious.

4. **Give the consumers easy questions to start.** The object is to get the consumers talking easily and naturally. Though the first questions should be easy, they should be open-ended so the interviewee doesn't simply answer the question with a one-word answer.

5. **Avoid leading questions.** If interviewees sense how you might answer a question, they may tell you what they think you want to hear. Be sure to phrase questions without giving any verbal or nonverbal clues about your position.

6. **Probe. Probe. Probe.** Consumers don't always know why they think, feel, or act a certain way. You'll want to use the word *why* repeatedly to get at deeply seated thoughts and feelings.

7. **Listen carefully to the answers.** Many times inexperienced interviewers will be so busy planning their next question that they will fail to pay attention to details and miss an opportunity to follow up on an important line of questioning.

8. **Make the interviewee work.** Even conscientious interviewees get tired or lazy. After 15 minutes or so, be sensitive to a decrease in the interviewee's attention or interest. Be polite, firm, and persistent. Reward them periodically with positive acknowledgment.

9. **Focus. Focus. Focus.** Interviewers also wear down. Make sure you hear the *last half* of any sentence or phrase.

10. **When finished, say thank you.** It's important you maintain professional standards. Be sure to leave the interviewee feeling positive about the experience.

---

clothing, *funny*-looking toys, *prestigious*-looking automobiles, or *youthful* brand images. Interviewers usually begin their questioning by asking about a product's or a brand's attributes.

Consequences can either be functional (more tangible in nature) or psychosocial (more subjective). When the advertising for Silkience shampoo suggests that using the product will leave hair soft, silky, and manageable, it is stressing functional consequences. If the advertising stresses how a woman's hair will make people admire her, it is stressing the psychosocial consequences. Consequences can also be described from both a negative and positive point of view. Advertisers seldom even imply that using their product will have undesirable consequences, but suggestions that using a competitive product will have negative consequences is a common practice. Advertisers will also play up the potential negative consequences of *not* using their product (for example, "You can pay me now, or you can pay me later"). In a depth interview, skillful interviewers will ask consumers why they want to avoid a specific "negative" outcome and then move "up" the means-end chain, or ladder, to questions about positive consequences and eventually about values.

Positive consequences are interpreted in terms of how a consumer benefits from using a product. Copywriters put a lot of emphasis on benefits in advertising copy. It is widely believed that consumers buy products more for their benefits than their attributes. This belief leads some advertisers to segment their markets, at least in part, in terms of the benefits consumers look for in a product. This approach, called *benefit segmentation,* influences both the message and media strategy. For example, the market for toothpaste consists mostly of consumers who hope to benefit from using a product that prevents cavities, freshens breath, or simply tastes good. Over the years, advertisers have consistently communicated the same general message regarding the benefit they hope to provide to toothpaste users. Some of the benefits and the advertisers that hope to provide them are as follows:

☐ Prevents cavities   Crest
☐ Freshens breath   Aquafresh
☐ Tastes good   Aim and Colgate

Students are probably much more familiar with the first two brand/benefit associations because benefit segmentation also influences media strategy. The target market for toothpaste that tastes good is mothers with small children—not college students (even though some college students have small children). Therefore, typical students are much less likely to be exposed to a media message about Aim than Aquafresh.

After learning which benefits the consumers are looking for, the interviewer can focus the questioning on how the benefits will affect the consumers' state of mind, or *values.*

Some scholars further refine values according to whether they are *instrumental values* (that is, they express preferred modes of conduct and behavior, such as being independent, loving, polite, responsible, or simply having a good time) or *terminal values* (that is, they express end states of mind or being, such as peacefulness, comfort, self-esteem, security, true friendship, or simply happiness).[14] An experienced interviewer will sequence the questions on the ladder, beginning with inquiries about a brand's attributes and ending with questions that elicit responses that identify the values the respondent hopes to obtain using the product. Figure 2–3 presents the different levels of meaning associated with product usage.

The laddering procedure works best when the interviewer is able to interact with a respondent in a one-on-one situation. With some modification, it can also be used with focus groups. Experienced interviewers use various techniques to elicit distinctions between one level of meaning and another. Respondents may not actually know the answer to a question, or the question may be probing a sensitive area. Sometimes the interviewer can simply redirect the question;

FIGURE 2-3   LEVELS OF MEANING ASSOCIATED WITH PRODUCT USAGE

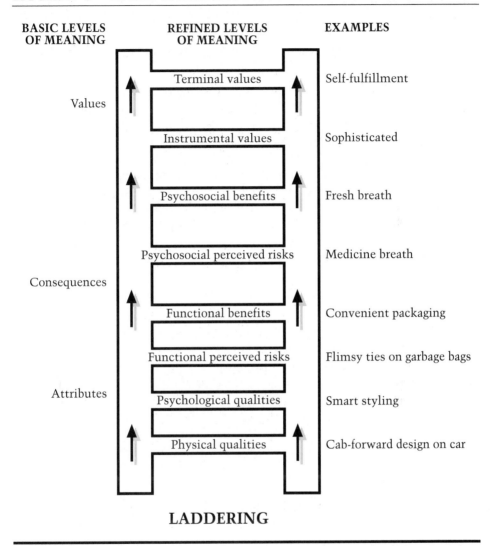

BASIC LEVELS OF MEANING	REFINED LEVELS OF MEANING	EXAMPLES
Values	Terminal values	Self-fulfillment
	Instrumental values	Sophisticated
	Psychosocial benefits	Fresh breath
Consequences	Psychosocial perceived risks	Medicine breath
	Functional benefits	Convenient packaging
	Functional perceived risks	Flimsy ties on garbage bags
Attributes	Psychological qualities	Smart styling
	Physical qualities	Cab-forward design on car

LADDERING

other times it may be helpful to use silence to give the respondent time to think or to displace tension. Sometimes it is helpful to change the context of the question from one involving the interviewee's motives or values to one involving a third person. Sometimes the laddering procedure will not result in eliciting responses that go beyond consumer benefits.[15]

Often, it is enough to simply begin most questions with the word *why*. Why is that important? Why don't you like that? Why do you think other people will think that? How does that make you feel? What does that mean to you? The dialogue below presents a laddering technique that could be used in research on a safety razor:

Interviewer:	What do you look for in a razor?
Respondent (female):	One that won't saw my legs off.
Interviewer:	What do you mean?
Respondent:	I don't like the blades if they're too sharp.
Interviewer:	Why?
Respondent:	Because I end up cutting my legs up around my knees.
Interviewer:	Why?
Respondent:	I guess I'm just too impatient. I'm usually in a hurry, and half the time I drop the razor, and when I go to pick it up, I get water in my eyes.
Interviewer:	Why do you drop the razor?
Respondent:	It just slips out of my hand. It's soapy.
Interviewer:	Is it more important to have a razor that isn't too sharp or to have a razor that wouldn't slip out of your hands?
Respondent:	I guess a razor that won't slip out of my hands. Then I could take more time and do a better job with my legs.
Interviewer:	Why is that important?
Respondent:	I like the way my legs feel, and I like knowing they look good.
Interviewer:	Why?
Respondent:	Everybody wants good-looking legs.
Interviewer:	Why is that important?
Respondent:	It feels good. It just does.

One-on-Ones The more academic name for this technique is the depth interview, but most people in advertising simply call this a one-on-one. This type of interview is generally used when information is going to be difficult to get with less costly techniques, such as surveys and focus groups. In these sessions, a trained interviewer interacts with an individual through a variety of loose, unstructured questions. The intent of the interviewer is to uncover hidden meanings, problems, attitudes, motives, and the activities of consumers, while carefully avoiding influencing the respondent. This type of interview is especially appropriate when:

1. A detailed probing of an individual's behavior, attitudes, needs, or wants is required.
2. A highly detailed, step-by-step understanding of complicated behavior or decision-making patterns (such as planning the family vacation) is required.

3. The subject matter is of a sensitive or embarrassing nature (such as personal hygiene products).
4. The subject matter is likely to be of a highly confidential nature (such as personal investments).
5. Strong, socially acceptable norms exist (such as baby-feeding philosophy), and group interaction may influence responses.
6. The interviews are with professionals (such as finance directors).[16]

Focus Groups A focus group interview is one of the more useful forms of a depth interview. The typical group consists of from eight to twelve members, although recently some major ad agencies report they are using as few as six people. The group members are selected and recruited to be representative of the consumer segment thought to be the target audience. The interview generally takes place in a comfortable room with a trained moderator guiding the discussion. Meetings often last between one and three hours, but an hour is fairly typical. The session is usually recorded and may even be viewed and videotaped from behind a one-way mirror.

The purpose of the focus group interview is to uncover some of the more hidden thoughts, feelings, and problems consumers have with respect to the product. The moderator operates with a rough outline of topical questions to keep the meeting focused on the topic. Moderators take great care not to inhibit discussion. Part of the value of a group interview will come from the interaction of the group members.

Student-directed focus groups sometimes encounter a problem that professionals usually are able to avoid. Experienced moderators know how to subtly steer a discussion to cover all the predetermined topics. Part of the technique involves interjecting a few pertinent words, phrases, or short sentences to redirect discussion so that it all appears very natural. This requires the moderator to listen carefully for the right moment to speak. Experience helps, but there is also some skill involved.

Because of their lack of experience, students are not likely to be as familiar as a trained moderator with the subtle issues associated with a topic. This lack of familiarity can come across as awkwardness, especially when students are nervous about moderating a focus group for the first time, as they usually are. The apparent awkwardness can be intensified if they begin to worry about when to introduce the next question and how to phrase it so that the transition from one topic to another question is a smooth one.

One solution is to have two student moderators. The first student asks a question and then listens intently for the right moment to introduce appropriate prompting comments. Meanwhile, the other student is following the conversation and mentally preparing for the next general question. When the moment is right, the second student asks the next general question as well as makes the subtle comments, such as words, phrases, or short sentences, that generate the freewheeling atmosphere that is characteristic of successful focus group interviews. From that moment on, the two students alternate questions.

Projective Tests This form of qualitative research is both a good way to learn about consumers and a powerful way to get information about the product. It is discussed in Chapter 3 under Product Analysis.

Survey Research

Although qualitative research is very good at generating ideas and providing insight on the consumer, the analyst usually runs a risk that the research findings may not be generalizable to a larger population base. Primarily for this reason, a more rigorous study involving survey research is frequently appropriate.

Survey research tends to imply the use of a questionnaire. The research is usually structured, quantifiable, and able to be administered by less-skilled personnel. This type of research is more likely to be done by the advertiser or a private research company than by an advertising agency. Among the most popular methods of acquiring data are telephone interviews, personal interviews, self-administered questionnaires, and mail questionnaires.

Telephone Interviews This technique is particularly useful in studies that require a broad cross-section of the population, such as a national sample. Its relatively low cost is sometimes offset by the difficulty of keeping individuals on the phone longer than 15 minutes. This method has largely replaced door-to-door personal interviews. It is widely used in advertising tracking studies that are designed to assess awareness levels, attitudes, and product usage. According to a survey of 140 corporate marketing research directors, telephone interviewing, especially used in conjunction with a WATS (Wide Area Telephone Service) system, was one of the two most popular data collection techniques, the other being the mall intercept.[17]

Mall Intercepts This is the most popular form of the personal interview. Respondents are either interviewed on the spot or escorted to a private area within the mall. Students often use a variation of this technique and interview consumers outside the mall because it is usually time consuming and difficult to secure permission to go inside. Although personal interviews can take place anywhere, including the home, malls offer many advantages. The interviewer usually works from a questionnaire, and large numbers of consumers can be interviewed in a relatively small period of time. This approach is especially useful when the testing procedure requires getting consumer reaction to visual stimuli, such as packaging, name-change alternatives, advertising concepts, and advertisements. Less-skilled personnel can administer the questionnaire.

The major disadvantage of this method is the representativeness of the sample. People who visit shopping malls are not necessarily representative of the rest of the population. On the other hand, mall shoppers are often precisely the cross-section of the population many advertisers are interested in reaching. A variation of the mall intercept is the *after-purchase intercept* where consumers are interviewed after they purchase a product.

Self-administered Questionnaires There are two basic types of self-administered instruments: a leave-behind questionnaire and a hand-delivered questionnaire. With the first type of questionnaire, consumers are invited to fill out a form at some central location, usually a retail store or a restaurant. To work well, some control should be maintained over which respondents fill the form out. The second type of self-administered questionnaire works much better.

With this method, a data collector personally delivers a questionnaire to the home of a preselected respondent who has been offered an incentive. The data collector informs the consumer that the questionnaire will be picked up after a period of time, usually a week. Having the questionnaire picked up helps to improve the representativeness of the sample, a major problem with self-administered questionnaires. This procedure is the primary method the Simmons Market Research Bureau uses to collect data on product usage, and it is especially useful and cost-effective when a large amount of information is to be collected.

As a rule, it is much better to have an interviewer fill out the questionnaire than the consumer. This puts the interviewer in control of the flow of information and reduces the likelihood of misunderstood questions. The interviewer can also control the pacing of questions and answers, thereby helping to ensure that the questions on the second half of a questionnaire receive the same consideration as the earlier ones.

Mail Questionnaires This method of gathering data is used primarily because of its low cost. A questionnaire can be mailed to potential respondents, attached to a product in the marketplace, or included within the body of a magazine or newspaper. The main disadvantage of this method is that it is very difficult to determine the extent to which nonrespondents are similar to respondents on the variables that influence product usage. Even if you match up both groups on the basis of demographic and psychographic criteria, it is difficult to determine how representative the results are.

This method is a variation of the self-administered questionnaire and has many of the same advantages and disadvantages. Some control over nonresponse is gained if the sampling units have been recruited to participate in a consumer panel. National Family Opinion, Inc. (NFO), is a leader in this area and successfully uses the mail questionnaire with an active panel base of more than 300,000 U.S. households. However, one recurring criticism of panels is that even if cooperation can be maintained over panel members, it is often a more difficult task to get a representative cross-section of the appropriate population to join the panel.

This method can be effective if the company offers the consumer a sufficient incentive to complete the questionnaire. To reduce nonresponses, some companies include a product sample with the questionnaire and offer to send the consumer additional coupons upon completion of the questionnaire. Other companies ask customers to fill out mail questionnaires when turning in their warranty agreements for new product purchases. Companies use this approach as a major source of information in developing a database on their customers. A major variation of the mail questionnaire is the diary that companies use to collect information on consumer purchases. Marketing Research Corporation of America (MRCA) uses the diary method to monitor the purchasing habits of its consumer panel, which consists of 7,500 households.

Finishing the Company and Consumer Analyses

Although this chapter is coming to a close, it does not mean that the company and consumer analyses are complete. Many of the analytical techniques to be discussed in Chapter 3 will shed additional light on the company and consumer. For example, many of the sources of information on the company can and should be used to gain insight on the competition, and many of the techniques recommended for the competitive analysis will also be of value in analyzing the company. It is also worth noting that many of the tests used to evaluate the product say as much about the consumer as they do about the product. In short, although we have separated the situation analysis into distinct sections, the information-gathering efforts described in each section should be used to further the search for insight on the problems and opportunities facing the company. This means that in the event the research foundation is separated into sections and assigned to different members of a team, information should be shared so that each section benefits from the cross-fertilization of the information obtained from other areas.

Endnotes

[1] Raymond Serafin and Bradley Johnson, "Saturn-alia in Springhill Next Summer," *Advertising Age* (October 18, 1993):1, 55.

[2] Thomas O'Donnell and Jill Andresky, "Are GM's Troubles Deeper than They Look?" *Forbes* (September 27, 1982): 131–135.

[3] Keith Morgan and Deborah Kelly-Milburn, "Internet Resources for Economics," *College & Research Libraries News* 55 (September 1994): 475–478.

[4] SRI International, *Values and Lifestyles* (Menlo Park, Calif.: SRI International, 1994): 3.

[5] SRI International.

[6] Judith Waldrop, "Markets with Attitude," *American Demographics* (July 1994): 3.

[7] For more information, see William C. Johnson, "Sales Promotion: It's Come Down to 'Push Marketing,'" *Marketing News* (April 1988): 2.

[8] David J. Curry, *The New Marketing Research Systems: How to Use Strategic Database Information for Better Marketing Decisions* (New York: John Wiley & Sons, 1993): 86.

[9] James F. Engel, Martin R. Warshaw, and Thomas C. Kinnear, *Promotional Strategy: Managing the Marketing Communications Process*, 8th ed. (Burr Ridge, Ill.: Irwin, 1994),14.

[10] Rita Koselka, "It's My Favorite Statistic," *Forbes* (September 12, 1994): 162.

[11] This information is based on personal interviews and personal correspondence with Michael Robinson, research director, Tatham Euro RSCG.

[12] For more information, see Lisa Fortini-Campbell, *Hitting the Sweet Spot: The Consumer Insight Workbook*, 2nd ed. (Chicago: The Copy Workshop, 1992): 159–170.

[13] Johnathan Gutman, "A Means-End Chain Model Based on Consumer Categorization Processes," *Journal of Marketing* 46 (Spring 1982): 60–72.

[14] Milton J. Rokeach, as quoted in J. Paul Peter and Jerry C. Olson, *Consumer Behavior and Marketing Strategy*, 2nd ed. (Homewood, Ill.: Irwin, 1987): 78.

[15] T. J. Reynolds and J. Gutman, "Laddering Theory, Method, Analysis and Interpretation," *Journal of Advertising Research* (February/March 1988): 16.

[16] Donald S. Tull and Del I. Hawkins, *Marketing Research: Measurement and Method*, 4th ed. (New York: Macmillan, 1987), 311.

[17] William R. Dillon, Thomas J. Madden, and Neil H. Firtle, *Essentials of Marketing Research* (Homewood, Ill.: Irwin, 1993): 154.

The Research Foundation II: Market, Product, and Competitive Analyses

THE MARKET ANALYSIS

It is widely understood in the advertising business that the mass market is becoming increasingly fragmented. This change does not necessarily mean that the role of national advertising has diminished. Rather, it underscores the importance of giving extra attention to local markets. One common line used with many variations is "Think globally, but act like a retailer."

The basic purpose of the market analysis is to determine the geographic areas that warrant special attention, either because they are problems or because they are most likely to respond favorably to the company's marketing communication program. In a sense, this section is simply an extension of the consumer analysis. Advertisers treat this topic separately for two reasons: (1) to help organize additional sources of information that focus primarily on geographic data, although they may include demographic and psychographic data, and (2) to help media planners identify geographic areas where they should allocate media dollars. The second point is becoming an important consideration as marketers increasingly narrow the focus of their communication strategy and tactics and look for markets that need extra emphasis.

A word of clarification: The term *market* may be used both to indicate a geographic area and as a descriptive term to refer to a population segment, such as a Hispanic market. The words *target market* usually refer to both a population segment and a geographic area. In some plans, this section would be referred to as a geographic analysis. That is common and very acceptable. We prefer using the word *market* for the section because it connotes a place where sales take place and where consumers live and buy.

PRODUCT-USAGE DATA

The importance of a market is usually determined by the amount of product usage and the number of current users in the area. If this information is unavailable or hard to come by, planners will usually select a market on the basis of the demographic and psychographic characteristics of the consumers living in the area. Wherever possible, however, purchase behavior should be used as a predictor of future sales.

A good place to start the analysis is with sales data that are internal to the company. If the company has analyzed its sales geographically, this information is likely to be available from the marketing department. If not, then the task will be much more difficult and will require the analyst to gather the information through records in the accounting area.

The amount and type of information will vary from company to company and usually depend on the research suppliers with whom the company works. For students, the information they can get usually depends on who is providing it and what the sources are willing to share. A student may be limited to what is available in a university library. Unfortunately, many important sources of market information, including share-of-market data, and resource tools, such as Nielsen's SCANTRACK and IRI's InfoScan, are not likely to be found in libraries. If the information is available, a common use of the data is to construct index numbers that indicate the relative value of a market.

Index Numbers

Index numbers are widely used measures to indicate a market's sales potential. In this section, we briefly look at three types of indexes: first, product-usage index numbers cross-referenced by the geographic areas reported by the Simmons Market Research Bureau (SMRB); second, a buying-power index, usually developed from data in the *Sales & Marketing Management Survey of Buying Power;* and, third, a brand-development index and its companion, a category-development index.

Simmons The SMRB provides information on product usage for some 800 brands, products, and services and cross-references them by broad classifications of geographic areas. The areas include nine geographic regions of the country (such as Midwest), four classifications of county size (such as County Size A), three metropolitan categories (for example, Metro Central City), and three areas of dominant influence (ADI) categories (such as Top 5 ADIs). The product-usage data are broken down by total usage and the percentage usage accounted for by the geographic segment. Of special interest are the index numbers for the geographic segments that indicate relative product usage and may be used as a very rough predictor of sales potential. Mediamark Research, Inc. (MRI), provides data similar to those of Simmons.

Buying-Power Index (BPI) This index is another handy measure that can be used to help predict sales potential. It is typically developed from data provided by *Sales & Marketing Management Survey of Buying Power* (see below), but it can be compiled from data from a variety of sources. The BPI is a multiple-factor index that uses a number of statistics associated with a market to indicate sales potential. The *Survey of Buying Power,* uses population, effective buying income (also called disposable income), and retail sales for its

FIGURE 3-1   SURVEY OF BUYING POWER

S&MM ESTIMATES: 1/1/94

POPULATION / RETAIL SALES BY STORE GROUP

METRO AREA / County / City	Total Population (Thousands)	% Of U.S.	Median Age Of Pop.	18-24 Years	25-34 Years	35-49 Years	50 & Over	Households (Thousands)	Total Retail Sales ($000)	Food ($000)	Eating & Drinking Places ($000)	General Mdse. ($000)	Furniture/ Furnish. Appliance ($000)	Automotive ($000)	Drug ($000)
CHARLOTTE-GASTONIA-ROCK HILL	1,255.0	.4833	33.6	10.3	16.8	23.6	24.1	478.2	10,157,043	1,727,418	1,019,950	1,067,775	592,912	2,537,587	435,115
York	141.1	.0543	33.2	11.1	15.3	23.1	24.2	50.8	1,057,711	208,514	101,118	111,990	67,916	217,391	52,122
• Rock Hill	46.3	.0178	30.3	16.2	15.8	18.9	23.7	16.3	639,135	119,759	58,633	102,062	40,144	110,736	27,607
Cabarrus, N. C.	105.3	.0406	35.7	9.3	15.1	23.5	27.7	40.0	807,455	154,754	61,877	98,053	60,572	215,938	22,707
• Concord	29.1	.0112	36.3	10.6	15.0	21.0	30.8	11.5	357,254	71,351	28,711	28,346	21,907	137,162	11,200
• Kannapolis	33.0	.0127	36.9	9.3	15.1	18.5	34.0	13.5	139,984	31,113	6,175	88	23,966	34,497	3,244
Gaston, N. C.	180.9	.0697	34.5	9.9	15.3	22.8	26.4	67.7	1,390,861	283,399	132,128	184,271	57,455	289,815	77,607
• Gastonia	58.6	.0226	35.0	9.2	15.1	22.0	28.1	22.4	939,251	156,679	89,863	161,791	36,878	196,260	44,806
Lincoln, N. C.	53.9	.0207	35.0	9.5	15.4	23.7	26.3	20.2	296,814	65,310	25,593	15,446	12,713	55,855	18,146
Mecklenburg, N. C.	566.2	.2181	32.7	10.8	18.9	24.2	21.5	222.7	5,574,118	827,930	612,194	531,692	347,630	1,511,728	212,781
• Charlotte	462.7	.1783	32.8	10.2	19.3	23.8	22.0	186.6	5,118,573	692,630	538,453	504,732	320,920	1,496,021	187,667
Rowan, N. C.	115.6	.0445	36.3	9.2	14.8	21.9	30.0	44.7	521,449	88,180	49,124	56,993	22,396	113,578	29,244
Union, N. C.	92.0	.0354	32.9	10.1	15.5	24.0	22.7	32.1	508,635	99,331	37,916	69,330	24,230	133,282	22,508
SUBURBAN TOTAL	625.3	.2407	34.2	10.1	15.4	24.3	24.6	227.9	2,962,846	655,886	298,115	270,756	149,097	562,911	160,591
COLUMBIA	474.0	.1826	32.0	12.2	17.5	23.6	21.2	172.2	4,184,297	636,520	466,695	550,197	287,224	1,015,492	131,930
Lexington	179.8	.0692	33.6	9.1	16.5	25.6	22.0	66.3	1,361,432	268,138	144,169	124,476	77,600	347,315	55,843
Richland	294.2	.1134	31.2	14.0	18.4	22.3	20.7	105.9	2,822,865	368,382	322,526	425,721	209,624	668,177	76,087
• Columbia	97.5	.0376	29.0	22.8	18.3	18.0	21.0	34.0	1,290,964	149,584	164,328	176,466	106,250	278,556	36,185
SUBURBAN TOTAL	376.5	.1450	32.9	9.4	17.5	25.0	21.2	138.2	2,893,333	486,936	302,367	373,731	180,974	736,936	95,745

S&MM ESTIMATES: 1/1/94

EFFECTIVE BUYING INCOME

METRO AREA / County / City	Total EBI ($000)	Median Hsld. EBI	A $10,000-$19,999	B $20,000-$34,999	C $35,000-$49,999	D $50,000 & Over	Buying Power Index
COLUMBIA	7,081,828	34,480	15.4	24.8	20.9	28.2	.1818
Lexington	2,760,268	36,983	14.0	23.9	22.9	30.4	.0665
Richland	4,321,560	32,883	16.4	25.2	19.8	26.8	.1153
• Columbia	1,331,143	26,795	19.9	25.1	16.0	21.1	.0421
SUBURBAN TOTAL	5,750,685	36,284	14.4	24.6	22.2	29.9	.1397
FLORENCE	1,482,919	28,268	18.2	23.8	18.0	21.8	.0428
Florence	1,482,919	28,268	18.2	23.8	18.0	21.8	.0428
• Florence	438,071	28,732	18.9	21.3	16.7	24.4	.0179
SUBURBAN TOTAL	1,044,902	28,115	18.0	24.7	18.5	20.8	.0249
GREENVILLE-SPARTANBURG- ANDERSON	12,189,712	31,508	17.3	24.7	20.1	24.4	.3189
Anderson	1,968,494	29,238	18.4	25.4	20.0	20.8	.0528
• Anderson	350,635	22,897	22.6	24.8	15.1	15.9	.0166
Cherokee	520,094	26,914	18.7	28.4	19.8	14.8	.0143
Greenville	5,194,691	33,809	16.3	23.8	19.8	28.3	.1344
• Greenville	975,076	28,401	18.3	23.7	16.8	23.6	.0392
Pickens	1,323,550	31,286	18.2	24.3	20.0	24.2	.0315
Spartanburg	3,182,883	30,946	17.5	25.2	20.5	22.9	.0859
• Spartanburg	613,442	26,159	18.3	23.1	16.6	20.6	.0246
SUBURBAN TOTAL	10,250,559	32,469	16.9	24.9	20.8	25.1	.2385

S&MM ESTIMATES: 1/1/94

EFFECTIVE BUYING INCOME

METRO AREA / County / City	Total EBI ($000)	Median Hsld. EBI	A $10,000-$19,999	B $20,000-$34,999	C $35,000-$49,999	D $50,000 & Over	Buying Power Index
Allendale	93,518	16,422	22.5	21.2	11.5	11.2	.0025
Bamberg	151,617	19,241	25.6	22.9	13.9	11.3	.0041
Barnwell	222,901	24,248	20.6	22.9	18.6	15.4	.0059
Beaufort	1,437,650	31,714	16.8	25.8	19.1	25.7	.0373
Calhoun	136,692	25,520	19.3	25.4	19.8	13.9	.0031
Chester	378,250	27,252	18.9	27.5	18.9	17.3	.0091
Chesterfield	415,233	23,896	21.6	25.9	17.1	14.6	.0107
Clarendon	259,583	20,134	22.6	25.6	13.3	11.4	.0072
Colleton	371,249	23,846	22.3	22.9	17.9	15.3	.0104
Darlington	748,974	25,996	19.6	24.3	16.9	19.6	.0191
Dillon	264,276	20,676	23.9	25.6	15.2	10.7	.0080
Fairfield	244,235	25,951	19.2	24.1	18.1	18.7	.0060
Georgetown	591,787	26,438	19.9	25.1	17.7	18.6	.0164
Greenwood	807,508	28,135	19.3	23.9	18.7	20.9	.0220
Hampton	164,156	20,083	24.1	24.0	16.1	10.0	.0049
Jasper	150,376	21,004	26.6	23.4	15.7	12.8	.0041
Kershaw	603,865	32,037	16.7	26.4	21.9	22.9	.0159
Lancaster	682,769	28,652	19.1	25.6	20.4	19.3	.0170
Laurens	698,569	28,191	20.0	27.5	20.3	17.3	.0169
Lee	144,765	19,219	23.8	25.5	13.8	9.0	.0043

Source: Reprinted with permission of Sales & Marketing Management, 335 Park Avenue South, NY, NY 10010-1789.

calculations. The *Survey of Buying Power* devotes a page in each issue to take readers step-by-step through the procedure for calculating a BPI, including how to allocate weights (that is, emphasis) to various factors. Another source for market statistics is SRDS (see below).

Sales and Marketing Management (S&MM) This useful source is widely available in most libraries, in part because it is relatively inexpensive. It's published monthly, but the most useful issue for market information is the August issue's survey of buying power (see Figure 3-1). This issue provides statistical information on each state, according to Metropolitan Statistical Areas (MSA), counties, and many of the larger cities. Statistics are provided for population, age groups, number of households, effective buying income (EBI), and retail sales for six types of retail stores (food, eating and drinking, general merchandise, furniture/furnishings/appliances, automotive, and drug).

S&MM also publishes a special October issue titled *Survey of Media Markets*. This issue provides statistics for geographical areas according to designated market areas (DMAs, which are Arbitron's designation for the 211 TV markets). *S&MM* also provides a ranking of metropolitan areas for each of ten retail merchandise lines. Figure 3–1 presents part of a typical page from the *Survey of Buying Power*.

SRDS In the monthly volumes covering spot radio, spot television, and newspapers, *SRDS* publishes market information similar to the statistics in the *Survey of Buying Power*. Data are presented for population, households, and effective buying income for the United States, geographic regions, and each state.

Brand-Development Ideas and Category-Development Index The brand-development index (BDI) and category development index (CDI) must be calculated using information from various sources. They indicate how well a brand does in a market relative to the number of people living in the area. So if a market accounts for 1 percent of the total population, it might be expected to account for 1 percent of a brand's or a category's total sales, if this were an average market. The formula looks like this:

$$\frac{\% \text{ of a brand's total U.S. sales in a market}}{\% \text{ of total U.S. population in a market}} \times 100 = \text{BDI}$$

If the index number is more than 100, it means that the brand is doing above average in this market. If the number is less than 100, the brand is not doing proportionately as well in this market as it is doing in other areas. In either case, the reasons for success in one market or a subpar performance in another should be investigated, if at all possible. A major reason a brand does well is because sales in the generic category are high. To assess this effect, a category-development index can be calculated. The formula is as follows:

$$\frac{\% \text{ of a category's total U.S. sales in a market}}{\% \text{ of total U.S. population in a market}} \times 100 = \text{CDI}$$

If the index number is more than 100, a preliminary judgment will be that the market is receptive to the product (that is, the category). If the number is less than 100, it does not necessarily mean that the market is not receptive to the category, but only that the market does not use the product to the same degree as do other markets. This situation calls for further analysis. Is there sufficient distribution in the market? Do the dealers in the market use low, medium, or high levels of promotional support in the market, especially sales promotion? How new is the product to the area? If marketing promotional levels have been weak, it may indicate a marketing opportunity that can be taken advantage of simply through an increase in promotional support. The essential point to understand is that CDIs and BDIs are a way to get you thinking about the relative importance of a market. They should not be used as the only justification for deciding to put more or less promotional effort in an area.

The next important step is to compare the BDI number with a CDI number. If the BDI is lower than the CDI and both indexes are still more than 100, then that means that the brand and the category are doing well, but consumers are more receptive to competitive brands. This finding is generally perceived as an opportunity because it is usually much easier to get consumers to switch brands than to get them to use a product for the first time. However, it would be a mistake to assume that a high BDI and a higher CDI automatically mean a marketing opportunity. In all cases, the analyst should take a closer look at the market and assess the amount of promotional support in a market as well as the history of the market's response to promotions.

DEMOGRAPHIC AND PSYCHOGRAPHIC DATA

Assessing market opportunities on the basis of product usage is the first step. The next step is to take the demographic and psychographic characteristics of the current users and look for similar characteristics in geographic areas around the country. Generally, the smaller the area you can identify, the more useful the information. Simmons and MRI, for example, provide demographic information on a regional basis, while some so-called geodemographic companies, such as Claritas, Inc. (with its PRIZM program), and Donnelly Marketing Information Services (with its ClusterPLUS), provide information on areas as small as block groups (250–550 households), blocks (25–50 households), and ZIP+4s (6–25 households).

Between the geodemographic sources and Simmons and MRI in terms of value are two syndicated sources of market information that are increasingly available in libraries: *The Lifestyle Market Analyst,* published by SRDS, and *The Sourcebook of ZIP Code Demographics,* published by CACI Marketing Systems.

SRDS's Lifestyle Market Analyst is a relatively new source of information. It is likely to become more widely available as it becomes better known because many libraries subscribe to SRDS for media rate information. This source provides demographic and lifestyle information on the DMAs, including county breakouts for the 10 largest DMAs. It includes a profile for each of 68 lifestyle interests, cross-referenced to the 211 DMAs. Figure 3–2 shows how demographic information is presented for the Gainesville, Florida, market, and Figure 3–3 presents the lifestyle information on Austin, Texas.

The Sourcebook of ZIP Code Demographics, published by CACI, contains statistics on all residential ZIP Codes in the United States. For each ZIP Code, it provides information on population, gender, age distribution, race, people of Hispanic origin, various kinds of household information, and family and household income. The information comes primarily from the U.S. census, but it also includes CACI's own estimates. A statistical summary is provided for each state.

FIGURE 3-2   SRDS: LIFESTYLE MARKET ANALYST

Gainesville, FL

Demographics
Base Index US = 100

Total Adult Population   191,194

Occupation	Population	%	Index
Administrative	16,825	8.8	75
Blue Collar	9,369	4.9	52
Clerical	12,619	6.6	84
Homemaker	21,987	11.5	79
Professional/Technical	53,343	27.9	113
Retired	37,474	19.6	97
Sales/Marketing	7,457	3.9	71
Self Employed	6,883	3.6	100
Student	25,238	13.2	528

Education (1990 Census)

Elementary (0-8 years)	10,741	8.1	78
High School (1-3 years)	18,564	14.0	97
High School (4 years)	32,619	24.6	82
College (1-3 years)	33,150	25.0	100
College (4+ years)	37,526	28.3	139

Race/Ethnicity

White	146,837	76.8	103
Black	32,885	17.2	151
Asian	4,015	2.1	68
Hispanic	6,883	3.6	36
American Indian	382	0.2	29
Other	191	0.1	100

Total Households   96,991

Age of Head of Household	Households	%	Index
18-24 years old	14,161	14.6	281
25-34 years old	19,689	20.3	102
35-44 years old	20,077	20.7	92
45-54 years old	14,549	15.0	86
55-64 years old	10,669	11.0	86
65-74 years old	10,572	10.9	89
75 years and older	7,274	7.5	77
Median Age	**42.3 years**		

Sex/Marital Status

Single Male	24,345	25.1	124
Single Female	26,576	27.4	112
Married	46,071	47.5	86

Children At Home

At Least One Child	23,569	24.3	81
Child Age Under 2	2,619	2.7	75
Child Age 2-4	5,528	5.7	72
Child Age 5-7	5,819	6.0	79
Child Age 8-10	5,916	6.1	78
Child Age 11-12	4,171	4.3	75
Child Age 13-15	6,595	6.8	84
Child Age 16-18	5,335	5.5	74

Home Ownership

Owner	59,455	61.3	95
Renter	37,536	38.7	110

Stage in Family Lifecycle	Households	%	Index
Single, 18-34, No Children	22,696	23.4	198
Single, 35-44, "	6,110	6.3	102
Single, 45-64, "	7,662	7.9	86
Single, 65+, "	7,856	8.1	81
Married, 18-34, "	5,528	5.7	119
Married, 35-44, "	3,104	3.2	97
Married, 45-64, "	11,639	12.0	85
Married, 65+, "	8,826	9.1	87
Single, Any Child at Home	6,595	6.8	89
Married, Child Age Under 13	9,796	10.1	78
Married, Child Age 13-18	7,177	7.4	77

Household Income

Under $20,000	39,572	40.8	145
$20,000-$29,999	16,197	16.7	108
$30,000-$39,999	12,027	12.4	90
$40,000-$49,999	8,826	9.1	80
$50,000-$74,999	12,221	12.6	71
$75,000-$99,999	4,462	4.6	64
$100,000 and over	3,686	3.8	61
Median Income	**$25,498**		

Income Earners

Married, One Income	25,218	26.0	92
Married, Two Incomes	20,950	21.6	80
Single	50,920	52.5	117

Dual Income Households

Children Age Under 13 years	5,335	5.5	76
Children Age 13-18 years	4,753	4.9	79
No Children	10,960	11.3	84

Age By Income

18-34, Income under $30,000	25,897	26.7	210
35-44, "	8,050	8.3	128
45-64, "	10,087	10.4	109
65+, "	11,736	12.1	81
18-34, Income $30,000-$49,999	4,850	5.0	75
35-44, "	5,722	5.9	91
45-64, "	6,401	6.6	85
65+, "	3,686	3.8	93
18-34, Income $50,000-$74,999	2,134	2.2	58
35-44, "	3,783	3.9	72
45-64, "	4,850	5.0	74
65+, "	1,455	1.5	88
18-34, Income $75,000 and over	970	1.0	50
35-44, "	2,425	2.5	61
45-64, "	3,880	4.0	66
65+, "	873	0.9	75

Credit Card Usage

Travel/Entertainment	13,773	14.2	100
Bank Card	73,616	75.9	104
Gas/Department Store	35,014	36.1	103
No Credit Cards	15,519	16.0	84

Source: THE LIFESTYLE MARKET ANALYST 1995, National Demographics & Lifestyles and SRDS.

FIGURE 3-3 MARKET PROFILES

Lifestyles   **Austin, TX**
Base Index US = 100

The Top Ten Lifestyles Ranked by Index

Use an Apple/Macintosh	185	Use an IBM Compatible	136
Science/New Technology	144	Career-Oriented Activities	134
Use a Personal Computer	143	Electronics	131
Running/Jogging	142	Frequent Flyer	128
Travel for Business	140	Science Fiction	127

Home Life	Households	%	Index	Rank
Avid Book Reading	162,780	40.6	107	37
Bible/Devotional Reading	74,173	18.5	99	141
Flower Gardening	109,856	27.4	84	198
Grandchildren	66,555	16.6	73	207
Home Furnishing/Decorating	81,791	20.4	101	53
House Plants	136,318	34.0	103	129
Own a Cat	125,894	31.4	120	36
Own a Dog	155,964	38.9	115	110
Subscribe to Cable TV	262,612	65.5	103	96
Vegetable Gardening	78,583	19.6	87	187

Good Life	Households	%	Index	Rank
Attend Cultural/Arts Events	68,560	17.1	126	10
Fashion Clothing	56,933	14.2	106	34
Fine Art/Antiques	48,513	12.1	119	7
Foreign Travel	68,961	17.2	121	17
Frequent Flyer	107,050	26.7	128	16
Gourmet Cooking/Fine Foods	74,574	18.6	109	27
Own a Vacation Home/Property	37,688	9.4	85	118
Travel for Business	109,054	27.2	140	5
Travel for Pleasure/Vacation	152,756	38.1	102	42
Travel in USA	144,738	36.1	103	34
Wines	58,136	14.5	123	16

Investing & Money	Households	%	Index	Rank
Casino Gambling	35,282	8.8	78	119
Entering Sweepstakes	56,933	14.2	101	141
Moneymaking Opportunities	51,320	12.8	108	44
Real Estate Investments	27,665	6.9	110	33
Stock/Bond Investments	63,348	15.8	100	49

Great Outdoors	Households	%	Index	Rank
Boating/Sailing	49,716	12.4	116	45
Camping/Hiking	98,630	24.6	109	84
Fishing Frequently	81,791	20.4	86	188
Hunting/Shooting	63,348	15.8	103	156
Motorcycles	25,660	6.4	85	184
Recreational Vehicles	27,264	6.8	84	181
Wildlife/Environmental	71,767	17.9	109	48

Sports, Fitness & Health	Households	%	Index	Rank
Bicycling Frequently	65,753	16.4	96	97
Dieting/Weight Control	78,583	19.6	96	157
Golf	74,574	18.6	94	111
Health/Natural Foods	69,763	17.4	116	20
Improving Your Health	95,823	23.9	101	56
Physical Fitness/Exercise	153,959	38.4	113	12
Running/Jogging	64,951	16.2	142	11
Snow Skiing Frequently	24,056	6.0	81	86
Tennis Frequently	28,466	7.1	122	17
Walking for Health	129,502	32.3	94	186
Watching Sports on TV	154,761	38.6	99	108

Hobbies & Interests	Households	%	Index	Rank
Automotive Work	58,937	14.7	96	179
Buy Pre-Recorded Videos	59,739	14.9	93	171
Career-Oriented Activities	49,315	12.3	134	4
Coin/Stamp Collecting	25,660	6.4	91	199
Collectibles/Collections	37,688	9.4	84	199
Crafts	98,229	24.5	88	198
Current Affairs/Politics	77,380	19.3	121	6
Home Workshop	95,022	23.7	95	183
Military Veteran in Household	89,409	22.3	89	198
Needlework/Knitting	54,527	13.6	78	206
Our Nation's Heritage	18,443	4.6	94	161
Self-Improvement	83,795	20.9	112	16
Sewing	68,961	17.2	91	196
Supports Health Charities	56,131	14.0	87	121

High-Tech Activities	Households	%	Index	Rank
Electronics	56,933	14.2	131	2
Home Video Games	46,508	11.6	98	133
Listen to Records/Tapes/CDs	214,901	53.6	108	8
Own a CD Player	230,137	57.4	114	13
Photography	77,380	19.3	103	48
Science Fiction	44,905	11.2	127	8
Science/New Technology	50,117	12.5	144	6
Use a Personal Computer	209,689	52.3	143	5
Use an Apple/Macintosh	66,154	16.5	185	5
Use an IBM Compatible	165,987	41.4	136	3

Source: THE LIFESTYLE MARKET ANALYST 1995, National Demographics & Lifestyles and SRDS.

Geodemographic Data

Geodemographic analyses are based on the principle that people who live in the same neighborhood tend to have similar characteristics. There are four major geodemographic computer-programming systems: PRIZM and ClusterPLUS, mentioned earlier, and ACORN by CACI, and MicroVision by Equifax: National Decision Systems. Each of these systems classifies geographical units of varying sizes according to information obtained from the U.S. Census Bureau. These areas are then delineated using demographic and behavioral data obtained from the U.S. census, syndicated research sources such as Simmons and MRI, and the system's own proprietary data-gathering procedures. The systems group areas throughout the United States with similar characteristics into categories so that advertisers can target geographically only those areas that contain their target audience (for example, affluent neighborhoods).

The newest generation of geodemographic systems can be linked to other research databases, including media consumption research, UPC scanner data, consumer panels, and lifestyle typologies (such as VALS 2). This kind of linkage means that an advertiser could define a target audience in terms of demographic and psychographic characteristics and then identify specifically where these consumers can be found geographically. The primary geographic unit is the postal ZIP Code; hence the use of these systems is often called ZIP-Code marketing. We'll examine the oldest and one of the most widely used systems: PRIZM.

PRIZM This system has been around since the early 1970s and has evolved since then along with the increasing sophistication of the data in the U.S. census. In the 1990s, Claritas factor analyzed the dozens of demographic and lifestyle variables in the census into six broad categories that represent most of the variance among different neighborhood types. These categories are

- ☐ Social rank (income, employment, education)
- ☐ Household composition (age, sex, family type, dependency status)
- ☐ Mobility (length of residency by owner or renter, auto ownership)
- ☐ Ethnicity (race, foreign birth, ancestry, language)
- ☐ Urbanization (population and housing density, such as urban, suburban, small city, town, rural)
- ☐ Housing (owner/renter status, home values, number of stories)

These six categories were then statistically analyzed to produce 62 so-called neighborhood types. Each of these neighborhood types has been assigned a nickname, such as blue-blood estates, executive suites, and pools and patios.[1] PRIZM uses maps and computer software to describe the location of these neighborhood types. The geographical areas are based on a comprehensive, computerized, digital street map of the United States that was used in the 1990 census and known by the acronym TIGER (for Topographically Integrated Geographic Coding and Referencing System).

The 62 neighborhood types, or clusters, are also grouped into larger clusters called a social group. Figure 3–4 presents the 15 social groups that represent almost all of the households in the United States.

FIGURE 3–4   PRIZM'S FIFTEEN SOCIAL GROUPS

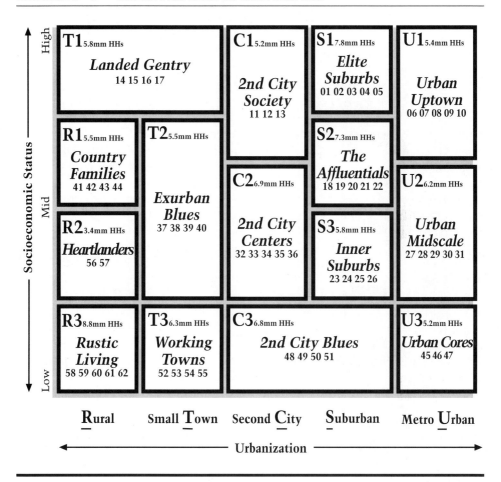

Source: Claritas, Inc., Arlington, VA.

Each social group is described in words, such as Elite Suburbs. The number under each social group indicates the number of the clusters in each category. For example, the Elite Suburbs, social group S1, consists of five clusters, numbers 01 through 05. Figure 3–5 presents a summary of the demographic and lifestyle characteristics of each of the clusters in this social group. (Note that these are not the five wealthiest neighborhood types.)

A significant part of the PRIZM system's power is its ability to identify small geographical units within each social group and cluster. The system uses U.S. census and Postal Service definitions to describe these geographical areas. Each of the geographical areas in Exhibit 3–1 is assigned to its appropriate neighborhood, or cluster.

The ability of the PRIZM system to deliver addressable names and mappable targets at the micromarket level has obvious advantages to advertisers,

FIGURE 3–5   PRIZM SOCIAL GROUPING

PRIZM

	Blue Blood Estates	Winner's Circle	Executive Suites	Pools & Patios	Kids & Cul-de-Sacs
Nickname					
Demographic Caption	Elite Super-Rich Families	Executive Suburban Families	Upscale White-Collar Couples	Established Empty Nesters	Upscale Suburban Families
Cluster Number	01	02	03	04	05
Percent of U.S. Households	0.8%	1.9%	1.2%	1.9%	2.8%
Predominant Adult Age Range	35-54	35-34, 55-64	25-34, 35-54	55-64, 65+	35-54
Key Education Level	College Grads	College Grads	College Grads	College Grads	College Grads
Predominant Employment	Professional	Professional	Professional	Professional	White-Collar Professional
Key Housing Type	Owners Single Unit	Owners Single Unit	Owners Single Unit	Owners Single Unit	Owners Single Unit
Lifestyle Preferences	Belong to a country club Own mutual funds $10,000+ Purchase a car phone Watch TV golf Read business magazines	Use a maid/housekeeper Have a line of credit account Eat Brie cheese Listen to classical radio Read travel magazines	Play racquetball Use financial planning services Own a camcorder/video camera Listen to jazz radio Read business magazines	Attend live theatre Own investments $50,00+ Drink Scotch Listen to news radio Read epicurean/leisure magazines	Buy trivia games Have 1st mortgage loan Own a piano Listen to soft contemporary radio Read infant/parenting magazines
Socio-Economic Rank	Elite [1]	Wealthy [2]	Affluent [8]	Affluent [9]	Affluent [10]
Race/Ethnicity	W [A]	W [A]	W [A]	W [A]	W [A]

Legend for Race/Ethnicity Category; first letter indicates key ethnic/racial type, [ ] letters indicate above average concentration.
W=White B=Black A=Asian H=Hispanic F=Foreign-Born

Source: Claritas, Inc., Arlington, VA.

EXHIBIT 3–1   **PRIZM CLUSTER ASSIGNMENTS**

Geographical Unit	Number in U.S.	Number of HH in Unit	Typical Size of Unit
ZIP Code	36,000	200–4,500	2,600
Tract	62,000	850–2,000	1,500
Block Group	225,000	250–550	400
Carrier Route	300,000	100–2,500	400
Block	6.8 million	25–50	30
ZIP+4	22 million	6–25	10

Source: Claritas, Inc., Arlington, VA.

especially in the planning of media strategy within a larger market. The ability to analyze markets at the microlevel block group or less has also been widely used for fundraising, site selection, and recruiting.[2] Exhibit 3–2 presents the PRIZM neighborhood types.

GeoVals SRI International developed GeoVals with Market Statistics, a firm that specializes in local-area information. It is based on the values and lifestyle segmentation system used with VALS II and discussed in Chapter 2. This system estimates the number and percent of each VALS segment in geographic units throughout the United States. The most common geographic unit is the ZIP Code, but information is also available on the basis of a specific post office, county, state, DMA, ADI, and MSA, as well as customized aggregates of ZIP Codes.[3]

The information is available on mapping software, such as Scan/US, or spreadsheet software, such as Excel or Lotus 1-2-3. Figure 3–6 presents a diagramatic view of the United States showing the percent of the VALS segments in the Augusta, Georgia, ZIP Code. Exhibit 3–3 on page 70 presents a simplified view of a spreadsheet showing the percent and number of households in Cloud County, Kansas, that fall into the eight VALS segments.

PRODUCT ANALYSIS

The basic questions to address in the product analysis center around how the many aspects of the product match up with consumers' needs, wants, problems, and interests. Not only does a product consist of physical and psychological qualities, but also its ability to satisfy needs and wants often depends highly on the way a product is marketed. Even simple products are surprisingly complex. Is this product the right size? Is it priced right? Is it in the right place? Consumers typically buy a product because of the whole package. They may say they are buying a product on the basis of price, but that is only because they have implicitly accepted that the product has met their minimum standards of quality.

Although consumers buy the package, an insightful analyst will usually think of the product as a whole but break it down into its component parts.

EXHIBIT 3–2   PRIZM NEIGHBORHOOD TYPES

Group	Cluster	Cluster Nickname	Group	Cluster	Cluster Nickname
S1	01	Blue Blood Estates	C2	32	Middleburg Managers
S1	02	Winner's Circle	C2	33	Boomtown Singles
S1	03	Executive Suites	C2	34	Starter Families
S1	04	Pools & Patios	C2	35	Sunset City Blues
S1	05	Kids & Cul-de-Sacs	C2	36	Towns & Gowns
Elite Suburbs			2nd City Centers		
U1	06	Urban Gold Coast	T2	37	New Homesteaders
U1	07	Money & Brains	T2	38	Middle America
U1	08	Young Literati	T2	39	Red, White & Blues
U1	09	American Dreams	T2	40	Military Quarters
U1	10	Bohemian Mix	Exurban Blues		
Urban Uptown			R1	41	Big Sky Families
C1	11	Second City Elite	R1	42	New Eco-topia
C1	12	Upward Bound	R1	43	River City, USA
C1	13	Gray Power	R1	44	Shotguns & Pickups
2nd City Society			Country Families		
T1	14	Country Squires	U3	45	Single City Blues
T1	15	God's Country	U3	46	Hispanic Mix
T1	16	Big Fish, Small Pond	U3	47	Inner Cities
T1	17	Greenbelt Families	Urban Cores		
Landed Gentry			C3	48	Smalltown Downtown
S2	18	Young Influentials	C3	49	Hometown Retired
S2	19	New Empty Nests	C3	50	Family Scramble
S2	20	Boomers & Babies	C3	51	Southside City
S2	21	Suburban Sprawl	2nd City Blues		
S2	22	Blue-Chip Blues	T3	52	Golden Ponds
The Affluentials			T3	53	Rural Industria
S3	23	Upstarts & Seniors	T3	54	Norma Rae-ville
S3	24	New Beginnings	T3	55	Mines & Mills
S3	25	Mobility Blues	Working Towns		
S3	26	Gray Collars	R2	56	Agri-Business
Inner Suburbs			R2	57	Grain Belt
U2	27	Urban Achievers	Heartlanders		
U2	28	Big City Blend	R3	58	Blue Highways
U2	29	Old Yankee Rows	R3	59	Rustic Elders
U2	30	Mid-City Mix	R3	60	Back Country Folks
U2	31	Latino America	R3	61	Scrub Pine Flats
Urban Midscale			R3	62	Hard Scramble
			Rustic Living		

Source: Claritas, Inc., Arlington, VA.

FIGURE 3–6   VALS SEGMENTS IN AUGUSTA, GA

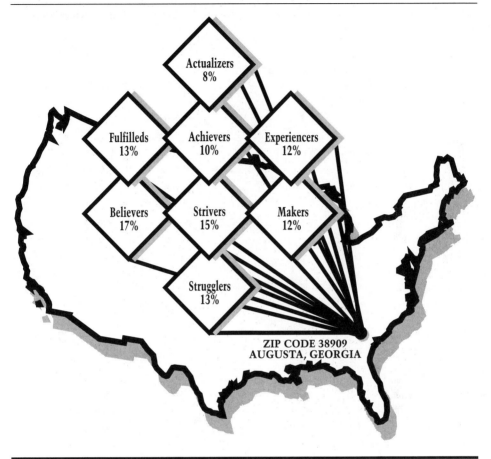

Source: Claritas, Inc., Arlington, VA.

The key to organizing the analysis of a product is to look at the fundamental elements in the marketing mix (that is, product, price, distribution, and promotion), and then consider four basic questions in any subsequent analysis:

1. Does the product package have the *ability* to give consumers what they want? (Or need, and so on)
2. Does the product package *promise* to deliver or address what consumers want?
3. Does the *delivery* of the product package match up with consumers' *expectations?*
4. Can the product package *exceed* consumers' expectations?

The first three questions tend to focus on potential barriers to a successful marketing program. A product without substance or real want-satisfying

EXHIBIT 3–3   SPREADSHEET OF EIGHT VALS SEGMENTS

| | | | *City: Concordia* | | *County: Cloud* | | *State: Kansas* | | | | | |
ZIP	Post office	County	Actualizers %	Fulfilleds %	Believers %	Achievers %	Strivers %	Experiencers %	Makers %	Strugglers %	Households %
Entire county			6.5	12.2	20.6	7.1	13.1	8.4	14.6	17.5	4414
66901	Concordia	Cloud	6.5	12.3	20.4	7.0	13.8	8.8	15.2	16.0	2788
66931	Ames	Cloud	5.8	10.2	18.0	10.8	13.4	9.8	15.2	16.8	76
66938	Clyde	Cloud	6.5	12.1	21.1	6.9	11.5	7.6	13.2	21.0	444
66948	Jamestown	Cloud	6.1	12.2	22.7	5.6	12.0	7.1	13.8	20.5	277
67417	Aurora	Cloud	8.7	13.8	19.3	11.8	11.2	7.8	13.0	14.3	110
67445	Glasco	Cloud	6.0	12.3	21.7	6.5	12.9	7.3	14.4	18.7	353
67446	Miltonvale	Cloud	6.2	11.9	20.1	7.5	11.5	7.6	13.1	22.0	366

Source: Claritas, Inc., Arlington, VA.

qualities is unlikely to be successful over a long term. If a product has special qualities but does not promote them, special opportunities may be lost. Opportunities can be perishable. Promising consumers one thing but delivering another can also lead to a product's diminished effectiveness. Perception is usually more important than reality. What gets delivered to consumers is not nearly as important as what they think they are receiving.

The fourth question focuses more on what the product could be—either real or perceived. The fourth question is the most difficult one to answer—both from the consumers' point of view and from the perspective of a marketing strategist. To get the answer requires imagination on the part of the researcher and the consumer.

LOOKING AT THE PRODUCT

To get a full appreciation of what consumers think or feel about a product, it is often helpful to compare it to its competition. In doing a product analysis, it may be useful to do some aspects of the competitive analysis at the same time. We separate these steps in this chapter primarily to help the reader see how the various parts of the situation analysis fit together and not because we feel they should be done sequentially. There are a number of useful ways to describe a product's qualities: concrete or abstract, physical or psychological, and tangible or intangible. In the advertising business, products are usually discussed in terms of their *attributes*, which tend to be physical, their *functions*, which are mostly physical and somewhat psychological, and their *images* or *brand personalities*, which are psychological.

Product Attributes

In evaluating a product, it is always helpful to understand how much of a product's want-satisfying qualities are tangible product attributes and how much of a product's qualities are intangible. If a product comes up short in the attribute area, then the solution to the problem of how to market the product is more likely to come from the research and development area than the marketing department. Problems concerning how to market intangible qualities, such as images and brand personalities, can be addressed with advertising and the communication mix. In analyzing a product's more tangible qualities, consider the following:

1. Product variety
2. Special designs
3. Differentiating features
4. Qualities (hidden and observable)
5. Packaging
6. Sizes
7. Services
8. Warranties
9. Returns[4]

Product Functions

In many product categories, consumers are less interested in a product's attributes, which they don't understand or don't want to understand, than they are in what the product can do for them. In the 1970s, commercials for some antiperspirants said the product contained aluminum chlorohydrate—a technical word, but not beyond the ability of consumers to remember. Today, the active ingredient in Arrid XX antiperspirant deodorant is aluminum zirconium pentachlorohydrexgly. Not surprisingly, all consumers want to know is that it keeps them "extra, extra dry."

Consider paper products. Charmin Ultra bathroom tissue is promoted primarily on the basis of its "Squeezably Soft & Thick" attributes. In contrast, Bounty paper towels have long been promoted on the basis of their absorbency—"The quicker picker-upper." In recent years, ads for Bounty have been emphasizing the towel's durability—"Look! It's Quilted." Of course, it's also possible to emphasize both attributes and functions. Ads for Kleenex Ultra facial tissues emphasize their "extra layer of softness" that provides a "soft, silky feel" to the skin.

For some products, the decision to emphasize the attribute or the function may depend on the target audience. The package of Edge Gel, a shaving preparation targeted for men with sensitive skin, prominently displays the message that the product is "for closer, more comfortable shaves!" Skintimate Shaving Gel for women, like Edge Gel, is formulated for sensitive skin and contains aloe vera. Yet, the Skintimate brand only mentions how the brand functions on the back of the package and in small print. Apparently, women understand the effects of aloe on sensitive or irritated skin better than men.

Brand Personality

People have long projected onto inanimate objects qualities that are normally associated with human beings. This is true for products, and it is especially so for brand products. In fact, it is the history of a brand, and all its associations, that often gives a product its distinctive personality. A brand name has value. It can be estimated subjectively through qualitative research or more rigorously in paired-comparison tests.

In a research setting, a whole range of questions associated with the brand or the brand personality can be addressed, including those focusing on purchasing intentions and price sensitivity. The research question can be as simple as "Which one do you prefer?" Exhibit 3–4 presents a brand valuation test for a fast-food chicken restaurant using this question in a taste test.

This type of test, which is usually done with matched samples, is used to estimate the value of the brand name. Presumably, the increased preference shown for Brand A in the second sample (where the brands are named) can be attributed to identifying the chicken as Brand A or Brand B. This valuation test (or a variation of this test) can be used to determine how much value the brand name adds to the product.

The next step is to understand how the product's attributes and brand personality contribute to its success (or lack thereof). To get this information,

---

EXHIBIT 3–4   BRAND VALUATION: WHICH PRODUCT DO YOU PREFER?

	1st Sample	2nd Sample
	Unnamed Chicken	Named Chicken
Brand A **(our chicken)**	50%	60%
Brand B **(the competitor's chicken)**	50%	40%

---

companies and agencies use a variety of techniques, including some already discussed, such as survey research, one-on-ones, and focus groups, as well as other techniques we will discuss.

PRODUCT TESTING

One of the best ways to evaluate consumers' thoughts about a product is to give them a product under real-life conditions and ask them what they think of it. Consumer testing focuses on consumers and attempts to understand their wants. Similarly, product testing seeks to understand a product's ability to satisfy a want. For this situation, there are three basic types of testing procedures:

1. *Monadic testing* presents consumers with one product at a time and requires them to make an evaluation without using any other product for comparison. (When scales are used as the testing instrument, it is sometimes called a noncomparative rating scale.) Monadic tests are designed to mirror real-life situations where consumers do not have competitive products to use as a basis for making comparisons. The idea is that consumers implicitly compare the product undergoing testing with other products they have considered in their lives. These tests are widely used in advertising, and examples will be provided shortly.

2. *Paired-comparison testing* presents the consumer with two (or more) products at one time and requires them to make an evaluation. Unlike monadic tests, which focus on the qualities and attributes of the product undergoing testing, paired-comparison tests focus on the differences between products. These will be discussed in greater detail in the section on competitive analysis.

3. *Projective tests* involve a much different way of collecting information about the product. This type of testing comes from clinical psychology. These tests are designed to get respondents to reveal their inner feelings and beliefs by getting them to project their own feelings and beliefs onto some situation that is ostensibly about someone or something other than

themselves. Naturally, this is often used to provide infomation about consumers. We include a description of these tests here because of their value in learning about brand personalities.

Monadic Tests

A wide variety of tests fall into this category. Most of them are some variation of a numerical rating scale and involve the measurement of the respondents' *predisposition* to respond to the product, usually in a favorable or unfavorable way. Some of the more commonly used scales are as follows:

1. *Semantic differential.* This is one of the most widely used tests in marketing research. The basic version consists of a series of bipolar adjectives usually separated by a 7-point rating scale. The test can be used to measure both a product's attributes and its image.

Example:

Brand X Rotisserie Chicken Restaurants

Friendly	___ ___ ___ ___ ___ ___ ___	Unfriendly
Clean	___ ___ ___ ___ ___ ___ ___	Messy
Modern	___ ___ ___ ___ ___ ___ ___	Old-fashioned
Expensive	___ ___ ___ ___ ___ ___ ___	Inexpensive

A variation of this technique uses phrases instead of bipolar adjectives.

2. *Stapel scales.* This test is a variation of the semantic differential scale. In this technique, respondents are typically asked to rate a product or a retail outlet according to the intensity of their agreement or disagreement with a product or a phrase. This test is fairly easy to administer and is often used in telephone interviews.

Example:

Telephone Interview

Please rate **Brand X Rotisserie Chicken** on the following qualities ranging from +5 to −5. (Sometimes a 0 is included as a neutral point, but some researchers feel it is better to make respondents choose a positive or negative value.)

+5	+5	+5	+5
+4	+4	+4	+4
+3	+3	+3	+3
+2	+2	+2	+2
+1	+1	+1	+1
tasty food	nutritious food	good value	distinctive flavor
−1	−1	−1	−1
−2	−2	−2	−2
−3	−3	−3	−3
−4	−4	−4	−4
−5	−5	−5	−5

3. *Likert scales.* Respondents are requested to indicate their agreement or disagreement with a series of statements. This is a relatively easy scale to construct and administer. Care should be taken to provide a balance in the number of favorable and unfavorable statements.

Example:

Brand X Rotisserie Chicken Restaurants

	Strongly Agree	Agree	Neither Agree nor Disagree	Disagree	Strongly Disagree
This store has great-tasting chicken.	_____	_____	_____	_____	_____
The counter personnel are unfriendly.	_____	_____	_____	_____	_____
The inside of the store is comfortable.	_____	_____	_____	_____	_____
Rotisserie chicken is good for you.	_____	_____	_____	_____	_____

4. *Purchase interest.* This test requires respondents to indicate on a 5- or 11-point scale the likelihood that they will buy a product or service. The correlation between actual consumer purchases of a product and consumers' indication that they intend to purchase it is less than perfect. Nevertheless, the technique is also called purchase intent.

Example:

Please answer the following question.

If rotisserie-baked chicken were available in your area, how likely would it be that you would purchase it?

_____ Definitely would buy.
_____ Probably would buy.
_____ Might or might not buy.
_____ Probably would not buy.
_____ Definitely would not buy.[5]

5. *Likability scales.* These tests are often used when the brand in question is essentially a parity product. In these cases, it is often felt that consumers make brand decisions on how well they "like" a product. The following itemized rating scale is one of a number of tests that can be used to test likability.

Example:

Please mark on the following scale how much you like Brand X Rotisserie Chicken.

_____ 100 Superior.		_____ 50 Neutral.	
_____ 90 Excellent.		_____ 40 Do not like it very well.	
_____ 80 Like it very much.		_____ 30 It's not so good.	
_____ 70 Like it quite well.		_____ 20 Do not like it at all.	
_____ 60 Like it fairly well.		_____ 10 It's terrible.	

Projective Tests

To get at the more elusive aspects of a brand's personality, many advertising agencies use projective techniques. Trained interviewers get consumers to reveal underlying attitudes, feelings, and motivations by having respondents project themselves into a situation. Some of the more widely used tests are as follows:

1. *Sentence completion.* This technique requires the respondent to complete a series of incomplete statements with the first word or phrase that comes to mind.

   Example:
   The best-tasting pizza usually comes with _____.
   The thing I like least about going out to eat pizza is _____.
   The thing I like most about eating pizza is _____.

2. *Story completion.* This technique is a variation of the sentence completion test. In this test, interviewers tell a respondent the details of part of a story and ask the respondent to fill in the rest.

   Example:
   A man and a woman are walking down the street with their 9-year-old daughter. They stop exactly between a Pizza Hut and a KFC restaurant to discuss which one to go into. What are they saying to each other? _____(Open ended)

3. *Word association.* This technique requires respondents to say the first word that comes to mind when they hear a stimulus word. In free word association, only the first word is important. In successive word association, a series of words is requested. Usually, a neutral word is inserted between the words in which the interviewer is most interested.

   Example:

Stimulus Word	Word Association	Successive Word Associations
pizza	_____	_____ _____ _____
Big Foot	_____	_____ _____ _____
inexpensive fast food	_____	_____ _____ _____
hamburgers (neutral)	_____	_____ _____ _____
healthy fast food	_____	_____ _____ _____
tasty fast food	_____	_____ _____ _____

4. *Role playing.* A respondent is asked to assume the role of another person or an object. One common technique involves asking the respondent to persuade reluctant customers to buy a product. The techniques that are used tend to reveal the respondent's attitude toward the product and potential customers.

5. *Pretend games.* Respondents are asked to imagine the product is an average person, a movie star, a sports figure, or a relative. Typically, the interviewer asks questions about where the people live, the kinds of houses they live in, and their ages. The responses are then used to provide definition to the brand's image or personality.

SEARCHING FOR PRODUCT OPPORTUNITIES

With many of the prior tests, the researcher is seeking to understand the extent to which the product's attributes and brand personality address consumers' needs and wants. Products that match up well with consumers' wants offer potential opportunity to a marketer. Researchers often incorporate the tests into their research plan but structure the procedures with minor modifications to improve the design's ability to predict opportunities. To identify opportunities with the existing product, a testing procedure may involve comparing an idealized description of the product concept with the actual product. To set this test up, consumers are intercepted in a shopping mall and given a series of tests (such as purchase interest test, a likability test, or a measure of perceived value) asking them to rate the product described on the test. Immediately following, they are given the product, and about a week later they are called up and given the same set of questions they were previously asked. The test-retest procedure is used to diagnose problems and identify opportunities. If the product does not meet consumers' expectations (that is, it underdelivers), then it may be sent back to research and development for further work. If the product exceeds their expectations (that is, it overdelivers), then this situation is viewed as an opportunity to exploit. This procedure can also be used to compare an idealized concept of the product (the first test) with the actual product (the second test).

Example:

	Version One	Version Two
Step 1	Rate the product concept.	Rate the product.
Step 2	Try the product.	Try the product.
Step 3	Rate the product again.	Rate the actual product.

Evaluating the Rest of the Marketing Mix

To get a complete picture of how the product is matching up with the needs and wants of the consumer, it is necessary to evaluate the rest of the marketing mix—the pricing, the distribution, and the promotion program.

Pricing Most of the information about consumers' sensitivity to price can be obtained while research is conducted on the product. Care should be taken that consumers' responses are not taken too literally. For example, consumers frequently indicate that a product's price is too high. The key question as to whether the price is a disadvantage can best be answered by market tests. Companies routinely vary the price of the product in isolated markets while holding other factors constant in order to gauge the effects of a market's sensitivity to price. This procedure is greatly facilitated with the use of scanner technology.

Distribution To understand a product's ability to match up well with consumers' needs and wants, analysis should focus on the extent to which the product is available, in a general sense, and conveniently available, in a specific sense. Judgments can be qualitative and based on simple observation, or they can be quantitative and based on scanner data indicating the percent of the all-commodity volume (that is, the total amount of sales in a given category) that can be accounted for by the outlets handling the company's product.

Promotion Although it can be helpful to separate advertising from the other forms of marketing communication, the distinction between advertising and sales promotion is increasingly blurred in consumers' eyes. Most of the evaluation in this area will come from consumer research. What do consumers think of the current advertising campaign? What do consumers think about coupons (a form of price discounting)? However, much of what consumers think and feel about the message strategy part of the campaign can be inferred from consumer and product testing, particularly those tests that focus on brand personality. In addition, large advertisers often use sophisticated tracking systems, such as Nielsen's ADPRO, to monitor the timing, frequency, and content of television commercials.

Although most of the effects of the creative part of the campaign can be inferred, the media effects should be measured. To do this kind of calculation requires understanding how the media plan will deliver the desired audiences and markets. The success of the plan often depends on how much money is being spent on advertising and whether this amount is sufficient to achieve the advertising objectives. Naturally, companies know how much money they are spending, but if the analyst is a student, then the best source to consult is one of the syndicated sources reporting competitive media expenditures, such as Leading National Advertisers Media Watch Multi-Media Service.

COMPETITIVE ANALYSIS

Consumers have a limited amount of purchasing power. What they do not spend on brand X, they will surely spend somewhere else. Even though this statement is not literally true, it is a good position to maintain to keep a company thinking competitively. In other words, a forward-thinking company should *always* be apprised of the competition, both direct and indirect. A company may be a weak competitor one day, and the next day it can undertake a course of action that can put its rivals out of business.

To begin a competitive analysis, it is important first to identify the options consumers consider in their purchasing decisions. These options include buying products that directly compete with each other in the same generic category and products that only indirectly compete with each other because they are in different categories. For example, the direct competition for wine coolers is other wine coolers, but the indirect competition may include wine, clear malt liquor, specialty mixed drinks, and breezers. The options also include not buying anything and postponing the purchase decision to a later time.

To do a thorough competitive analysis, rival companies and their brands should be understood in as much depth as the analyst's company. In practice, this may not be feasible, or practical. At a minimum, companies usually try to get a basic understanding of their rival's resources and the real and perceived comparative distinctions among the brands that compete with the company's own brands.

Many of the tests and procedures that were discussed in the company analysis (see Chapter 2) and in the preceding description of product analysis are also appropriate in this section. These procedures include one-on-ones and focus groups interviews. Projective tests can also be useful to gain insight into the brand personalities of competitive products. Many of the monadic tests, especially the semantic differential and the Stapel scales, can be be used to compare one product with another simply by repeating the test for each competitive brand. This section will emphasize the tests and techniques that are comparative in nature.

PRODUCT COMPARISONS

These evaluations often form the basis for the strategic decisions, especially positioning, that will follow as the campaign develops. We will examine two types of comparisons: perceptual mapping, which examines where a company or brand fits in consumers' perception of the product category, and attitude scales, which are used to compare one brand or company to another.

Perceptual Mapping

This technique is to help the analyst understand how a product is positioned in consumers' minds. Tests to implement perceptual mapping range from a simple technique, which is what we will discuss in this section, to more complicated multidimensional scaling techniques that require computer software to calculate.[6]

Perceptual mapping is often used to get a feel for a brand's image. The image a brand has is the result of a number of factors, including the physical and functional aspects of the brand, the psychological qualities associated with the brand's heritage, and the totality of all the images associated with competitive brands. A perceptual map helps to define a brand's image by putting it into the context of how consumers perceive the brand with respect to competitive brands. An image takes on a finer shade of meaning when an analyst can see how respondents rate a brand compared to a competitive one.

A perceptual map shows these distinctions by rating various brands on two dimensions at the same time. For example, a retail store can be evaluated at the same time on the basis of friendly/unfriendly service and high-quality/low-quality merchandise. Although not all of a brand's image or personality can be explained by two dimensions, this rating usually gives the analyst some feel for how consumers perceive the various brands with respect to each other. In perceptual mapping, the researcher will often choose which dimensions to use with respondents, based on his or her experience. In multidimensional scaling, the testing makes no assumptions with regard to the dimensions that are appropriate for the brands being examined. The dimensions are usually derived from judgments respondents make about the similarity of brands or their preference for the brands based on various attributes or qualities.

Figure 3–7 presents a perceptual map for various performers based on an informal test conducted in an undergraduate class on advertising principles. Naturally, the map would likely look considerably different with an older age group.

Comparative Rating Scales

As we discussed in the section on product testing, one of the basic types of product tests that can be used to evaluate the competition is the comparative attitude rating scale. Listed below are three examples:

1. *Rank-order rating scales.* In this test, the respondent is asked to rank order a number of products (or retail stores) on the basis of some specific criterion. The ranking may be on the basis of overall quality, but usually the criterion is a specific attribute or quality.

    Example:

    Please rank the following restaurants from 1 to 5 according to which one has the best-tasting chicken. Use a 1 to indicate the best.

    _____ Boston Rotisserie Chicken
    _____ Popeye's
    _____ KFC
    _____ Church's
    _____ Brand X Rotisserie Chicken

2. *Fractionation rating scale.* The test requires a respondent to rate several products on the basis of some criterion by comparing them to one specific product. Usually, the specific product is the brand leader or the company's brand. The objective of this test is to give the analyst an idea of how similar or different consumers consider the various brands.

    Example:

    If the Brand X Rotisserie Chicken restaurant is assumed to score 100 points on "fast service," how would you compare each of the following restaurants to it?

    | Brand X Rotisserie Chicken _____ | KFC _____ |
    | Boston Rotisserie Chicken _____ | Popeye's_____ |
    | Church's _____ | |

3. *Paired-comparison rating scale.* This test is simple in concept, but somewhat more complicated to implement. It requires the respondent to compare two products to each other and select one on the basis of some criterion. If there are only two brands, then the testing procedure is a fairly

FIGURE 3–7   PERCEPTUAL MAP

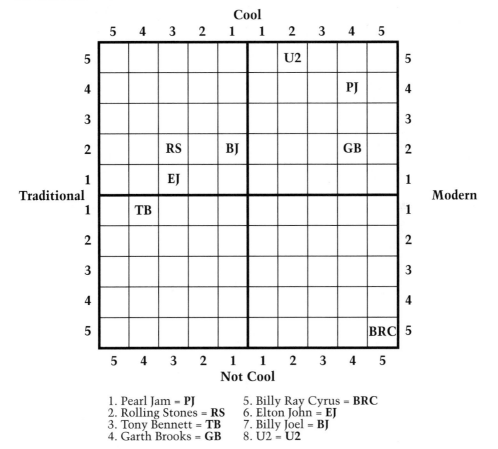

Cool

	5	4	3	2	1	1	2	3	4	5	
5							U2				5
4									PJ		4
3											3
2			RS		BJ				GB		2
1			EJ								1
1		TB									1
2											2
3											3
4											4
5										BRC	5

Traditional   Modern

| | 5 | 4 | 3 | 2 | 1 | 1 | 2 | 3 | 4 | 5 | |

Not Cool

1. Pearl Jam = **PJ**   5. Billy Ray Cyrus = **BRC**
2. Rolling Stones = **RS**   6. Elton John = **EJ**
3. Tony Bennett = **TB**   7. Billy Joel = **BJ**
4. Garth Brooks = **GB**   8. U2 = **U2**

Please consider the above acts and plot their initials
where you think they best fit on the map.

simple one requiring the respondent to indicate a preference for one brand over another. A comparison is made for each attribute that is thought to be important in the product category. However, if the number of brands in the test is greater than 2, then the number of comparisons *for each attribute* goes up dramatically according to $[n(n-1)/2]$ This means for 3 brands the number of paired comparisons would be 3 (4 brands = 6, 5 brands =10); 6 brands would require 15 comparisons *for each rated attribute.* To set this procedure up, it might be helpful to consult a marketing research text.[7]

This test can be especially useful when a company is considering two or three versions or recipes of the same product. It is also used when a company believes it may position a brand against a specific competitor.

Double-Checking Prices and Distribution

Analyzing the competition on the basis of price and distribution is fairly similar to the way you analyze the product. You can obtain much of this information as you analyze the product. Because the information will often be obtained in the product analysis, it is usually a good idea to double-check each competitor's prices and distribution strengths and weaknesses as you would the company in the product analysis.

Promotion Comparisons

To be comprehensive, the competitive analysis should include an understanding of the competition's marketing communications activity. Although data on some of the activity may be difficult to get, information on advertising is usually easier to obtain.

Competitive advertising can be divided into information about the message and about the media. Because most advertisers and students will not have access to the Ad Tracker database that provides the information for Nielsen's ADPRO, most analysts usually construct their own database, even if it is a lot less sophisticated. One common method popular among students is to keep a file of all competitive advertising. The print ads can be tear sheets, and the broadcast spots can be brief summaries. Usually it is helpful to do an informal content analysis of ads to track competitive positioning, themes, images, attributes, and objectives.

To get information on competitive media activity, it is possible to systematically monitor the major media. However, this is time consuming and not likely to be comprehensive. The most rigorous approach is to consult one of the syndicated sources of media expenditures, such as Competitive Media Expenditures' *Leading National Advertisers*. Figure 3–8 presents a partial page from *Leading National Advertisers*.

The most effective use of this information was summarized by the staff of *Media Decisions* more than twenty years ago. Although there have been tremendous changes in the media world within the last decade, the information is still very much on target.

1. The expenditure figures can show you regionality and seasonality, and how these factors are changing for all competitive and potentially competitive brands.
2. The data can give you a fix on ad budget size and media mix market by market.
3. You can use the data to spot new product tests and to track new brand roll-outs.
4. You can infer from where the money is being spent how competitors view their target audiences, how they profile their brands, and where they seek to position themselves in your marketplace.
5. You can watch spending patterns of the opposition—TV flighting, radio rotation, position practices in magazines, or day of week in newspapers.

FIGURE 3-8   *LNA/ARBITRON MULTI-MEDIA SERVICE (JANUARY–MARCH 1993)*

COMPANY/BRAND $

PARENT COMPANY/BRAND	CLASS CODE	10-MEDIA TOTAL	MAGAZINES	SUNDAY MAGAZINES	NEWSPAPERS	YEAR-TO-DATE ADVERTISING DOLLARS (000)						
						OUTDOOR	NETWORK TELEVISION	SPOT TELEVISION	SYNDICATED TELEVISION	CABLE TV NETWORKS	NETWORK RADIO	NATIONAL SPOT RADIO
ADAM & EVE VIDEOS												
ADAM & EVE (WISC)	G619	211.4	211.4	--			--	--	--	--	--	--
ADAM & EVE VIDEOS VIDEO CASSETTES	G61V	96.8	96.8	--			--	--	--	--	--	--
COMPANY TOTAL		308.2	308.2	--			--	--	--	--	--	--
ADAMS COMMUNICATIONS CORP												
KEZK RADIO STATION	B430	53.2	--	--			--	53.2	--	--	--	--
ADIDAS												
ADIDAS GENERAL PROMOTION	A119-8	73.1	19.6	--			35.2	--	--	18.3	--	--
ADIDAS SPORTING FOOTWEAR MEN	A132-1	63.0	61.6	--			--	1.4	--	--	--	--
ADIDAS SPORTING FOOTWEAR MEN & WOMEN	A132-3	16.8	16.8	--			--	--	--	--	--	--
ADIDAS SPRTING FOOTWEAR & SPRTWEAR M & W	A132-3	35.1	--	--			--	8.8	--	26.3	--	--
COMPANY TOTAL		188.0	98.0	--			35.2	10.2	--	44.6	--	--
ADIROMDACK COLONIAL FURNITURE												
ADIRONDACK COLONIAL FURN (MH)	G714	53.6	--	--			--	53.6	--	--	--	--
ADIROMDACK MANAGEMENT												
ADIRONDACK DIET BEVERAGE	F222	0.2	--	--			--	0.2	--	--	--	--
ADIRONDACK DIET RASPBERRY LINE SELTZER	F222	4.0	--	--			--	4.0	--	--	--	--
ADIRONDACK REG RASPBERRY LINE SELTZER	F221	16.6	--	--			--	16.6	--	--	--	--
ADIRONDACK REGULAR LEMON LINE SELTZER	F221	23.1	--	--			--	23.1	--	--	--	--
ADIRONDACK REGULAR RASPBERRY	F221	3.4	--	--			--	3.4	--	--	--	--
ADIROMDACK REGULAR SOFT DRINKS	F221	3.7	--	--			--	3.7	--	--	--	--
ADIROMDACK SELTZER	F221	22.4	--	--			--	22.4	--	--	--	--
COMPANY TOTAL		73.4	--	--			--	73.4	--	--	--	--
ADLERS COLEMAN E & SONS												
ADLERS (MH)	G714	11.7	11.7	--			--	--	--	--	--	--
ADLERS (WISC)	G619	19.1	19.1	--			--	--	--	--	--	--
ADLERS WATCHES	G712	85.2	85.2	--			--	--	--	--	--	--
COMPANY TOTAL		116.0	116.0	--			--	--	--	--	--	--
ADMINISTAFF												
ADMINISTAFF TEMPORARY PERSONNEL	B119	27.6	--	--			--	--	--	--	--	27.6
ADMIRALS COVE REAL ESTATE												
ADMIRALS COVE REAL ESTATE	B230	53.5	53.5	--			--	--	--	--	--	--
ADOLFO												
ADOLFO APPAREL WOMEN	G711-2	49.6	49.6	--			--	--	--	--	--	--
ADOLFO WEARING APPAREL WOMEN	A119-2	70.3	70.3	--			--	--	--	--	--	--
COMPANY TOTAL		119.9	119.9	--			--	--	--	--	--	--
ADORAMA												
ADORAMA (WISC)	G619	745.7	745.7	--			--	--	--	--	--	--
ADRAYS APPLIANCE CNTER												
ADRAYS APPLIANCE CENTER	G714	26.4	--	--			--	26.4	--	--	--	--
ADSERT GROUP INC												
ADSERTS MEDIA SERVICES	G900	602.9	602.9	--			--	--	--	--	--	--
ADT LTD												
ADT SECURITY SYSTEMS HOME	H525-5	2,332.7	--	--			--	--	2,332.7	--	--	--
ADT SECURITY SYSTEMS INDUSTRIAL	H525-7	3.0	--	--			3.0	--	--	--	--	--
COMPANY TOTAL		2,335.7	--	--			3.0	--	2,332.7	--	--	--
ADVANCE BOOKS												
ADVANCE BOOKS PUBLICATIONS	B410	126.3	--	--			--	--	--	--	126.3	--

Source: © Copyright 1993 by Leading National Advertisers, Inc., Publishers Information Bureau, Inc., and The Arbitron Company.

6. Once you have complete knowledge of what your enemies are up to, you can make better decisions as to where to meet them head-on and when to outflank them.

7. In new-product and line-extension planning, expenditure data are essential to estimate how much it will cost to get into a market, who's already there, and which competitive product types are growing fastest in the new product's market segment.[8]

FINISHING THE ANALYSIS

The title to this subsection is somewhat of a misnomer because an analysis should be an ongoing process. However, practically speaking, there are deadlines to meet and expense budgets to maintain—research can be expensive. Following the analysis of each of the major sections, there should be at least an informal sense of where the problems and opportunities lie. Frequently, this is a formal procedure, and a summary of the problems and opportunities is done following the completion of all the analyses.

ENDNOTES

[1] Some of this information is from promotional material by Claritas, Inc.

[2] David J. Curry, *The New Marketing Research Systems: How to Use Strategic Database Information for Better Marketing Decisions* (New York: John Wiley, 1993), 255.

[3] This information comes from SRI International fact sheets.

[4] Adapted from Philip Kotler, *Marketing Management: Analysis, Planning, Implementation, and Control*, 8th ed. (Englewood Cliffs, N.J.: Prentice Hall, 1994), 98.

[5] For more information on 11-point scales, see William R. Dillon, Thomas J. Madden, and Neil H. Firtle, *Essentials of Marketing Research* (Homewood, Ill.: Irwin, 1993), 279.

[6] Thomas C. Kinnear and James R. Taylor, *Marketing Research: An Applied Approach*, 3rd ed. (New York: McGraw-Hill , 1987), 536.

[7] Donald S. Tull and Del I. Hawkins, *Marketing Research: Measurement and Method*, 4th ed. (New York: Macmillan, 1987), 286.

[8] "Do You Know Your Competitive Brand Data?" *Media Decisions* (August 1975): 60.

Equity, Problems, Opportunities, and Objectives

In a chronological sense, the first major decisions in a campaign evolve out of the background analysis, which includes company, consumer, market, product, and competitive analyses. It should be clear, however, that because the information-gathering function is an ongoing process, decisions are continually subject to change. In other words, even though a decision is made following an analysis, that decision and other decisions are subject to numerous revisions as new information is received.

Following the background analysis, the first major conclusion reached should be how much value there is in either the company's name or in the names of the products it sells. This value, or equity, strongly influences both the company's problems and their opportunities, which are the second and third conclusions to reach following the analysis.

The problems and opportunities should reflect the amount of equity the company has either in its corporate name or in the brands it sells. After a thorough review of the background information and a clear identification of the problems and opportunities, the problems and opportunities get translated into objectives.

The campaign objectives are then used to provide direction to the rest of the campaign. Organizationally, the campaign should proceed roughly as shown in Figure 4–1.

PURSUING BRAND EQUITY

Businesses do not want consumers to comparison shop. This statement is as true for large firms as it is for small retail operations. Companies may tell consumers they want them to shop around, but they don't mean it. They would prefer consumers buy their products or shop in their stores because of what their name means or has meant. These names have value, or equity, to a company in the same way that a firm has equity in the property it owns. After reviewing the background analysis, the analyst should at least have a general idea of how much equity a company has and how much it can acquire.

Companies put brand names on products to distinguish them from other products. Naming a product provides consumers with something tangible they

FIGURE 4–1   ORGANIZATION OF CAMPAIGN OBJECTIVES

Situation Analysis

↓

Equity

↓

Problems

↓

Opportunities

↓

Objectives

↓

Target Market

↓

Strategy
(such as message and media)

↓

Tactics
(such as message and media)

can use to associate with thoughts, feelings, and images. If these associations are positive, the advertiser has gained some measure of control over consumers' future purchases and, possibly, over the influence they have with other consumers. These associations provide advertisers with a value they can use to persuade consumers to buy their product. This value is independent of the product's physical or even psychological qualities and is called a product's **brand equity.**

For example, telling someone you own an expensive electric guitar says something about the kind of instrument you own. It might also suggest you are a "cool" individual if you go on to say the guitar is a leading brand such as Gibson instead of a minor brand like Silvertone (that is, a legendary Sears brand). If you expand further and state you have a Les Paul preferred model, many music lovers and musicians would recognize immediately that you own the preferred brand of many legendary rock and blues guitarists and would extend you deferential acknowledgment. Consumers are usually willing to pay a premium price because of the extra value they get out of the Les Paul name. The name has become a company asset.

AVOIDING PRICE COMPETITION

Companies want repeat business for their current products and for their new, improved versions. Most firms do not like to compete strictly on the basis of price. Price competitors often devote so much of their effort to being the low-cost producer that they have insufficient resources left over for product development. This situation can be profitable as long as the firm keeps its costs low. Invariably, firms lose their low-cost advantage, frequently because competitors shift their manufacturing facilities to countries with lower labor costs or because another company has simply found a way to operate more cheaply. Advertisers invest in developing brand equity, especially as competitive products approach parity, to avoid price competition. The more value a company can add to its brands, the less likely it will have to compete on a price basis.

COMPETING ON THE BASIS OF QUALITY

Companies also strive to compete through product innovation. This type of competition has become difficult to achieve in many consumer goods categories. Even when a firm is able to develop differentiating qualities for its products, it seldom takes very long for the competition to duplicate the product. When Procter & Gamble developed the first soft-chewable cookies, it test marketed them before distributing the product nationally. By the time the product went into national distribution, Nabisco, Keebler, and Frito-Lay all had comparable products in the marketplace.[1]

National brands also face formidable competition from private labels along a variety of fronts. General merchandise retailers, such as Wal-Mart, sell generic equivalents under their own house labels, and Foot Locker, a specialty retailer, sells its own brand of sportswear and sneakers under its ITZ brand.[2] Private label suppliers, such as Perrigo, which does more than a $600 million business on personal care and over-the-counter products, and Sovex Inc., which specializes in cereal knockoffs, continue to encroach into product categories where traditional brands have been dominant.[3] The major brands are also competing against themselves as companies such as Ralston-Purina and Keebler have introduced private-label products into markets in which they already have major brands. Apparently, they are willing to cannibalize the sales of their own brands because of the perception, "if they don't enter the private label market, another company will."[4]

BRAND NAMES REMAIN IMPORTANT

The result of this multifaceted competition is a dynamic marketplace that redefines the status quo with unprecedented quickness. The traditional notion of carefully and deliberately building brand loyalty through heavy doses of consumer advertising, liberal amounts of sales promotion, and solid, intensive promotion work within the distribution channel has largely been refined by the notion that all of these activities will continue to be important in the next century—and *more*—but they will all have to be done much more quickly.

The traditional analogy of building brand equity as a mason builds a wall upon a strong foundation should be reconceived as a hunter sighting a target at point-blank range. The target is surprisingly difficult to hit because not only is the target moving quickly, but so is the hunter. Still, the target can be hit.

Progressive companies understand that achieving brand equity will continue to be an important corporate goal, but they also appreciate that they cannot rest upon past achievements. Successful companies of the future will not build brand equity so much as they will *pursue* brand equity.

An important function of the situation analysis is to assess the company's brand equity. To both pursue and build brand equity, a successful campaign will have to solve problems and exploit opportunities.

DEFINING PROBLEMS AND IDENTIFYING OPPORTUNITIES

Problem solving is such an omnipresent aspect of doing business that the management style of some firms seems geared to reacting to problems or, in its more extreme form, crises. These companies seem to be perpetually fighting fires. One of the qualities of a good strategic thinker is the ability to anticipate, so sound strategic planners try to avoid fires by focusing on prevention.

In marketing, a **problem** is any barrier or situation that makes it difficult to achieve an objective, whether past, present, or future. For a company to survive it must be able to solve its problems and achieve its objectives. Usually, marketing problems are best discussed in terms of how they relate to sales or market share. Perhaps the most common cause of most marketing problems is communication, or its more commercial version, promotion. Of all the variables in the marketing mix, promotion is the easiest to manipulate.

There are only so many things one can do with the price, distribution, or product line. It is impractical to keep changing these elements every week, month, or even year. With promotion, there are new messages, changes in media, and changing audiences to consider continually. Because of the complexity inherent in the promotion area, many of the marketing problems can be traced to communication or message problems. Is the company transmitting the most persuasive message? Is the medium used the most cost-efficient? To what extent are consumers aware of the products? Some of the marketing problems may be traced also to difficulties with distribution, pricing, or product development. If so, the reader may want to consult one of the many books on marketing management for more details.[5]

If a company is very good at solving its problems, it can turn them into marketing opportunities. For a company to be a leader in its field, it must be able to consistently capitalize on its opportunities. An **opportunity** is a situation or a circumstance that potentially can give the company a marketing

---

EXHIBIT 4–1   VIEWING A PROBLEM AS AN OPPORTUNITY

      Product: Arm & Hammer baking soda
      Problem: Its use for cooking limits its market potential.
Opportunity: Develop new uses for the product (for example, as a freshener in refrigerators and freezers).

      Product: Miller Lite beer
      Problem: Male heavy drinkers perceive low-calorie products as not very masculine.
Opportunity: Associate the product with very masculine men.

      Product: Heinz ketchup
      Problem: Product pours too slowly for some users.
Opportunity: Associate slow pouring with richness.

      Product: Smuckers jelly and jam
      Problem: Has a funny sounding name.
Opportunity: Suggest that the quality must be especially good to overcome the funny name ("With a name like Smuckers it has to be good").

---

advantage. Opportunities are based on assumptions that a company both wants to take advantage of a situation and can.

Listed in Exhibit 4–1 are some classic examples of companies that were able to transform a marketing problem into an opportunity.

Sometimes the difference between a problem and an opportunity depends on how one looks at a situation. The thick consistency of Heinz ketchup can be viewed as either a problem or an opportunity. People who correctly see opportunities where others only see problems are viewed as good leaders. When leaders see opportunity where others cannot imagine them, they get elevated to visionary status.

Not surprisingly, problems cannot be transformed neatly into an opportunity merely by taking an optimistic attitude. Factors internal and external to the firm can have a significant bearing on the extent to which a firm can capitalize on its opportunities.

EXTERNAL FACTORS

Often a number of conditions under which a firm has little control can have a profound influence on a firm's ability to take advantage of an opportunity. The political and legal environment, especially in foreign countries, can make it difficult, and sometimes next to impossible, for firms to get even the simplest venture started.

The cultural and social conditions of a state, region, or country are usually so pervasive as to make it inadvisable for firms to buck existing trends. McDonald's understood that in opening restaurants in India, a country where most of the people do not eat beef, it would have to operate significantly differently than it does in the United States. One difference in India is that it sells vegetable-based burgers. Similarly, what might sell well in Nashville may not do well in Seattle. It does not take a sophisticated market-research study to predict that grits are not likely to do as well in the Northwest as they do in the Southeast, no matter how much promotion they receive.

It is also wise to look at economic conditions. Introducing an expensive product during a recession may be possible but probably not as easy as during a period of economic expansion.

INTERNAL FACTORS

In evaluating whether to pursue an opportunity, a firm needs to be careful to differentiate between a vision and a dream. In marketing, the word *visionary* has come to refer to someone who sees an opportunity and understands whether the company has sufficient resources to take advantage of it. Dreamers also see opportunities, but they are unrealistic about a company's ability to develop and execute successful strategies to see the dream come to fruition. To pursue opportunities, firms usually need adequate resources in three major areas: finance, production, and marketing.

Financial Resources

To compete even on a local level, companies are often best advised to have enough financial resources to initiate action and to sustain the activity over a period of time. Many small-business people underestimate the cost of doing business. For example, restaurants selling pizza can get by with a relatively small overhead as long as they restrict their sales to within the store. If they expand their business to include home delivery, they require considerably larger financial resources. To speed up the baking of the pizza, which it will have to do in order to be competitive, the operation will probably require a conveyor oven, which sells for around $25,000. To get a decent return on the total investment, the company will likely have to draw business from an area larger than its current customer base.

With this kind of investment, the company runs the risk of getting in over its head, particularly when it faces the prospect of significant promotional expenses. The small pizza operation that thought it would be able to compete on the basis of word-of-mouth publicity is faced with financial demands it is unable to meet. Businesses like this can and do lose a lot of money. On a national scale, financial requirements become even more important.

Production Resources

Thinking up new product concepts or services is a lot easier than producing the product or implementing the service. As the saying goes, "The devil is in the details." In the fast-food business, many people will tell you that operational details, including management, doom more restaurants than the product concept. New product ideas do not become opportunities unless the company has sufficient resources to ensure that a quality product gets produced at a competitive cost. In the short run, the firm needs managerial expertise, technological competence, and physical facilities. In the long run, a firm can acquire or buy these things, but opportunities generally do not last over an extended period of time.

Marketing Resources

The Ford Motor Co. was reputed to be one of the most dominant companies in the history of the world. Yet many of the readers of this book think of Ford as the number-two automobile company behind General Motors. The difference is that Henry Ford's genius was in his ability to marshal production resources to sell cars, and the genius of Alfred Sloan of General Motors was in marketing. Henry Ford's myopic view that the company only sell black automobiles regardless of consumer wants is nearly unthinkable today. It does underscore the importance of having marketing-savvy people in decision-making positions.

UNCOVERING OPPORTUNITIES

Following the analysis of the background information (see Chapters 2 and 3), it should be apparent that opportunities may exist in each of the areas analyzed: the company and its resources, the consumer, the market, the product (including its price, distribution, and promotion), and the competition. The analyst should be ever on guard to be sure that opportunities within the consumer area receive prominence over the other areas. The classic mistake is to confuse what the company would like to sell to consumers with what the consumers want to purchase. When seeking out opportunities, consider those that are associated with the following:

☐ Changing consumer needs, wants, or interests
☐ Changing consumer lifestyles
☐ Emerging markets in the United States
☐ Emerging markets overseas
☐ Established markets overseas
☐ Product advantages
☐ Service strengths
☐ New uses for existing products
☐ New technologies
☐ Pricing advantages
☐ Distribution strengths
☐ Marketing and promotional strengths[6]

One of the most important opportunities to identify is where the business is going to come from. This opportunity, of course, refers to the **target market,** or **target audience.** This decision helps provide the foundation upon which the campaign is built. Some planners make the mistake of defining the target market immediately following the consumer analysis. This decision should be deferred until *all* the analyses are complete to be sure the company has sufficient resources to satisfy the consumers' needs, wants, or interests.

The Target Market Decision

Engel, Warshaw, and Kinnear discuss three basic options with regard to this decision: undifferentiated marketing, differentiated marketing, and concentrated marketing.[7] The **undifferentiated market** essentially treats the audience as one mass market. A company must use sufficiently broad but still fairly dramatic creative appeals to be effective with so many diverse subgroups in this overall category. As the marketplace has become increasingly competitive, this approach has decreased in use because rival firms undercut it by targeting a subgroup in the market with a focused and usually more effective appeal. A variation of this option is to target only the largest segment of the overall market, usually the so-called heavy half.

The **differentiated market** is probably the most widely used option today. With differentiated markets, companies may (1) divide the market into segments, usually called *primary, secondary,* and *tertiary markets;* (2) identify a target market and refer to target groups within that category; or (3) simply call all targets *market segments.* Cigarette companies have long used a segmented market approach, as do many companies that offer multiple brands in product categories where the products are similar. A good part of the early success of General Motors can be traced to its strategic decision to divide the overall car market into segments and to develop products that catered to the differentiated market segments.

The **concentrated market** is also referred to as a market niche. This option assumes that a firm will achieve more success targeting a smaller segment in the overall market than by competing directly against the market-share leader in all segments. The niche marketer runs a risk by conceding the largest segment of the market to another company, usually a larger one. The market-share leader that has built up brand equity over a broader base may decide to confront the niche marketer head-on with a new product. The leader would be trading on its brand equity to acquire market share from the smaller market while maintaining the same market share in the larger segments. Gatorade, the leader in the sports drink market, undoubtedly realized that once Coca-Cola and Pepsi Co. decided to enter the sports beverage market, share erosion was all but inevitable.

Delineating the Target Market

It is important to be sensitive to how information about the target market will be used. The creative people look for insight into the consumer to help them develop and craft persuasive messages; the media planners and buyers look for some special piece of information that they can use to deliver these messages efficiently. At the early stage in the campaign, the determination of the target market is largely done in outline form. Later, the creative and media personnel will use the information discussed in the consumer analysis (see Chapter 2) and their own resources to define the target audience or market in greater detail. Typically, the target market should be defined, or delineated, considering at least some of the following criteria:

☐ Demographic variables
☐ Psychographic variables (including lifestyle)
☐ Product usage (for example, heavy, medium, or light)
☐ Brand loyalty
☐ Benefit segmentation
☐ Consumers' needs and wants
☐ Consumers' interests
☐ Consumers' problems
☐ Consumers' motivations

SETTING OBJECTIVES

After the target market has been defined, then the next step is to translate the opportunities into objectives. Setting objectives is one of the key decisions in any campaign, and it is also one of the hardest. The basic problem is twofold: First, the planner must determine what advertising, or any other form of communication, can accomplish that will lead to sales; and second, how one can determine the specific causal relationship between advertising and sales.

Most business people will tell you that their objective in advertising is to sell the product. They may also look at you in a peculiar fashion as though you have been in an ivory tower too long if you fail to recognize what for them is fairly obvious. A standard academic response is to agree that the ultimate goal is generating sales but to add that it is also important to understand the communication effects that need to be accomplished for sales to result.

One analogy looks at the football coach who enters the locker room at half-time as he prepares to address his team, which happens to be losing. What does he tell them? Try harder. Concentrate. Most modern coaches know that this type of old-style motivational speech can actually produce counterproductive results with the team becoming overly tense and tight. Coaches know that they have to be prepared *before* they enter the locker room with a full analysis of the situation. If the basic problem is that the team is not completing enough passes, then the coach needs to determine the reason why and whether any coaching adjustments can be made to correct the situation. Is the offense too predictable, resulting in defensive linemen who rush the quarterback without concern for stopping the running backs? Are the offensive linemen not providing the quarterback with enough time to throw carefully? Is the quarterback simply inaccurate? The coach's message to the players must address the specific problem.

The solutions to the team's problems are a lot like the objectives one can set for an advertising campaign. There are many different things one can try to accomplish, but individually the achievement of one goal is unlikely to guarantee winning or sales. So the coach might suggest to the offensive coordinator to mix up the offense to include more running plays, to the receivers he may suggest different pass routes, to the linemen he may adjust their blocking assignments, and to the quarterback he may ask him to sit down. Or the coach can do what a lot of advertisers do: Keep trying, keep the faith, and hope things will work out.

Setting objectives is a discipline that presents many problems. In addition to trying to measure them, some people feel that the process of researching, determining, and writing the objectives takes more time than they can afford. Others worry that setting specific objectives may make them more accountable than they would like. Setting and writing the objectives can also be difficult. Aside from generating sales, creating awareness, improving images, and generating sales leads, executives often feel unsure about what else they can say. Some of the problems with understanding objective setting are due to semantic confusion, but most of the difficulty results from an inadequate understanding of the various principles that underlie the setting of objectives. Most of the principles in the following section have evolved out of George Odiorne's classic work on management by objectives (MBO).[8]

DEFINITION OF OBJECTIVES

An objective is the desired end of an action—what one expects to accomplish. In MBO terminology, an objective is an effectiveness standard. In an advertising or marketing campaign, all of the strategies and tactics, including creative ideas, are designed to achieve certain results. These results are the objectives, although a practitioner may not call them that.

Some authors, Russell H. Colley in particular, distinguish between an objective and a goal; an objective is general or long term in nature, and a goal is specific or short term in nature.[9] Most advertising texts do not make this distinction. The suggestion that an objective is general may confuse some people who are familiar with MBO literature because MBO literature states that objectives should be specific. Therefore, in the interest of clarity and simplicity, the terms *goal* and *objective* will be used interchangeably, unless otherwise indicated, to indicate a desirable, specific end. When the desired end is general or broad in nature, words such as *long run, long term, broad, general,* or *ultimate* will precede the terms *objective* and *goal* to add precision to their meaning.

FUNCTION OF OBJECTIVES

An objective is established to provide an individual, a group of individuals, or a unit in an organization, such as a department, with *direction* in a problem-solving situation. The setting of objectives serves to communicate to all those charged with the responsibility of achieving the objectives exactly what is expected of them. Logically, an objective should be set so that if it is achieved it will solve some problem or an aspect of a problem. The achievement of an objective may also provide evidence that the firm is capitalizing on an opportunity.

An objective is also established to provide for *accountability.* Objectives serve as standards against which the output or performance of a person or a unit can be evaluated. In the production area of a firm, setting objectives is a long-established practice. For example, in many factories, production goals (sometimes referred to as quotas) are established for individuals and departments. In the production area it is relatively easy to set objectives because the output is a tangible item.

In advertising, it is often difficult to establish a direct causal relationship between advertising and sales because advertising is only one of the many variables that influence sales. Many people disagree about the nature of objectives in advertising. Some people say they should be stated in terms of sales; others want them defined in terms of communication effects, such as awareness or attitude shift.

MARKETING VERSUS ADVERTISING GOALS

Most advertising is simply designed to sell a product or service. However, people do not automatically buy a product after they are exposed to an ad. First, they have thoughts or feelings about a product, and *then* they buy it. Advertising and other types of marketing communication directly affect consumers' mental processes. Advertising can be thought of as a stimulus that produces a response or an effect.

If the objective is to provide *direction* to the strategist, then it must indicate specifically what thoughts or feelings an ad should evoke. These thoughts and feelings can be defined in terms of communications criteria, such as awareness and attitude. In other words, if advertising can stimulate an awareness or a favorable attitude in a consumer, then these effects may trigger a purchase response. Therefore, it makes little sense to set sales as an objective for advertising because these communications effects must occur in order for a sale to take place.

The effects that intervene between advertising and sales are usually the goals that advertising, or any other type of marketing communication, should strive to accomplish. These goals, indirect in nature, can be thought of as **communications objectives.** In most situations, advertising objectives should be formulated as communications objectives.

There are exceptions to this advice. New procedures are being developed and refined with scanner technology that increasingly allow a researcher to isolate the particular effect of advertising on sales. These procedures combine data from consumer panels with information from both in-home and retail scanners of UPC-coded items. The consumer data include information on broadcasting and print exposure, sales promotion activities, and price information. Because the data on media exposure, sales promotion, pricing, and product usage all come from the same sample, it is called single-source data.

The two largest systems, SCANTRACK from A. C. Nielsen and InfoScan from Information Resources, Inc. (IRI), have been discontinued. These systems, according to one report, were expensive and time-consuming, sometimes requiring more than six months to produce usable results at a cost of $200,000 to $300,000 per test.[10] These systems, however, are still evolving. By mid-1995, IRI had replaced InfoScan with BehaviorScan, a more modest system using eight geographically dispersed test markets to collect data.

In some types of direct marketing, researchers are also able to trace a sale to a specific advertisement. However, unless an advertiser uses a single-source system, it is usually easier to evaluate the effectiveness of advertising by measuring the achievement of communications goals than by measuring sales.

Even with single-source data, there are still numerous unmeasured variables that can affect a sale. The effects of advertising frequently interact with a consumer's response to a product's quality, price, service arrangements, and distribution to produce a combined effect that stimulates a sale. Some uncontrollable variables are also at play, such as the economic and political environment, competitive activity, and even the weather. Thus, it is often difficult to isolate the effect of advertising on sales, particularly because advertising often affects sales over a lengthy period of time. Therefore, advertising objectives formulated in terms of communications criteria provide a better measure of accountability than objectives formulated in terms of sales.

Still, it is hard to convince many people that sales are not the relevant measure. Some of the more often quoted words in the literature belong to Michael Halbert, formerly of Du Pont, whose comments nearly 30 years ago continue to reflect the feelings of many people in the business today:

> When a study using one of the goals just mentioned [namely, increase awareness] is published and reported at a meeting, I sometimes get the unsocial urge to question the author with, "So what?" If he has shown that advertising does, in fact, increase brand name awareness or favorable attitude toward the company, on what grounds does this increase a justifiable use of the company's funds? The answer usually given is that more people will buy a product if they are aware of it or if they have a favorable attitude. But why leave this critical piece of inference out of the design of the original research?[11]

Many years have passed since Halbert first made these remarks, and only now are appropriate research designs beginning to emerge that can trace the effect of advertising to sales. But for many products, a meaningful measuring system does not exist.

Until measurement problems are overcome (including expense), planners should consider setting advertising objectives in terms of communications criteria. These criteria should be formulated to provide a critical link tying advertising to sales.

Some advertisers would rather define advertising objectives in terms of sales because they are using single-source systems or because they have difficulty accepting the value of using communications criteria for their advertising objectives. We then suggest using communications criteria as the core elements in the creative objectives.

PLANNING THE OBJECTIVES

To devise effective strategy, the planner must determine precisely the role that advertising and related communications play in the purchase decision. This role is sometimes called the *communication task.* Over the years, there have been a number of attempts to conceptualize the effects of communication and to relate them to consumer behavior. Implicit in these efforts is the notion that consumers pass through a number of stages on their way to a purchase decision.

Russell H. Colley in his so-called DAGMAR approach (an acronym for Defining Advertising Goals for Measured Advertising Results) suggested there were five steps through which a brand must climb to gain acceptance: unawareness, awareness, comprehension and image, attitude, and action.[12] Robert Lavidge and Gary Steiner suggested six steps: awareness, knowledge, liking, preference, conviction, and purchase. Their model, which has received wide exposure, further examined the sociopsychological underpinnings of each of these steps.[13]

Each of these models discusses psychological constructs such as attitude, knowledge, and comprehension. These constructs exist within consumers' minds, and where they are not directly observable and are difficult to measure. Just as Colley and Lavidge and Steiner do not see eye-to-eye on the abstract and complex nature of these concepts, there are other differing opinions about the importance of the various communication criteria discussed in their models and their effect on influencing sales. There are also differing opinions about whether consumers need to pass through *each* step on the way from awareness to a purchase decision. Must consumers understand how a product operates before they make a purchase? And how important is liking the product (or a commercial)? Is awareness a sufficient achievement to stimulate consumers to buy? How important is the brand image versus the physical qualities of the product?

The answers to these questions are important because they provide the core elements of a campaign's objectives. The answers are probably also beyond the scope of this book. What seems more probable is that advertising practitioners determine that a communication effect, such as awareness or image, is needed to stimulate sales. Whether or not it is a stage in a hierarchical sequence of steps is less important.

COMMUNICATION TASKS

It may be helpful to think of each communication task as consisting of both a communication effect and an action word that indicates what is supposed to be done with respect to the effect. For example, awareness is a common communication effect. Words such as *establish, maintain, increase,* or *change* would be action words that indicate the desired status of the effect. So one might *increase* or *establish* awareness, *change* an image or attitude, *maintain* or *increase* brand preference, and *increase* the levels of trust or liking in a brand. Exhibit 4–2 includes some common communication effects and associated action words.

EXHIBIT 4–2   OBJECTIVES AND THEIR ACTION WORDS

Desired Communication Effect	Action Associated with Effect
Awareness (top-of-mind) (brand) (specific product qualities) (of ingredients) (the omission of ingredients)	Establish, maintain, or increase.
Comprehension or understanding	Establish, maintain, or increase.
Conviction or believability	Establish, maintain, increase, or reinforce.
Trust	Establish, maintain, increase, or reinforce.
Attitude	Establish, maintain, reinforce, or change.
Image	Establish, maintain, reinforce, or change.

Writing the Objectives

Communication objectives should be put into written operational form. This step facilitates communication by providing a common set of short-term, intermediate, and long-term goals to guide decision making. It also establishes standards that clearly indicate the basis on which a campaign will be evaluated. By communicating the objectives in writing, the likelihood of a misunderstanding or misinterpretation of what is expected is reduced and possibly eliminated.

The task of writing objectives, however, is not easy. It takes skill, care, and a thorough understanding of the principles that underlie the setting of sound objectives. The following section discusses ten salient criteria to consider in planning and writing objectives.

A Conceptual Foundation for Setting Objectives

The principle that objectives should be specific and measurable is well established in advertising literature. However, students and practitioners may still encounter a number of problems unless they consider the following criteria.

Unit Oriented Objectives should be set for each unit in an organization that performs a task in a business environment. In advertising, the relevant tasks generally are associated with the marketing, advertising, creative (message), media areas, and other types of marketing communication, such as sales promotion and public relations. Even though one person or department may be responsible for decisions in more than one area, it is helpful to set separate objectives for each area. A typical campaign report should include marketing,

---

EXHIBIT 4–3   LINKING OBJECTIVES

---

1. *Corporate objective:* to increase the rate of profit from 5 percent to 7 percent of sales by the year 2000.
2a. *Financial objective:* to secure $10 million in capital to finance the construction of a new production facility within the next six months.
2b. *Production objective:* to produce 100,000 cases of Fruit Juicy by the end of the first quarter.
2c. *Marketing objective:* to increase sales of Fruit Juicy 300 percent compared to the previous year by the end of the year.
3. *Advertising objective:* to establish top-of-mind awareness in 70 percent of the target market by the end of October 1996.
4a. *Creative objective:* to establish in the minds of the target market an association between the trade character, JUICE MAN, and Fruit Juicy.
4b. *Media objective:* to reach 85 percent of the target market by the end of the year.
4c. *Sales promotion objective:* to get 20 percent of the target market to play the tropical sweepstakes game during the first quarter.

---

advertising, creative, media, and marketing communication objectives as long as there are strategies and tactics to achieve the goals.

Objectives should not be set for a unit unless the unit (or department) can achieve the desired result by itself. A common mistake is to confuse marketing goals with advertising goals. For example, "to sell X number of units" is clearly a marketing objective because selling a product requires a combination of variable activities, such as those associated with product quality, price, distribution, and promotion, that are not normally under the control of the advertising unit. Objectives should be set so that the tasks necessary to achieve the goals are clearly the responsibility of a specific unit.

A staff member working within a unit deserves to be rewarded not only on his or her contribution to a unit but also on the unit's contribution to the aggregate even if the overall effort may be a failure. Formulating objectives that are unit oriented helps to provide for each unit's accountability.

Unit Linked All efforts that are oriented toward goals should be linked with one another. The creative plan and the media plan in an advertising campaign each has its own set of objectives, and they should be compatible. These goals must be directly connected to an advertising objective that in turn is tied into a marketing objective. Similarly, marketing goals must be compatible with production goals and finance goals and directly linked to corporate goals. Suppose, for example, the firm Acme's New World Drinks had recently introduced a beverage. Exhibit 4–3 illustrates how its corporate goals might be linked to advertising goals.

In an actual campaign, a number of objectives would be written for each unit; the examples in the exhibit show how objectives link together. From this perspective, one can see how the objectives of an advertising campaign are usually linked to sales even though a sales figure is not established as an objective of the advertising effort.

The linking of objectives avoids *overlap*, a situation in which two units are responsible for accomplishing the same thing. Overlap often occurs when a goal like increasing sales is written for both marketing and advertising objectives. *Underlap* occurs when no unit is assigned the responsibility of achieving a result, as sometimes occurs with sales promotion. The marketing unit may expect the advertising unit to develop the program and vice versa. Writing objectives that are unit linked should avoid overlap and underlap.

Output Oriented Many written statements of the objective incorrectly focus on an activity, or *input*, rather than on the desired result, or *output*. In other words, the strategy and tactics are confused with the objective. For example, part of a creative approach may be to use an appeal to consumers' desire for safety as part of the overall message strategy. An input-oriented objective might read, "to associate Brand X with safe or security-inspiring situations," and an output-oriented objective would rephrase the statement to read, "to develop within the target market a feeling that Brand X is a safe product." Both statements have approximately the same meaning, but input-oriented statements focus on what it takes to achieve a desired result, which is part of the strategy. An output-oriented statement is the desired result of an activity. Focusing on the desired results rather than the activity is a better indication of advertising effectiveness because the purpose of a campaign is to achieve results. Output-oriented statements are expressed in a way that *lend themselves to evaluation.*

Time Bounded An advertising campaign is usually completed within a specified period of time, frequently one year. The progress made in the campaign should be reviewed at various points during the campaign. Objectives should reflect an expectation that specific results will be achieved by specific dates. For example, one might set as an advertising objective, "to achieve brand awareness for New World fruit drinks in 50 percent of the target market within the first three months of the campaign" (or by a specific date). A second objective might be to achieve 70 percent awareness by the end of the second three-month period. Time-bounded objectives establish benchmarks that allow a campaign to be evaluated, or *tracked*, over a period of time.

Realistic Objectives should be neither overambitious nor underambitious. They should be realistic and attainable. Some executives may set their objectives at levels that they do not expect to achieve but just to give them something to shoot at. In MBO terminology this situation is an *overload*, a condition that presents definite problems when trying to evaluate the effectiveness of a unit. Unrealistic objectives only indicate what the planner would *like* to achieve, not what *can* be achieved. Even worse, if a firm is using the objective-and-task method of determining the size of the advertising budget, it will set the objectives and then figure out the cost of achieving them. Unrealistically high objectives may increase the budget out of proportion to the value received in achieving the goals. An *underload* exists when a firm sets its objectives at a level so low that they can be achieved with little or no effort. Objectives that are unrealistic fail to communicate exactly what is expected from the advertising effort.

Common Effectiveness Certain responsibilities relating to effectiveness are common to most units. Such responsibilities as to organize, to plan, to reach the target market efficiently, to be creative, or to do the best job for the least amount of money are standards of effectiveness referred to as common effectiveness. They are usually an implicit part of a standard job description. An employer or client expects these standards from an employee or an agency. Establishing these standards as objectives is only stating the obvious.

Singularity of Purpose For purposes of clarity and ease of evaluation, each objective should be worded so that only one result is associated with each statement. For example, a message strategy may be designed to get prospects to associate "economy of operation" and "high quality" with a particular brand. Is this one objective or two objectives? Having separate objectives prevents the confusion that may occur when half of a dual objective is achieved. Objectives that are stated in paragraph form or objectives that include three or four desired results in one statement only have to be separated in the evaluation phase of campaign anyway. Otherwise, the researcher ends up having to clarify the results by saying, "We achieved this part of the objective but not that part." It is much better to separate multifaceted goals into distinct ones at the beginning of a campaign than at the end.

Measurable If an objective is to provide for accountability, it must be measurable. Problems with measurement account for much of the reluctance to quantify objectives. Measuring communications criteria is still an imprecise science. Many decision makers undoubtedly feel that there is not much sense in quantifying objectives if the measurement techniques are weak. Nevertheless, even when measurement problems are too difficult to overcome or too costly to solve, it is still advisable to quantify objectives whenever possible, because it adds precision to the sense of direction provided to the unit.

Although it is possible to quantify objectives for the major decision-making areas in advertising, quantifying objectives in the creative area may not make as much sense because of the subjective nature of many message variables such as image and attitude. Because the specific relationship between these communications criteria and a marketing goal (such as sales) is seldom precisely known, it is no wonder that copywriters and art directors feel uneasy when the "quant jocks" evaluate their work. A secondary problem could also occur if the copywriters take measurement too seriously and develop ads that score high on the tests but not so well in the marketplace.

An inexperienced decision maker, and in particular students, may regard attempts to quantify objectives as strictly arbitrary and usually just guesstimates. The students may be right if inexperienced evaluators are doing the work. Talking about such things as establishing new levels of awareness is difficult unless the planner knows what the existing levels are. As one becomes more experienced, quantifying objectives becomes more realistic and meaningful.

Inexperienced decision makers can use the following process to develop precision in quantifying advertising objectives:

1. Estimate the marketing objectives.
2. Determine the specific role advertising should play in the overall marketing mix.
3. Set the appropriate advertising (or communication) objectives. If the budget has not been set, it becomes primarily a matter of figuring out what it will cost to achieve the objectives (measured by estimating media costs). If the budget has already been set, then the decision maker compares the cost of achieving the media objectives with the size of the budget. If there is a difference, then some revision of the media objectives would have to take place (or there would have to be an increase or decrease in the size of the budget).
4. Revision of the media objectives should be followed by corresponding revisions of the advertising and marketing objectives. Most beginners and students underestimate how many times objectives need to be revised. In fact, all objectives may need to be in a continual state of revision until the planning of the advertising campaign is completed. When the planning is completed, the objectives should remain firm.

Specific Formulating specific objectives helps provide a sense of direction for the unit and establishes benchmarks against which the unit's effectiveness can be evaluated. Using words such as *increase, maximize, satisfy,* or *optimize* without specific quantification is vague and leads to problems in evaluating the campaign. For example, if the advertising objectives are stated as "to maximize (or increase) awareness," what is the standard of success? To make everybody in the market aware of the brand or only as many people as would be economically practical? Writing specific objectives helps avoid these measurement problems.

Cost-Effective Objectives should always be planned with the idea in mind that they are worth achieving. Because of the difficulty in relating the achievement of communications criteria to sales, it is easy to overlook the cost of achieving the goal. Unless some type of marginal analysis is employed, the planner must remember that the process of setting objectives *is still the result* of executive judgment. Some objectives may be too expensive to accomplish.

Testing for Sound Objectives
During the planning stage or after the objectives have been written, it is helpful to test their soundness by asking the questions listed in Exhibit 4–4 for *each* objective. Following each question is the aspect of each objective that is being evaluated.

Reviewing the Decisions
After the objectives are set, the marketing communication strategy can be developed. Before moving on, it is sometimes helpful to review all key

---

EXHIBIT 4–4   QUESTIONS TO ASSESS THE SOUNDNESS OF OBJECTIVES

---

1. Is this something my _____(insert marketing, advertising, creative, media, or the like) plan can accomplish by itself without underlap or overlap? (Is this unit oriented?)

2. Is this objective linked to an objective in another unit, area, or department? (Is this unit linked?)

3. Is this sentence a statement of a strategy or tactic, or is it something I want my_____(insert marketing, advertising, creative, media, or the like) plan to accomplish? (Is this output oriented?)

4. Is there a specific date by which I expect to achieve this goal? (Is this time bounded?)

5. Is this objective realistic and attainable, or is it overambitious or underambitious? (Is this realistic?)

6. Is this objective something I would expect of every_____(insert marketing, advertising, creative, media, or the like) plan? (Is this common effectiveness?)

7. Is this objective too complex? Can it be separated into a number of simpler objectives? (Does this have singularity of purpose?)

8. Can we measure this objective? (Is this objective measurable?)

9. Is this objective as specific as it can be? (Is it specific?)

10. Is the value of this objective to the_____(insert marketing, advertising, creative, media, or the like) plan commensurate with the cost of accomplishing it? (Is this cost-effective?)

---

decisions. The most important of these decisions is the definition of the target market. The target may consist of a single segment of the overall population of consumers, or it may consist of multiple segments, as in primary and secondary targets. These segments are the prime prospects for the company's products.

The next decision is really a set of decisions. It involves setting the objectives. At this stage, the marketing objectives should be fairly firm, but the advertising objectives should still be fairly flexible. Later, after the media strategy and tactics have been decided, the advertising objectives can be firmed up.

Both the marketing objectives and the advertising objectives should reflect the problems and opportunities that were uncovered in the situation analysis. Of the many problems and opportunities, special attention should be paid to the amount of value, or equity, associated with the names of the company and its products.

ENDNOTES

[1]Matthew Heller, "The Great Cookie War," *Madison Avenue* 27 (January 1985): 100.

[2]Mathew Grimm, "Foot Locker Sneaks Private Label into Sneaker Race with Converse Adidas," *Brandweek* 34 (August 16, 1993): 1, 6.

[3]John McManus, "Don't Count Prosperity as Ally Versus Store Brands," *Brandweek* (February 7, 1994): 14.

[4]Fara Warner, "Going Private: Keebler Heads into Private Label after Disastrous 1992," *Brandweek* (February 1, 1993): 1, 6.

[5]Philip Kotler, *Marketing Management: Analysis, Planning, Implementation, and Control, The Prentice Hall Series in Marketing,* 8th ed. (Englewood Cliffs, N.J.: Prentice Hall, 1994).

[6]For additional information on opportunity analysis, see Robert J. Hamper and L. Sue Baugh, *Strategic Market Planning* (Chicago: NTC Business Books, 1994), Chapter 5.

[7]James F. Engel, Martin R. Warshaw, and Thomas C. Kinnear, *Promotional Strategy: Managing the Marketing Communications Process,* 8th ed. (Burr Ridge, Ill.: Irwin, 1994), 162.

[8]G. S. Odiorne, *Management by Objectives: A System of Managerial Leadership* (New York: Pitman, 1965), 204.

[9]Russel H. Colley, *Defining Advertising Goals for Measured Advertising Results* (New York: Association of National Advertisers, 1961), 6.

[10]William Wells, John Burnett, and Sandra Moriarity, *Advertising: Principles and Practice,* 3rd ed. (Englewood Cliffs, N.J.: Prentice Hall, 1995), 694.

[11]Michael Halbert, "What Do We Buy with Our Advertising Dollar?" Speech presented at the Ninth Annual Seminar in Marketing Management, Miami University, Oxford, Ohio, 1961.

[12]Colley, *Defining Awareness,* 37–38.

[13]Robert J. Lavidge and Gary A. Steiner, "A Model for Predictive Measurements of Advertising Effectiveness," *Journal of Marketing* 25 (October 1961): 61–62.

Building the Marketing Communication Strategy

If you call a large ad agency or advertiser, instead of reaching the executive you dialed, you are likely to get voice mail. If you persist and get through to a secretary, he or she will probably tell you that the person you called is in a meeting. Do these people really need so many meetings? What could they be spending so much time discussing? One answer is that they have to evaluate research, discuss objectives, plot strategy, and then do it all over again—unlike a textbook, where once something is discussed, the readers move on to the next chapter until they reach the end of the book. In advertising, once you've thought through something, you have to rethink it—and then you have to rethink it all over again. Revision is a way of life in the advertising business.

If you are working on a campaign while you are reading this book, you should understand that as you consider strategy options in this chapter, you may want to go back and redo your research, rethink your target market, and reset your objectives. You may not want to revisit everything, just some of it. In the business world, a dynamic market dictates that a campaign be updated continually to meet changing conditions in the environment. Beyond that, revision is simply part of a normal process of fine-tuning your work to produce professional results.

THINKING ABOUT STRATEGY

A basic premise in this book is that advertising or any communication strategy should not be created in a vacuum. Only after an analysis of the situation and a systematic delineation of the problems and opportunities is it time to make decisions. This approach does not mean that every situation should be subjected to rigorous quantitative techniques, but it does mean that decisions should be the result of a careful analysis. If the problems and opportunities can be determined with some insight, the decisions about defining the target market and setting the objectives should evolve naturally out of the analysis. After the target market and objectives have been determined, you should start thinking about strategy.

The strategy will largely consist of message and media options as well as the various marketing communication tools, such as sales promotion, direct marketing, and public relations, to deliver and display the message. However, before the strategy is conceptualized, it is highly important to have a firm understanding of the ideas and decisions that form the base upon which the strategy is developed. We call this base the **strategic foundation.**

Building a Foundation for the Development of Strategy

The strategic foundation consists of the following four elements that work together to provide a platform upon which a successful marketing communication strategy can be built:

- ☐ Management of brand equity
- ☐ Marketing communication expenditure
- ☐ Positioning of messages
- ☐ Targeting and delivery of messages

The strategic foundation is a type of decision making that *precedes* the development of the message and media strategy. The strategic foundation provides the core elements of the strategies that will eventually be developed, expanded, and refined by creative and media personnel.

Each element in the strategic foundation plays out over a period of time, both during the campaign period and from one campaign to another. This separation of short-term effects from long-term ones is not easy and may only be a matter of judgment, *but it is necessary to comprehensively evaluate the effectiveness of a campaign.* Strategically, each of the above elements has both short-term and long-term ramifications.

This chapter will focus on the decisions involving the management of brand equity, the first element of the strategic foundation. Most of what we have to say about the message and media components of the marketing communication strategy will be contained in the subsequent chapters.

Brand equity considerations are easily the most important part of a communication strategy. If a brand loses its equity, it may not survive. Yet many marketing communication campaigns focus more on positioning, targeting, and budgeting decisions than on managing a brand's equity because the campaigns tend to be short-term in nature and of immediate concern. Overworked managers can easily lose sight of long-term effects when faced with making daily decisions. Often management needs to be educated and convinced about the strategic importance of long-term planning.

Until recently, McDonald's Corporation did little research to measure the effectiveness of its advertising. Apparently, the company believed it would be too difficult to evaluate its numerous ads by measurement. The bulk of McDonald's advertising is designed to reinforce the brand's core equities: family, good-tasting food, value, fast service, convenience, and cleanliness. These words all reflect ideas and values that are easy to understand but difficult to measure, especially considering the effects a McDonald's commercial has over an extended period of time. McDonald's is now doing research in this difficult area, not because it has become easier but because it is even more convinced of the strategic importance of managing the brand's equity.

Decisions about the advertising expenditure make up the second element in the strategic foundation. Although very important, we decided not to discuss them in detail because they tend to be more corporate decisions than marketing or advertising ones. Their relevance is particularly minor in a typical advertising campaigns class where the size of the advertising/marketing communication budget is usually predetermined.

Expenditure decisions do, however, have both short- and long-term ramifications. The appropriations decision is of long-term strategic interest. To compete in some categories, a firm must be able to marshal sufficient financial resources. On the other hand, budgetary decisions about how to allocate the money are short-term operational decisions only indirectly concerned with long-range strategic planning.

The elements of the strategic foundation that deal with positioning and targeting correspond to what is frequently referred to in an advertising agency as the creative and media areas. These concepts will be looked at in greater detail in Chapters 6 (on message strategy), 7 (on media strategy), and 8 (on related marketing communications).

Positioning, or the way the firm presents the brand in its various forms of communication, can be planned to achieve short-term or long-term effects. Sometimes it can do both. When McDonald's advertises a promotion tied to Barbie dolls and Hot Wheels, ostensibly it is advertising for the short term. The toys are presented as fun and exciting and only available for a limited amount of time. However, by presenting the toys in a wholesome, family environment, the company is also reinforcing one of its core equities and enhancing the value of the brand over a much longer period of time.

The targeting decision can also have both short-term and long-range ramifications. On a daily basis, targeting decisions usually devolve to questions about the efficiency with which the media are delivering messages to target audiences. Of more strategic concern, targeting focuses on the extent to which the messages are delivered to the right target. In 1990, Oldsmobile began a clever and still memorable 18-month campaign to reposition the brand to appeal to a younger market. It was called "This is not your father's Oldsmobile." The consumers' response was clear: "Oh yes it is!" The problem wasn't so much the advertising as it was the product. General Motors was trying to distinguish the Oldsmobile from its other brands and models, mostly Buicks, by giving it a more youthful image. Consumers liked the advertising. They just didn't believe it.

At this point it might be helpful to look at each of the four elements of the strategic foundation in some detail.

MANAGING BRAND EQUITY

Brand names have value, or equity, and are an asset every bit as important as the mortar and brick in the building housing the company. Like an investment property, brand equity must be managed. Brand equity is all about the *value* in the company's names and symbols. This means that a brand's opportunities must be cultivated and nurtured, its position in the market reinforced and intensified, and its problems dealt with by protecting and defending the brand from any situation that would undermine its status in the marketplace.

David A. Aaker, in his widely influential book *Managing Brand Equity,* discusses five categories of largely intangible assets and liabilities upon which brand equity is based:

1. Brand loyalty
2. Name awareness
3. Perceived quality
4. Brand associations
5. Other proprietary assets such as patents, trademarks, characters, and channel relationships[1]

Brand Loyalty
Establishing, building, reinforcing, and intensifying brand loyalty are easily the most important aspects of managing brand equity. There is an axiom in marketing that suggests it is easier to keep customers than to get new ones. Consumers fall into routines and will often buy a product simply out of habit, especially if they are satisfied. The cost of acquiring new customers is typically greater than maintaining existing customers. Existing customers also help expand demand by promoting the product through word-of-mouth publicity. If a company takes the proper steps to satisfy its customers, it is amazing how loyal consumers can be to a brand. Exhibit 5–1 compares the leading brands of various products in 1925 with the leaders in 1985 and 1994. With only a few exceptions, the leaders today are still the same as they were in 1925 and 1985.

Simply being a leader, however, is no guarantee of long-term success. The saying "The bigger they are, the harder they fall" applies to companies as well as giants. Eastern Airlines, a leader in the 1970s, is out of business. Not all companies can be the leaders in their field. Enlightened companies understand that brand loyalty doesn't automatically follow brand-share leadership. As Figure 5–1 illustrates, firms seek to gain control over consumers by moving them along a continuum beginning with brand awareness and ideally ending with brand insistence.

Brand awareness can range from a point where consumers are barely familiar with the brand name to a point at which the brand is the first word that comes to the consumer's mind when the product category is mentioned. Simple brand awareness is only a very mild form of control whereas *top-of-mind awareness* can be a distinct advantage, particularly in a generic category where the differences among products are slight. In some consumer groups or areas of the country, a brand may have high top-of-mind awareness because the brand name is used as a generic term.

In Tennessee, a lot of Coca-Cola is sold to people who use the word *coke* as a generic equivalent for soft drinks. Several years ago, a young man asked an acquaintance of one of the authors to pick up a couple of cases of "cokes" for

EXHIBIT 5–1   THE LEADING BRANDS

Product	1925	Position in 1985	Position in 1994
Bacon	Swift	Leader	Number 3
Biscuits	Nabisco	Leader	Leader
Breakfast cereal	Kellogg	Leader	Leader
Cameras	Kodak	Leader	Leader
Chewing gum	Wrigley	Leader	Leader
Chocolates	Hershey	Number 2	Leader
Mint candies	Life Savers	Leader	Number 2
Razors	Gillette	Leader	Leader
Shortening	Crisco	Leader	Leader
Soap	Ivory	Leader	Number 5
Soft drinks	Coca-Cola	Leader	Leader
Soup	Campbell	Leader	Leader
Tea	Lipton	Leader	Leader
Tires	Goodyear	Leader	Leader
Toothpaste	Colgate	Number 2	Number 2

Sources: For 1925 and 1985 data, the source is Thomas S. Wurster, "The Leading Brands: 1925–1985," *Perspectives* (Boston: The Boston Consulting Group, 1987). Quoted in David A. Aaker, *Managing Brand Equity;* 1994 data courtesy of Information Resources, Inc.

a picnic. When she arrived at the park with two cases of Coca-Cola, the young man asked her why she hadn't bought any Pepsi, which was his favorite, uncharitably she laughed. Later, he conceded that from time to time he was served Coke simply because it was the first word that came to his mind, and, to him, it really didn't matter very much.

Most consumer brands fall into the classification *brand acceptance.* Consumers typically find several brands in product categories satisfactory and appear willing to base their purchase decisions on a sale price or a coupon. Increasingly, the nationally advertised brands are discovering that consumers are extending their level of acceptance to include many store brands and private-label merchandise.

Brand preference is a measure of loyalty that most companies would like their brands to achieve. A brand can achieve leadership in a category even when it is only slightly preferred. Budweiser is clearly the number-one beer in the United States, a position that reflects the preference consumers have for the

FIGURE 5–1   BRAND CONTINUUM

Brand
Awareness → Brand
Acceptance → Brand
Preference → Brand
Insistence →

brand. How strong is this preference? Even though many beer drinkers claim to "love" their Bud, it is highly likely that they would quickly order some other brand if Budweiser were unavailable.

The ideal level of brand loyalty is *brand insistence.* This means consumers will take no substitutes for the brand. So if a store is out of Budweiser, it's out of beer. Schlitz used a variation of this line in the 1970s: "When you're out of Schlitz, you're out of beer." It's a nice line that speaks of a highly desirable state of brand loyalty, but as legend has it, it was originally spoken by a Budweiser beer salesman. Apparently, after ordering a Budweiser and learning that the bar was out of his brand, he cried, "When you're out of Bud, you're out of beer." A copywriter at Leo Burnett reportedly heard the line and used it on the Schlitz campaign. Unfortunately for Schlitz, nice line that it was, it did not save the brand from declining from the second best-selling beer to a point where it is virtually out of the beer business.

Perhaps, the ultimate level of brand insistence has been attained by Harley-Davidson. Not only will potential buyers wait months to purchase the brand, but buyers belong to owners' clubs, attend Harley Davidson rallies, wear shirts with the company logo, and tattoo their bodies with the brand name. Obviously, it is unrealistic to expect this kind of loyalty for the average product.

Cultivating Brand Loyalty The key to developing brand loyalty is to get consumers to make an emotional attachment to the company or its brands, or both. Companies that consistently produce better products than their competitors have a much easier time developing this emotional bond. However, a better product is often a matter of opinion and a function of perspective. In the 1990s, many companies cultivate brand loyalty by extending the marketing concept to giving people not only what they want but also "more"—more attention, more recognition, more satisfaction—in short, more *value.* Some companies attempt to formalize this approach by giving it a special name: *relationship marketing.*

Relationship Marketing The key to developing a relationship with consumers is attitude. The firm must be willing to provide extra value to consumers in return for greater brand loyalty. This is a simple paraphrase of the Stuart Smalley pop psychology phrase of the 1980s: "If you want to be loved, give love." Many brands have substantial amounts of brand equity without resorting to warm and fuzzy marketing, but many companies find that a more caring consumer-oriented approach is good for business. As the differences among products appear to be getting smaller each year, companies are searching long and hard for ways to provide extra value to consumers.

Companies can forge a positive relationship at all three stages of a consumer's experience with a brand: (1) before the purchase, (2) while the consumer is using the product, and (3) after a customer has stopped using or purchasing the brand. Pepsi Cola and Nike are two advertisers that make extensive use of the relationship concept.

For years, Pepsi has invited consumers to join the Pepsi generation using a fun, even funky, approach. Its message is simple: If you're conservative or stodgy, drink Coke. If you're hip, join us. In recent years, Nike has segmented its approach to selling athletic shoes. To reach men, it has used a traditional campaign with famous athletes, like Michael Jordan and Bo Jackson, often in humorous situations. To appeal to women, it shows the product less than in its advertising for men, if it appears at all. Instead, the ads use a lot of empathic copy to discuss, if not celebrate, what it is like to be a woman, especially one who works out. The message is simple and subtle: "We understand real women. If you're in the market for a pair of shoes, who understands your needs and wants better than us?"

Companies that use the relationship marketing approach understand that making the sale is only part of the transaction. Consumer satisfaction can be a transitory thing. What satisfied a consumer yesterday, happened yesterday. Consumers are continually exposed to all kinds of promotions. Consumers who sign up with MCI receive regular calls from the company checking whether the service is satisfactory.

Saturn prides itself on being a different kind of a company. From its inception, Saturn has worked hard to demonstrate its commitment to being sensitive to the way consumers like to be treated. General Motors literally bet a large part of its future on this division. If they couldn't get it right there, then they might not have been able to get it right anywhere.

First, the company trained its dealers to work with the salespeople so they were less pushy and more laid back. Next GM cooperated with the media in letting them know about the delays on the production line, which were to make sure each car was just right. Then when a car broke down in a far-off place like Alaska, hundreds of miles from a dealer, the company flew a repairperson in to fix it. Naturally, the company carefully documented these events for promotions; it's not enough for a company to care—the consumer has to know it cares.

Saturn also inaugurated an owners' club. These clubs are not uncommon in the auto industry; Saab, Corvette, Mustang, and Porsche are only some brands that have had clubs for years. Usually, the cars in these clubs are sporty, foreign, or expensive. Saturn had none of these qualities. In 1994, Saturn mailed out 700,000 invitations to attend a "homecoming" celebration in Spring Hill, Tennessee, about an hour's drive from Nashville.[2] Amazingly, 30,000 people paid $34 per ticket to attend the festivities and take a tour of the factory, some arriving in caravans from Florida, California, and even Taiwan. Why? Is it the car? Not likely. Evidently, people liked the attention and recognition and a chance to attend a gigantic party (tame as it was). People bought the Saturn experience as much as they bought the car.

Companies are also beginning to understand the importance of pursuing a relationship with customers after they stop buying. Terry Vavra, in his book *AfterMarketing,* argues that some of a company's best prospects are the consumers who no longer buy the company's products or services. He gives three reasons.[3] First, there is a wealth of information to be learned from previous customers: Were they dissatisfied with the product or service? Did they switch for a lower price? Have they simply moved on to new interests or wants in their lives?

Second, it is often cheaper to get back old customers than to acquire new ones. Many firms have accumulated a considerable database of previous customers. Instead of purging files of inactive customers, it may be cheaper and easier to retarget old customers than to launch a campaign aimed at winning new ones.

Third, with the information obtained from old customers, a firm can often fix the problems that led customers to buy elsewhere. Consumers who purchased from a company more than once probably have residual positive feelings about a company even after they go elsewhere. Prospecting for new business with old customers is simply a way to rekindle the warmth associated with an old relationship.[4]

Staples, an office supplies store, builds its database of customers by offering them membership cards that entitle them to a special discount. These cards enable the store to track purchase behavior; identify monthly patterns, including responses to various promotions; and detect whether each customer has decreased or stopped purchases. With this information, Staples is able to mount marketing-oriented countermeasures aimed at regaining business.[5]

Name Awareness

Awareness is an aspect of brand loyalty, but it is important enough as a tactical and strategic concern to merit special attention. Simple awareness by itself does not contribute much to brand loyalty. However, without awareness there can't be any loyalty. This premise may be why awareness seems to be the primary objective of so much advertising. In a survey of more than 3,000 directors of advertising designed to look at the way decision makers set objectives, more directors stated awareness as an advertising objective more than any other criterion.[6]

Awareness and Value   David Aaker suggests that awareness contributes to a brand's equity in at least four ways:

1. A name provides an anchor to which you can attach other associations.
2. A recognizable name provides a sense of familiarity that people usually like.
3. A well-known name signals that there is substance and commitment behind it.
4. A well-known name signals that others have found the brand worth considering.[7]

Exhibit 5–2 presents a list of names with some common associations. If you are familiar with the names, you will probably make similar associations. If you are unfamiliar with a name, you may not have a clue as to where the association is coming from. Of course, familiarity doesn't always generate good feelings; sometimes it breeds contempt, as the saying goes. Even in cases where there are negative associations, however, people may be willing to pay attention to the names because they assume others have.

Stages of Awareness   Awareness can vary on a continuum from no awareness to extreme awareness. However, this is not how it tends to be measured. Figure

EXHIBIT 5-2   NAMES AND COMMON ASSOCIATIONS

Domino's	fast delivery
Crest	fights cavities
JiffyLube	fast service
Wal-Mart	low prices
Jerry Lewis Telethon	Muscular Dystrophy Association
Bono	cool music
Pearl Jam	angst music
Uno's, Due's, and Gino's	deep-dish pizza

5–2 presents a continuum of the different stages of awareness. Below the first line is another continuum displaying how these stages of awareness get measured conceptually. The distinction between the stages and measurement can be important for both strategic and operational purposes.

Using a commonsense approach to discussing strategy, you may simply say that you would like consumers to be very aware of the brand name. When the copywriters and media buyers devise their plans to achieve this aim, however, they may have different ideas about what "very aware" means. To avoid this confusion, a planner may suggest a much more specific goal, such as "We would like X percent of our target market to be able to recall the brand name." Brand *recognition* is the weakest form of awareness, and it is measured simply by asking respondents, usually by phone, if they recognize any of the names an interviewer tells them. *Recall* is measured by asking respondents to name a brand within a product category without any prompting or aid. Both recognition and recall are memory tests. Many planners do not feel comfortable using memory tests both for methodological reasons and because the evidence is not compelling that high scores on a memory test translate into increased sales.[8]

Top-of-mind awareness is basically measured in one of two ways: (1) Respondents are asked to indicate the first word that comes to mind when prompted by a product category, or (2) top-of-mind status is simply assigned to the first brand mentioned in a recall test.

Top-of-Mind Awareness Top-of-mind awareness can be a distinct advantage to a brand in certain categories. It usually helps to be the first name considered for impulse items and products in categories where many of the brands are comparable in quality and have achieved brand acceptance. Pizza is often an impulse item. Pizza is also a good example of a product category in which many brands have achieved brand acceptance. Even bad pizza seems to sell, sometimes well. In many markets, when people think about delivered pizza, instead of saying, "Let's order pizza," they will simply say, "Let's call Domino's." Is this because Domino's makes great pizza? Probably not. Over the years, Domino's has invested substantial sums of money in building its equity, so that when consumers think of delivered pizza, they think of

FIGURE 5–2   STAGES OF AWARENESS

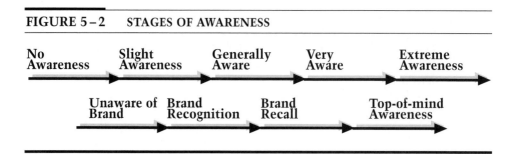

Domino's first. Domino's might not hold such a preeminent position in consumers' minds if its products were more expensive, if the quality differences among the national brands were greater, or if consumers had a more discerning palate.

The "uncola" campaign for 7-UP is a reflection of the strategic importance advertisers place on top-of-mind awareness. In the early 1970s, 7-UP uncovered in its consumer research the not too surprising information that consumers were consistently mentioning either Coca-Cola or Pepsi first in any top-of-mind awareness test. What bothered 7-UP most about these findings was that the pattern also was true for consumers who preferred 7-UP over Coke and Pepsi. No doubt marketers at 7-UP agonized over sales that were lost simply because consumers thought of one of its competitor's brand names first. So for more than 20 years, 7-UP has periodically run the "uncola" campaign in an attempt to get consumers to stop automatically thinking of a cola when they want a soft drink.

Perceived Quality

An image of quality is an important part of brand equity. Once you have a quality image, it becomes an asset that is an integral part of brand loyalty. Getting this image can be an elusive goal. Companies with substantial research and development (R&D) functions learn early in their work that there is more to an image than what one sees. R&D people use the qualities that consumers find desirable in competitive products as a benchmark, or standard for their own product. Then they try to produce a product that is better than the one in their specifications, or specs. If a company can come up with a comparable or even superior product, it's won only half the battle. The rest of the job is convincing consumers.

Al Ries and Jack Trout in their book, *The 22 Immutable Laws of Marketing,* suggest that "marketing is not a battle of products, it's a battle of perceptions."[9] The best product will not automatically become the market leader. It's not how good a product is; it's how good people *think* it is. The magazine *Consumer Reports,* which rates the quality of products, provides ample evidence nearly every issue that the highest-rated products are not necessarily the brands with the largest market share.

What makes a quality desirable can also be a matter of opinion. In California, consumers prefer smaller, crisper-handling cars, whereas in the Midwest buyers prefer cars that are bigger and more comfortable to drive. What makes a quality desirable can also be a matter of which company has the best chance to get its image registered with consumers. Apparently, once consumers get an impression or image of a person, product, or place, they tend to keep the image and its associations for a long time. Ries and Trout argue that it is "better to be first than it is to be better. It's much easier to get into the mind first than to try and convince someone you have a better product than the one that got there first."[10] As evidence they cite a number of famous firsts and some not-so-famous seconds. Exhibit 5–3 lists some of their examples along with others.

It is hard to know why the first company to make an impression has such an advantage over other companies. One guess is that as consumers become satisfied with a brand, they have little motivation, reason, or incentive to pursue further information. For example, Whitehall Labs was the first company to take advantage of the Food and Drug Administration's approval allowing ibuprofen to be sold as an over-the-counter drug. In its early advertising, it introduced Advil as the same pain reliever that consumers had been buying under the prescriptive name Motrin. Later when Upjohn decided to market Motrin IB as an over-the-counter drug, consumers did not flock to the "real thing." Apparently, they were satisfied with Advil. Consumers' perception of Advil's quality is sufficiently high to ward off competition from brands that are equivalent and, in many instances, cheaper. In 1994, Advil was the number-one selling brand of ibuprofen.[11]

Brand Associations

Companies also actively manage the equity in a brand through associations with its proprietary names. Associations can influence perceptions, increase brand awareness, and build brand loyalty. The type of associations companies promote can be almost infinite in scope. Some of the more common associations are with celebrities, places, characters, ideas, or words.

The use of celebrities to endorse a product or simply appear in a commercial is widespread. Sales of Gatorade increased significantly when Michael Jordan signed on to appear in the company's ads. The target market, overwhelmingly male, related to the line "Be like Mike." Other products find positive associations with geographic regions, states, and cities. Jimmy Dean Breakfast Sausage and Bryan sausage both play up their southern heritage while Northern Bathroom Tissue associates with the North. Louisiana Hot Sauce and generic products such as California raisins, Idaho potatoes, and Washington State apples associate with states. Cities are also popular associations. There's Old Milwaukee beer, L.A. Gear sportswear, K.C. Masterpiece barbecue sauce, Philadelphia Brand cream cheese, OshKosh clothing, and Raleigh, Winston, and Salem cigarettes.

Companies also associate with characters. The characters can be animated, such as the Green Giant and the Keebler elves, or live, such as the Maytag repairman and Mikey, the little boy who says he likes Life cereal.

EXHIBIT 5 – 3   FAMOUS FIRSTS

Famous Event or Product	Famous First	Not-So-Famous Second
First person to fly solo across the Atlantic	Charles Lindbergh	Bert Hinckler
First cellophane adhesive tape	Scotch	3-M
First person to walk on the moon	Neil Armstrong	Buzz Aldrin
First sport drink	Gatorade	Unknown
First president of the United States	George Washington	John Adams
First brand of English muffin	Thomas	Unknown
First female to receive a "10" in Olympics	Nadia Commenici	Nelli Kim

---

When the Mikey campaign was first run in the early 1980s, it featured two adolescent boys trying to decide if they should eat a bowl of Life cereal. The boys decided to give it to their younger brother, Mikey, as an acid test because Mikey "doesn't eat anything." When the camera zoomed in on Mikey's cherubic face joyously eating the product, his brothers made advertising history by exclaiming, "He likes it." As soon as the people at Quaker Oats, parent company of Life cereal, saw the commercial, they knew it was magic. They rushed the spot on the air without pretesting it, something they rarely did. Later Quaker Oats tested the commercial, and it did poorly both in terms of the communication measures the company was using and in its sales impact. Consumers could recall the ad but had difficulty recalling the brand advertised. Someone at Quaker came up with the brilliant idea of putting "Mikey's" picture on the Life cereal package and announcing that this was "Mikey's cereal." During the first 18 months following the start of Mikey advertising, sales increased 25 percent. Today Mikey is a young adult who regularly appears on talk shows.

Competing against a corporate giant is rarely easy. Competing against a company with the size and history of AT&T must be especially daunting. AT&T spends more than $500 million on advertising and over the years has built up considerable brand equity. Part of its equity is based on consumers' confidence in AT&T's technological abilities. Consumers are generally aware that the U.S. phone system is the envy of the world, and AT&T largely gets the credit. To break into this market, both MCI and Sprint have been aggressive price discounters. Both companies realize that eventually they will need to compete on some basis other than price. To get into this market, both companies have been essentially buying market share with price discounts. To stay in this market, MCI has been relying on a number of innovative marketing promotions, especially its Friends and Family campaign.

Sprint has also launched a number of marketing initiatives, but it has also spent substantial sums of money to build brand equity by associating its name with an idea. The idea is simple: Sprint has invested in an extensive network of fiber-optic cable. Its reception is so clear, "you can hear a pin drop." The message is designed to allay consumers' concern that the telephone reception on Sprint might be inferior to that of AT&T. The pin association is presented both visually and orally, and for the most part represents an investment to produce short-term sales as well as long-term equity.

Simple word associations can be so strong that a single word or two can be indelibly associated with a brand in the minds of consumers. Budweiser is known as the king of beers. It's a powerful association, and it belongs to Budweiser. Even if it weren't trademarked, a company would be foolish to try and use it. There simply wouldn't be any credibility. Consider the following: "Pabst, the king of beers" or "Stroh's, the beer of kings." Or how about "Miller Genuine Draft: the royalty of bottled beer." In fact, by its association with royalty, Budweiser has preempted the use of all terms that denote royalty. It's unlikely there will ever be a "prince of beers" and certainly not a "queen of bottled beer."

Consider the following associations:

Ivory	floats
Domino's	delivers
Lee's	fit
Michelin	cares
The Club	protects
John Deere's	run

How about two words:

Charmin	squeezably soft
Avis	tries harder
Crest	fights cavities
Allstate	good hands
United Air Lines	friendly skies
Apple/Macintosh	user friendly

The best word associations are probably those that communicate the message in a word or two. Sometimes a word or two will be used less for its literal associations and more for the associations it stimulates. In the summer of 1994, a story, perhaps apocryphal, was circulating within the Chicago advertising community. Four executives from a top-10 ad agency were quitting the business to enter the microbrewed beer business. Their chief asset was an association. Allegedly, they were going to call their beer Naughty Boy. The copy and visuals would be simple: Two attractive women walk up to a bar. The first woman says, "I'll have a Naughty Boy." The second woman leans forward and with emphasis says, "Make that two Naughty Boys." Tacky? A gratuitous use of sex appeal? Probably. But still it would be a powerful use of an association, even for the beer business. As the beer business shows signs of fragmenting into smaller segments, or niches, this kind of ad could build awareness.

As good as some associations are, their value in maintaining brand equity may be limited over a long term. As advancements continue in the field of computer software, other companies may take over Apple's "user friendly" association. An association based upon a physical quality may be more difficult for a company to maintain once a company loses its distinctness.

The fact that Ivory soap floats has nowhere near the value today as it did when it was introduced by Procter & Gamble in 1881. At the time, floating soap did not exist. A worker accidentally fed air into a mixture of soap, and the company was unaware of its buoyant properties until customers tried to reorder the "floating soap."[12] Today other soaps float, and people take more showers. Times change.

A bigger potential problem occurs when a company voluntarily gives up its associations before they have lost their effectiveness. A maxim in the agency business is that clients usually get tired of a strategy or slogan long before it loses its effectiveness. Clients may simply be eager to try new ideas, or they may feel the agency is not doing enough to earn their compensation. There is also a temptation to capitalize on the equity in a brand by entering a new category.

In 1993, Miller Lite was the second best-selling brand of beer, Budweiser was easily first, and Coors Light and Bud Light both came in a distant third. In 1991, Miller changed its advertising campaign in an attempt to make up the considerable distance between Budweiser and Miller Lite with a new campaign that used the tagline "It's it and that's that." They were trying to suggest that consumers were drinking Miller Lite for itself and not because it was a beer with fewer calories. The message simply wasn't credible. Taste may be subjective, but do any beer drinkers actually prefer the taste of a thinner (light) beer to a full-bodied (regular) beer? It was a nice idea, but the opportunity simply wasn't there. In 1994, Bud Light overtook Miller Lite as the second best-selling brand of beer.[13]

Other Proprietary Brand Assets

Another important part of a brand's equity is assets (or liabilities), such as patents, trademarks, characters, and channel relationships.

Patents and Trademarks Many companies have exclusive ownership of distinctive assets that contribute to a brand's equity. Until late 1993, Monsanto owned the patent rights to aspartame, a sweetener the company branded under the names Equal, when sold in packages, and Nutrasweet, when used as an ingredient in other products. Many people thought that after the patent ran out other companies would enter the market with a cheaper generic equivalent, which would also be aspartame. These people forgot the lessons learned with Tylenol.

Many companies can easily duplicate acetaminophen, the generic name for Tylenol, but consumers won't buy very much of it. Tylenol is not only far and away the best-selling brand of acetaminophen, but it also sells more than twice as much as the next best-selling, over-the-counter pain reliever, Advil. Doctors rarely recommend acetaminophen; they simply say Tylenol.

Similarly, Monsanto shrewdly managed its asset so that even after it no longer owned the patent, the brand was still protected. Monsanto set up a separate company, The Nutrasweet Co., to manage the brand and give it corporate identity. It invested heavily in advertising and required the thousands of products that use Nutrasweet as an ingredient to list the brand name and its symbol on their labels. The only way a new company could compete would be on price, and even then it is likely that Monsanto would meet any competitor's low price. A competing company would have to overcome both consumer loyalty to the Equal brand and resistance within the production areas of companies reluctant to change their advertising and packaging to reflect the absence of Nutrasweet. As a result, no significant competition to Nutrasweet appears on the horizon.

In Chapter 1, we spoke about the value of using characters to lend continuity to a campaign. Characters can also be used to manage the equity in a brand. Putting Mikey's face on the box of Life cereal and Morris's picture on the outside of a can of cat food can stimulate sales in the short term and have lasting effects over an extended period of time. The effects can also be permanent.

Characters In 1950, the Minnesota Valley Canning Company changed its name to the Green Giant Company to reflect its use of the Green Giant character in its advertising. The giant first appeared in the company's ads in 1925, hunchbacked and looking like a "fugitive from a Grimm's fairy tale." Later it evolved into an amiable character, somewhat obscure but, most of all, imaginary. Leo Burnett added the word *Jolly* to a proof of a *Ladies Home Journal* ad, and the company has kept the word in its vocabulary ever since.[14]

Channel Relationships The relationship within the channel of distribution is another important influence on a brand's equity. This relationship, along with the various messages consumers receive from other marketing communication tools, directly influence the image of the company, which in turn influences brand loyalty, perception of quality, and brand association. For example, salespeople put a high premium on the value of their contacts. Frequently, it's not what you know or what you have to sell as much as it is who you know and how much people like working with you. Personal relationships can be very important. Over time, a network of relationships tends to become institutionalized. Companies within a channel of distribution get accustomed to working with certain suppliers and may also have to pay to change their suppliers. New vendors may require company employees to learn new product specifications, new procedures, and new contacts within their organization. If the company uses any of the supplier's equipment, as often is the case with vending operations, changing suppliers can be a significant inconvenience.

Not only are channel relationships important, but also the extensiveness of the channel networks can be a positive influence on what consumers and channel members think of a brand. Gatorade is the number-one sport drink with substantial brand equity, but when Coca-Cola entered the market with Powerade and Pepsi with All Sport, Gatorade might have been nervous. Both Coca-Cola and Pepsi have substantial resources to spend promoting their products and extensive distribution networks that can make their products available in many locations that are not available to Gatorade. These networks add value to the brand's image because consumers and dealers know Coca-Cola and Pepsi are considerable forces to be reckoned with in the marketplace.

In the early 1990s, United Air Lines ran a commercial that touched upon the importance of personal relationships. The spot used a slice-of-life dramatic approach featuring a CEO addressing his employees in a serious tone of voice. The company had lost a major customer apparently because the company "no longer knew who we were." In the spot, the CEO passes out plane tickets (presumably from United Air Lines) and urges his executives to get to know the customers better.

PROTECTING BRAND EQUITY

Underlying the development of all communication strategy should be an understanding that the protection of the brand name is of paramount importance. Whereas managing brand equity is part of the strategic foundation that is used to build the marketing communication strategy, protecting brand equity is a philosophy that pervades *all* strategic and tactical thinking.

Brands can be a fragile asset for a company. Consider the current status of once proud names, such as Miller Highlife, Schlitz, Luv's (in Canada), Wordstar, and White Cloud. A brand can be a strong player one year and next to nowhere within a few years. At the local level, business people need to work hard to shore up the erosion of their company names. If all the local hardware or garden supply store has to offer is merchandise and equipment, then it surely will be squeezed out of business by Wal-Mart and Kmart.

Through all the steps in building the strategic foundation and while pursuing its strategy and tactics, companies need to be sure that their names are protected. Figure 5–3 presents a diagrammatic view of the relationships involved in managing and protecting brand equity.

Short-Term Thinking versus Long-Term Investment

Much has been written about the differences between Japanese and American businesses. Japanese companies tend to be more concerned about the long term, whereas American firms tend to pay more attention to the company's stock prices, which usually reflect short-term performances. The performances of many brand managers are evaluated on a quarterly basis. If sales haven't reached marketing goals toward the end of a quarter, many managers will run price promotions, such as trade discounts, consumer rebates, coupons, and price reductions. These promotions eat into profit margins and send a not too subtle message to consumers: Our position is not very strong, they say, so we're lowering prices. If you can't buy now, wait around; we'll probably lower them again. Price promotions undermine consumers' confidence in their perceptions of the brand's worth. The value in having a brand with equity is that consumers are generally willing to pay a premium for a strong name.

Investing in advertising promotion to build a brand's equity or keep it from eroding is a lot more difficult to measure than short-term behavioral effects,

FIGURE 5-3   MANAGING BRAND EQUITY

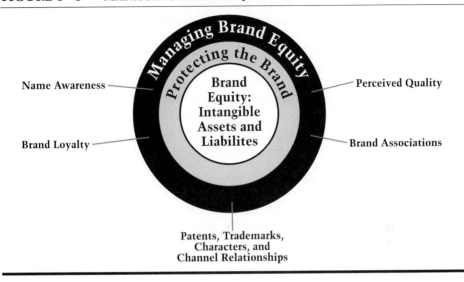

Name Awareness

Brand Loyalty

Brand Equity: Intangible Assets and Liabilites

Perceived Quality

Brand Associations

Patents, Trademarks,
Characters, and
Channel Relationships

such as coupon redemptions, price promotions, or 1-800 inquiries. Focusing on brand equity is more long term in nature because the effects of advertising to build a brand tend to accumulate over an extended period of time. But long term may be interminable to brand managers working their way up the corporate ladder. It is easier for them to document their accomplishments with something that is easily measured than it is with something that can be as vague and difficult to measure as brand equity.

A focus on short-term performance may also be a problem with investment managers in the stock market. Toward the end of the annual or semiannual accounting period when companies send out reports to shareholders, many fund managers dress up their holdings, to use the trade's terminology, by dumping poor-performing stocks and buying that year's winners. The problem with this approach is that the stellar performers are frequently purchased after their price has been run up, and the losers are sold after their prices have hit bottom. Investment managers who should know better and who are evaluated on their portfolio's performance do it anyway because they know many investors only look at the fund's holdings when they get their semiannual reports.

Who Protects the Names

If brand managers cannot be relied on to protect the brand's long-term interest, whose responsibility is it? The answer should be everyone's, but in most companies that's not the case. Most companies consider it easier to measure short-term effects than long-term effects, and the results make a decision maker's position more defensible and less subject to the demanding scrutiny of a client or supervisor. Much of what is written about setting and writing objectives, including what we have written, works better with short-term effects.

At a minimum, the protection of the brand should be the responsibility of the marketing director and, in advertising, the advertising director. In 1981 McDonald's replaced its advertising agency, Needham, Harper Worldwide, with the Leo Burnett Co. This move stunned the advertising business because Needham had won numerous awards for its creative efforts, and *Advertising Age* had named it the "Advertising Agency of the Year for 1977." Sales were doing fine at McDonald's, but, according to insiders, McDonald's had posed a number of marketing questions to Needham, which usually responded with more creative executions. What McDonald's wanted was more insight on strategic planning. In what directions should they take the brand? How might they capitalize on the brand's equity without undermining its value? McDonald's was thinking long term, and Needham was focusing on the short term.

The transition from Needham to Burnett appeared to be smoother than it really was. Although Burnett did provide the desired marketing information, the early Burnett ads were not consistent with the way McDonald's had been promoted. McDonald's had to educate Burnett about McDonald's approach to protect the brand equity. What is somewhat surprising about this situation is that until 1993, McDonald's had used little to no research to measure the effectiveness of its advertising and acted largely according to its judgment. With a major retail operation like McDonald's, you can often see the effects of an ad or campaign in the marketplace. Although you may not be able to statistically validate the effects, an experienced manager can make a reasonable judgment. Fortunately for McDonald's, they have had that kind of judgment.

On the agency side, the guardianship of a brand's equity should nominally belong to the account executive (AE). However, AEs are a lot like brand managers in that they are so involved in day-to-day details, such as checking copy, approving coupons, and reviewing media schedules, that they, too, run the risk of sacrificing long-term equity for short-term performance. Account supervisors, who rank higher than an AE, should do a better job of focusing on brand equity because they are likely to be more experienced than an account executive and are less involved with day-to-day details.

In large to very large agencies, the research director plays an important role in protecting the brand by tracking perceptions of it in the market. Although it is still difficult to isolate the effect of advertising and other forms of communication on the brand's equity, researchers can often provide more rigorous reasons that an ad should be changed or rejected. Perhaps, in recognition that building brand equity is a long-term strategic concern to a brand and to give the director of research some clout in trying to deal with it, many research directors also carry the title director of strategic planning.

Not all accounts are large enough to merit the attention of an account executive, a supervisor, or a research director. Responsibility for the guardianship of smaller brands falls on the upper management of the agency.

Spelling Out Brand Protection

Protecting the equity in a brand can be viewed as either a core element in a strategic plan or as a mind-set that should pervade all aspects of any campaign. We prefer to assume that protection of the company's names should be of paramount importance in all activities and need not be spelled out in a firm's marketing plan. Protecting equity is somewhat different from managing brand equity. Protecting equity implies a defensive strategy, whereas managing equity suggests a proactive strategy. A company that is trying to build brand X for Acme Mfg., for example, may recommend an action that could damage the brand or the company name. To manage Acme's equity, someone might interject, "That's not Acme" (meaning, that's not the way we do things around here) or "That's not the brand X way" (meaning, that's not the way we do things for the brand either). Usually, on a day-to-day basis, the questions that come up deal more with managing than protecting brand equity.

However, when a public-relations disaster occurs, companies often adopt a circle-the-wagons approach, in which they try to protect the brand name from all sides. In 1990, traces of benzene, a toxic liquid, were found in Perrier bottled water, forcing a global recall of all supplies of the company's bottled water. At the time Perrier was the brand leader with more than a 50 percent market share. There appeared to be little that could be done to protect the brand. Consumers assumed the problem was in the company's product because benzene, a carcinogen, had entered the water in the production process.[15] Nearly three years later, the Perrier brand had sunk to less than a 4 percent market share, ranking number eight in the bottled-water category, according to Nielsen.[16] However, the best-selling brand of bottled water continued to be a product sold by the Perrier Group of America, only in 1994 the brand name was Arrowhead instead of the company's best-known name, Perrier.[17] In other words, the only way Perrier could find to manage the crisis was to concentrate on another name and let Perrier drop.

In 1993, reports came out of Seattle, Nashville, and New Orleans that syringes were found in cans of Pepsi and Diet Pepsi. Within days, Pepsi Cola put together a team of 11 high-ranking executives to handle the crisis. It took out ads in more than 200 local newspapers as well as national publications such as the *New York Times* and *USA Today* to reassure consumers that it was "simply not logical to conclude that a nationwide tampering had occurred" based on the production process and other factors. Within days, the media were generally reporting that the stories were probably a hoax. Later research showed no significant effect on sales.[18]

THE MARKETING COMMUNICATION EXPENDITURE

The decision about how much money to set aside for marketing communications is simple in concept but much more complicated in practice. This decision is of strategic interest because it has a profound influence on the way a company can compete. Companies compete both in terms of the quality and the quantity of the messages they disseminate. The size of the advertising budget, usually called the *appropriation,* can influence the creativity involved in the message strategy, but it may have an even greater impact on media. Although creativity can flourish independent of expenditures, media exposure cannot. One common viewpoint is expressed as follows:

**Share of media expenditures
equals
Share of media voice
equals
Share of mind and heart
equals
Share of market.**

Of course, this view only works within a certain range of expenditures. Beyond a certain level of expenditures, each additional dollar spent on advertising or promotion is unlikely to generate sufficient sales to cover expenses and still contribute to net profit. It is relatively easy using marginal analysis to understand the relationship between advertising expenditures and sales in retrospect; it is a lot more difficult to predict this relationship in advance.[19] Determining the optimum amount of money to spend for advertising may be one of the most difficult tasks facing advertising and agency planners.[20]

A complete discussion of all the variables that can influence the appropriation and how to determine the optimal level of expenditures is beyond the scope of this book. Such a discussion would include modeling procedures using multiple regression analysis to explain and predict the relationship between advertising and sales over time.

The typical reader of this book does not usually deal with these issues, and the size of the budget is usually a given in advertising campaigns classes. Agencies, also, do not usually determine the advertising appropriation but receive it from their clients. It is, however, important that the amount of money set aside for marketing communications be appropriate for the expected tasks: solving problems and exploiting opportunities. To provide a rough idea about how these decisions are made, we'll look at some traditional methods for determining the appropriation and some of the factors that influence their size.

TRADITIONAL APPROACHES TO DETERMINING THE APPROPRIATION

A number of widely used methods appear in advertising textbooks. It is important to understand that a company doesn't necessarily use one method. It is likely that companies use a combination of methods.

All You Can Afford

The use of this method appears to be on the decline. The chief advantage of this method is that it is simple, and, for companies of limited resources, it may be the only option. Its main disadvantages are lack of a rational basis for the decision and insufficient resources to generate enough advertising exposure to stimulate an impact in the marketplace. In 1975, San Augustine and Foley found that this was the second most widely used method by large advertisers.[21] In 1981, Patti and Blasko reported that this method had fallen to the sixth position in popularity.[22] Still, approximately 20 percent of the respondents reported using this method. Many companies reported using more than one method. It is likely that many companies started out using another method and wound up using this one due to budgetary constraints.

Percentage of Sales

This widely used method involves multiplying past or anticipated sales by a certain percentage to determine the amount of money to be appropriated for the marketing communication budget. This percentage can be obtained from a variety of sources: industry contacts, trade associations, trade publications, government data, conferences, and conventions. This method is an especially useful one if the decision maker's expertise does not lie within the area of marketing or advertising. If the percentage used as the multiplier is typical of successful firms in the field, then this method is likely to be a good one, depending on the degree to which the advertiser is similar to other companies. Its main disadvantage is that sales are usually used to determine the advertising expenditure. When sales are high, the advertising budget will be high. When sales are low, the budget will also be low. Logically, the situation may require the exact opposite, especially when sales are low.

Competitive Parity

This method uses the competition's expenditures as a benchmark against which the company determines its strategy. Companies use this approach for at least two reasons: First, a company may assume that if the competition is successful, it must know what it is doing, including appropriating the best amount for a budget; and second, a company may feel that it needs to match the competition's expenditures to be competitive.

The limitations of this method vary according to how similar the companies in the category match up. Companies that appear to be similar from afar may have significant differences when scrutinized up close.

Objective and Task

This approach is the most logical method, but it is probably also the most difficult one to use. It is used by nearly two-thirds of the largest advertisers.[23] To use this method, a planner first defines specific objectives. The next step involves determining the various tasks required to achieve the objectives. The last step, also the easiest, involves estimating the cost of implementing the tasks.

This approach is logical because it links marketing communication expenditures to the achievement of specific goals. If the objectives are defined in terms of behavioral objectives such as sales, then the first step, defining objectives, is relatively easy, but the second step is difficult, determining the marketing communication tasks that will likely achieve the objectives.

In the case of sales goals, many of the marketing communication tools, such as advertising, could influence sales. Determining which variable had which effect often leaves a gap in the linkage between sales goals and a specific communication tool, such as advertising or sales promotion. To solve this problem, some advertisers define their communication objectives (at least their message-oriented ones) in terms of communication criteria, such as top-of-mind awareness or attitude change. This makes the link between the objectives and the communication tasks much clearer. It still leaves difficult questions pertaining to the degree to which the achievement of communications criteria, such as attitude change, will result in the achievement of marketing goals, such as sales.

Although the objective and task method is more complicated than many of the other approaches, it attempts to deal with questions the other methods leave unanswered. In 1975, one study of large advertisers reported that only 12 percent of the companies used the method.[24] By 1981, a similar study indicated that the percentage using this method had increased to 62 percent.[25] In 1983, a related study of computer-based advertising budgeting practices of large advertisers reported that 80 percent of companies used this method.[26]

POSITIONING THE MESSAGE

Positioning is the next important element of the strategic foundation. It is highly interrelated with the management of brand equity and budgetary decisions. Positioning refers to the way advertisers try to get consumers to think of their products. Consumers seem to have a perceptual map in their minds that places, or positions, one product in relation to another according to their similarities or differences.

Chevrolet, for example, is usually thought of as a family car; Volvo as a safe, durable car; and Cadillac as a luxury car. Consumers also make fine distinctions within subcategories. Cadillacs are not simply luxury automobiles; they are also cars that have a more traditional image, conveying status and prestige, a car that might be purchased by a banker or a small-business owner. In contrast, a Lexus has a more contemporary luxury image, a car you might expect an investment counselor or a CEO of a midsize company to own.

Positioning reflects the decisions that companies make to intentionally influence the images that consumers have of their products and, sometimes, even those of the competition. For example, Pepsi would like consumers to believe that it is a product for hip, young-minded people. In contrast, it likes to portray Coca-Cola as an older, more conservative, and somewhat stodgy brand.

In Chapters 2 and 3, we discussed some of the procedures and tests you can use to determine consumers' perceptions of a brand. A goal of many of these activities is to determine and understand a brand's image or personality. This information can then be used to change, reinforce, or intensify the image. The brand's image or its personality can be the result of many factors, including advertising, pricing policies, signage, packaging, and the want-satisfying qualities of the product. Positioning is action oriented. It's what companies do to influence what people think. A brand or a company's image takes time to establish, but, once it is implanted on the consumers' perceptual map, it remains firmly established—sometimes even when the company would like to see it changed.

Sears has long had the reputation as a seller of quality merchandise, especially for appliances and hardware. However, in the 1980s it was having a difficult time dealing with two major problems. Its merchandise, especially soft goods, was often perceived as a little too conservative. Sears was also being undercut badly by discount merchandisers such as Wal-Mart. In some stores, nearly half of all revenue was generated by items on sale.

In the spring of 1989, Sears changed its pricing structure to a policy featuring fewer sale items and everyday low(er) prices (EDLP) on most items. Sears achieved some success with this move, but, after an initial spurt in business, stores were allowed to run more sale items. Over the years, Sears had trained its customers to expect sale items; that was part of the consumers' perception of how Sears operates. Despite heavy promotion announcing the new plan, Sears relented, and its pricing policy began to increasingly resemble the old structure.

Sales continued to be a problem. In 1993, Sears restructured its clothing and apparel lines, updating them with a more contemporary look. It then introduced the lines with the very successful advertising campaign, "Come see the softer side of Sears."[27]

Positioning decisions are strategic in nature and provide the direction for a campaign to follow. Positioning usually implies that the company is willing to sacrifice some component of the overall market to be more effective with a narrower focus. Miller Lite beer became the number-two brand of beer by narrowing its focus to beer drinkers who prefer beer with fewer calories. This is a fairly large market. Any attempt to reposition the brand to appeal to all beer drinkers is destined to fail, as the company found out, because consumers will likely continue to think of Miller Lite as a beer with fewer calories (or less substance). And Miller runs the risk that it will appeal less to calorie-conscious beer drinkers by broadening its appeal. (In 1994, Miller Lite lost the number-two position to Bud Light. Miller wound up third in beer sales.)

Positioning a Product

Various authors have noted that there are at least seven different ways to position a product:

1. By product characteristics or customer benefits. (Lee Jeans is the "brand that fits.")
2. By a price-quality relationship. (Sears is a "value" store.)
3. By use or application. (Cortaid Cream "relieves itches.")
4. By product user. (Miller is for blue-collar workers.)
5. By product category. (7-UP is a soft drink like the colas, not a mixer.)
6. By cultural symbol. (Harley-Davidson, "Born in the U.S.A.")
7. By competitor. (Avis positions itself with Hertz.)[28]

After the basic positioning strategy has been determined, it is up to the copywriters and the art directors to execute a message strategy with creative tactics. The development of the message strategy and tactics will be covered more extensively in Chapter 6.

Targeting the Message

Targeting is the last element supporting the strategic foundation. In its broadest sense, targeting the message involves both the people to whom the message is aimed and the means by which the message gets delivered. At this stage in the development of a campaign, the target market has typically already been determined. Nevertheless, during the development of strategy, new opportunities may present themselves that call for either a reexamination or a modification of the target market. This is another example of how the development of a campaign can be an ongoing process.

For example, in 1992 when Coca-Cola hired CAA out of Hollywood to produce television commercials, it was looking for breakthrough advertising. Coca-Cola's strategy was simple: Hire famous, highly creative film directors to produce highly creative television commercials. The spots were often highly creative, very visual, and mostly unrelated except for the tagline "Always Coca-Cola." Although the campaign has been criticized for not having enough continuity, the company's response has been that it is using different spots to appeal to different market segments.[29]

Whether this strategy was in place before the spots were produced is moot for this discussion. It is easy to argue that the decision to determine the target audience, or markets, should be made before the strategy and tactics are determined; however, it is also common and strategically sound to modify the positioning and targeting strategies as new opportunities develop.

The targeting decision usually ranges from a point where a company will use one message, or appeal, for all consumers to a point at which the company uses separate messages for different market segments. Figure 5–4 presents typical targeting options.

When a company makes a decision to position its message, it logically follows that it will be segmenting at least part of the market. By influencing consumers to think of a product a certain way, a company is suggesting to consumers not to think of the product a different way. When Pepsi positions its products as youth oriented, it is targeting its messages to segments of the overall population who are young, who think young, or who would like to be young.

Companies that use one message to appeal to a mass audience tend to be companies whose products are used across broad demographic categories, such as Wesson with its oil, Hunt with its tomato paste, and Nabisco and its crackers. To be successful with this approach, the message should be general or diffuse enough to allow a variety of consumer groups to read into it a benefit that appeals to them. Campbell Soup's "Soup is good food" is an example of this type of message. This approach usually works best for the market leader in a category. Campbell Soup sells more than 50 percent of all canned soup. As product categories become increasingly competitive and as the products within the generic class approach parity, companies usually opt for a strategy positioned around a message that appeals primarily to a portion of the overall market.

Companies that use multiple messages to target multiple market segments tend to be large companies. In many cases, these companies are simply applying

FIGURE 5–4   TYPICAL TARGETING OPTIONS

the marketing concept to an increasingly fragmented market. In the "Always Coca-Cola" campaign, Coca-Cola used a variety of musical formats, such as rock, rap, and country, to send different messages to various segments with the same general, low-keyed theme: No matter what's going on, Coca-Cola is always around. To be successful with different messages, a company must be sure to tie each message into the brand's core equities, as Coca-Cola does.

Developing a Marketing Communication Mix

There has been a great deal written in recent years about the importance of integrating the components of marketing communication into a marketing communication mix. Surprisingly, there has been very little written about how much of the marketing effort or budget should be devoted to advertising and how much to other types of marketing communications. Companies offer little insight. The same company that will divulge proprietary information off the record will seldom provide any usable information about how it allocates money to different types of promotion. Generally, companies say they use judgment based on experience. Other times they will indicate they use marketing mix or advertising and marketing (A and M) models, but "they are proprietary." These models may be sophisticated, but the usual impression companies give is that the models are rudimentary or even crude.

A Media-Oriented Approach One approach to determining the marketing communication mix is to view each type of communication as a means of delivering messages or impressions to consumers. Each promotional tool can then be evaluated in terms of the exposure it generates for the brand. Values can be assigned to the importance of traditional media criteria, such as cost-efficiency, competitive share of voice, and optimal reach and frequencies, and an allocation model can be constructed. There are at least a couple of problems with this approach. Some forms of marketing communications, such as sales promotion and public relations, are difficult to measure. Any type of quantitative analysis would only be as good as the measurements. However, the main problem with this approach is that it is difficult to integrate a value for message content into a quantitative model.

A Message-Oriented Approach Some scholars have argued that it is wrong to evaluate media channels in terms of vehicle exposures. Instead, promotional tools should be evaluated on the basis of the information they communicate.

Therefore, each medium, or type of marketing communication, can be looked at in terms of its ability to deliver certain types of information. For example:

Network television	delivers a strong brand identity.
Brochures	deliver specific information.
Radio	reminds consumers to act.
Yellow Pages	move consumers to specific buying locations.
Public relations	provides information that is more highly credible.
Infomercials	provide in-depth persuasive information.
Store displays	stimulate action at point of sale.[30]

Both the media- and the message-oriented approach require substantial amounts of judgment. Although it is possible to do a mathematical model to apportion amounts of money to marketing communication tools, expectations of a rigorous approach probably await further research developments. In-depth coverage of marketing communication strategy and tactics will be covered in Chapter 8.

Advertising Media Strategy

In the development of an integrated marketing communication plan, the strategic decision about the marketing communication mix should precede any decisions about what kind of media to use. However, advertising usually will be the dominant form of marketing communication. For this reason, media strategy will be covered in depth in Chapter 7. Related types of marketing communication, such as sales promotion, public relations, and direct marketing, which typically supplement traditional media such as radio, television, magazines, and newspapers, are described in Chapter 8.

ENDNOTES

[1]David A. Aaker, *Managing Brand Equity* (New York: Free Press, 1991), 16.

[2]Raymond Serafin and Bradley Johnson, "Saturn-alia in Spring Hill Next Summer," *Advertising Age* 64 (October 18, 1993): 1, 55.

[3]Terry G. Vavra, "After-marketing: How to Keep Customers for Life Through Relationship Marketing," *Brandweek*. This article is an excerpt from *AfterMarketing* by Terry G. Vavra.

[4]Terry G. Vavra, "Learning from Your Losses," *Brandweek* (December 7, 1992): 21.

[5]Vavra, "Learning from Your Losses," 20.

[6]Donald E. Parente, "A Look at the Way Advertisers Write Objectives," unpublished working paper (1995), 9.

[7]Aaker, *Managing Brand Equity*, 63.

[8]Alan D. Fletcher and Thomas A. Bowers, *Fundamentals of Advertising Research*, 3rd ed. (Belmont, Calif.: Wadsworth, 1988), 176.

[9]Al Ries and Jack Trout, *The 22 Immutable Laws of Marketing: Violate Them at Your Own Risk* (New York: HarperBusiness, 1993), 18.

[10]Ries and Trout, *The 22 Immutable Laws*, 3.

[11]Pam Weisz, "Major Brands on Defensive," *Superbrands* (October 17, 1994), 118-119.

[12]Aaker, *Managing Brand Equity*, 1.

[13]Ira Teinowits, *Advertising Age* 65 (May 6, 1994): 3, 55.

[14]The information on the Green Giant character is abstracted from unpublished, undated, and unnumbered material on "Enduring Campaigns" from the Leo Burnett Company, Inc.

[15]"News Makers 1990," *Advertising Age* 61 (December 24, 1990): 5.

[16]Bruce Crumley and Elena Bowes, "Perrier Moves to Publicis," *Advertising Age* 63 (November 30, 1992): 53.

[17]*SuperBrands* (1989–1994).

[18]Marcy Magiera, "Pepsi Weathers Tampering Hoaxes," *Advertising Age* 64 (June 21, 1993): 46.

[19]For more information on marginal analysis, see David A. Aaker, Rajeev Batra, and John G. Myers, *Advertising Management,* 4th ed. (Englewood Cliffs, N.J.: Prentice Hall, 1992), 469.

[20]Jack Z. Sissors and Lincoln Bumba, *Advertising Media Planning,* 4th ed. (Lincolnwood, Ill.: NTC Business Books, 1993), 365.

[21]Andre J. San Augustine and William F. Foley, "How Large Advertisers Set Budgets," *Journal of Advertising Research* 15 (October 1975): 11–16.

[22]Charles H. Patti and Vincent Blasko, "Budgeting Practices of Big Advertisers," *Journal of Advertising Research* 21 (December 1981): 23–29.

[23]Patti and Blasko, "Budgeting Practices," 23–29

[24]San Augustine and Foley, "How Large Advertisers," 11–16.

[25]Patti and Blasko, "Budgetary Practices," 23–29.

[26]Kent M. Lancaster and Judith Stern, "Computer Based Advertising Budgeting Practices of Leading U.S. Advertisers," *Journal of Advertising* 12 (1983): 6.

[27]Elaine Underwood, "Weathering the Storm," *SuperBrands* (1995): 123.

[28]Aaker, *Advertising Management,* 151.

[29]Bob Garfield, "Coke Ads Great, but Not Always," *Advertising Age* (February 15, 1993): 60.

[30]Adapted from Ron Kaatz, "An Integrated Media Planning System," in *Advertising: Its Role in Modern Marketing,* Dean M. Krugman, Leonard N. Reid, Watson Dunn, and Arnold M. Barban, 8th ed. (Fort Worth: The Dryden Press, 1994), 327.

Finding Your Creative Way: Strategies and Ideas

During World War II, Winston Churchill asked the commander of the British Navy for the strategy to be used in winning the war against the Germans. Churchill wanted the strategy written on one side of a piece of paper. Think about that. Think about all that was at stake—the people, the traditions, and the entire country. Yet, one side of a piece of paper would do just fine.

Think, too, of what must have taken place in the mind of the person writing that strategy. Think of all he must have known and all he must have considered. Think of his mental process in boiling out the extraneous and keeping the vital.

This is not unlike your task when you sit down to formulate your creative plan. The creative plan is a tiny document, really, often no more than one side of a piece of paper. But what's on the paper represents the essence of extensive knowledge and profound thought.

KNOW WHAT YOU HAVE: THE IMPORTANCE OF RESEARCH

The creative plan doesn't just happen. It's not the result of sleight of hand, nor is it a sudden and welcome bolt of divine inspiration. It's always the result of digging and picking, thinking and rethinking, probing and imagining. Such acts cannot be rushed. You should plan time to dig and pick at the research provided to you. You should plan time to work your way through that mass of information that is most often presented in your situation analysis and research findings, as described in Chapters 3 and 4. The question, of course, is, through all the digging and picking, the thinking and rethinking, how do you know what to look for in the information?

THINK LIKE A DETECTIVE

Think of yourself as a problem solver, a detective of sorts always on the lookout for clues. You'll find them in the situation analysis and research. They won't always seem obvious, just as clues aren't always obvious. They'll be there, cowering, hiding perhaps, but they'll be right under your nose, and it's your job to see them. You'll have to see them clearly enough to spot that here is something that could give you an edge. It is a means for matching your product with the needs and wants of your consumer, your target audience.

Often, your search for clues takes you right back to the root of it all, the marketing of the brand. Notice how often the advertising you see reflects the rapidly changing marketing environment we discussed in previous chapters. For example, who would think that Tide, the leading laundry detergent in both powders and liquids, would need to rethink its position in the marketplace? After all, at the close of 1993 Tide owned a whopping 37.4 percent of the powdered detergent market and 25.1 percent of the liquid detergent market. Why fix something if it's not broken?

Despite this apparently rosy picture in 1993, there were some clues that the bloom on Tide's rose was indeed beginning to wither. A 7.4 percent sales decline for the year led to a reformulation of the Tide brand, a similar reformulation to the one Cheer, the second-leading detergent, had completed in order to experience a 14.5 percent surge in sales in the powdered detergent market. Tide's reformulation was based on a technological advance that reduced fuzz buildups in fabrics, thus keeping them newer looking.[1]

Think about this profile of the Tide situation. With the marketplace changing rapidly, Tide could ill afford to rest on its laurels. It didn't simply have to keep pace with its competition, but it had to outsmart and outgun its competition. Such is the kind of information you'll find in the situation analysis and research findings. The information hints at the possibility of problem-solving demonstrations in the creative executions, and these demonstrations can lead to a desired end of newer-looking clothes coming out of the dryer. This kind of information leads to opportunities, and opportunities lead to creative breakthroughs.

More than 14,000 new supermarket products have been introduced for each of the past 10 to 15 years, but less than 5 percent of those products offer an innovation to differentiate them from the competition.[2] Yet, each has its own story to tell. Each faces stiff competition right from the start. Each exists in a live-or-die world. And each must adjust and innovate or die. So it is with Tide, anything but a new brand but one eager to hold its crown as the royalty of laundry detergents.

The core of the research lies in the stack of papers and spreadsheets sitting on your desk. Inside those papers and sheets are clues, special facts, and data that can serve as the foundation for your creative plan and, ultimately, your creative idea. Consider, for example, Ikea's approach to advertising. Ikea is a modern furniture retailer that appeals to upbeat and young adult shoppers. It sells moderately priced products that are trendy and hip.

In the early 1990s, Ikea knew that the 46 million people in Generation X—the 18- to 29-year-old typical college student and recent graduate—spend an estimated $125 billion annually. They're getting married (average age is 26.3 for males and 24.1 for females). They're not inclined to buy a home but still need furnishings. Indeed, 20 percent of them plan to buy furniture in the next year, compared with 17 percent of the 30- to 40-year-olds and 16 percent of older adults. According to Stuart Himmelfarb, vice-president at the research firm,

Roper Starch Worldwide, "Many [between 18 and 29] have jobs that aren't careers, because of the difficulty in finding a first job. So for them, their leisure time is a lot more an expression of their selves than work is, and they want their homes to be as nice as possible."[3]

So what do these facts about Generation X mean for Ikea's creative plan and idea? In a word, style. In fact, style has become the thematic center of Ikea's successful spot TV campaigns, so much so that a future bride in a recent spot claims with pride that "Ikea's cool because they have tons of styles to choose from."

As you look at the Ikea spot in Figure 6–1, unpeel the many layers of creative decisions made on the basis of research. For example, throughout this book's first five chapters we've been advising you to keep a watchful eye on your target audience. Certainly, Ikea did. Notice the careful selection of the woman in the spot. She's not the kind of person you're likely to see featured in *Modern Maturity* magazine. Instead, this newly married woman is young and in her mid- to late-20s. As her visit to Ikea unfolds along a narrative storyline of shopping and planning, the script embeds Ikea's wide modern and contemporary selection of styles. If you think back to what Ikea knew about the target market, you'll see the immediate connections to the creative idea. And if you unpeel the idea, you'll see the creative planning behind it, all based on research findings.

In Chapter 2 we outlined the steps in planning your research and developing your situation analysis. Winding its way through that outline was a common theme of interrelated variables, where the consumer interrelates with the product or the product interrelates with the competition. No variable stood alone, although the research isolates them for the purposes of organization and description. However, it is important to understand that as you work your way to a creative plan, you must consider all of the variables as they interrelate. All of them stand in context to one another.

At the same time, it should have been clear to you just how crucial an understanding of your target market is to assuring a well-constructed strategy of a creative plan and idea. At the center of it all stands the target market, your audience.

KNOW YOUR TARGET AUDIENCE

Your research gives you concrete data about your audience, usually demographic data such as gender, age, income, and education level. These hard data are important for you to consider. They help to frame your view of the audience. But your research gives you less concrete data, or information, as well. Often, this information is more important than the raw demographic data, simply because it reaches closer to the heart of consumers' attitudes and decisions in the competitive marketplace of products, goods, and services. It guides you "inside" your audience, to the mind and heart where those attitudes and decisions originate and crystallize.

Think back, for example, to Chapter 4 and the discussion about Heinz ketchup. Surely, the H. J. Heinz Co. could manufacture a more fluid, runny, or

FIGURE 6–1

watery ketchup. If the company did, consumers might use more of it than they do the thicker ketchup. Yet, the company knew what their consumers wanted in a ketchup, including substance, richness, and thickness. The Heinz example speaks as much to the need to understand your product class and brand as it does to the need to understand your target audience. What is it your consumers want with the product class and your brand? It's here, in determining the wants and needs of the consumer, that demographic data take a back seat to research findings more focused on psychographics and, especially, consumer attitudes.

Consumers' Attitudes

An attitude is a mental construct that consumers have of a product or brand. It is a composite of consumers' perceptions, feelings, and beliefs toward that product or brand. Generally, an attitude can be viewed as a structure containing three parts, as shown in Figure 6–2.[4]

Notice how the three-part structure suggests the fluid movement or interrelationship of each part. The cognitive part relates to thinking. The affective part relates to feeling, and the conative part relates to acting. Yet, each part exerts influence on the others, while the consumer's attitude toward the product or brand always reflects the coordinated influence of one or more of these parts. For example, we tend to buy (conative) when we like (affective) a product or brand, and that liking is based on our thoughts (cognitive) about it.

There is a distinct connection between the consumer and the product or brand. At the same time, however, the consumer, or your target audience, resides at the center of that connection, creating either rationally or emotionally an attitude toward the product or brand. That attitude can be a matter of like, dislike, brand loyalty, or any of a number of mental constructs formed in relationship to the product or brand.

In your research you will find suggestions of the consumer's attitude toward your product or brand as well as toward your competition. You are also likely to find suggestions of why that attitude exists, the reasons for the attitude. Think back to Heinz ketchup, for example, and the probabilities that Heinz

---

FIGURE 6-2   **EFFECT OF ADVERTISING ON CONSUMERS: MOVEMENT FROM AWARENESS TO ACTION**

Related Behavioral Dimensions	Movement toward Purchase	Example of Types of Promotion or Advertising Relevant to Various Steps
Conative: The realm of motives. Ads stimulate or direct desires.	Purchase ⬆ Conviction	Point-of-purchase Retail store ads Deals "Last chance" offers Price appeals Testimonials
Affective: The realm of emotions. Ads change attitudes and feelings.	Preference ⬆ Liking	Competitive ads Argumentative copy "Image" copy Status, glamour appeals
Cognitive: The realm of thoughts. Ads provide information and facts.	Knowledge ⬆ Awareness	Announcements Descriptive copy Classified ads Slogans Jingles Skywriting Teaser Campaigns

---

Source: Reprinted from "Effect of Advertising Consumers: Movement from Awareness to Action," *Journal of Marketing*, American Marketing Association, Robert Lavidge and Gary A. Steiner, October, 1961.

---

knew that consumers liked slow, thick, rich ketchup. Consumer analysis would indicate consumers' preferences, and their attitudes would make the brand attribute of thickness or slowness more appealing as a possible thematic focal point in the creative strategy and eventual tactical considerations.

As you work your way through creative planning, you should focus on your target audience and look for something that telescopes or zeroes in on the audience's attitude toward your product or brand and your competition. Within that construct, you should look closely at the specific product attributes, benefits, or features that prompt or energize that attitude.

KNOW YOUR PRODUCT

The importance of knowing your product surfaced frequently in the previous discussion about knowing your audience. After all, you're searching for a link, a so-called hot button that stimulates your audience to a connection with your product. To find that link, you must get inside your product to know its attributes, features, and benefits. In your research, you will find extensive information on the product, which breaks it down to its many components and relates those components—the attributes and features—to the all-important benefits. In a nutshell, your job is to be on the lookout for the appropriate match between what the product offers and what consumers need or want.

Attributes, Features, and Benefits

Whether it's a product, goods, or a service that you're advertising, it has qualities, specific components, or characteristics that help the product perform in the marketplace. These qualities have been described in various ways by practitioners and scholars, but the general model includes a triad of attributes, features, and benefits.[5]

Think of attributes as what the product has. Think of features as what the product does. And think of benefits as what the product means because of what it has or does. For example, Heinz ketchup has a combination of certain ingredients and a manufacturing process (attributes) that make it slower coming out of the bottle (feature) than other brands of ketchup. The attributes and feature lead to the benefit, which may be described as richer taste. Ideally, the benefit should be competitive in that it solves the consumers' problem better than the competition does. Recently, the benefit has also been termed a consumer consequence because it is the result for the consumer.

Consider, for example, the laddering approach to attributes that was described in Chapter 2. Attributes led to consumer consequences and ultimately to personal values. Even within the attributes and consequences you can subdivide categories so that some attributes become physical or pseudo-physical and some consequences become functional or self-involved. Of course, as you move up the ladder from attributes to personal values, you're moving away from the focus on the product to a tighter focus on the consumer and how that product affects the consumer.

Important to your considerations of attributes and features that lead to benefits is the need to find the differentiating factor for your product. What is it that separates or differentiates your product from those of the competition? Again in the case of Heinz ketchup, the slowness in coming out of the bottle differentiates Heinz from its competition. However, not all attributes and features or the benefits leading from them are equal. Some are more important than others, and the key to which are important is always what consumers need or want. Again, your research will identify areas of importance or unimportance. Meanwhile, as you dig and pick at your research, you should be sensitive to finding points of difference between your product or brand and those of the competition. Eventually, this information will help you identify your brand personality and position.

KNOW YOUR COMPETITION

Imagine creating a campaign or strategy for anything—a political election, a football game, a job search—without studying your competition. It doesn't make much sense, does it? Because your advertising campaign exists in a competitive marketplace of visible ad ideas, you need to know your competition so that you can make your product stand out as the most appropriate choice for the target audience. "Know your competition" means you must know everything you can about your competition's marketing, advertising, and promotion. What has the competition done in the past? What is it doing now? What does its advertising suggest about the product and audience? What does its advertising tell you about the positioning and strategy? Has its advertising been successful; if so, how and why and, if not, why not?

Your research should contain a competition analysis. Dig deeply into that analysis and find out what makes your competitor's product and advertising tick. What are the key attributes, features, and benefits communicated to the consumer? Is the target audience your target audience? If so, how and why and, if not, why not? How is the brand different from or the same as yours? And ultimately, what is the consumer's attitude toward the brands (yours and the competition's) in both positive and negative ways?

One of the most important discoveries you can make in knowing your competition is just how you can differentiate and ultimately position yourself. By seeing and understanding what the competition is doing, you'll be better prepared to carve out your own position in the marketplace, one that doesn't overlap or try to accomplish something that has already been accomplished.

Consider, for example, the case of MCI. After the 1984 breakup of the Bell System, AT&T owned the lion's share of the long-distance calling market. Always a highly visible advertiser, AT&T commanded the market with a no-nonsense, businesslike approach featuring the actor Cliff Robertson as a leading spokesman. Robertson projected an image of both grace and strength, cordiality and firmness. He fit perfectly with the no-nonsense, traditional image of AT&T. Then along came MCI.

In 1990 MCI claimed a 13 percent market share of the long-distance calling business. But in three short years (1990–1993) that share increased to 20 percent despite the fact that AT&T typically outspent MCI on advertising by a six-to-one margin. Still, MCI's spending of $103 million in 1992 helped move it steadily up the market-share ladder.

What did the trick for MCI was its Friends and Family campaign beginning in 1991, which put the company on a nonstop marketing roll. Within the next three years, that campaign spurred the Friends of the Firm campaign for small business, the Friends Around the World campaign for international long-distance calling in 1994, and the Best Friends campaign, which says the caller receives a 20 percent savings on calls to a selected person and a 40 percent savings if the other person belongs to MCI. Notice, however, that the key strategic position for MCI against AT&T centers on Friends. The word itself conjures up images of closeness, warmth, and good feelings. It suggests humanness and personalism to create an emotional attachment between MCI and its audience. As the audience feels warm and fuzzy all over in its conversations with favored friends and relatives, it has MCI to thank. The emotional attachment to MCI flows naturally.

As chief executive officer of MCI, Bert Roberts makes the MCI advertising focus clear when he says: "We've come at it from the point of view of what the consumer needs and wants, and everything springs from that."[6] These are crucial words in understanding the importance of research to creative planning. MCI knew its target audience's needs and wants, particularly those needs and wants that may not have been addressed by AT&T. And that knowledge is the key. In short, MCI knew its competition.

Research indicated that AT&T was perceived as formal, dignified, businesslike, efficient, professional, and at times even distant or aloof. AT&T owned this particular image and position. Not a bad image and position, mind you, especially because it was AT&T's exclusively. However, this image and position left elbow room for MCI to wriggle into the consumer's mind and focus on the consumer's needs and wants for personalism, warmth, and cost-savings.

To know your audience, product, and competition is critical to the effectiveness of your creative strategy and tactical considerations. Without such knowledge, you will be shooting in the dark, and your chances of hitting the moving target shrink immensely. But with research at your side, you can glean the important data and information so that your advertising is strategically correct in its match of what you promise your target audience, what your brand can provide, and how both the promise and provision differentiate you from your competition. Figures 6–3A, B, and C show three ads, one from Heinz ketchup, one from Timberland shoes, and one from MCI. Look behind and through those ads with an analytical frame of mind. You're sure to see that the ads reflect abundant knowledge about the target audience, the brand, and the competition.

To differentiate itself through its brand image, Heinz features the slow ketchup. But what does *slow* mean to consumers? In a word, it means quality, and that is precisely how Heinz wants its ketchup perceived. The slowness in the ketchup suggests a thickness and richness of ingredients and preparation. All those traits point toward what the consumer wants from ketchup. And because Heinz ketchup has become known for that slowness, it occupies a special place in the consumers' minds, one reserved for Heinz only and one where the competition cannot compete.

With Timberland shoes any one of a number of brand attributes or features, such as price, style, or color, could have become central to the ad. Instead, Timberland relies on what the shoe gives the consumer in respect to safety. Research made it clear to Timberland that its deck shoes were used in precisely that place, the deck. And when you're on the deck of "a boat that's bucking like a rodeo bull," the traction from your shoes takes on enormous importance. This doesn't mean that Timberland forsakes the stylish-benefit appeal, but that appeal becomes secondary to the overriding safety-benefit appeal.

With MCI, the Friends and Family ad reflects the consumers' wants when it comes to long-distance calling.

FIGURE 6–3A

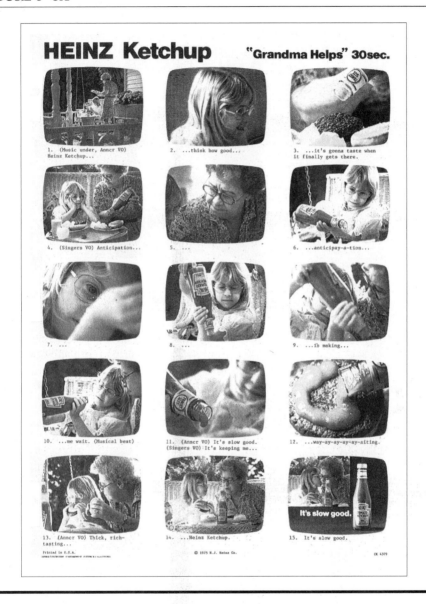

KNOW WHAT YOU MEAN TO THE CONSUMER: THE IMPORTANCE OF BRANDING AND BRAND POSITIONING

Perceptions are the reality when it comes to branding and positioning. But perceptions can be shaped, reinforced, or changed. In making these revisions,

FIGURE 6–3B

advertising comes into play, especially on the creative side. It is what the copy and visuals (creatives) say, and how they say it, that help create the perceptions consumers have of products and brands. Those perceptions transform into the reality of the marketplace. Your job, then, is to control those perceptions.

BRANDING

Although David Ogilvy has been one of the most vigorous advocates for the importance of brand image over the past three decades, the branding concept has evolved considerably over the past few years. It has been dissected, analyzed, and reconstructed with various definitions and parts. At its core, however, are brand image and brand equity.

Brand Image and Brand Equity

Brand image has been defined as as a "cluster of attributes and associations that consumers connect to the brand name."[7] Brand image contains three component parts: the image of the maker (the corporation making the product), the image of the product (the product itself), and the image of the user (the consumer using the product). The parts interact, at least to a degree, and contribute to the overall brand image.

Brand equity has been defined more from a managerial than a consumer perspective. It results from the brand image and includes the value of the brand. This value can be based on finances (additional cash flow from associating a brand with the product or service) or consumers (the degree of consumer loyalty to the brand).[8]

FIGURE 6–3C

From the standpoint of the creative for your campaign, it is critical that your big idea and its execution reflect the carefulness of a branding strategy, particularly in terms of your brand's image. For example, consumers perceive products and services, with the exception of new ones of course, in meaningful ways. Depending on the past advertising and the past experiences consumers have with your brand and its competition, certain brand personalities emerge. They are based on your consumers' perceptions of the brands, which "typically capture a person's personality."[9]

To understand brand personality as it leads to image, think of it on a personal level—your own. You have a personality, and no doubt it has led to your image within your circle of friends and associates. What is that image? Or, if you wish to construct an image over time, years from now how would you like to be known? You may want to answer that question by completing this statement: I would like to be known as a(n) _____ .

How would you fill in that blank, either personally or professionally? Personally, would you fill it in with "good person," "loyal friend," or "understanding partner," or any one of a number of other alternatives? Professionally, would you fill it in with "creative genius," "superb writer," "positive spirit among my colleagues," or, again, with any one of a number of other alternatives?

Maybe you would like to fill in the blank with most, if not all, of those answers. But that's not what the brand image is. With brand image, your answers are limited to what other people perceive of you. These perceptions are based on your personality traits, which allow your friends and associates to create an overall meaning of you, your image.

Now, assume you fill in one answer. You would then consciously arrange your actions and behaviors to fit the brand image you want. So, if you wanted to be known as a positive spirit among your colleagues, you would behave in a positive way. You would, indeed, become a yay-sayer not a nay-sayer. You would see problems as opportunities and not as insurmountable obstacles. You would applaud the achievements of others. In short, your actions would mirror the brand image you claimed as yours, in much the same way that advertising (the visible presentation of a product's personality) mirrors the brand image of that product. This is what David Ogilvy meant when he argued for the long-term importance of the brand image in the advertising.

And if you expanded your self-description, how would you define the personality that led to the image? Friendly? Outgoing? Soothing? Adventurous? Exciting? Such descriptors also apply to products and contribute to the overall perception of a brand's image.

Typical in brand imaging is the association of feelings or emotions with the brand, sometimes termed *emotional bonding.* With this type of association, the consumers' perceptions play a leading role in aligning the brand with affective or emotional predispositions, again based on past advertising, promotion, and experience. Often, advertising that seeks this kind of bonding is executionally based, in that how you say something (that is, execute it) is more important than what you say. But emotional bonding can evolve from several creative approaches. For example, your creative may use a functional, symbolic, or experiential approach depending on what your product has and does and what the consumer wants or needs from it.[10] With a functional approach, you concentrate on intrinsic product attributes, such as speed or performance. With a symbolic approach, you concentrate on extrinsic attributes, such as style or pr estige, as did the Ikea ad example we described earlier. And with the experiential approach, you concentrate on the consumer pleasure derived from the product, such as relaxation, excitement, or romance. Vacation cruises fit in well here.

You should strive to create this kind of consumer bonding with your brand. As we discussed with managing brand equity in Chapter 5, successful brands create emotional attachments for their consumers, whether through relationship marketing or positive and enduring brand associations. Important, too, is that the messages your creative delivers tie in closely with your brand's core equities.

Brand imaging touches on all of these considerations and relies for the most part on the consumers' perceptions, which consumers develop from contact with the products' attributes, features, and benefits. In a sense, the consumer connects, often emotionally, with the brand, thus forming those perceptions. Through that connection, the brand gains equity in the competitive marketplace.

Think of *brand equity* as you would the equity in a home, a business, or other kind of investment. In those investments the equity represents what the value is to you as the owner and generally is expressed in terms of dollars. So, for instance, if you own a home that's worth $100,000 in the marketplace and you owe the bank that holds the mortgage $75,000, you have an equity of $25,000. You own that amount of money. So it is with products and brands.

Accrued through advertising, promotion, and consumer experiences, your brand has certain equity or value in the minds of your consumers. Often this equity can be expressed in terms of the degree or level of consumer brand loyalty, a difficult achievement in this age of product and brand parity and proliferation. Equity can also be expressed in terms of brand name awareness, perceived brand quality, or brand associations.[11]

Brand equity is the accrued result of your brand's image. It specifies exactly what your brand owns in the marketplace, either in terms of share of market and consumer loyalty or more abstract, less tangible values, such as perceived brand quality or unchallenged and unique brand associations. Your goal is to protect and manage that equity, primarily by linking your creative messages with the most positive attributes, features, and benefits associated with your brand.

BRAND POSITIONING

Advertising changes so quickly that key concepts or terms that were hot yesterday cool off considerably today. Yet, some concepts are so solid at their base that they endure the test of time. Positioning is one of those concepts. It became a key element in advertising's strategic foundation in the 1970s, eventually giving up some ground to new orientations, such as brand image and equity, in the 1980s and 1990s. Today, advertisers consider positioning and brand image and equity as integral and related elements in advertising. Positioning describes advertisers' actions in trying to place their product in one place, or position, in relation to another according to their similarities or differences. (See Chapter 5.)

To understand positioning, think of it this way: You're in a crowded room, and you're trying to find a place to stand and be comfortable. The room is your typical consumer's mind, crowded to the hilt with all sorts of competing products, brands, and messages. How do you find a place there that's yours alone and where you can feel comfortable? This search for a place is the essence of positioning.

Perhaps you'll have to elbow or wriggle your way to a good place, perhaps preempting someone else who has an eye on that place (the "best" or leadership position, according to Bruce Bendinger in his *Copy Workshop Workbook*). Perhaps you'll have to wrestle head-to-head for the place you want (the "against" position, according to Bendinger). Perhaps you'll have to be content with a little room in a bigger space where others want to be, simply because it is special or highly desirable (the "niche" position). Perhaps you'll have to move to a different place, one not so crowded (the "new" position).[12]

Each of the positioning variations relates to what place you'll occupy in the consumer's mind—the position you'll own. Will you be faster? Fastest?

Crunchier? Crunchiest? Shinier? Shiniest? More reliable? Most reliable? Newer? Newest? Of course, the list could go on. But the point is that positioning demands you find and occupy in the consumer's mind a certain place that is clear, unmistakable, valued by the consumer, and yours alone. Positioning provides a direction or center point for your campaign around which your creative plan and the creative elements such as graphics or copy revolve.

You can't simply guess at the position you want to occupy. You must rely on research, particularly on the integration of advertising's role within the marketing mix. Once again, this demands imaginative insight into your research.

The Link to Research

As your group prepares the plans book and the presentation to your client, knitting becomes an important activity. To knit is to link, or tie together, the various parts of what you're producing. The goal is to produce something unified in which the beginning foreshadows the ending, and, in the middle, the various parts thread together, reaching back to the beginning and ahead to the ending.

Your determination of the position your advertiser should claim or hold serves as a key thread in the overall campaign, including your plans book and presentation. If the position seems remote or distant, perhaps isolated and surprising, then it suggests a lack of campaign focus and unity. Worse, it suggests that you haven't done your homework and haven't built your creative decisions on a sound or solid foundation. Here's where imaginative insight into your research comes into play.

Remember what research provides you: information on the competition, product, brand, and target audience. That information can help you narrow each category, so that with the target audience, for example, you can gain insight into demographic and psychographic forces motivating your consumer to believe or act in a certain way toward the competition or your brand. Recall the earlier discussion of Ikea and what it knew before it prepared its creative strategy and executions. It knew about Generation X and the attitude of that prospective audience toward furniture. It even knew why that attitude existed. The knowledge enabled the company to choose its position.

Within your research lies the seed for your brand positioning and for your creative plan and executions.

Is It Unique? Is It Right?

Understanding the competitive environment and consumers' needs and wants opened the door for MCI to initiate its Friends and Family campaign. But before the company could open the door on that campaign, it had to understand what the research could tell the company about its position and, eventually, its creative approach in making that position clear and meaningful to the target audience. To a large extent, an advertiser must undertake a thoughtful and considered analysis of the research. It must consider what it implies or suggests about the positions left unoccupied by the competition and what it specifies and emphasizes about consumers' needs and wants. The unoccupied position is unique, the needs and wants are important, and one without the other is inadequate. The advertiser needs a workable match between the two—between the uniqueness of the position and the important needs and wants. If there is a workable match, the advertiser's position crystallizes.

The following list highlights slogans and copylines that reflect unique positions important to consumers. As you read the list, read between the words and lines. Get behind them to the research prompting their use. As with all good ads, once you look behind and through them, you're sure to see a solid foundation of research.

When it absolutely, positively has to be there overnight.

Melts in your mouth, not in your hand.

Four out of five dentists recommend.

How do you spell Relief?

The choice of a new generation.

It keeps going and going and going . . .

We're number two.

Because so much is riding on your tires.

Each of these copylines reflects the advertiser's brand position. You could probably name most, if not all, the advertisers: Federal Express, M&M candies, Crest, Rolaids, Pepsi, Eveready Batteries, Avis, and Michelin. Notice, however, how the lines differ in what they suggest about the brands. Notice, too, how often you can boil down the position of each brand to one or a few words. For instance, with Federal Express you get reliable speed, nothing less and nothing more. With M&M's (the familiar Rosser Reeves USP), you get clean combined with a taste sensation. With Crest you get health. With Rolaids you get relief. With Pepsi you get up-to-date. With Eveready you get durability. With Avis you get service and care (because they're number two, they must give it). And with Michelin you get safety. Each of the lines establishes the brand's position in the consumers' minds, occupying a place of importance relative to the product class and the competition. Also, as you study the lines, carefully notice how they state or imply benefits to the consumers. They match what the product does with what consumers need or want. In so doing, each line carves out the position for the brand, so that if you need or want safety in tires, then Michelin will be your brand of choice.

Advertisers position their products in the marketplace by integrating their creative side with the position they want for their product. For instance, when Pepsi makes its claims about a new generation, it's positioning itself as a youthful and contemporary soft drink. Far be it from Pepsi not to include youthful and contemporary imagery, sound, and sensual stimuli in its advertising or related promotions, all of which are cutting-edge, energetic, and invigorating.

Or, in the case of Michelin, the position of safety first dominates the overall brand image as conveyed in the ad shown in Figure 6–4.

FIGURE 6–4

For years Michelin has been using the copyline "Because so much is riding on your tires.®" You've heard and seen the copyline in ads on television, billboards, and in print. It has become so entrenched in our minds that no other tire could possibly occupy the same position with respect to safety, particularly for children. Now, if you read the copy in the ad, you'll see that Michelin builds its brand equity by associating price with quality. If you were the parent of a beloved child, then the last thing you'd want is for your child to ride on suspect tires. The ads say you wouldn't get that with Michelin. Instead with Michelin you get a secure feeling that your loved ones are safe. Safety is what Michelin stands for, and that is what the advertising says and means to the consumer.

Notice, too, the symbolic associations that help create the consumers' "emotional bonding" with the Michelin brand. The child embraced securely and safely within the tire prompts a warm, fuzzy feeling, with Michelin positioned as a trusted babysitter in the consumers' minds.

And finally, notice how the consumer resides at the center of the ad's appeal. Buy Michelin, and you will not experience guilt. Instead, you will experience emotional and psychological satisfaction derived from knowing that you have done your best for your family.

The ads shown earlier in this chapter also show branding and positioning strategies at work. For example, notice how Heinz ketchup occupies the slow ketchup position, one of leadership within the product category. Also notice how that position reflects the brand image of quality and assumed goodness. With Timberland, too, notice how the brand occupies the safe-shoe position, one again of leadership. The same is true of Ikea, with style, and MCI, with friendly and caring. With all of these advertisers, notice how the consumer resides at the center of the ad appeals. In the end, it's what the consumer needs or wants, identified through the brand image and the brand position, that makes for successful advertising.

Underlying all of this discussion and analysis of branding and positioning is the match between your brand and the consumer. What is it your brand offers that is both unique and right? What is it that makes your brand different from that of the competition or from what the competition has been saying in its advertising? And more important, what is it that makes your brand important to the consumers' needs and wants?

CREATING A PLAN: THE IMPORTANCE OF STRATEGY

Look inside any successful creative idea in advertising, and you're sure to see a plan. That plan relies on strategy, and the strategy relies on research. Creative plans simply do not materialize out of thin air. Instead, they are the culmination of thoughtful and perceptive analysis of the research. Often, this analysis means digging deep beneath the obvious. After all, the obvious was just that to your competitors. But your job is to go beyond the obvious, all the way to the meaningful and often hidden core of a match between your brand and your audience. Your job is to find a match that proves to be both unique (original) and right (on strategy).

The creative plan is an articulation of your strategy. Think of it as a map. Just as you would use a map to guide you to your destination on the road, so, too, you use your creative plan to guide you to your destination in the competitive marketplace of advertising ideas. This map outlines or profiles the important strategic considerations for the campaign's creative thrust, which ultimately drives the message. The map tells you how you're going to get where you want to go, which is the objective. So, in essence, creative planning includes the communications goal and the strategy, or map, for achieving that goal.

There are many formats and structures available for creative plans, and different agencies use different plans. Each has its own focal points and terminology, which are often adapted to meet the requirements of that particular agency. Within this diversity, there is considerable agreement about the plans' main elements. The consumers, or target audience, play a major role in the plans. Plans also require that you know certain key facts about your products and competition.

In the pages that follow you'll see a number of plans that established agencies have used. Note the variations in the plans and the variations in their titles. Indeed, they also vary in how they originate creative emphases within a campaign. Despite these differences, you'll notice the common ground to the plans. Each focuses attention on the target audience. Each focuses attention on an attainable goal that clarifies what the advertising is supposed to achieve. Each zeroes in on the product, particularly the product benefit and copy points (reason why or support) that match with what the audience needs or wants. Common to most of the plans, too, is the clarity of what the competition is doing and the tone, manner, or personality the advertising should reflect. Then, within the individual plans, you'll notice that other emphases are given, such as so-called mandatories (those copy points that must be included) or the problem to be solved by the advertising.[13]

You can use any of these plans or modify them by adding or deleting elements from each for your purposes. Notice, though, how each of the plans emphasizes creative guideposts for your thinking. In a large sense, the plans provide you with a map to guide your brainstorming and eventual selection of creative ideas, those thematic centers for your advertising and promotion. Plans keep you from driving blindfolded, which no agencies want when someone else's money and possible survival are at stake.

The Y&R Creative Work Plan

1. Statement of Key Fact
2. Definition of Problem
3. Advertising Objective
4. Creative Strategy
   a. Prospect Definition
   b. Principal Competition
   c. Promise/Consumer Benefit
      1) What it will do for the consumer
      2) Competitive
      3) Motivate
      4) Not written in ad terms
   d. Reason Why

The Chiat/Day Creative Brief

1. What is the opportunity and/or problem the advertising must address?
2. What do we want people to do as a result of the advertising?
3. Whom are we talking to?
4. What's the key response we want?
5. What information/attributes might help produce this response?

6. What aspect of brand personality should the advertising express?
7. Are there media or budget considerations?
8. This could be helpful...

The Leo Burnett Strategy Worksheet

1. To convince _____
2. That _____
3. Because _____
4. Support _____

The DDB/Needham "R.O.I." System

1. What is the purpose of the advertising?
2. To whom will it be addressed?
3. What competitive benefit will be promised, and how will that promise be supported?
4. What personality will distinguish the brand?
5. Media

The Wells Rich Greene Plan[14]

Creative Strategy:
A. Target Audience
B. Objective
C. Creative Strategy
    1. To convince _____
    2. To buy _____
    3. Instead of _____
    4. Because _____
D. Support
E. Considerations (mandatories)
F. Tone
G. Rationale

The Roman and Maas Creative Strategy Plan

1. Objective
2. Target Audience
3. Key Consumer Benefit
4. Support
5. Tone and Manner

The A. Jerome Jewler Creative Platform
1. Objectives
2. Target Audience
3. Key Selling Idea
4. Key Benefits
5. Creative Strategy Statement

The Jim Albright Creative Strategy (a hybrid of the Y&R and Bozell plans)
1. Client
2. Key Fact
3. Consumer Problem to Overcome
4. Advertising Goal
5. Principal Competition
6. Target Market
7. Creative Strategy (the promise)
8. Reason Why
9. Mandatories

As you review the eight creative plans or maps, notice how they dovetail at key points. For example, each plan mentions the consumer or the target audience, the very center of your considerations and thoughts about what message you will deliver. If you go back to your research, you'll find a wealth of information and perspectives about that audience. What do they like? What do they use in your product class? Why do they like what they do? Why do they use what they do? What are their needs and wants?

Also each plan concentrates on the brand. What does it provide for the consumer (the benefit)? What is the key fact behind the brand and the need for the advertising? What does the brand have that can substantiate the benefit? What personality will distinguish the brand?

Through all of these considerations, the advertising fits in with certain opportunities and goals or objectives, which are also articulated. This helps keep you on course when you generate and select your big idea.

To see how each plan guides creative thinking, consider the three ads in Figures 6–5A, B, and C.

In the ad for Trojan condoms (Figure 6–5A), the advertising opportunity presents itself clearly. In this day of the insidious AIDS virus, the opportunity is there for brands such as Trojan to gain customers. But, all is not so simple. Based on the ad, the target audience has a problem with condoms, namely, the way they feel. The Trojan ad meets the problem head-on, exclaiming in the target audience's own style of language to "Get Real" so that both partners relax. In studying the ad, it should be clear that certain key facts and problems inspired Trojan to advertise. The benefits to the audience are implied, but they're also strong, given what is known today about AIDS.

FIGURE 6–5A

"It doesn't feel as good."

GET REAL

With a condom, you'll both relax. And that feels good, too.

New Trojan® Ultra Texture.
Designed for
a unique sensation.

Free Sample
Call 1-800-277-4383

Helps reduce the risk

All information kept confidential. Sample will be mailed in a discreet envelope. Offer good until August 31, 1994 or while supplies last. Must be 18 years or older.
Limit one offer per name or address. No P.O. Boxes. Offer good only in the USA and void where prohibited, restricted or taxed.

In a similar way, the Wrigley's ad in Figure 6–5B also suggests an opportunity for the brand. With the current sentiment and, in some cases, regulations against smoking in public places, in this case stadiums, the opportunity presents itself for Wrigley's to increase its market share as an alternative to smoking. Other Wrigley ads provide different contexts, such as places of business or restaurants.

As you analyze the Trojan and Wrigley ads, you can understand just how pointed they are in terms of capitalizing on a marketing and advertising opportunity and then tailoring their messages to a specific target audience. It should come as no surprise, for example, that the Trojan ad appeared in *Rolling Stone* magazine, and the Wrigley's ad appeared in *Sports Illustrated.* In both ads the medium and its targeted readers influenced the creative decisions about what to say, and what you say is one of the prime considerations of your creative plan.

In the third ad, the guiding idea for Blue Fox suggests a target audience of people who like to fish. Based on the creative execution (see Figure 6–5C), the plan called for a strategy of convincing this audience that the Blue Fox bug lures act, smell, and taste like the real thing. Anyone who has fished knows how important natural elements are to catching fish. Indeed, the Blue Fox ad spends considerable time supporting this benefit for the consumer. Real food is

FIGURE 6–5B

used in manufacturing the lures. Natural scents improve the lures' capacity to attract fish. And all through the copy, the connection to real and natural components of a fish's diet is emphasized. Clearly, the creative plan acted as a guideline, getting advertisers to stress that connection while they used a playful, fun tone to associate the Blue Fox brand with fishing as recreation and leisure.

FIGURE 6-5C

With each of the three ads, you can see the components of the creative plan at work. Starting with a key fact, that is, creating an opportunity for a problem to be solved, and from a benefit to be promised and supported, the ads reflect the inner workings of a creative plan. At the same time, the ads align themselves with brand image, suggesting different qualities and personalities for each of the advertisers. This leads to the brand position, so that if you want relaxation with sex, you'll buy Trojan; if you want a substitute for smoking, you'll buy Wrigley's; and if you want real, natural-looking lures, you'll buy Blue Fox.

STORMING FOR IDEAS: THE COMBINATION OF UNIQUE AND RIGHT

There is no magic formula for generating ideas. There is only you and your creativity. But there are ways you can unlock the door to your creativity. First, understand the creative process so you won't suffer undue anxiety when you face the familiar block or wall to your creativity. Second, create a mind-set for yourself that welcomes imagination and creativity. And third, understand and then use idea-generation techniques as a means for stimulating creative ideas.

THE CREATIVE PROCESS

Research indicates that creative people work their way through a process en route to creative ideas. This process includes four basic stages: preparation, incubation, illumination, and verification. There have been hybrids of this basic model of the process, but by and large the process includes these four stages.[15]

The creative process begins with a *preparation* stage during which you orient yourself to the problem at hand and gather information. This step is much like the review and careful analysis of research findings and perspectives, which we described earlier.

Following this kind of preparation you enter into the incubation stage. *Incubation* is the uncomfortable stage. It is the one in which you toss and turn in trying to organize the information and use it as a catalyst for an idea. Incubation is also a brewing stage, when your subconscious is working diligently away on the problem and your imagination begins to grab hold. It's at this stage that you suffer the most, simply because you're struggling for ideas, especially the right idea.

Following incubation comes the *illumination* stage. During illumination, you feel the relief and excitement after the personal storm of incubation. It is when you find ideas and feel relieved and excited because they seem to be plentiful after they've worked their slow, arduous way up through your preparation and incubation.

The final part of the process is the *verification stage*. Verification is the stage at which you immerse yourself in the most appealing idea, tinker inside it, and consequently bring it to fruition.

Don't expect that as you work your way through the creative process, the steps will be as linear and pure as they are described here. Rather, you'll end up going back and forth, shifting from one possible idea to another or gathering more research on which to base your final idea. But the result will surely be ideas. They will come, but they will often come despite how hard you try to force their appearance. Often, they will seem to come of their own accord, rising out of some mysterious depths in your psyche. And that will certainly be true, for you will have prepared yourself for their appearance.

The Right Mind-set

You might not be able to control the sudden appearance of ideas, but you can control the environment that stimulates them. That environment includes both internal and external influences that nourish your imagination so that it is ready and fit to generate ideas. Internally, for example, you will need to be fearless and adventurous, willing to take risks, and playful in how you perceive the world around you, including your product and consumer. You will also need to defer judgment when you storm for ideas. In this respect you should be open, not closed. You should not pass judgment as ideas emerge. Instead, you should embrace them all, logging them as you go, aware that what may seem to be a lukewarm idea today could well transform itself into a hot idea tomorrow. And finally, your senses will need to be sharp and in tune with your world, for it is your senses that often provide you with the connection to an idea.[16]

Externally, you will need to manipulate the environment to suit your creativity's purposes. For instance, creative people are often bound by rituals, primarily of time and place. There are certain times, such as early morning or late evening, when they are more creative than other times, and there are certain places that stimulate creativity. In this respect, you need a place that is your own and lends itself automatically to your creativity.

Having the right mind-set is no easy matter, but you can work on it. You can surround yourself with environments, mentally and physically, that lend themselves to your creativity. Research indicates that, above all else, creative people are independent thinkers. They are able to form unique and playful connections that result in ideas that lift themselves out of the ordinary. But you cannot cultivate this creativity if you're afraid, inclined to play it safe, captive to the views and opinions of others, or too set in the way you think. Instead, big ideas appear when you're open, receptive, fearless, independent, and flexible.

Idea-Generation Techniques

To take some of the mystery out of creativity, understand how your mind creates ideas. Fundamentally it's a matter of connections. The mind takes one reality, connects or merges it with another, and the result of that connection is a new idea. For example, associations represent a common denominator to many creative ideas. Often, these associations are symbolic in nature, using emotional symbols to convey something important about the brand image, consumer benefit, or both. The Michelin ad we discussed previously is a good example. The baby in the tire symbolizes consumers' most important cares and concerns. It symbolizes family, responsibility, dedication, and love, all bound up in a bundle of meanings conveyed through that particular image. The creative minds behind the ad connected all that was important to the consumer and that Michelin could offer with an everyday reality, a baby, which symbolized the consumer benefit.

Symbolic Associations

This connecting process relies on your ability to match important brand attributes or consumer benefits with phenomena from the real world. It also relies on your playful approach to all of the considerations in your advertising strategy, ranging from media choice and time to consumer demographics and psychographics. By way of these connections, your mind finds the links among the brand, the consumer, and the media.

Figures 6–6A and B show two ads from a popular series for Absolut vodka. In Figure 6–6A, the Absolut bottle appears as a basket containing fruit, which

FIGURE 6–6A

ABSOLUT KURANT.

suggests a product innovation or line extension from Absolut. In Figure 6–6B, the bottle is contoured into the Brooklyn Bridge. Both ads are in keeping with the personality of all Absolut ads—wry, distinctive, original, and memorable.

Consider how the creative mind behind the Absolut ads formed associations through connections. The bottle's form or shape led the way to the association. Connecting that form with similar forms from the real world (a basket and a bridge) spurred the eventual creative idea. The Absolut bottle gains the visual spotlight because it is presented in a unique way that avoids the commonplace and ordinary. The result has been a distinctive brand image and position for Absolut in the consumers' minds that can be measured by Absolut's extraordinary 1,750 percent increase in sales between 1979 and 1987. Bear in mind, too, that the increase in sales occurred while Absolut was raising, not lowering, its prices.[17] This type of growth can happen when you create a symbol with such endurance and appeal that it both protects and manages your brand's equity.

FIGURE 6–6B

You create associations in many different ways, and each one can provide you with the seeds for exciting ideas. When you look for associations, you're asking what something is like. In the Absolut case, the form of the bottle was like a basket and a bridge. But you can expand the possibilities by logging all of your brand's attributes and benefits and consumer benefits and then asking yourself what they are like. The answers lead you to possible ideas.

Bear in mind that the range of your associations should be large. Associating the physical qualities or attributes of your brand (form, size, color, mechanical workings, ingredients, and the like) with phenomena from real life lead to ideas, but so will associating all of the functional, symbolic, and experiential attributes or brand concepts. This means making associations between such concepts as brand performance, style, prestige, or experiences with real-life phenomena. So, too, associating the senses with your brand or the brand and consumer benefits leads to ideas. What does the brand taste like?

FIGURE 6–7

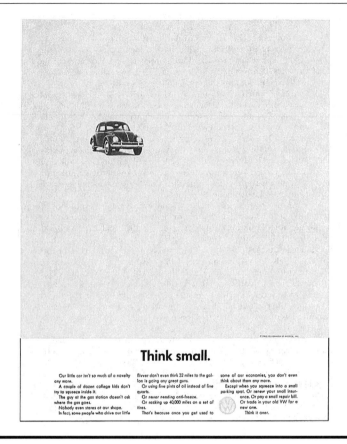

Smell like? Feel like? Sound like? You can ask similar questions using the consumers' experiences with the brand as the focus.[18]

Associations are a means for activating connections in your mind. To connect your brand with the consumer and with your big idea is your ultimate goal during this stage of the creative process.

Opposites and Wordplays

Still another means for generating ideas involves doing the opposite of what might be expected.[19] Because one of your primary goals is to stand out from the vast crowd of competing ads, then doing the opposite of what's expected yields creative ideas. Black-and-white television ads, for example, run counter to color television. Or, in the case of the famous and timeless Volkswagen ad in Figure 6–7, "Think Small" is the opposite of the more accepted motto of "Think Big."

Wordplays represent another technique for generating ideas by bucking convention. You create a twist on what's expected when it comes to words.

FIGURE 6–8

Often, brand names (a key to developing effective branding) lend themselves nicely to wordplays. Brand performance can do the same. For example, in Figure 6–8 an abbreviated storyboard for a TV spot for Price Pfister Company, a maker of bath fixtures, shows how the company name can be used to great advantage if you simply play with it.

In the Alka-Seltzer ad in Figure 6–9, you see a wordplay suggesting brand performance through the sounds of "Plop Plop Fizz Fizz."

The wordplays in both ads create memorability of both brand and brand performance, establishing brand image and reinforcing consumer benefits. Notice in the Alka-Seltzer ad, for instance, how the consumers' benefit of relief is associated with the sound and performance of the Alka-Seltzer brand. And in the Price Pfister ad, the wordplays of *pfabulous* and *pforged* suggest brand quality connected to and associated with the brand name.

The key to your idea generation is playing—keeping loose. The actual generation of your ideas should be fun. Just recall how many ads you see that are fun. No doubt they've been generated from minds having fun along the way. But this doesn't mean that your ideas aren't serious business. Indeed, a great deal of serious business is at stake with your ideas. And that means money. Your ideas represent the expenditure of money. So you need to be sure your creative idea reflects the right strategy. To do that, you have to do some more connecting—namely, connecting the creative idea with the most appropriate message your brand will deliver.

FIGURE 6–9

You don't undertake any creativity for creativity's sake here or being different for the simple sake of difference here, either. Instead, your blockbuster idea needs to be firmly grounded in sound strategic thinking, and that means being right, or on strategy. This, after all, is priority one. Even as you look behind the ads you've viewed to this point, despite their creativity, originality, fun, or cleverness, you're sure to see strategy. You're sure to see pointed, no-nonsense thinking that connects the idea with central and vital concepts or knowledge about the brand and consumer.

MATCHING IDEAS AND STRATEGY

Leo Burnett once said, "If you want to be different, you can come down in the morning with a sock in your mouth." It's easy to be different with your ads, but it's not so easy being different and on strategy at the same time. The key to an effective creative idea is to have it be both unique and on strategy.

If you reflect on the ads you've seen in this chapter, you'll notice how they all center on a tightly focused strategy. As we discussed, you articulate that strategy through your creative plan. The plan then acts as a guide for your selection of the creative ideas you generate. In a sense, your selection depends on how well you're able to match the idea with the plan.

KEEPING YOUR EYE ON THE PLAN

The success of your creative idea hinges on how well it reflects the creative plan. At the same time, the success of the plan hinges on how well, and often how imaginatively, you interpret your research findings. Notice that there is a process implied here, from research to plan to idea. One builds on the other, so that ultimately they are inextricably linked to one another.

Think back to the Michelin ad in Figure 6–4. We considered it primarily in terms of brand positioning. If you unpeel the layers of the ad and look through and behind it, you're sure to see the ties to research and the creative plan. For instance, if you were using the Roman and Maas Creative Strategy Plan containing objective, target audience, key consumer benefit, support, and tone and manner, then the Michelin ad suggests preference of the Michelin tire as a desired effect in its objective. Persuasion of a target audience occurs after the audience has gone through various steps ranging from awareness to interest to preference and finally to conviction for the product. The objective of the ad is to get the target audience to prefer Michelin and not simply become aware of it.

In considering the target audience, notice how the ad points to a specific individual who is married, with young children. Furthermore that individual is serious about family responsibilities. That individual may be considered a striver and achiever, especially when you notice that the brand's price consideration defers to quality.

The benefit the individual gains from Michelin centers on comfort, but not of the riding kind. The ad projects an emotional comfort that comes from the security of knowing that one's family members, particularly one's children, are protected.

In turn, the benefit is supported primarily by the combination of copy and graphics. The copy stresses Michelin's quality within the framework of how Michelin tires compare with other tires. Within the copy, reference to steel cables, machinery, and x-ray quality-control checks act as additional support or explanation for the benefit. In respect to graphics, the dominant symbol of a child in the tire implies the benefit without really stating it, creating a feeling of warmth acting as support for the Michelin claims.

In regard to tone or manner (the personality of the ad), key descriptors such as reassuring, bold, direct, and comforting describe the ad's "feel," initially directing the copywriter and artist to include and exclude certain appeals or messages.

Recall the discussions about branding and positioning in this and the preceding chapter, and notice how the Michelin ad reflects careful and wise considerations about managing brand equity and positioning the message. For example, as the visible product of the Michelin company's strategies, the ad creates a price/quality relationship that builds and reinforces the brand's core equities, such as consumer perceptions of brand quality and consumer associations between the brand and safety for one's family.

Yet, if the ad had simply stated much of what you've read in our retracing of the Roman and Maas plan, it would have been dull, lifeless, and ordinary. It would have sounded like a business plan, devoid of an imaginative spark igniting powerful meanings in the consumers' minds. Instead, the creative minds behind the ad (and the campaign at large in its success over the years) added the creative spark that lifted the ad out of the ordinary—how many times have you seen a child inside a tire?—and into the realm of the imaginative and provocative. But despite the pedestrian language in the plan, the ad's creative idea matches it, and it, in turn, follows from the research.

Knowing Your Promise or Benefit

Along with the creative plans' common emphases on consumers and the brand, each plan highlights an objective or purpose for the advertising. Similarly, each plan highlights a promise or benefit, primarily from the consumers' point of view. In determining the creative slant (the idea that will act as the thematic focus for your campaign), remember that its success depends on the appropriate benefit. Think of the benefit as the answer to the question, What's in it for me? In this case, the "me" is the consumer, your target audience.

Often in advertising the benefit disappears behind the dazzle of an exciting creative idea. But that's not what happens with the best advertising. In the most successful ads, the benefit steps out and is not upstaged by the idea. The benefit drives the meaning of the ad, even though its conveyance is through the creative idea. Again, the Michelin ad illustrates just this point. The baby in the tire acts as the core of the creative idea, but it is not a creative idea for the sake of creativity. Instead, the creative idea reflects the meaningful and clear benefit that you will feel secure, comfortable, and guilt-free when you buy Michelin tires.

As you review the ads in this chapter, notice how the creative ideas convey the benefits: the safety benefits in Timberland shoes and Trojan condoms, the taste benefit in Heinz ketchup, the substitute satisfaction benefit in Wrigley's gum, the relief benefit in Alka-Seltzer, and even the benefit of belonging to the trendy and upscale Absolut vodka club.

At the very center of an ad's success you will find the benefit, which answers the question, What's in it for me? Indeed, as you craft your ad and consider the most strategic idea to govern it, the critically important determinations for you to make are to find and then convey the most appropriate benefit. Simply put, the benefit motivates your target audience. And as a key message, the benefit gets inside that audience, mainly because those consumers allow it. If you need to be sure about one thing in your creative plan and then eventually in the message you want conveyed in your ads, be sure about the benefit.

Think of the concept of benefit broadly, so that you keep your mind focused on your target audience when making those all-important creative decisions. A benefit provides satisfaction for that audience, a kind of filling of the audience's want or need. But as we all know, satisfaction can take many forms, ranging from the sensory (taste, smell, feel, sight, sound) to the psychological or emotional (safety, status, belonging, convenience). Naturally, not all brands provide the same benefits. Nor do different audiences have the same wants or needs. Your job is to match what your brand provides with what your target audience wants or needs from the brand. Robin Woods, head of Segmentation Marketing Ltd., notes just this emphasis on matching the product (what it has or does) with what the consumers need or want, most notably in the form of a benefit.[20] For Woods, you must satisfy five conditions to have a solid benefit brand position:

1. You need a position that is based on consumer needs that are primary in the selection of one brand over another.
2. You must tell consumers why your brand meets their needs better than every other brand it competes against.
3. No other brand can be substituted for your brand and give the consumers the same message.
4. No other product class can be substituted for your brand and leave the consumers with the same message.
5. Your message can be precisely and specifically communicated to consumers.

Notice in Woods' list how the success of your strategy (and eventual ad execution) depends to a large extent on meeting consumer needs (the benefit your product provides) and differentiating your ad approach or creative idea from others. We've called that being unique and being right, which are central concerns for you as you craft your ads.

KNOWING YOUR CREATIVE APPROACH

Once you have a tight hold on your plan, especially on the benefit for the consumer, you need to decide on the best creative approach to meet your objective. Charles H. Patti and Charles F. Frazer cite seven creative approaches that can serve as a guideline for your crafting of ads. (See Exhibit 6–1.)

The *generic strategy*, which makes no competitive or superiority claims, is best used for products or brands that dominate a category. It is easily identifiable with a market leader and can rely on a combination of attributes and benefits, with little or no comparison to others made.

The *preemptive claim* preempts or upstages the competition by advertising a point of difference for your brand. Competing brands may provide similar benefits or have similar attributes, but they have not advertised those benefits or attributes. Thus, you preempt them by being the first to lay claim to the key benefit or salient attributes.

The *Unique Selling Proposition (USP)* is used when there is a distinct competitive advantage, namely a differentiating factor for your brand. Rosser

EXHIBIT 6–1   CREATIVE STRATEGY ALTERNATIVES: A SUMMARY

Strategy	Description	Most Suitable Conditions	Competitive Implications
Generic	Straight product or benefit claim with no assertion of superiority	Monopoly or extreme dominance of product category	Serves to make advertiser's brand synonymous with product category; may be combated through higher-order strategies
Preemptive	Generic claim with assertion of superiority	Most useful in growing or awakening market where competitive advertising is generic or nonexistent	May be successful in convincing consumer of superiority of advertiser's product; limited response options for competitors
Unique Selling Proposition	Superiority claim based on unique physical feature or benefit	Most useful when point of difference cannot be readily matched by competitors	Advertiser obtains strong persuasive advantage; may force competitors to imitate or choose more aggressive strategy (e.g., "positioning")
Brand Image	Claim based on psychological differentiation; usually symbolic association	Best suited to homogeneous goods where physical differences are difficult to develop or may be quickly matched; requires sufficient understanding of consumers to develop meaningful symbols/associations	Most often involves prestige claims that rarely challenge competitors directly

Positioning	Attempt to build or occupy mental niche in relation to identified competitor	Best strategy for attacking a market leader; requires relatively long-term commitment to aggressive advertising efforts and understanding consumers	Direct comparison severely limits options for named competitor; counterattacks seem to offer little chance of success
Resonance	Attempt to evoke stored experiences of prospects to endow product with relevant meaning or significance	Best suited to socially visible goods; requires considerable consumer understanding to design message patterns	Few direct limitations on competitor's options; likely competitive response: imitation
Affective	Attempt to provoke involvement or emotion through ambiguity, humor, or the like, without strong selling emphasis	Best suited to discretionary items; effective use depends upon conventional approach by competitors to maximize difference; greatest commitment is to aesthetics or intuition rather than research	Competitors may imitate to undermine strategy of difference or pursue other alternatives

Source: Charles H. Patti and Charles F. Frazer, *Advertising: A Decision-Making Approach* (New York: The Dryden Press, 1988), 304.

Reeves made this technique famous with M&M candy's slogan "Melts in your mouth, not in your hands." This strategy is difficult in today's highly competitive environment that is defined by explosive product and brand proliferation. Still, as you examine what your brand has and can do in relationship to the competition, you should be watchful for positive and useful differentiating factors.

The *brand image strategy* relies on factors not inherent to a brand. Specific product attributes are relatively meaningless. Instead, the advertising should build, reinforce, or change the target audience's attitude toward the brand, primarily by concentrating on psychological or emotional appeals.

Product positioning is a strategy that calls for carving out a niche for your brand in the consumers' minds relative to the competition. It's a means for differentiating your brand from that of the competition and is especially helpful for new brands or those wishing to gain on the competitive leaders in market share.

The *resonance approach* relies on target-audience associations where fond or positive memories or feelings are associated with the brand. Obviously, the lack of differentiating factors for your brand would make this approach appropriate.

An *affective strategy* seeks to form an emotional attachment between the brand and the consumers. Highly charged and symbolic images or words, often combined with music in broadcast, evoke heightened emotional response from the consumer. Such a strategy is useful for brands with little to differentiate them in the marketplace or whose success depends on the emotional attachment of consumers.

Although these seven strategies or approaches provide you with formulas of sorts, it is important to understand that they often overlap. For example, you may be inclined to use a *brand image strategy* in combination with a *resonance approach,* particularly if your brand lacks distinct differentiation based on attributes and seeks to create emotional ties with the consumer. To these strategies or approaches you can also add Leo Burnett's famous "inherent drama," where your goal is to find a dramatic centerpiece, often a narrative or story, in which the brand or product turns out to be the hero.

As you can imagine, the range of questions for your creative decisions is vast, especially when you begin to consider the relationship of various ads at different times or the dynamic interplay of graphics and copy in one ad or a combination of ads. Should you emphasize the product in use? Should you use a strong, charged symbol? Should you show the price/quality relationship? Should you dwell on product characteristics or attributes? Should you preempt your competition? Should you acknowledge your competition in the hopes of positioning yourself effectively against them? Should you rely solely on a key benefit?

The list of questions could go on, of course, but the key question for you to remember is this: What is there about your brand that satisfies a salient want or need of the target audience? If research tells you that something exists, if you're confident that it's critical to the selling of your product, if it fits with the objective in your strategy, and if you've found an original, creative idea or means to carry the message, then this is probably the most promising route for you to take. Notice, though, how that decision greatly depends on a host of variables that demand careful consideration and thought.

To see how such variables stimulate this kind of intense consideration and thought, consider one of the most talked-about advertising campaigns in recent years, the campaign for Saturn.

The Case for Saturn

In 1990 a new car company introduced a new car, the Saturn. The company selected Hal Riney & Partners as the advertising agency of record for the Saturn, and it established a two-pronged campaign attempting, in the words of Hal Riney, "to build a personality of the car that's comfortable."[21] The agency determined that the car was not to be sold on the basis of American heritage, price, comparison to Asian imports, rebates, or low-cost financing. Others had done that already, and Saturn was determined to be a different kind of company manufacturing and selling a different kind of car. Surely, then, its advertising could not simply follow the lead of others. It had to be different, and it was.

Saturn's initial advertising talked about the company and its commitments, not about the car. Launched six months prior to the Saturn's introduction in showrooms, the advertising sought to create awareness and trust in Saturn. It did so by spotlighting those individuals who made the car, particularly in their commitment and dedication to the task. Television ads featuring transmission designers or labor and management personnel working together suggested a family atmosphere in which people care and do their best. Copy lines such as "Imagine, labor and management working together" and "Seems to me that when you see where your part fits in the big picture it means a lot more" flavored the scripts with a homey, honest, and trustworthy feeling. These ads were unlike the razzle-dazzle or sleekness associated with many car ad campaigns. They needed to be different because Saturn was a different kind of company.

Following the initial campaign launch, the second year's advertising shifted ground and began focusing on people who bought Saturns. One well-known commercial featured a customer in Alaska who bought a Saturn sight unseen but then had trouble with a seat belt attachment. In the ad a Saturn technician flies 2,500 miles to Alaska to fix the problem. He claims, "We couldn't very well bring her car to us, so we went to her." This kind of testimony to service positioned Saturn as a company reconfiguring the way automotive companies relate to their customers and do business. Again, it was not a typical creative approach, especially in light of the proliferation of high-powered, sleek car ads, but it worked. Targeting a younger audience (around 40), the Saturn campaign for the first two years more than doubled purchase consideration of the Saturn among prospective car buyers. Meanwhile, awareness of the Saturn increased from 4 percent in 1990 to 85 percent by 1992.[22]

Figure 6–10A, which features a Saturn safety engineer, and Figure 6–10B, which shows a Saturn customer, reflect the homey, personal, caring, and

FIGURE 6-10A

warm tone or manner associated with the brand's image and personality. As such they are different from typical car ads and are consistent with the goal of portraying Saturn as a different kind of company and car. In their friendliness and personalism, the ads tap into the consumers' emotional centers, resonating with attachments we have to hard-working people and to ordinary, regular people who happen to live a bit on the fringe. This emotional reaction allows us to project ourselves onto those people so that we form a connection of sorts, a kind of human bond that is then associated with the Saturn.

Important, too, is that each ad complements the other. Notice, for instance, the consistencies of typeface, basic layout, and copy style. This type of continuity, or coordination, produces echoes of meaning for those coming in contact with the ads. Playing off one another, the ads sweep to a thematic center, holding fast in their essential appeal. This tightness and control of the core creative idea looms as critical to your campaign development.

UNIFYING YOUR ADS

Because an advertising campaign contains various ads for diverse media, the tendency is to treat each ad independently, almost as if it exists in a vacuum. This, of course, is not the case. Rather, each ad builds on or complements the

FIGURE 6–10B

others regardless of the medium in which they're placed. Because of their complementary nature, the Saturn ads are reminiscent of each other. Just as they build on each other in print, the same type of concentrated focus on Saturn employees and customers dominated the storylines in the television commercial. Similarly, as you advance into promotional or specialty items, the same holds true. You continue to link your thematic center, the big idea controlling and governing your creative approach.

BENDING TO THE CENTER

In many cases the meaning of a thematic center or idea can be reduced to a single word or a few words that are reflected in the slogan or tagline. For example, with Federal Express the single word meaning would be *fast*. With Heinz ketchup the single word meaning would be *slow*. This reduction of the meaning of your ads to one or a few choice words helps keep you focused and on strategy and at the same time provides unity for the campaign.

The same holds true within a single ad. As you read the many ads in this chapter, for instance, you probably noticed how the copy and graphics tied together to create a unified whole. For instance, in the Michelin ad the copy connects with the headline, especially in the copy's beginning and end. This type of connection is a familiar and successful formula for writing ad copy, regardless of its length. The basic circle (one of the most unifying shapes in the universe), in which the beginning and end echo the headline and the controlling theme and idea, reduces and tightens the core of meaning for the reader or listener. Combine with this a complementary graphic, such as the baby inside the tire, and the meaning tightens even more.

Think of this unifying approach to your ads as a tactical consideration in which you bend to the center of the ad's meaning and idea.[23] Consider again the ads you've seen and read in this chapter and recall how the headlines, copy, and graphics tie together in unified and coordinated package with a single meaning and idea. Now, recall the graphics, the lead visuals, and headlines for two of those ads and consider the following excerpts from body copy:

For Timberland: "Just be aware that we engineered these shoes so you dance on a very different surface. The storm-blackened foredeck of a boat that's bucking like a rodeo bull." Or, "the number of leading edges exceeds the traction capacity of traditional boat soles by a good 50%." Notice how the second line provides support for the benefit and claim.

For Volkswagen: "Except when you squeeze into a small parking space. Or renew your small insurance. Or pay a small repair bill. Or trade in your old VW for a new one… Think it over." Notice how centered the benefits are on the single word *small.*

Even with ads that have little or no body copy, the importance of unity remains critical to the ad's execution. In the Absolut vodka ads, for instance, the trendy creative idea requires little verbal support. Even still, however, the headlined words reinforce the ads' spunky, offbeat, wry attitude. "Absolut Kurant" and "Absolute Brooklyn" play into the transformation of shapes to fit the Absolut bottle, but do so in a clever, offbeat way.

This kind of tonal, graphic, and copy consistency, where all of the ads' elements bend to the center of the theme and idea, create a unified impression and meaning in the target audiences' minds. In a sense, it's a matter of keeping things simple and not trying to do too much. This simplicity and single-mindedness can make your ad unmistakable and clear. In fact, the same basic rule applies even when you're developing multiple ads for a campaign, including those that span media and time.

CAMPAIGN CONTINUITY

In much the same way that you focus on a tight and meaningful circle for the structure of an individual ad, in a campaign development in which an ad is one of many, it still must contribute to the whole of the campaign. In the Saturn case, for instance, the two ads highlighting employees and customers reinforce each other and don't depart from the basic theme or idea. As varia-

FIGURE 6–11

tions on the theme or idea, you can stretch to new motifs or executions, but the core remains the same. Again, consider the Absolut ads and how each is strongly reminiscent of the other. Add to this the many other Absolut ads, and you're sure to find the same continuity, despite the slight variations targeted to different geographic regions, other market segments, or product-line extensions.

Translating all of this for your needs is simple. Keep to the center of your theme and idea. You can vary, twist, or tweak the graphic or visual representation, depending on how the strategy may shift over time, just as Saturn moved from its initial launch with the employees at the heart of the message to the customer at the heart. Keep ad elements, such as basic layout, typefaces, and copy style, as consistent as possible from one ad to the next or even one medium to the next. This continuity will ensure campaign unity, keep your message simple and understandable, and help build and reinforce your brand's image and position over time.

To pull our discussion and examples together, consider the campaign pieces in Figure 6–11. The pieces include brochures and print ads for Saturn. Combine these with the ads you've seen for Saturn in this chapter, and you'll notice the core themes and ideas that carry over from one piece of an ad campaign to another.

As you develop your campaign, keep in mind this need for unity and continuity within the campaign's elements. It's always easier to change your ads. Indeed, your client may be tired of the campaign and want just that, often much before the campaign has had the time to work itself inside the minds of your target audience. Guard against that happening. If your core theme is strategically right and your creative ideas present that theme in a unique and captivating way, then time will prove their worth.

ENDNOTES

[1] Jennifer Lawrence, "P&G Makes a New Push with Tide," *Advertising Age* (February 7, 1994): 12.

[2] Julie Liesse, "Despite Risks and Little Time, Marketplace Superstars Emerge" [Special Report: Brands in Demand], *Advertising Age* (February 7, 1994): S-1.

[3] Junu Bryan Kim, "Generation X Gets Comfortable with Furnishings, Housewares" [Special Report: Marketing to Home and Family], *Advertising Age* (January 10, 1994): S-2.

[4] David A. Aaker, Rajeev Batra, and John G. Myers, *Advertising Management*, 4th ed. (Englewood Cliffs, N.J.: Prentice Hall, 1992), 196–202.

[5] For a thorough discussion of product attributes, see Aaker, Batra, and Myers, *Advertising Management*, 203–213. Almost any textbook devoted to advertising creative strategy or campaign planning will include discussion of features, attributes, and benefits from the point of view of consumers and the products. For example, see Don E. Schultz, *Strategic Advertising Campaigns*, 3rd ed. (Lincolnwood, Ill.: NTC Business Books, 1990), 292–309, particularly pages 292–293 for a discussion on the importance of a benefit-oriented advertising strategy.

[6] Kate Fitzgerald, "Adman of the Year: Roberts Brings Real Branding to Long-Distance Phones" [Special Report: 1993 Year in Review], *Advertising Age* (December 20, 1993): 8–9.

[7] Alexander L. Biel, "Converting Image into Equity," in *Brand Equity and Advertising: Advertising's Role in Building Strong Brands*, ed. David A. Aaker and Alexander L. Biel (Hillsdale, N.J.: Lawrence Erlbaum Associates, 1993), 67–82.

[8] David A. Aaker and Alexander L. Biel, "Brand Equity and Advertising: An Overview," in *Brand Equity and Advertising*, ed. Aaker and Biel, 1–8.

[9] Rajeev Batra, Donald R. Lehmann, and Dipinder Singh, "The Brand Personality Component of Brand Goodwill: Some Antecedents and Consequences," in *Brand Equity and Advertising*, ed. Aaker and Biel, 83–96.

[10] Amna Kirmani and Valarie Zeithaml, "Advertising, Perceived Quality, and Brand Image," in *Brand Equity and Advertising*, ed. Aaker and Biel, 143–161. See especially 153–154.

[11] Discussions and analyses of branding can be found in a number of books, including those by David A. Aaker (some noted in this chapter's notes); *Branding: A Key Marketing Tool*, ed. John M. Murphy (New York: McGraw-Hill, 1987); and John H. Murphy II and Isabella M. Cunningham, *Advertising and Marketing Communication Management* (Fort Worth, Texas: The Dryden Press, 1993).

[12] Bruce Bendinger, *The Copy Workshop Workbook* (Chicago: The Copy Workshop, 1993), 46–53.

[13] The creative plans come from various sources, including Bruce Bendinger's *The Copy Workshop Workbook*, 154–159; Jim Albright, *Creating the Advertising Message* (Mountain View, Calif.: Mayfield Publishing, 1992), 28–29; A. Jerome Jewler, *Creative Strategy in Advertising*, 4th. ed. (Belmont, Calif.: Wadsworth Publishing, 1992), 72–75; Kenneth Roman and Jane Maas, *The New How to Advertise* (New York: St. Martin's Press, 1992), 2–3.

[14]Jim Avery, *Advertising Campaign Planning: Developing an Advertising-Based Marketing Plan* (Chicago: The Copy Workshop, 1993), 129–131.

[15]For reference to the various stages in the creative process, see Graham Wallas, "Stages in the Creative Process," in *The Creativity Quest,* eds. Albert Rothenberg and Carl R. Hausman (Durham, N.C.: Duke University Press, 1976), 69–73; Alex F. Osborn, *Applied Imagination: Principles and Procedures of Creative Thinking,* rev. ed. (New York: Scribner's, 1957), 114–116; James Webb Young, *A Technique for Producing Ideas* (Lincolnwood, Ill.: NTC Business Books, 1975).

[16]For a discussion about creating the right mind-set for creativity and using the senses (imagery and associations) to generate ideas, see James L. Marra, *Advertising Creativity: Techniques for Generating Ideas* (Englewood Cliffs, N.J.: Prentice Hall, 1990), 92–108, 137–144; Sandra E. Moriarty, *Creative Advertising: Theory and Practice* (Englewood Cliffs, N.J.: Prentice Hall, 1986), 21–27.

[17]Norman Smothers, "Can Products and Brands Have Charisma?" in *Brand Equity and Advertising,* ed. Aaker and Biel, 97–111.

[18]For a thorough discussion and outlining of the technique of association, see Marra, *Advertising Creativity,* 109–136; Moriarty, *Creative Advertising,* 3–4.

[19]Marra, *Advertising Creativity,* 162–184.

[20]Robin Woods, "Why Has Advertising Gone Blank?" *Brandweek* (February 22, 1993): 14–17. Excerpted from *What's in It for Me? A Marketer's Guide to Establishing an Equal Partnership with Customers* (New York: Amacom, 1993).

[21]Hal Riney, speech delivered at the American Advertising Federation Convention, Portland, Oreg., June 15, 1992.

[22]Riney, speech.

[23]For a discussion of theme and pulling ad elements, including copy, to a thematic center, see James L. Marra, *Advertising Copywriting: Techniques for Improving Your Writing Skills* (Englewood Cliffs, N.J.: Prentice Hall, 1993), 230–261.

7

Media Strategy and Planning

Chapter 1 described in general terms the elements, or factors, that constitute an advertising campaign. It further showed how advertising plans, in today's highly competitive and ever-changing business world, must be linked and integrated with the entire marketing communication spectrum. The next five chapters brought in a number of topics that the advertising campaign planner must take into account in developing strategies and tactics:

☐ The research and information bases of the plan
☐ The consideration of brand equity, the definition of problems and identification of opportunities, and the setting of general campaign objectives
☐ The development of a general campaign strategy and determination of a budget
☐ The linking of a creative plan with a strategy

Although all of the topics discussed in the first six chapters are critical to the development of an advertising campaign, the *message* strategy and *media* strategy together with the tactical execution of these strategies are at the heart of any advertising campaign. Creative or message strategy was discussed in Chapter 6, and this chapter treats the parallel subject of media. Creative and media strategies must be integrally linked as a synergistic whole. The greatest creative idea is doomed to failure if it is placed in media that do not effectively reach the intended audience. Placing an ineffective message in the "right" medium would also fail.

To get across the idea of the relationship between message and media strategies, along with other marketing and advertising variables, try a little experiment of your own. Scan the television schedule for today and watch a program on a commercial station you think you would enjoy viewing (limit it to a 30-minute program, especially if you need to be working on your advertising campaign assignment). During the program, watch (or don't watch!) the commercials as you normally would. Assess the quality of those you do watch. If you judge particular commercials to be especially good (let's hope that at least one will be good), ask yourself what made the commercial successful:

☐ Was it the quality of the brand's characteristics?
☐ Was the commercial for a product or brand you especially have wanted to buy recently or for a brand you now buy?

□ Was it the creativity and communication capabilities of the message content?

□ Was it because of the commercial's placement in this particular program?

□ Or was it a combination of several things, or yet something else?

You may have come up with some answers to these questions, but before you could answer the questions you had to watch the commercials. The point is that before a commercial or advertisement can truly be successful and effective, there must be an audience—and indeed an audience that the advertiser wants to reach—for the message. The advertising message cannot communicate its intended effect unless the desired people have a chance to read it, hear it, or view it. Reaching the appropriate audience requires making the right *media decisions* in the advertising campaign process.

SETTING THE STAGE

Before media planners can choose the right vehicle for advertisers, they must know their choices. This task has become more formidable in recent years. As the number of media increase, only one thing seems sure: The role of the media planner is becoming more and more vulnerable.

INCREASING IMPORTANCE OF MEDIA

In today's world of advertising, most executives believe the creative strategy is the major determinant of success, at least in relation to media. Yet, the importance of media, in relation to the message and other functions, has clearly risen over the past 20 or so years. Barban, Cristol, and Kopec noted in the 1976 edition of their book:

> Too often, and among too many advertisers and agencies, the Media Department is looked upon as a support function instead of as a vital problem-solving arm of marketing and advertising management. Media planning has frequently been a hero in delivering marketing results but seldom gets the credit it deserves.[1]

Almost 20 years later, the same authors observed:

> Among professional advertising people, there is a wide range of opinions when you ask about the importance of the media function and the respect paid to media practitioners. Our own view is that the assessment of media as an advertising activity continues to increase in significance; however, it is not yet an equal partner with other functions.[2]

It is likely, though, that in the near future, probably within 10 years, the media function will be coequal with the other major advertising factors. With an increasing demand by advertising practitioners that what they spend on advertising be justified in dollar-and-cents terms, it is reasonable to expect that all advertising activity will be viewed in a like manner.

Changes in the Media World

Just a few years ago, media planners had fairly straightforward choices among media. The media mix proposed for a particular advertising campaign came from a stable set of alternatives. A planner, for example, could consider using television and radio (local or network), magazines, newspapers, direct mail, out-of-home media, and perhaps some miscellaneous media such as specialties and directory advertising.

Today, not only are there a host of new, nontraditional media, but the growth and extension in variety of the traditional media have also grown exponentially. These changes have added enormous complexity to the media task and require the planner to be not only alert to new opportunities but also to think in the most creative ways possible. Among the so-called traditional media, today there are more than 1,300 commercial television stations, 11,000 commercial radio stations, almost 12,000 cable systems, approximately 1,600 daily newspapers, 7,000-plus magazines, and more than 10,000 outdoor panels in the top 300 markets of the country. Making media selections among these traditional media types alone is a formidable task.

If you add to these traditional media types the category nontraditional media, the task of media selection becomes even more complex. A media expert expressed some of the following views about this phenomenon:

> In a rapidly changing media environment, all of us are seeking greater operating efficiencies and more effective ways of doing business.... Agency media departments today must realize that they are in the communications business instead of the advertising media business. The range of media options related to marketing communications is exploding.... To be of value to a client, you must be able to provide customized communication programs designed specifically for the client's business—not geared solely to traditional media or traditional agency media.[3]

In developing a customized communication program, today's media planner must consider such media as:[4]

- **Online computer services,** for example Prodigy, where advertisements are interspersed with information content. Online computer services are part of a whole array of nontraditional media. These online services are usually referred to as interactive media because a potential buyer can interact with the message content, including placing an order. Several interactive television experiments were being conducted in a half-dozen U.S. cities in the middle 1990s.[5] See Figure 7–1 for the advertisement of a company specializing in interactive television. Note the last paragraph of the advertisement, where mention is made of the *advertising* opportunities with this system.
- **In-store media,** including advertisements on shopping carts, at ends of aisles, and on the shelf where the brand resides (a variation of this is to have a coupon dispenser next to the brand). Figure 7–2 shows an advertisement for a company that focuses on in-store media and marketing.
- **Event marketing,** whereby a company and its brands can participate in the sponsorship of a particular event, such as a sports festival or rock concert.

FIGURE 7–1   ADVERTISEMENT FOR INTERACTIVE NETWORK

Source: Courtesy of Interactive Network

Although traditional media, like television, may also cover these events, advertisers have the added opportunity of reaching thousands of on-site audience members.

☐ **Direct broadcast satellite (DBS) systems** involve sending a signal directly via satellite into subscribers' homes through a small antenna receiver dish. If

FIGURE 7-2   ACTMEDIA DISCUSSES THE VALUE OF USING IN-STORE MEDIA TO CARRY AN ADVERTISING MESSAGE

Source: Courtesty of ACTMEDIA

successful, this system would have a major impact on standard television and cable as we know them today. DBS systems also have the capacity to be interactive. Some major media companies, including those owned by media mogul Rupert Murdoch, are investigating this nontraditional media area.

Although there are many other types of nontraditional media, these examples should serve to point out the need for a media planner to be alert to these new avenues for delivering advertising messages.[6] That such new media will be important in the future Professor Robert Ducoffe of the Baruch College in New York made clear in a recent study. Ducoffe asked advertising executives to evaluate which media will be more important to the advertising industry within the next 10 to 15 years. Exhibit 7–1 shows some of the key results.

Seventy percent or more of the executives surveyed named nontraditional media as being more important in the years ahead. Among the traditional media only *direct mail*, which itself has increasingly become nontraditional through innovative techniques and technological advancements, was named by more than 50 percent of the executives. Magazines, newspapers, and television networks were at the bottom of the list.

Only by being familiar with the various traditional and nontraditional media can a planner begin to develop media planning strategies and implement those strategies through tactical execution. Recall that *strategy* provides the direction for all those involved in the campaign to follow and the framework within which they should operate. Media *tactics* are those specific activities and decisions required to implement the strategy.

MEDIA PLANNING

If you looked at a wide assortment of media plans by advertising professionals, you would discover that there is no one way to write the strategic part of the plan. The specific approach taken varies according to the company or person doing the plan, the product or service category being advertised, the marketing circumstances, external conditions that are likely to exist for the duration of the plan, and a host of other factors.

Nevertheless, there are some common areas that are included in almost every media plan. How these areas are worded and how they are organized within the plan may vary, but typically certain basic content must be included in the strategy part of a media plan. These common areas are:

☐ Marketing background (or situation analysis)
☐ Media objectives
☐ Target audience
☐ Media mix

These four key areas, or elements, of a media plan serve to organize this section. We will discuss each element in some detail, with the goal of providing you with an approach to writing the media part of an advertising campaign. Along with these major planning elements, there also are a number of other matters that usually are included in the media section of a campaign, including the tactical execution of the strategy. We will discuss these other factors at the end of this section.

EXHIBIT 7–1   **ADVERTISING EXECUTIVES' EVALUATION OF VARIOUS MEDIA IN THE NEXT 10 TO 15 YEARS**

Media Type	Percent Saying Media Type Will Be Important
Interactive television	88%
Cable	87
Electronic information services	71
Computer networks	70
Direct mail	55
Magazines	30
Newspapers	21
Broadcast television networks	16

Source: *Advertising Age* (July 11, 1994): 3.

ASSESSING THE MARKETING BACKGROUND

The marketing background, or situation analysis, consists of a series of content areas that generally serve as the backdrop or factual basis for setting the media objectives, deciding the target audience to be delivered during the campaign, and determining the mixture of media types and classes to be used to reach the desired audience.

Some of the background areas discussed here may not appear in the media part of the campaign plans book but are included elsewhere in the plan as background for the campaign as a whole. We include them here, however, because the media planner typically must take them into account in setting media strategies.

Examining Marketing Research

Most advertising campaigns are based on research, ranging from a huge amount of available information to basing the campaign solely on past experience (indeed, past experience is a type of research, albeit informal). The media strategist must look at all of the information available and determine what applies to the media decisions and in what way.

The specifics of research for the overall planning of campaign strategy were discussed in Chapters 2 and 3. We will not dwell extensively on what was said earlier, but you are encouraged to reread those chapters and ask yourself how what was presented there has application to media decisions. Here we focus on three specific areas of research that can have direct effect on media planning—consumer/product research, market analysis, and competitive activity.

Consumer/Product Research   For many product categories, as well as for specific brands, there is a wealth of syndicated research data for perusal. MRI and SMRB, for example, are two major syndicated research companies that provide sizable information on product/brand usage patterns, demographic and psychographic characteristics of product/brand users, and media consumption. Such information can provide a media planner with vital insights into how to target media audiences and which media types and vehicles to use in a plan.

Note the MRI table in Figure 7–3. The data are excerpted from MRI for the product category ready-to-eat cookies. The figure shows product user, demographic, and media usage patterns with similar information for specific brands of cookies.

Analyzing such research data does not in itself provide the planner with a clear-cut decision—in the final analysis decisions are based on judgment—but the information can be most helpful in formulating a decision. Let's say that MRI or SMRB data show a particular product class (for example, gourmet frozen foods) to have a large number of users having a certain kind of lifestyle (or psychographic) orientation (say, many consider themselves to be "sophisticated," "food connoisseurs," "devotees of the arts," and "always on the go"). By cross-checking with the media patterns of specific magazines, having a qualitative feeling that certain magazines orient their editorial content to this type of person, or doing both, an efficient match can be made between a targeted audience and a specific media vehicle.

Market Analysis Market analysis is that type of research that looks to the manner in which products and brands are used within *geographic* units. The geographic units analyzed can range from rather large units (such as an entire marketing region of the country, like the East Central states), to an individual state (say, Illinois), to a specific city (Chicago). In many instances, it also is possible to deliver messages geographically only to certain ZIP Codes within a city (perhaps you want to reach areas in which average income within a ZIP Code is especially high). Note in Figure 7–3 how cookies are used (in this example, who buys cookies) in the four broad census regions of the country (Northeast, North Central, South, and West).

The idea of looking at such patterns for media purposes is to determine if certain geographic units are worth targeting with a media effort. (Keep in mind that most media can be purchased in very specific locales. Network television can blanket the country with a message, but spot television can be bought in approximately 230 individual markets. As you likely already know, this situation of national- versus local-buying potential occurs in almost all media categories.) Yet, even when you have precise data on geographic areas, the media decisions to make are not automatic.

Let's say that MRI data show frozen dinner users in the East Central states to be a sizable number of people who also have a greater-than-average propensity to use frozen dinners (that is, a high index). Should we devote special attention to the East Central; that is, should we run extra advertising here? Maybe, maybe not. What you ultimately decide is a matter of judgment and based on a number of things. For example, your particular brand may already being doing especially well in the East Central because of a strong sales force there. Additional advertising weight may not produce worthwhile results. Or you may have a price advantage in the East Central due to the location of

FIGURE 7-3 SAMPLE DATA FROM MEDIAMARK RESEARCH INC. (MRI)

Base: Female Homemakers	Total U.S. '000	Keebler's Chips Deluxe				Keebler's E.L. Fudge Sandwich				Keebler's Magic Middles				Keebler's Rainbow Chips			
		A '000	B Down %	C Across %	D Index	A '000	B Down %	C Across %	D Index	A '000	B Down %	C Across %	D Index	A '000	B Down %	C Across %	D Index
All Female Homemakers	84728	6670	100.0	7.9	100	5662	100.0	6.7	100	3912	100.0	4.6	100	2623	100.0	3.1	100
Women	84728	6670	100.0	7.9	100	5662	100.0	6.7	100	3912	100.0	4.6	100	2623	100.0	3.1	100
Household Heads	32168	1992	29.9	6.2	79	1515	26.8	4.7	70	1194	30.5	3.7	80	642	24.5	2.0	64
Homemakers	84728	6670	100.0	7.9	100	5662	100.0	6.7	100	3912	100.0	4.6	100	2623	100.0	3.1	100
Graduated College	14659	1172	17.6	8.0	102	1054	18.6	7.2	108	908	23.2	6.2	134	764	29.1	5.2	168
Attended College	15978	1230	18.4	7.7	98	1284	22.7	8.0	120	943	24.1	5.9	128	501	19.1	3.1	101
Graduated High School	35718	2982	44.7	8.3	106	2610	46.1	7.3	109	1715	43.8	4.8	104	1057	40.3	3.0	96
Did not Graduate High School	18373	1286	19.3	7.0	89	715	12.6	3.9	58	346	8.8	1.9	41	300	11.4	1.6	53
18-24	7416	381	5.7	5.1	65	398	7.0	5.4	80	255	6.5	3.4	74	129	4.9	1.7	56
25-34	20322	1798	27.0	8.8	112	1754	31.0	8.6	129	1063	27.2	5.2	113	873	33.3	4.3	139
35-44	17985	1926	28.9	10.7	136	1819	32.1	10.1	151	1497	38.3	8.3	180	847	32.3	4.7	152
45-54	12051	780	11.7	6.5	82	806	14.2	6.7	100	581	14.9	4.8	104	378	14.4	3.1	101
55-64	10650	999	15.0	9.4	119	435	7.7	4.1	61	306	7.8	2.9	62	213	8.1	2.0	65
65 or Over	16304	786	11.8	4.8	61	450	7.9	2.8	41	210	5.4	1.3	28	182	6.9	1.1	36
18-34	27738	2179	32.7	7.9	100	2152	38.0	7.8	116	1317	33.7	4.7	103	1001	38.2	3.6	117
18-49	52394	4423	66.3	8.4	107	4467	78.9	8.5	128	3138	80.2	6.0	130	2129	81.2	4.1	131
25-54	50357	4504	67.5	8.9	114	4380	77.4	8.7	130	3141	80.3	6.2	135	2098	80.0	4.2	135

(continued on following page)

FIGURE 7-3 SAMPLE DATA FROM MEDIAMARK RESEARCH INC. (MRI; CONTINUED)

Base: Female Homemakers

					Boxes or Packages/Last 30 Days													
		All				Heavy More Than 3				Medium 2-3				Light Less Than 2			
	Total U.S.	A	B	C	D	A	B	C	D	A	B	C	D	A	B	C	D
	'000	'000	% Down	% Across	Index	'000	% Down	% Across	Index	'000	% Down	% Across	Index	'000	% Down	% Across	Index
All Female Homemakers	84728	59122	100.0	69.8	100	17366	100.0	20.5	100	22136	100.0	26.1	100	19620	100.0	23.2	100
Women	84728	59122	100.0	69.8	100	17366	100.0	20.5	100	22136	100.0	26.1	100	19620	100.0	23.2	100
Household Heads	32168	20560	34.8	63.9	92	5150	29.7	16.0	78	7413	33.5	23.0	88	7996	40.8	24.9	107
Homemakers	84728	59122	100.0	69.8	100	17366	100.0	20.5	100	22136	100.0	26.1	100	19620	100.0	23.2	100
Graduated College	14659	10165	17.2	69.3	99	2906	16.7	19.8	97	3646	16.5	24.9	95	3610	18.4	24.6	106
Attended College	15978	11772	19.9	73.7	106	3179	18.3	19.9	97	4905	22.2	30.7	118	3687	18.8	23.1	100
Graduated High School	35718	25456	43.1	71.3	102	7502	43.2	21.0	102	9705	43.8	27.2	104	8249	42.0	23.1	100
Did Not Graduate High School	18373	11729	19.8	63.8	91	3776	21.7	20.6	100	3879	17.5	21.1	81	4074	20.8	22.2	96
18-24	7416	4948	8.4	66.7	96	1083	6.2	14.6	71	1720	7.8	23.2	89	2145	10.9	28.9	125
25-34	20322	15084	25.5	74.2	106	4278	24.6	21.1	103	5825	26.3	28.7	110	4982	25.4	24.5	106
35-44	17985	13593	23.0	75.6	108	4702	27.1	26.1	128	5051	22.8	28.1	107	3840	19.6	21.4	92
45-54	12051	8554	14.5	71.0	102	2837	16.3	23.5	115	3207	14.5	26.6	102	2511	12.8	20.8	90
55-64	10650	6906	11.7	64.8	93	1894	10.9	17.8	87	2898	13.1	27.2	104	2114	10.8	19.8	86
65 or Over	16304	10036	17.0	61.6	88	2572	14.8	15.8	77	3435	15.5	21.1	81	4029	20.5	24.7	107
18-34	27738	20032	33.9	72.2	103	5360	30.9	19.3	94	7545	34.1	27.2	104	7127	36.3	25.7	111

18–49	52394	38597	65.3	73.7	106	11795	67.9	22.5	110	14454	65.3	27.6	106	12349	62.9	23.6	102
25–54	50357	37232	63.0	73.9	106	11816	68.0	23.5	114	14083	63.6	28.0	107	11333	57.8	22.5	97
Census Region:																	
North East	17224	12701	21.5	73.7	106	4702	27.1	27.3	133	4504	20.3	26.1	100	3495	17.8	20.3	88
North Central	20965	14851	25.1	70.8	102	3825	22.0	18.2	89	6336	28.6	30.2	116	4691	23.9	22.4	97
South	29718	20592	34.8	69.3	99	6031	34.7	20.3	99	7367	33.3	24.8	95	7194	36.7	24.2	105
West	16821	10978	18.6	65.3	94	2808	16.2	16.7	81	3929	17.7	23.4	89	4241	21.6	25.2	109
Daily Newspapers:																	
Read Any	49736	34764	58.8	69.9	100	10469	60.3	21.0	103	13144	59.4	26.4	101	1150	56.8	22.4	97
Read One Daily	40196	28241	47.8	70.3	101	8278	47.7	20.6	100	10899	49.2	27.1	104	9064	46.2	22.5	97
Read Two or More Dailies	9540	6523	11.0	68.4	98	2191	12.6	23.0	112	2245	10.1	23.5	90	2086	10.6	21.9	94
Sunday Newspapers:																	
Read Any	55721	39701	67.2	71.2	102	12161	70.0	21.8	106	14813	66.9	26.6	102	12727	64.9	22.8	99
Read One Sunday	49960	35306	59.7	70.7	101	10759	62.0	21.5	105	13172	59.5	26.4	101	11375	58.0	22.8	98
Read Two or More Sundays	5761	4395	7.4	76.3	109	1402	8.1	24.3	119	1641	7.4	28.5	109	1352	6.9	23.5	101

These data include how people use the product category (ready-to-eat cookies) based on their demographic and media usage patterns.

Source: Courtesy of Mediamark Research Inc. (MRI)

your production facilities, and adding more advertising here may not noticeably affect unit sales. However, it also is possible that by placing some extra advertising in this region, you could increase market share.

Thus, although doing market analysis does not in itself show you the precise media decisions you should make, it does provide a basis for assessing the situation and making judgments.

Competitive Activity This research area is of critical importance to media strategy and tactics, and almost always is a part of any media plan. Competitive activity research involves looking at what competing brands have been doing about their media selections. There are a number of syndicated research services that provide such information, most notably the Leading National Advertisers (LNA) MediaWatch Multi-Media Service. A variety of books discuss these services in depth.[7]

Competitive analysis can provide the media planner with some of the following kinds of information:

☐ *How much are brand competitors spending for their media effort?* Although the figures available in sources such as LNA are not always precisely accurate (due to media prices being negotiated on an individual basis), you can get a general idea as to what companies are spending on a brand. You can see, for example, that Brand X generally outspends Brand Y by 50 percent. This type of analysis can result in what often is called the share-of-voice, or advertising share, of brands in a category. Let's say that LNA *MediaWatch* data show the following media expenditures for a particular year:

Brand	Amount Spent Last Year	Share of Voice
A	$12.6 million	34%
B	$10.9 million	30
C	$8.6 million	24
D	$4.4 million	12
TOTAL	$36.5 million	100

Such data provide a general idea about how these four brands are spending in the media that LNA monitors. Thus, we see that Brand A is the brand leader in terms of media expenditures with 4 percentage points greater advertising share than Brand B, and we can make similar observations for the other brands in this category. A sample page from *LNA/MediaWatch Multi-Media Service* is shown in Figure 7–4.

Several things to keep uppermost in mind when using competitive data include (1) dollar figures are not precisely accurate, (2) only certain media are monitored (LNA currently reports data for 10 media types), and these mostly are traditional media, and (3) the data always are from the past, and there is no way to predict absolutely that a brand will spend in the future exactly what it did in the past.

☐ *What are the media mixes of brand competitors?* Because LNA reports the estimated expenditures of brands according to the amount spent in each of

FIGURE 7-4   A SAMPLE PAGE FROM LNA/MEDIA WATCH MULTI-MEDIA SERVICE

LNA/MEDIAWATCH MULTI-MEDIA SERVICE
January - December 1993

CLASS/BRAND $

QUARTERLY AND YEAR-TO-DATE ADVERTISING DOLLARS (000)

CLASS/COMPANY/BRAND		CLASS CODE	10 MEDIA TOTAL	MAGAZINES	SUNDAY MAGAZINES	NEWSPAPERS	OUTDOOR	NETWORK TELEVISION	SPOT TELEVISION	SYNDICATED TELEVISION	CABLE TV NETWORKS	NETWORK RADIO	NATIONAL SPOT RADIO
F163 COOKIES & CRACKERS--							*CONTINUED*						
DELICIOUS FOODS INC (CONTINUED)													
DELICIOUS COOKIES	92 YTD	F163	250.5	--	--	--	10.0	157.9	49.1	--	33.5	--	--
COMPANY TOTAL	Q1		19.4	--	--	--	--	--	19.4	--	--	--	--
	Q2		12.0	--	--	--	--	--	12.0	--	--	--	--
	Q3		127.2	--	--	--	--	--	53.4	--	73.8	--	--
	93 YTD		158.6	--	--	--	--	--	84.8	--	73.8	--	--
	92 YTD		288.5	--	--	--	10.0	157.9	67.1	--	33.5	--	--
GENERAL MILLS INC		F163											
BETTY CROCKER DUNKAROOS COOKIES	Q1		717.7	--	--	--	--	217.8	460.7	--	39.2	--	--
	Q2		1,604.8	--	--	--	--	--	1,412.2	--	192.6	--	--
	Q3		2,180.2	--	--	--	--	--	2,085.6	--	94.6	--	--
	Q4		1,705.9	--	--	--	--	--	1,647.4	--	58.5	--	--
	93 YTD		6,208.6	--	--	--	--	217.8	5,605.9	--	384.9	--	--
	92 YTD		2,519.9	--	--	--	--	--	2,519.9	--	--	--	--
GF INDUSTRIES INC		F163											
SUNSHINE CRACKERS	Q1		18.9	--	--	--	--	--	18.9	--	--	--	--
	Q4		40.7	--	--	--	--	--	40.7	--	--	--	--
	93 YTD		59.6	--	--	--	--	--	59.6	--	--	--	--
	92 YTD		67.4	--	--	--	--	--	67.4	--	--	--	--
SUNSHINE VANILLA WAFERS	Q1		17.4	--	--	--	--	--	17.4	--	--	--	--
	93 YTD		17.4	--	--	--	--	--	17.4	--	--	--	--
	92 YTD		--	--	--	--	--	--	--	--	--	--	--
COMPANY TOTAL	Q1		36.3	--	--	--	--	--	36.3	--	--	--	--
	Q4		40.7	--	--	--	--	--	40.7	--	--	--	--
	93 YTD		77.0	--	--	--	--	--	77.0	--	--	--	--
	92 YTD		139.2	--	--	71.8	--	--	67.4	--	--	--	--
GRAND METROPOLITAN PLC		F163											
PILLSBURY SLICE N BAKE COOKIES	Q4		1,321.7	1,275.5	--	46.2	--	--	--	--	--	--	--
	93 YTD		1,321.7	1,275.5	--	46.2	--	--	--	--	--	--	--
KOHLBERG KRAVIS ROBERT & CO		F163											
NABISCO BUGS BUNNY & TEDDY GRAHMS GRM SN	Q3		294.5	294.5	--	--	--	--	--	--	--	--	--
	93 YTD		294.5	294.5	--	--	--	--	--	--	--	--	--
NABISCO BUGS BUNNY GRAHAM SNACKS	93 YTD	F163	858.8	--	--	--	--	--	--	--	--	858.8	--
												858.8	
NABISCO CHIPS AHOY & RITZ CRACKERS	Q1	F163	9.6	--	--	--	--	--	9.6	--	--	--	--
	Q3		12.5	--	--	--	--	--	12.5	--	--	--	--
	93 YTD		22.1	--	--	--	--	--	22.1	--	--	--	--
NABISCO CHIPS AHOY COOKIES	Q2	F163	3,019.2	--	--	--	--	2,576.9	16.0	297.0	129.3	--	--
	Q3		5,103.5	--	--	--	--	3,901.2	117.6	784.1	300.1	--	--
	Q4		514.6	--	--	--	--	--	150.8	60.9	23.6	--	--
	93 YTD		8,657.3	--	--	--	--	6,757.9	284.4	1,142.0	453.0	--	--
NABISCO CRACKERS	Q3	F163	512.4	--	--	36.1	--	--	--	--	239.2	273.2	--
	93 YTD		512.4	--	--	36.1	--	--	--	--	239.2	273.2	--
	92 YTD		36.1	--	--	--	--	--	--	--	--	--	--
NABISCO ENTERTAINERS CRACKERS	Q3	F163	30.9	--	--	30.9	--	--	--	--	--	--	--
	93 YTD		30.9	--	--	30.9	--	--	--	--	--	--	--
NABISCO FAT FREE NEWTON COOKIES	Q1	F163	1,369.8	--	--	--	--	1,002.5	205.2	87.4	74.7	--	--
	Q2		1,349.6	--	--	--	--	1,128.1	88.7	51.0	81.8	--	--
	Q4		0.5	--	--	--	--	--	0.5	--	--	--	--
	93 YTD		1,739.2	--	--	--	--	1,457.2	34.6	95.5	151.9	--	--
	92 YTD		3,103.8	--	--	--	--	2,640.9	22.1	283.9	308.4	--	--
										141.7	299.1		
----CONTINUED----													

From these data a planner can compute the share of voice for the brands shown as well as their media mixes.

Source: Courtesy of Leading National Advertisers (LNA)

10 media types, a planner can determine the media mix of a brand. Thus, a brand spending $10 million in a particular period—$5 million in network television, $2.5 million in consumer magazines, and $2.5 million in newspapers—has the following media mix:

Network television	50%
Magazines	25
Newspapers	25

Figure 7–5 shows this media mix in the form of a pie chart, which is a useful way to present the media mixes of various competitors.

Competitors' media mixes in past periods can be analyzed in order to help a planner decide on the media mix for the brand's approach in the current campaign.

☐ *What are the specific media buying patterns of brand competitors?* Along with the general media data reported in sources such as the *LNA MediaWatch Multi-Media Service,* several companies, including a number owned or affiliated with LNA, provide extensive detail on media spending. For instance, in the example above, we said that a brand spent $5 million (half the total media budget) in network television. Another source would tell us how this $5 million was allocated within network television, including such things as:

Which networks and programs were purchased

When commercials were run

Length of commercials bought

A planner might use many other types of marketing research to provide insight into the media situation. The ones discussed above exemplify how research information serves as a background for making specific media decisions.

Understanding the Marketing Mix

Along with evaluating marketing research, the media planner must have a clear understanding of the marketing mix of the brand in question. Typically, someone other than the media planner develops the marketing mix or strategy. The media person, however, must be fully versed in marketing and be able to develop media plans from marketing strategy.

As you will recall from your study of the field of marketing, a marketing mix is that set of variables that constitutes a brand's strategy.[8] The marketing mix usually is referred to as the four Ps of marketing and includes the broad areas of **p**roduct, **p**lace, **p**rice, and **p**romotion. Let's take a brief look at how these marketing mix variables can interact with media decisions.[9]

Product Starting with the product part of the marketing mix, we recognize that product decisions involve a large number of things, including a product's characteristics, its stage in the product life cycle, and all aspects of a brand's image and position in the market.

FIGURE 7–5   A BRAND'S MEDIA MIX

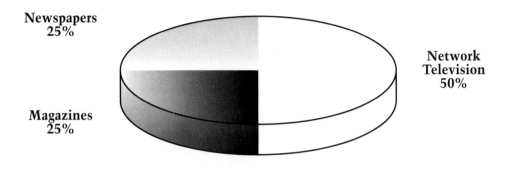

Newspapers
25%

Network
Television
50%

Magazines
25%

A pie chart is an effective way to show a brand's media mix.

For example, if the brand you are advertising has a complicated set of attributes—maybe it's a new electronic device—you may need to consider print media, which provide the prospective consumer an opportunity to read leisurely about the details. Or, if you desire using television extensively in your media mix, 60-second commercials (or even longer infomercials) may be needed to explain your brand's characteristics.

The product life cycle also can have a direct impact on media decisions.[10] Say you have a brand in the introductory stage of the cycle. You likely are going to want to promote as much *awareness* of your message as possible. So reaching the largest possible degree of your target audience is desirable. Media selections will have to reflect this objective. If the product is in the mature stage of the life cycle, on the other hand, media choices likely will focus on repeating the message as often as possible to your audience.

And the image, or personality, a brand holds among a target segment, or a brand image that is sought by the marketer, can readily interact with media decisions. If you are advertising a brand of the upscale Calvin Klein women's cologne, for example, *Vogue* magazine might be a reasonable choice, whereas *Modern Romances* might not.

Place Place is a marketing-mix variable that deals with the channel of distribution through which a brand is sold. A planner considers many things about a brand's distribution channel when establishing media strategy.[11]

Many brands are not distributed uniformly throughout the country, and distribution may be stronger in certain geographic areas than others. Thus, media placement will have to take this into account. If your brand has strong distribution in metropolitan areas but not in less populated cities and towns, media decisions likely will be affected.

Another distribution factor is the type of retail outlets in which your brand is sold. If, for example, your brand is sold in prestigious, exclusive retail stores—which also likely relates to the kind of image you seek for the brand—your choice of media vehicles will have to match the brand image.

The opinion of your distributors also can affect media decisions in that members of the channel of distribution, retailers and wholesalers, can be a target along with those who buy the brand at the retail level. There typically are many media through which an advertiser can reach distributors, business magazines being one major media type used. In addition to delivering messages directly to your distributors, you also may need to consider their opinions about media used to reach your final target audience. For example, if many of your dealers are sports fans, you may want to schedule things such as *Sports Illustrated* or *Monday Night Football* in your media mix.

Price The interrelation between the price aspect of a marketing mix and media decisions is somewhat more indirect than the other "**P**" variables. Yet, price does have to be taken into account in developing media strategy.

In setting a suggested retail price, the marketer considers the *profit margin* such a price provides the dealer. If the margin of profit is small compared to that of other competing brands, the marketer may have to assume a major responsibility for advertising or promoting the brand. On the other hand, a large relative profit margin may require the marketer to rely heavily on his or her dealers to advertise the brand. Either alternative affects the advertising budget, which has a direct impact on media decisions because media expenditures usually are about 90 percent of total advertising.

Pricing as a marketing variable also interacts with product characteristics, thus relating to media choices. For example, a brand that is priced at the high end of the price continuum in the product category often reflects a desire to create a certain brand image. In turn, media decisions will be influenced. Consider the advertising for, say, Calvin Klein's Obsession versus Revlon's Charlie. The media choices for these two brands, in part due to the pricing strategies of each—one is considerably more expensive than the other—likely will be noticeably different.

Promotion Promotion, as one part of the marketing mix, perhaps is *the* most important "**P**" factor in terms of affecting media strategy and planning.[12] It ranks so high because promotion includes advertising, of which media clearly is a major component. Figure 7–6 graphically shows the relationships among marketing, promotion, and advertising mixes, each of which affects the media strategy.

As the figure shows, promotion includes, in addition to advertising itself, sales promotion, personal selling, public relations, and publicity. Each of these promotion-mix elements must be considered in developing media strategy.

Sales promotion includes such things as coupons, premiums, contests, sweepstakes, and cents-off packages. Such sales promotion techniques are typically used to encourage consumers to try a brand for the first time or use it again if they've switched brands. A sales promotion can of course be used without any advertising, but often promotions are in fact advertised. Thus, this consideration must be a part of the media strategy: Which media should be used to advertise the promotion? For example, although coupons can be distributed in many ways not involving media (for example, on a package or in a coupon

FIGURE 7–6   RELATIONSHIPS AMONG THE MARKETING, PROMOTION, AND ADVERTISING MIXES

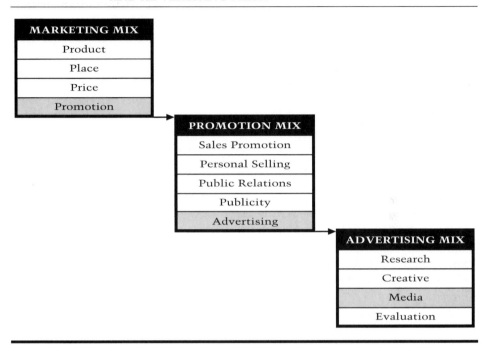

Source: From Donald W. Jugenheimer, *Advertising Media: Strategy and Tactics,* Copyright © 1992 Wm. C. Brown Communications, Inc., Dubuque, Iowa. Reprinted by permission of Times Mirror Higher Education Group, Inc., Dubuque, Iowa. All rights reserved.

dispenser on a grocery gondola), they also can be delivered through newspapers, magazines, and direct mailings. One type of newspaper advertising, free standing inserts (FSIs), was created primarily to distribute coupons.

Personal selling, as a promotion-mix variable, often can affect advertising that is focused on specific geographical areas. For example, your sales force may be weak or nonexistent in a particular region. If so, you may want to substitute advertising to compensate for this weakness. Obviously, you will have to choose media that can be efficiently bought on a regional basis. Another way in which personal selling can influence media decisions is through the ratio that is established between personal selling and advertising. Say, for example, a marketer places much greater emphasis on selling than advertising. With a limited promotional budget, there may be only modest funds available for media purchases, which may preclude the use of high-cost media such as network television.

Public relations and *publicity* are promotion factors that are similar to advertising and also often involve the use of media. Both advertising and public relations share a responsibility for communicating an image about a product or service, but public relations has a much broader role. Public relations can be defined as "the firm's communication and relationship with various publics, including employees, prospective recruits, industry partners, prospective and current customers, suppliers, the financial and investment community, government officials, and the society in which it operates."[13] Publicity involves using the mass media to convey information about a company or organization, but, unlike advertising, it does not pay for the media at specified advertising rates, and the sponsor is not identified. Not only must the advertising for your brand or company be coordinated with the public relations strategy, but also media-placed advertisements often are used to carry the public relations message.

Advertising decisions that interrelate with media include the objectives that are set for the advertising plan, the positioning sought for the advertised brand, and the message content of the advertising.[14]

Most advertising objectives or goals relate to communication: What should the advertising be accomplishing in terms of the communicative aspect of the message? A brand just entering the marketplace likely is virtually unknown by prospective consumers. The advertising goal may be to create, within a certain period of time, an awareness of the brand. The goal, for example, might be "achieve awareness for Brand A among at least 50 percent of those targeted within the first two months of the campaign." In another product category, a particular brand may seek to achieve an objective more closely related to sales, say, "have two-thirds of the targeted audience indicate a strong preference for our brand." The nature of the communication goal sought relates directly to media decisions in that different media types and vehicles deliver audiences in a variety of ways.

The position of a brand relates to how it is viewed in the consumers' minds. Thus, positioning potentially affects all aspects of a brand's marketing mix. As such, media implications are largely indirect. The position first has an impact on one or more other marketing-mix variables and, in turn, these variables have an impact on media decisions. For example, if a cookie brand emphasized it was "low in sugar and fat content, with 30 percent reduced calories" and thus was "'healthy' to eat," we might conclude that its position was in the "wellness" or "health" category. Thus, *Cooking Light* magazine might be a logical media vehicle to consider.

What you include in a brand's message content usually will have a direct effect on media decisions. For example, if your creative strategy is to emphasize reminding your target market about the brand, media decisions should focus on achieving repetition of the message as opposed to disseminating the message to more and more prospects (as you will note later, this is called a frequency strategy). Another message-media relationship is the nature of the message itself. A brand that wants to communicate its "news worthiness" might logically use newspapers; if television were preferred, you might want to select a news program as the vehicle (for example, *48 Hours, Dateline,* or the local evening news broadcast).

Taking Constraints into Account

Along with assessing marketing research and understanding the marketing mix as part of the marketing background, the media planner should take into account any constraints. Constraints (also referred to as *uncontrollable influences*) are those factors over which the media planner has no direct control yet must nevertheless consider when decisions are developed. Typical constraints include:

☐ Management policies and amount appropriated for advertising
☐ Economic conditions
☐ Competitor efforts
☐ Legal and cultural environment
☐ Media environment
☐ Weather and cataclysmic conditions

A media planner typically is given a specific amount of money to spend for media and must operate within the budget. This budget is a constraint imposed by higher management on the planner. Similarly, management often has policies about how its company should operate, and some of these policies can affect media choices. If a company wants to be perceived as "responsible, trustworthy, and a good corporate citizen," for example, there may be a desire to avoid certain kinds of media vehicles, such as television programs with a lot of violence.

Economic conditions, likewise, can influence media decisions. If sales of the brand you are advertising are affected by recessions, such conditions will have to be forecast for the period of the media plan. Under circumstances where the economy can adversely affect brand sales, not only will your messages have to be hard hitting, but media selections must also reflect the situation.

Although you cannot control what competitors are going to do regarding advertising plans, you nevertheless have to consider their strategies in developing your brand's media plan. If you learn that certain competitors usually use a specific set of magazines to advertise their brands, for example, you will need to consider their strategies. Usually, how your brand is positioned will be influential here. Thus, if you have a media budget comparable to most of those competitors' budgets and you want to compete with them on a head-to-head basis, you may want to choose to advertise in the same magazine vehicles.

Legal constraints are fairly straightforward in terms of influence. Products such as tobacco and liquor are not permitted in certain media. Cultural factors are somewhat more subtle as to their effect on media decisions, and such influences often change over time. A few years ago, the advertising of condoms would have been unacceptable to many media vehicles. With growing concern about AIDS and the practice of so-called safe sex, media today are more likely to accept such product advertising. Cultural influences can be especially tricky in international markets, and planners must be knowledgeable about each country in which they schedule media.

Media planners often must consider weather and related matters in developing media strategies and tactics. Here are a few examples:

☐ Many products are sold on a seasonal basis—snow skis, lawn mowers, sun-screen—and the media schedule must be related to sales peaks and valleys.

☐ Seasonality also can be related to geography—antifreeze likely will be advertised much earlier in the upper Midwest than in the Deep South, thus affecting media choices in a very direct way.

☐ An airline likely will cancel its advertising immediately following a major airline tragedy. Advertisers also often suspend advertising during natural disasters, such as floods and tornadoes, because to advertise under such cir-cumstances might create negative feelings among consumers.

The media environment is yet another uncontrollable variable that can affect media decisions, although there are opportunities here to have some influence. Planners often will want to know where their advertisement or commercial will be placed within a vehicle. If you were advertising Kraft salad dressings in a magazine, you may want the advertisement to appear opposite an article on salad preparation. But if you were the planner for GMC truck advertising, you probably would not want your commercial to appear on a news program the day a recall for the brand was being reported.

SETTING MEDIA OBJECTIVES

The setting of media objectives in a careful and precise way is essential to the success of any media effort in a campaign's plan. Without knowing exactly what you want to accomplish through your media strategy and tactics, the success or failure of the plan cannot be determined.

We discussed some general aspects of objectives, or goals, in Chapter 4, and almost everything said there also applies to media objectives. In particular, recall that objectives should be output oriented, time bounded, realistic and attainable, have common effectiveness and singularity of purpose, and be measurable, specific, and cost-effective.

Also, refer to the discussion about advertising versus marketing goals in Chapter 4. In setting media objectives it is essential to keep in mind that goal-setting for an advertising campaign is hierarchical: Marketing objectives are set first, followed by advertising communication objectives, and in turn media goals are derived from these "higher" sets of desired outputs. This hierarchy of objectives once again stresses the synergism of an advertising campaign and the need for each specialist, such as the media person, to have an understanding and appreciation of all critical components.

To understand better the setting of media goals, let us review some key concepts upon which these goals are based.

Key Concepts to the Setting of Media Objectives

A certain lexicon is used in the setting of important media goals: reach, frequency, and continuity as well as the related ideas of gross impressions and gross rating points. These terms explain different facets in the measurement of the media objectives. Let's be sure we understand what each term means.

Reach Reach can be defined as the number of different people or households exposed to a media schedule within a given period of time, or those who are exposed at least once to the schedule. The period of time can vary according to the type of media used, but generally a four-week period is used. Let's say we have the following information about a particular network television schedule:

☐ Targeted audience is women, ages 18 to 49; there are approximately 62 million in this target.

☐ Our schedule for the month of November is ten 30-second commercials bought on four different weekly television programs. The specific schedule is

two commercials on *Roseanne* (in weeks one and three of November)
two commercials on *Matlock* (in weeks one and three of November)
two commercials on *Seinfeld* (in weeks two and four of November)
four commercials on *60 Minutes* (in each of the four Sundays of November)

☐ Our computer program tells us that *34 million* 18- to 49-year-old women were exposed to at least one of the ten broadcasts of these four programs (some of the women were exposed to two broadcasts, some to three, and so forth).

Thus, we can state that the *reach* of this schedule is *34 million* targeted women. We also can say that 34 million, of a possible 62 million, were exposed to a broadcast at least once, or 54.8 percent (34 million ÷ 62 million × 100 = 54.8 percent). Reach can be expressed as an absolute number (34 million) or a relative number (54.8 percent).

Reach, when used in setting media objectives, is a precise way of stating the *extent* of a desired media effort. If we have an advertising goal of delivering a high level of awareness of our brand's existence, for example, that may translate to a goal of high reach, perhaps as much as 85 percent to 95 percent of the targeted audience. By knowing the level of reach we want to deliver at a particular time, we attempt to accomplish the goal through our media selections.

Frequency Frequency is the number of times a person or household is exposed to a media schedule within a given period of time. Frequency can be expressed in two ways: as a straight average or as a distribution *(frequency* or *exposure* distribution). If frequency is computed as an average, say, 2.19 for the television schedule noted, it means the average 18- to 49-year-old woman was exposed to the schedule 2.19 times during the four weeks in November. (Keep in mind that an average is a statistical artifact; no individual woman could be exposed to 2.19 messages.)

A frequency or exposure distribution, arrived at by using a computer program that accurately estimates reach and frequency figures, might look like this:

Number of Exposures	Number Women Age 18–49 Exposed	Percent Exposed
1	13,500,000	21.8%
2	9,700,000	15.6
3	5,600,000	9.0
4	2,900,000	4.7
5	1,300,000	2.1
6	600,000	1.0
7	240,000	0.4
8	105,000	0.2
9	40,000	0.06
10	15,000	0.02

Whereas 34 million women were exposed at least once, we now can see that 13.5 million women received only one of the ten possible exposures (this is 21.8 percent of all of the 62 million in the target audience), 9.7 million were exposed twice, 5.6 million three times, and so forth. The average of this distribution is 2.19 exposures.

Frequency permits media objectives to be stated in terms of the *repetition* of messages to a target. There often are times within a plan when we want to deliver as many messages as possible to get across certain things about the brand to our target. Repetition thus might be useful in achieving attitude change among prospects in order to get a high level of brand loyalty.

Continuity Media practitioners use the term *continuity* in a variety of ways. We mean continuity to be the manner in which media messages are scheduled over the campaign period. For example, we could state our continuity pattern as follows:

> *To introduce our brand's new advertising theme to the target audience for the first two months of the campaign (say, January and February), followed by a three-month period of focusing on brand attributes (March, April, May), doing no advertising at all during the low sales months of summer (June, July, August), having a big back-to-school push in September because of peak sales, and complete the campaign cycle by maintaining brand loyalty during the last period of the campaign (October, November, and December).*

The continuity used for a particular media plan depends on several factors, many of which are unique to the particular marketing situation. Yet, there usually are two key things a planner always must consider in establishing the timing pattern—the advertising communication objectives and the seasonality of sales for the product category (and perhaps even the particular brand). We might further look to the concept of continuity by showing three general scheduling strategies—continuous, flighting, and pulsed. Figures 7–7A, B, and C show three graphs (media schedule) of the three approaches.

A *continuous* continuity pattern is one in which about the same amount of money is spent in each period of the campaign. Such a strategy might be related to a brand with a relatively fixed share of market, with sales fairly equal across each month or period.

FIGURE 7–7A   THREE PATTERNS OF MEDIA CONTINUITY

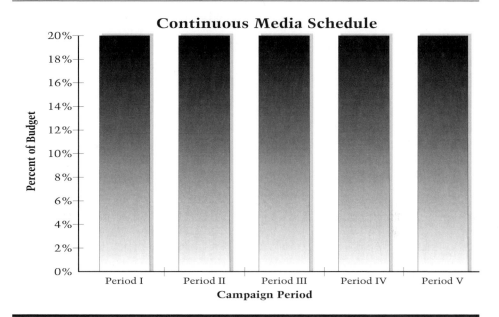

In a *flighting* strategy advertising varies from period to period. During certain times of the campaign, there is no advertising at all. This approach often is considered for a brand with a limited budget relative to competitors and a varying sales pattern throughout the year.

A *pulsed* schedule is similar to flighting—advertising varies from period to period—but there is at least some advertising media scheduled in each period. For example, a heavy media effort may be placed just before peak sales periods, yet at other times you would continue media messages in order to maintain top-of-mind brand recognition.

Gross Impressions Gross impressions are the *total* number of people or households exposed to a media schedule within a given period of time. The term describes the sum of all vehicle exposures and counts every exposure in a schedule, even multiple exposures to the same person or household. This means that gross impressions include duplication of audience. Consider the sample November television schedule of 10 commercials from our discussion of reach and frequency. A computer estimating program might report that we delivered 75 million gross impressions, or a total of 75 million message deliveries, some being multiple exposures to the same women ages 18 to 49. The 75 million impressions gives us an idea of the total magnitude of our media schedule.

Gross Rating Points Gross rating points (GRPs) are identical to gross impressions, but they are expressed as a percent of a total population. Thus, 75 million gross impressions to a target audience of 62 million women ages

---

FIGURE 7–7B   THREE PATTERNS OF MEDIA CONTINUITY

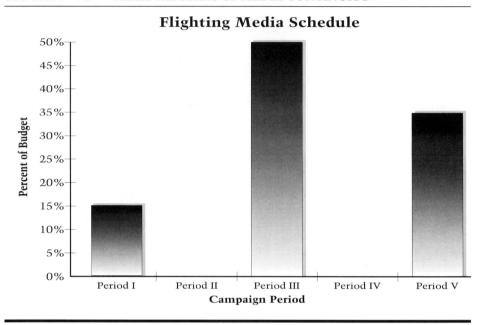

Flighting Media Schedule

---

18 to 49 would be 121 GRPs (75 million ÷ 62 million × 100 = 120.96 percent = 121; although a "percent," GRPs are not typically shown with a percent sign). Like gross impressions, GRPs indicate the magnitude of a media schedule. In our example of 121 GRPs we could compare that with a similar schedule that, say, delivered 200 GRPs, a notable increase in total weight.

The mathematical relationships of the concepts discussed, with examples from the sample scheduled we've been using, are

> Gross Impressions = Reach (expressed as an absolute number) × Average Frequency

In our example:

> Gross Impressions = 34 million reached × 2.19
> = **74.5 million** (rounded to 75 million gross impressions)

> Gross Rating Points = Reach (expressed as a percent) × Average Frequency

In our example:

> GRPs = 54.8% reached × 2.19 = **120** (because of rounding errors, the 120 GRPs computed from this formula is not precisely the 121 GRPs computed above from the number of gross impressions)

FIGURE 7–7C   THREE PATTERNS OF MEDIA CONTINUITY

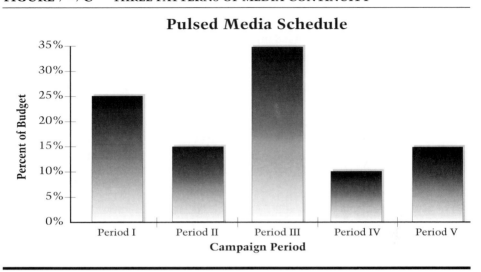

Pulsed Media Schedule

As mentioned, there are computer programs that provide planners with estimates of reach, frequency, GRPs, and the like. Such computer software is used extensively in the advertising media industry. A software package that is especially useful for student advertising campaigns is *Media Flight Plan—IM*, 3rd edition, by Dennis Martin, of Brigham Young University, and Dale Coons, vice-president of media research for the Lintas: Campbell-Ewald advertising agency. This program is used to assist media planning as part of an advertising campaign. A brief explanation of the *Media Flight Plan—IM* is given in Exhibit 7–2, and the software can be ordered from Deer Creek Publishing (address and phone indicated at bottom of exhibit).

Balancing Reach, Frequency, and Continuity

A planner typically must arrive at a balance among reach, frequency, and continuity in setting media goals. With a prescribed amount of money available for a campaign, a media person must decide on the relative importance of reach versus frequency for particular time periods. As mentioned, the idea behind a pulsed or flighted schedule is to conserve campaign funds for the most effective time periods. Within a given time period, the planner must gauge the relationship between reach and frequency.

For example, in introducing a new brand—where advertising communication goals might attempt to achieve a certain level of awareness—a planner may decide to reach as many of the target audience as possible early in the campaign. To accomplish this within a certain budget may mean the planner will recommend relatively low levels of message repetition (that is, frequency) during this time period. This is not to say, though, that reach and frequency always must be

---

EXHIBIT 7–2   *MEDIA FLIGHT PLAN III*

Revisions in *MFP III* Text Aim for Simplicity

MFP's new Third Edition is divided into six major sections:

- **I** Marketing/Media Planning Tools and Syndicated Data
- **II** Marketing Spreadsheet Excercises
- **III** Computer Basics for IBM and Mac: Power Level I
- **IV** How to Write a Media Plan: Three Chapters
- **V** Marketing/Media Case Studies
- **VI** Advanced MFP Applications: Power Levels II, III, and IV

The philosophy that drives *MFP*'s new Third Edition has not changed—that is, media flowcharts and reach/frequency are secondary in importance. Intelligent reasoning and thinking *before* you print the flowchart is the real goal. The biggest changes in *MFP III* will be evident in four ways: 1) Most exercises have been rewritten or revised with a singular focus—relevance to marketing-driven media planning. 2) *MFP III* was tested in the classroom for three semesters to improve both clarity and simplicity. 3) The three chapters on "Writing a Media Plan" are enhanced by richer content and consideration for student needs. 4) *MFP III* has three challenging, new case studies plus two final exam cases in the *Instructor's Answer Guide*.

Integrated Marketing Impacts *MFP III*

The evolution of integrated marketing is having a profound effect on how campaign planners perceive the term *media* itself. One of the biggest questions today is "What is media?" TV and radio are no longer bought automatically according to broad demo groups. Instead, multiple subtargets are broken out and defined by behavior as well as demographics. Indeed, each subtarget is ranked according to profitability for the brand. Only after conducting intense marketing research can the planner begin to identify the best media to reach these subtargets.

To complicate the media task further, mass audience TV cannot do the job it used to. It is no longer the most effective way to sell and persuade many subtargets—hence, the demand for more integrated marketing. This in turn is causing a rapid growth in direct media, sales promotion, event marketing, and marketing public relations (PR). Some interactive media, via the internet, is already showing up on some agency flowcharts.

Key to *Media Flight Plan III:* Four Criteria

Given the mercurial state of today's real media world, the primary goal for *Media Flight Plan III* is to be flexible enough to encourage strategic campaign planning. It is intended for university courses, and attempts to meet these four criteria:

1. Relatively easy and fast to learn
2. Simulate the real-world environment of media planning
3. Encourage experimentation and creative thinking
4. Adaptable to integrated marketing non-traditional media needs

Let's evaluate *MFP* based on those four criteria:

First Criterion: Ease of Use

Media Flight Plan III is available on both IBM and Macintosh platforms. Its first objective is to introduce students to hands-on media planning to help reduce student anxiety. Professor Carla Lloyd, Syracuse University, said, "Media used to be the torture chamber of advertising courses. *Media Flight Plan* has helped eliminate much of the drudgery and anxiety associated with this course." (See Endnote 1.) Another reviewer wrote, "*Media Flight Plan* is easy to understand with a good tutorial to warm up." (See Endnote 2.)

"Ease of use" is nicely illustrated when buying spot markets. It used to take students several hours to find costs/ratings for multiple media in spot markets and then many hours longer to perform the calculations. This task now takes about a minute with *MFP III.* You simply check off the spot markets you want, and the software finds all the data and does all the calculations. The computer screen for spot markets from *MFP III* looks similar to the figure below.

```
Select Markets by Pressing Space Bar

MARKET NAME                          RANK          %US POP
Abilene-Sweetwater, TX                157            0.1
Albany, GA                            153            0.1
Albany et al., NY                      51            0.6
Albuquerque, NM                        52            0.6
Alexandria, LA                        173            0.1
Alpena, MI                            210            0.1
Amarillo, TX                          127            0.2
Anniston, AL                          194            0.1

SCROLL FOR MORE MARKETS BELOW
```

Second Criterion: Simulating the Real World

Since the real world of media planning is Gross Rating Point (GRP) driven, *MFP III* follows that model. All planning and buying are based on the GRP model, and the *MFP III* text includes a hands-on exercise that teaches how the GRP model works.

Another real-world feature is the use of beta-binomial reach curves. A sophisticated BBD model has been constructed especially for *MFP III* by R. Dale Coons, Vice-President Media Research and Information Services, Lintas: Campbell-Ewald.

The 25/75 Media Planning Model

In the real world, media directors spend most of their time planning, not computing. This model suggests that human resources should be focused on the one thing humans do best, creative thinking. Only humans can analyze campaign problems and think creatively about media strategy. So, let the computer do the mechanical, redundant work. The 25/75 model suggests that a maximum of 25 percent of student time be spent on the computer. Seventy-five percent should be invested into analysis of marketing problems, creative problem solving, and writing media strategies. *Media Flight Plan III* was originally designed to fit this 25/75 model.

Third Criterion: Creativity and Experimentation

Now, you're ready to play "what if." Here you actually start buying GRPs in the media of your choice. *MFP III* displays the immediate effect on your reach/frequency goals. Since the combinations of GRP levels and media choices is infinite, experimentation is required in *Media Flight Plan III,* just as in real-world media planning software. And, more importantly, creativity is demanded as students experiment with possible combinations.

(continued on following page)

EXHIBIT 7–2 *MEDIA FLIGHT PLAN III* (CONTINUED)

Fourth Criterion: Adapting to Integrated Marketing

MFP III easily adapts to the use of nontraditional media, for example, sales promotions, event marketing, and marketing PR. Everything from blimps to beach towels can be integrated into your campaign. All buys will show up on your media flowchart, although reach/frequency curves will not be calculated since they are unreliable for most non-traditional media.

MFP—IM's Four Power Levels

MFP—IM is divided into four power levels based on campaign needs. Each level adds a layer of sophistication to your media plan. Levels I through III are all quite easy to use. The fourth level is truly demanding and somewhat complicated, intended only for experienced media practitioners with a working knowledge of media.

> **Power Level I—The Basics**   Not only is this the easiest level of the program, but it's also the most important. You always start here even if you plan to use other power levels. Level I requires you to set up the basics for your plan, for example, target audience demographics, launch month, budget. The following figure illustrates how "Media Basics" appear on the computer screen.

> **Media Basics**
> * Target
> * Scope
> * Calendar
> * Spot Markets
> * Budget
> * Ad Types

> **Power Level II—Naming Vehicles and Controlling Costs**   Once you learn the basics, you can easily add another level of sophistication to your media plan. Level II gives

---

Source: From the introduction of *Media Flight Plan III* published by Deer Creek Publishing; 3990 North 480 East, Provo, Utah 84604; phone # or fax: (801) 225-0702. It is a copyrighted software/course-

---

traded off in a particular period. In some situations you may want to achieve high levels of both reach and frequency at the same time. To accomplish this, however, will require either an especially large media budget or a continuity plan where there are periods of no advertising, or a combination of both. Think about certain brands that you often see advertised and in a host of media types (where others also can be reached by the advertising)—say, McDonald's, Coca-Cola, and Pepsi. Such brands have especially large media budgets compared with those of other advertisers and therefore can reach large numbers of people fairly often. Media budgets of this magnitude are the exception rather than the rule.

Formulating Media Objectives

A major consideration—probably the most critical aspect—in setting media goals involves the levels of reach and frequency sought during specific time periods. Yet, planners must consider numerous other factors. Figure 7–8, from you the power to name vehicles. You can type in recommended titles for *any* medium, for example, *Elle, Rolling Stones, Late Show with David Letterman.* These titles will appear when you print your flowchart. Because it is optional, you are *not* required to provide media/vehicle costs in Power Level II. A special database automatically estimates mean costs per GRP for each medium you buy. However, if you want to enter your own costs for specific vehicles, Level II allows that option.

Power Level III—Integrating Marketing with Media Planning   This is where the truly integrated campaign takes shape. As noted earlier, *MFP III* allows everything from blimps to beach towels to be integrated into your campaign. But since most integrated media are promotional in nature, valid reach/frequency curves are rarely available at this level, even in the professional world. Nevertheless, *MFP III* will calculate nontraditional media into your total budget. It will even print "beach towels" on your flowchart. But, it will *not* calculate "beach towels" into the reach/frequency estimates.

Power Level IV—For Media Experts Only   If you have the time and available cost/rating information, *MFP III* allows you to customize costs and ratings for any medium. Although more demanding than the other three power levels, this level is not difficult if you follow the tutorial carefully. However, you will need the following before attempting Power Level IV:

1. *Media Market Guide* or similar publication that provides essential cost and rating data (*Media Market Guide* cost is approximately $130)

2. *MFP III* does all the calculations for you, but in some media you will need to calculate the average rating cost per point.

Endnote 1: Dennis Martin and Carla Lloyd: *Impact of Computer Software on Advertising Media Courses,* from presentation to annual conference of *Association for Education in Journalism & Mass Communications,* Boston, Summer 1991.

Endnote 2: Professor Janet Dooley: "Software You Can Use," article published in *American Advertising Federation Adviser,* Washington, D.C., February/March 1991.

ware package developed by Professor Dennis G. Martin, Brigham Young University, and R. Dale Coons, Vice-President Media Research/Director Information Services, Lintas: Campbell-Ewald.

a media planning book by Sissors and Bumba, outlines several of the questions planners must review in setting their media strategy.

In Figure 7–8 the media objectives are set forth in the boxes on the left, and the questions that lead from these objectives to media strategies are noted in the boxes on the right. The approach can be most helpful to you in arriving at meaningful strategies as you set media goals for your advertising campaign. Note that two of the boxes deal with reach, frequency, and continuity—the fourth box, "What balance of reach to frequency is needed?" and the eighth, "Which kind of scheduling patterns suits our plans?"

Along with these areas of media goals, Sissors and Bumba point out other important considerations in formulating media objectives:

☐ Competitors' use of media
☐ Influence of our brand's creative strategy

FIGURE 7–8   QUESTIONS TO CONSIDER IN SETTNG MEDIA OBJECTIVES

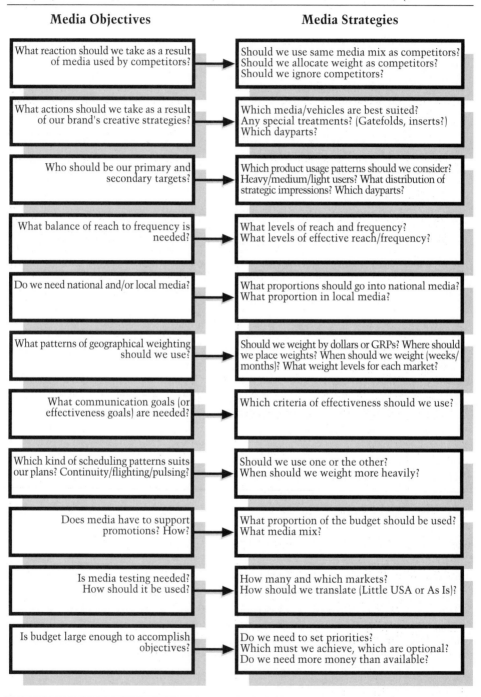

Media Objectives	Media Strategies
What reaction should we take as a result of media used by competitors?	Should we use same media mix as competitors? Should we allocate weight as competitors? Should we ignore competitors?
What actions should we take as a result of our brand's creative strategies?	Which media/vehicles are best suited? Any special treatments? (Gatefolds, inserts?) Which dayparts?
Who should be our primary and secondary targets?	Which product usage patterns should we consider? Heavy/medium/light users? What distribution of strategic impressions? Which dayparts?
What balance of reach to frequency is needed?	What levels of reach and frequency? What levels of effective reach/frequency?
Do we need national and/or local media?	What proportions should go into national media? What proportion in local media?
What patterns of geographical weighting should we use?	Should we weight by dollars or GRPs? Where should we place weights? When should we weight (weeks/months)? What weight levels for each market?
What communication goals (or effectiveness goals) are needed?	Which criteria of effectiveness should we use?
Which kind of scheduling patterns suits our plans? Continuity/flighting/pulsing?	Should we use one or the other? When should we weight more heavily?
Does media have to support promotions? How?	What proportion of the budget should be used? What media mix?
Is media testing needed? How should it be used?	How many and which markets? How should we translate (Little USA or As Is)?
Is budget large enough to accomplish objectives?	Do we need to set priorities? Which must we achieve, which are optional? Do we need more money than available?

Source: Jack Z. Sissors and Lincoln Bumba, *Advertising Media Planning,* 4th ed. (Lincolnwood, Ill.: NTC Business Books, 1993), Figure 1–3, p. 11.

☐ Target or targets (primary versus secondary) of the media plan
☐ National versus local media
☐ Geographic weighting of media effort
☐ Influence of communication goals
☐ Relation of media to sales promotion
☐ Need for media testing
☐ Influence of budget size

By carefully thinking through all of these variables, the media planner can arrive at a realistic establishment of the media objectives for the plan at hand.[15]

IDENTIFYING TARGET AUDIENCES

The target audience—those people advertisers want to reach—is at the very heart of an advertising campaign. Identifying that audience is an important strategy that requires first selecting prospect groups and target markets.[16]

Prospect groups include individuals who have some likelihood of purchasing a particular product. Planners want to identify anyone who might be a prospect for purchasing a brand within a product category. Because this group is so diverse, nonspecific, and generally large, we usually need tighter criteria for targeting.

Target markets is the term used to identify the geographic locations of customers and prospects. The geographic locations might include a region of the country (say, the Southeast), a specific state (Georgia) or city (Atlanta), or various other geographic boundaries (for example, a metropolitan or county area, a specific ZIP Code, and the like).

Jugenheimer, Barban, and Turk define target audiences succinctly: "*Target audiences* are certain prospect groups, living in the selected target markets, who are identified for special advertising emphasis. Media planners and buyers must then select the media vehicles that best expose these target audiences to the advertising message."[17] Thus, it is the identification of target audiences that becomes a critical area of focus for media strategy.

Variables for Profiling Target Audiences

Profiling target audiences within a media plan typically is done in terms of several types of variables: (1) demographic, (2) psychographic, (3) lifestyle, (4) product/brand usage, and (5) geodemographic. These variables can be used singly or in assorted combinations.

Demographics Identifying a target audience by demography is one of the most common methods used in media planning, primarily because there is extensive information available on media audiences. The major syndicated media research firms, such as MRI and SMRB, provide a large number of demographic characteristics. Typical demographic variables used in many media situations include age, gender, income, education, and occupation. Thus, we might find a targeting strategy that states:

The primary targeted audience is women, between the ages of 25 and 34. This primary target is weighted 75 percent.

A secondary target is women, between the ages of 18 and 24, which is weighted 25 percent.

Such a targeting profile shows precisely to whom the planner wants the media effort directed. In this example, there are actually two targets—women 25 to 34 and 18 to 24—and weights are assigned (75 percent and 25 percent) to each. Such a targeting definition permits the media buyer to execute the plan as efficiently as possible. If the plan consisted solely of magazines, for example, the buyer would search mainly for those magazines that most effectively provided audiences of women in these age groups. (Do keep in mind that most media vehicles cannot deliver an audience with absolutely no waste coverage— even direct mail cannot do this—so the idea is to make buys that are as *optimal* as possible.) The readership of specific magazines by women according to four age groupings appears as a page from an MRI report in Figure 7–9.

Psychographics   A somewhat newer approach to targeting media audiences involves identification of prospects according to behavioral characteristics, or psychographics. In measuring the psychographic profile of consumer groups, the researcher attempts to classify people according to such things as their common beliefs, opinions, interests, personalities, and behaviors. For example, some people might be classified as "economy minded," others as "impulsive" (in their shopping behavior), and yet others as "experimenters."

The idea behind such groupings is that a person's shopping behavior is more influenced by sociopsychological factors than it is by their demographic characteristics. Some limitations, though, in using psychographics in media decisions are (1) the research used to detect psychographic traits is questionable in terms of its reliability, and (2) a lot of data about *media* usage is not currently available. Nevertheless, advertisers and advertising agencies today are experimenting with behavioral approaches to improve their media-planning processes. The Leo Burnett advertising agency is using an innovative approach, according to an article in *Advertising Age:*

> **Behavioral segmentation:** *An approach that flips the traditional media-planning process by first finding the target audience, then finding the reasons and motivations for their purchase and usage patterns. . .*
>
> *Burnett uses a proprietary tool called Buyer Strategy Detection to sort consumers and non-consumers of a brand.*
>
> *"In the past, we typically boiled down who was using the product to big groups, like women 25–54—and said, well, here's what people think, then here's what they do," Ms. Spittler [Jane Spittler, vice-president and director of media research at Leo Burnett] says. "But behavior is what we want to affect."[18]*

Lifestyles   According to Jugenheimer, Barban, and Turk, "Lifestyle profiles are intended to reflect the consumer's priorities—that is, they measure commitment of time, money, and energy to activities, interests, and viewpoints. To gain perspective, lifestyle surveys cover all sorts of things we do and care about."[19] Some examples of lifestyle profiling are:

☐ Activities (such as sports, recreation, and entertainment)

☐ Preferences (such as social causes and political perspective)

☐ Interests (such as music, books, hobbies, and the like)

FIGURE 7–9 MEDIAMARK RESEARCH INC. (MRI) PROVIDES MAGAZINE READERSHIP ACCORDING TO DEMOGRAPHIC CHARACTERISTICS

BASE: WOMEN	TOTAL U.S. '000	18-24 A '000	B % DOWN	C % ACROSS	D INDEX	25-34 A '000	B % DOWN	C % ACROSS	D INDEX	35-44 A '000	B % DOWN	C % ACROSS	D INDEX	45-54 A '000	B % DOWN	C % ACROSS	D INDEX
All Women	96399	12883	100.0	13.4	100	22335	100.0	23.2	100	19151	100.0	19.9	100	12912	100.0	13.4	100
American Baby	2698	682	5.3	25.3	189	1399	6.3	51.9	224	438	2.3	16.2	82	*95	.7	3.5	26
American Health	2368	*135	1.0	5.7	43	*486	2.2	20.5	89	732	3.8	30.9	156	413	3.2	17.4	130
American Legion	1520	*21	.2	1.4	10	*110	.5	7.2	31	*267	1.4	17.6	88	*294	2.3	19.3	144
American Way	446	*72	.6	16.1	121	*77	.3	17.3	75	*98	.5	22.0	111	*101	.8	22.6	169
Architectural Digest	2123	*277	2.2	13.0	98	410	1.8	19.3	83	626	3.3	29.5	148	*369	2.9	17.4	130
Audubon	1182	*64	.5	5.4	41	*321	1.4	27.2	117	*302	1.6	25.5	129	*136	1.1	11.5	86
Baby Talk	2107	867	6.7	41.1	308	737	3.3	35.0	151	*216	1.1	10.3	52	*207	1.6	9.8	73
Barron's	*354	*104	.8	-	-	*33	.1	-	-	*36	.2	-	-	*89	.7	-	-
Bassmaster	577	*127	1.0	22.0	165	*224	1.0	38.8	168	*125	.7	21.7	109	*35	.3	6.1	45
Better Homes & Gardens	26515	2736	21.2	10.3	77	6010	26.9	22.7	98	6405	33.4	24.2	122	3736	28.9	14.1	105
BHG/LHJ Combo (Gr)	42754	4001	31.1	9.4	70	9264	41.5	21.7	94	10500	54.8	24.6	124	6291	48.7	14.7	110
Black Enterprise	957	*96	.7	10.0	75	*255	1.1	26.6	115	*323	1.7	33.8	170	*114	.9	11.9	89
Bon Appetit	3973	*334	2.6	8.4	63	758	3.4	19.1	82	993	5.2	25.0	126	677	5.2	17.0	127
Bride's and Your New Home	3867	1573	12.2	40.7	304	922	4.1	23.8	103	610	3.2	15.8	79	*464	3.6	12.0	90
Business Week	1836	*317	2.5	17.3	129	491	2.2	26.7	115	543	2.8	29.6	149	*153	1.2	8.3	62
Byte	*477	*114	.9	-	-	*104	.5	-	-	*144	.8	-	-	*60	.5	-	-
Cable Guide/TV Time (Gr)	9905	2100	16.3	21.2	159	2627	11.8	26.5	114	2237	11.7	22.6	114	1386	10.7	14.0	104
Car and Driver	732	*194	1.5	26.5	198	*296	1.3	40.4	175	*124	.6	16.9	85	*64	.5	8.7	65
Car Craft	*152	*20	.2	-	-	*37	.2	-	-	*44	.2	-	-	*12	.1	-	-
Colonial Home	1906	*225	1.7	11.8	88	*384	1.7	20.1	87	513	2.7	26.9	135	*243	1.9	12.7	95
Conde Nast Limited (Gr)	21312	4689	36.4	22.0	165	5267	23.6	24.7	107	4652	24.3	21.8	110	2977	23.1	14.0	104
Conde Nast Traveler	883	*51	.4	5.8	43	*214	1.0	24.2	105	*234	1.2	26.5	133	*152	1.2	17.2	129
Conde Nast Women (Gr)	31339	11000	85.4	35.1	263	8189	36.7	26.1	113	5759	30.1	18.4	93	3638	28.2	11.6	87
Consumers Digest	2355	*244	1.9	10.4	78	*418	1.9	17.7	77	679	3.5	28.8	145	*393	3.0	16.7	125
Cooking Light	2516	*158	1.2	6.3	47	579	2.6	23.0	99	521	2.7	20.7	104	587	4.5	23.3	174
Cosmopolitan	11949	3483	27.0	29.1	218	3493	15.6	29.2	126	2495	13.0	20.9	105	1161	9.0	9.7	73
Country Home	5151	*569	4.4	11.0	83	1338	6.0	26.0	112	1392	7.3	27.0	136	781	6.0	15.2	113
Country Living	8018	*721	5.6	9.0	67	1823	8.2	22.7	98	2118	11.1	26.4	133	1524	11.8	19.0	142
Country Music	2529	*377	2.9	14.9	112	720	3.2	28.5	123	*490	2.6	19.4	98	*427	3.3	16.9	126
Delta's SKY Magazine	649	*169	1.3	26.0	195	*90	.4	13.9	60	*124	.6	19.1	96	*112	.9	17.3	129
Discover	2105	*437	3.4	20.8	155	541	2.4	25.7	111	*349	1.8	16.6	83	*237	1.8	11.3	84
Disney Channel Magazine	3977	*494	3.8	12.4	93	1419	6.4	35.7	154	1194	6.2	30.0	151	*470	3.6	11.8	88
Ebony	6374	1217	9.4	19.1	143	1841	8.2	28.9	125	1494	7.8	23.4	118	754	5.8	11.8	88
Elle	3595	1478	11.5	41.1	308	899	4.0	25.0	108	562	2.9	15.6	79	*425	3.3	11.8	88
Endless Vacation	908	*81	.6	8.9	67	*72	.3	7.9	34	*324	1.7	35.7	180	*111	1.4	19.9	149
Entertainment Weekly	2095	*626	4.9	29.9	224	581	2.6	27.7	120	*530	2.8	25.3	127	*97	.8	4.6	35
Esquire	1203	*168	1.3	14.0	104	*355	1.6	29.5	127	*300	1.6	24.9	126	*132	1.0	11.0	82
Essence	3710	811	6.3	21.9	164	975	4.4	26.3	113	994	5.2	26.8	135	*424	3.3	11.4	85
Family Circle	23529	2087	16.2	8.9	66	4823	21.6	20.5	88	5436	28.4	23.1	116	4203	32.6	17.9	133
Family Circle/McCall's (Gr)	39715	3979	30.9	10.0	75	8068	36.1	20.3	88	8926	46.6	22.5	113	6839	53.0	17.2	129
Family Handyman	1232	*80	.6	6.5	49	*267	1.2	21.7	94	*263	1.4	21.3	107	*290	2.2	23.5	176
Field & Stream	3318	*407	3.2	12.3	92	934	4.2	28.1	121	883	4.6	26.6	134	*437	3.4	13.2	98
First For Women	5362	1220	9.5	22.8	170	1803	8.1	33.6	145	1220	6.4	22.8	115	801	6.2	14.9	112
Flower & Garden	2890	*192	1.5	6.6	50	*579	2.6	20.0	86	625	3.3	21.6	109	*539	4.2	18.7	139
Flower & Grdn/Workbench (Gr)	3877	*216	1.7	5.6	42	793	3.6	20.5	88	951	5.0	24.5	123	716	5.5	18.5	138
Food & Wine	1968	*286	2.1	13.5	101	546	2.4	27.7	119	466	2.4	23.7	119	*361	2.8	18.3	137
Forbes	1378	*356	2.8	25.8	193	*203	.9	14.7	64	*325	1.7	23.6	119	*172	1.3	12.5	93
Fortune	1387	*230	1.8	16.6	124	*374	1.7	27.0	116	*300	1.6	21.6	109	*200	1.5	14.4	108
4 Wheel & Off Road	*384	*104	.8	-	-	*80	.4	-	-	*137	.7	-	-	*31	.2	-	-
Glamour	10108	3287	25.5	32.5	243	2881	12.9	28.5	123	1884	9.8	18.6	94	1125	8.7	11.1	83
Golf Digest	1392	*245	1.9	17.6	132	*388	1.7	27.9	120	*331	1.7	23.8	120	*109	.8	7.8	58
Golf Digest/Tennis (Gr)	2169	*458	3.6	21.1	158	582	2.6	26.8	116	535	2.8	24.7	124	*187	1.4	8.6	64
Golf Illustrated	750	*77	.6	10.3	77	*272	1.2	36.3	157	*196	1.0	26.1	132	*76	.6	10.1	76
Golf Magazine	1192	*99	.8	8.3	62	*316	1.4	26.5	114	*305	1.6	25.6	129	*123	1.0	10.3	77
Good Housekeeping	25099	2410	18.7	9.6	72	6051	27.1	24.1	104	5564	29.1	22.2	112	3868	30.0	15.4	115
Gourmet	3137	*281	2.2	9.0	67	592	2.7	18.9	81	753	3.9	24.0	121	562	4.4	17.9	134
GQ (Gentlemen's Quarterly)	1758	*808	6.3	46.0	344	*479	2.1	27.2	118	*295	1.5	16.8	84	*153	1.2	8.7	65
Guns & Ammo	801	*187	1.5	23.3	175	*371	1.7	46.3	200	*187	1.0	23.3	118	*13	.1	1.6	12
Hachette Magazine Ntwk (Gr)	32446	5258	40.8	16.2	121	7547	33.8	23.3	100	7102	37.1	21.9	110	4970	38.5	15.3	114
Hachette Men's Package (Gr)	4090	*622	7.2	22.5	169	1265	5.7	30.9	133	859	4.5	21.0	106	635	4.9	15.5	116
Harper's Bazaar	2566	*586	4.5	22.8	171	*560	2.5	21.8	94	472	2.5	18.4	93	*401	3.1	15.6	117
Hearst Combo Power (Gr)	37734	3882	30.1	10.3	77	9089	40.7	24.1	104	8721	45.5	23.1	116	5642	43.7	15.0	112
Hearst Home Delivery (Gr)	17908	1549	12.0	8.6	65	3952	17.7	22.1	95	4620	24.1	25.8	130	3147	24.4	17.6	131
HG (House & Garden)	4633	*322	2.5	7.0	52	1132	5.1	24.4	105	1190	6.2	25.7	129	725	5.6	15.6	117
Home	3452	*489	3.8	14.2	106	830	3.7	24.0	104	906	4.7	26.2	132	513	4.0	14.9	111
Home Mechanix	636	*35	.3	5.5	41	*166	.7	26.1	113	*148	.8	23.3	117	*151	1.2	23.7	177
Hot Rod	1096	*557	4.3	50.8	380	*203	.9	18.5	80	*203	1.1	18.5	93	*87	.7	7.9	59
House Beautiful	5623	*334	2.6	5.9	44	1080	4.8	19.2	83	1420	7.4	25.3	127	976	7.6	17.4	130
Hunting	*504	*18	.1	-	-	*161	.7	-	-	*157	.8	-	-	*85	.7	-	-
Inc.	661	*193	1.5	29.2	218	*68	.3	10.3	44	*265	1.4	40.1	202	*88	.7	13.3	99
Inside Sports	555	*144	1.1	25.9	194	*119	.5	21.4	93	*118	.6	21.3	107	*69	.5	12.4	93
Jet	4912	1043	8.1	21.2	159	1170	5.2	23.8	103	1129	5.9	23.0	116	692	5.4	14.1	105
Kiplinger's Personal Finance	974	*42	.3	4.3	32	*128	.6	13.1	57	*134	.7	13.8	69	*256	2.0	26.3	196
Knapp Signature Coll. (Gr)	6096	*611	4.7	10.0	75	1168	5.2	19.2	83	1619	8.5	26.6	134	1046	8.1	17.2	128
Ladies' Home Journal	16239	1265	9.8	7.8	58	3254	14.6	20.0	86	4095	21.4	25.2	127	2555	19.8	15.7	117
Life	10363	2107	16.4	20.3	152	2718	12.2	26.1	113	2429	12.7	23.4	118	1217	9.6	11.9	89
Mademoiselle	6053	2613	20.3	43.2	323	1403	6.3	23.2	100	1035	5.4	17.1	86	*521	4.0	8.6	64
McCall's	16186	1892	14.7	11.7	87	3245	14.5	20.0	87	3490	18.2	21.6	109	2636	20.4	16.3	122
Men's Fitness	*149	*5	-	-	-	*38	.2	-	-	*59	.3	-	-	*34	.3	-	-
Metropolitan Home	1565	*147	1.1	9.4	70	*349	1.6	22.3	96	520	2.7	33.2	167	*224	1.7	14.3	107
Metro-Puck Comics Network	25853	3945	30.6	15.3	114	6084	27.2	23.5	102	4939	25.8	19.1	96	3584	27.8	13.9	103
Midwest Living	1349	*63	.5	4.7	35	*318	1.4	23.6	102	*273	1.4	20.2	102	*289	2.2	21.4	160
Mirabella	1618	*477	3.7	29.5	221	*351	1.6	21.7	94	*309	1.6	19.1	96	*286	2.2	17.7	132
Modern Bride	2880	1284	10.0	44.6	334	622	2.8	21.6	93	*467	2.4	16.2	82	*256	2.0	8.9	66

Source: Courtesy of Mediamark Research Inc. (MRI)

Identifying target audiences according to lifestyle characteristics is similar to using psychographics, and the two approaches often are treated as one. By the same token, lifestyle research has the same limitations when used for media purposes.

Product/Brand Usage Profiling target audiences according to the usage level of a product category or specific brand is used to a great extent in media strategy. The method is as popular as defining by demography, and in fact the two variables typically are used together. Refer back to the MRI data in Figure 7–3. Three levels of cookie usage by female homemakers are shown: "heavy" users (who stated they use more than three boxes or packages in the past 30 days), "medium" users (two to three boxes/packages), and "light" users (less than two boxes/packages).

Note also that some demographic characteristics (education, age, and census region) of female homemaker cookie users are shown according to product usage levels (MRI also profiles a number of other demographic characteristics, but only a sample of these appear in the figure). We can use such data to provide an estimate of the *size* of a target audience and its *propensity* for using a product.

Thus, if we considered targeting our media to "Female Homemakers (FH), between the ages of 25 and 54, who are heavy users of ready-to-eat cookies," MRI estimates that such a target consists of 11,816,000 women (see column A under heavy users). These 11.816 million FH are 14 percent of all FH (11.816 million ÷ 84.728 million total FH × 100), 20 percent of FHs who use cookies (11.816 million ÷ 59.122 million FH who use cookies × 100), and 68 percent of all FH heavy users of cookies (11.816 million ÷ 17.366 million FH heavy users of cookies; note that the 68 percent is given in column B of the MRI table).

We also can note from the MRI data that this target has a greater propensity than average to use ready-to-eat cookies, since the index is 114 (that is, 14 percent above an average index of 100). Observing all of this information does not in itself tell us to whom to direct our media effort. Deciding the actual target audience is a decision the media planner must ultimately make. He or she will ask a host of questions about a possible target before making the final decision, including some of the following:

☐ Is the size of the target sufficient to meet marketing sales goals and advertising communication objectives?

☐ Can a large enough portion of the target audience be reached efficiently, with an adequate level of frequency?

☐ Is the possible target logical in regard to the strategy of competing brands? (Note in Figure 7–3 the sample data for four brands of Keebler cookies.)

☐ Does our media budget permit adequate delivery of messages to the possible target?

Geodemographics With media vehicles becoming more and more localized according to geography, it is logical that planners would attempt to combine geographical patterns with demographic characteristics. For example, many consumer magazines today offer an advertiser wide choices for geographical pinpointing of target markets. You can buy an advertisement that will appear only in a particular region of the country (say the Southwest), or a state (Texas), and some magazines will even permit a metropolitan area split (Dallas). Other media types long have been structured to permit localized buys—spot television and cable, spot radio, newspapers, and out-of-home media, to name a few.

A number of research services have been developed to meet the desire of planners to use geodemographics in profiling target audiences. Such services report a variety of profile characteristics, such as income, education, occupation, ethnic affiliation, population density, and type of housing. Information for such characteristics often is presented according to every ZIP Code in the United States.

Matching Target Audiences with Media Choices

Regardless of the variable or variables used to profile target audiences, the media planner ultimately must choose the target audience and then match that with available media. The difficulty in doing this is that information that permits a direct match often is not available. For example, if you target "economy-minded women ages 20 to 55" and decide to use outdoor posters in the 50 largest cities of the United States, you likely will not have much usable information on how well that target is delivered by outdoor advertising. Your rationale for such a strategy may have to be based on intuition and creative logic or through using informal surveys of possible prospects.

Matching is possible with the demographics, and product-usage information syndicated research services, like MRI and SMRB, provide media planners for defining target audiences. Figure 7–10 shows graphically how the matching process might proceed under such situations.

Thus, if you use a syndicated source to define your target in demographic terms, you will attempt to select media vehicles that most closely approximate the target description. This matching process is shown on the left side of the figure. When a target audience is defined in product-usage terms, two options for matching become available (see right side of the figure). The most direct approach is to match the target audience with media vehicles according to the exposure level of users. If data exist for such a match, the planner will likely use this option. Another less direct approach involves a two-step process: Seek the demographic profiles of media vehicle audiences and seek the demographic profiles of the various levels of users. Audience profiles are then matched with the profiles of product users.

According to Barban, Cristol, and Kopec, the less direct approach is desirable if the following conditions prevail:

(1) Information on product users' media exposure is not available; (2) creative strategy relies heavily on a knowledge of the target market's demographic characteristics; (3) demographics significantly influence other marketing elements, such as distribution; or (4) frequency of use is unknown as in the introduction of a new product, in which case the planner would focus on total usage in the product category as a basis for media-market matching.[20]

ESTABLISHING THE MEDIA MIX

Thus far, we have discussed three of the four key areas, or elements, of a media plan: assessing the marketing background, setting media objectives, and identifying target audiences. We now look to establishing the media mix by

FIGURE 7–10   APPROACHES TO MATCHING TARGET AUDIENCES WITH MEDIA CHOICES

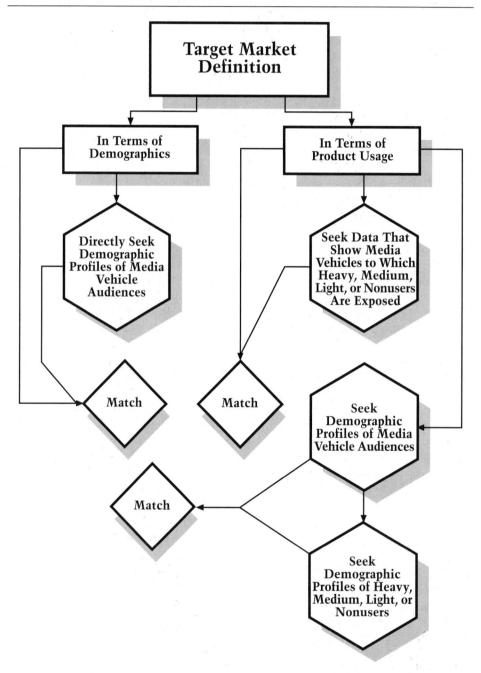

Source: Arnold M. Barban, Steven M. Cristol, and Frank J. Kopec, *Essentials of Media Planning: A Marketing Viewpoint,* 3rd. ed. (Lincolnwood, Ill.: NTC Business Books, 1993), Figure 3.8, p. 49.

deciding the different media types to include in the plan and their relative importance (see Figure 7–5 for a pie-chart graph of a media mix).

The balance of the media types for a plan logically flows from the marketing background, the media goals, and the target audiences to whom the plan is directed. Even if only a single media type is chosen—say, network television—there typically will be a mix. The mix might consist of the balance among television dayparts—that is, available segments in a 24-hour schedule. For example, a planner may spend 35 percent of the budget on daytime programs, 50 percent on evening programs, and 15 percent for late evening television. Or, even if the planner chooses only one daypart (say, evening programs), there might be a mix among different programming formats: situation comedies, action drama, and news magazines.

Factors to Consider for Media Weighting

There are several factors a planner likely will consider in determining the weighting of a particular set of media.

Target Audience A media planner typically will have to decide on different media based on the size and composition of the target audience or audiences to whom the media effort is directed. A narrow target might be reached effectively by a single media type, but an assortment of different media may be required to reach a diverse population. The planner and media buyer will usually look to audience data to see how different media vehicles deliver specific targeted audiences. For example, *Redbook* magazine may be quite efficient in reaching your target and thus would be a part of your mix. Yet, the number *Redbook* delivers may be only a small proportion of the total audience sought, and you will have to bring in several other magazine vehicles, say, *Ladies Home Journal* and *McCall's*.

Target Market/Geographic Region As mentioned earlier, a target market relates to the *geographic* location of customers and prospects. In developing a media mix, with appropriate weights among media types, the planner must look to the size and potential product or brand use of differing geographic areas. Some media types deliver audiences directly on a national scale, for example, network broadcast media (television, cable, and radio) and many magazines. However, other media types can be bought in a variety of geographical ways. Thus, daily newspapers are available in more than 1,500 local cities, television can be purchased on more than 1,300 individual stations in around 230 markets in the United States, and so forth.

A planner must take into account the various potentials of certain geographic areas in arriving at media weights. Consider for some particular product category the following information about product usage by major marketing regions:

Region	Number of Users of the Product Category	Index of Product Users
Northeast	22 million	89
East Central	13 million	83
West Central	22 million	119
South	37 million	111
Pacific	17 million	89

The South is the largest region in terms of product users, 37 million. Also note that the relative use of this product in the South is above average (the index of 111 indicates an 11 percent above average use). This information might suggest to a planner to add some extra media effort to southern markets. Yet, the planner also will note that all five regions have sizable numbers of users (the East Central is the lowest but has 13 million product users), and none of the regions is dramatically above or below average (index ranges from 83 to 119). In the final analysis, interpreting such data is subjective, and a planner's decision must be justified on the basis of the analysis and intrinsic logic.

Timing Pattern The weighting of media types also must take into account the continuity, or timing, pattern for the plan. If timing involves pulsing, with media effort varying from period to period, the choice of media types and vehicles likely will vary according to the period. For example, if you are using a media mix of network television (65 percent of budget) and national magazines (35 percent of budget), you might use both media types during peak periods but only one of the two types at the low periods. Such strategy, of course, will be reflected in the media objectives as well.

The interaction of the timing pattern with media weights is discussed by Barban, Cristol, and Kopec as follows:

> *Any evaluation of the alternative strategies of continuous advertising, flighting, and pulsing should address the following considerations beyond the omnipresent budget constraints: (1) seasonal sales skews, (2) repurchase cycle, (3) product life cycle, (4) competitive advertising patterns and level, (5) reach and frequency objectives, and (6) the desire to dominate a medium (relative to competition).[21]*

Media Types A fourth factor in weighting decisions of necessity involves the media types used in the plan. You must decide the relative amount of emphasis to place on the various media types used. Even if only one media type is used, there are weighting considerations within the single type (for example, weight among television or radio dayparts, different classes of magazines, and the like).

One of the difficulties in making such decisions is the differential costs associated with each medium. A $1 million schedule of television and newspaper ads is different from a $1 million schedule of, say, radio and newspaper ads. Although the same amount of money in each mix is allocated to newspapers, newspapers are more important in the mix with television than with radio—$1 million of radio commercials will provide a much greater level of message repetition than $1 million invested in television. Thus, by comparison, newspapers will appear to have more impact in the television-newspaper mix than in the radio-newspaper mix. In the final analysis, however, these decisions are subjective, but with a goal of effectively matching the vehicles of each media type with the target audiences.

Linking the Media Mix with Other Strategies

Although there are countless ways to compose a media mix, two quite varied approaches delineate the situation. Media mix strategies can be viewed as being either concentrated or assorted.

A *concentrated* mix is one in which you typically use a single media type, say, network television. You also can think of a concentrated mix as including one or a very limited number of vehicles within a media type (say, only *Sports Illustrated* as your magazine choice).

Concentration provides some of the following benefits:

effect on competitors — by focusing your media effort in a very limited way, there is a strong chance of dominating that medium relative to competition. Thus, your advertising likely will have greater impact in the minds of consumers exposed to that medium or vehicle.

effect on dealers — by limiting media buys, dealers may readily note your advertising and be impressed by its concentrated effort. Perhaps you have chosen to put most of your money into a single vehicle—say, an important miniseries on television or a blockbuster event such as a Super Bowl game. This may have a desirable effect on the retailers and wholesalers in the channel of distribution.

effect on media — by concentrating your media money in a single type, and a few vehicles, you often will gain a negotiating advantage with the media. They may be more inclined to offer better prices or merchandising help because you are spending the bulk of your media dollars with them.

effect on production costs — there likely will be certain economies of scale associated with a concentrated media buy. If you use both television and magazines, for example, the cost to produce commercials and advertisements will be greater than if you used a single media type. The same may be true if you spread your vehicle buys over a large base.

An *assorted* mix is using several media types in the media mix by spreading dollars across a large base of media opportunities. Certain situations may more logically warrant this approach than a concentrated one. For example, if a target audience is subdivided into several components, you will be more likely to use an assortment of media. A primary target of "working mothers" and a secondary target of "working mothers' children," for example, may logically break down into magazines for the primary target and Saturday morning television for the secondary.

Assorted mixes can result in some of the following advantages:

effect on target audiences — with many media types today, especially some of the nontraditional media, focusing on increasingly smaller audience segments, an assortment of media facilitates delivering different messages to different people. The more that targeted audiences are split, the more likely this approach will be used.

effect on message content — if you would like to communicate with the same prospects but in different psychological contexts, assortment makes sense. This approach might be used where there is a lengthy period through which messages take a prospect through the communication cycle, from initial awareness of a brand to getting a prospect to intend to make a brand purchase. Each of these stages may best be presented in different media.

effect on reach and frequency goals — whereas a concentrated mix often results in frequency being more easily attainable than reach, an assorted approach can affect both. Most typically, however, assortment translates into reach being extended beyond that which a concentrated mix provides. Because there are heavy and light users for each medium, adding a second (or third or fourth) medium will usually extend the reach of a single medium. For example, you may get a reach of 75 percent against the target with a network television buy. By shifting some of the money spent in television to magazines, the television reach may go down somewhat, but the combined television-magazine delivery may increase to, say, 80 percent.

The effect of an assortment on frequency comes about through a balancing of exposure opportunities. In some concentrated media schedules, frequency exposures are particularly high at the low and high ends of the distribution. In other words, the number of the target audiences exposed is relatively large for those who get one and two exposures only, as well as by those getting the largest possible number of exposures. If additional media are added, the extremes of the exposure distribution usually are reduced, with a corresponding increase in the midrange exposures. This process smooths out the overall frequency distribution and may result in a more effective achievement of media objectives.

CONSIDERING OTHER MEDIA FACTORS

The major considerations in developing a media plan consist of assessing the marketing background, setting media objectives, identifying target audiences, and establishing the media mix. Media planners should also consider tactics, contingency plans, and alternatives, as well as the rationale, integration, and summary of the plan. These elements, each in its own way, are essential to making sure that the plan works. Our discussions of these considerations are of necessity relatively brief, and we encourage readers to refer to the sources indicated for further understanding.

Tactical Execution of Media Strategy

Even if your media strategy is perfect for the situation, you will not get the desired results if the plan is not properly executed.[22] And the fact is that the tactical execution of media strategy is a time-consuming and detailed process. We usually refer to the development of media strategy as media planning, which contrasts with media buying, or tactics. Let's look at some of the key things involved in media tactics.

A successful media buyer has a set of skills that permits efficient execution of a plan. Included are such things as (1) a clear and careful understanding of media audiences, including the sources that provide audience information along with the strengths and limitations of such data; (2) the ability to estimate media costs in advance of actual purchasing; (3) a thorough knowledge of computer hardware and especially software, which is becoming more and more prevalent in the media field, even among very small advertising organizations; (4) a capacity for negotiating media buys, because very few media vehicles today simply list their prices and expect a buyer to pay the card rate; and (5) the ability to monitor media buys on a postanalysis basis to determine if the original estimates of vehicle delivery were accurate and to use such feedback as the basis for future improvement of the process.

Once workable media objectives are set, target audiences identified, including perhaps a multiple target with relative weights among the units, and a media mix is proposed, along with the necessary weighting of the various media types and components, all of this strategy must be executed. To do this, a media buyer goes through a matching process with the aim of arriving at the most efficient buys possible. Let's look at an example: Suppose the media strategy for Milky Way II—a reduced-calorie version of regular Milky Way candy bars—has the following plan elements:

☐ Media objectives are set in order to achieve high-reach and medium-frequency levels during the first four-month period of the campaign (called the introduction). The remaining eight months of the campaign are directed toward achieving a good level of brand loyalty and purchase intention by focusing on high levels of frequency with medium levels of reach.
☐ The target audience for Milky Way II is
  Primary (weighted 75 percent): young adults ages 18 to 24
  Secondary (weighted 25 percent): mothers of children ages 5 to 12
☐ The media mix consists of
  Young-adult magazines, weighted 75 percent of budget
  Late-night television, weighted 25 percent of budget

The media buyer with this information would proceed to do several things. First, he or she would decide which media vehicles within magazines and on late-night television should be purchased. Should the buyer purchase *Cosmopolitan, Elle, Glamour, Rolling Stone, Mademoiselle,* or *Sports Illustrated,* or, more likely, some combination of these or other magazines? For late-night television, will the *Late Show with David Letterman* suffice, or should others be considered? When making these decisions as efficiently as possible, the buyer should try to match audience delivery of vehicles with the audiences targeted.

Second, the buyer would consider the media *units* to be purchased: 1) Should full-page color advertisements be purchased, or 2) are 15-, 30-, or 60-second commercials needed? Not only does the buyer have to consider reach and frequency goals here, but he or she likely will discuss choice of units with the people who are writing and producing the advertisements and commercials. For Milky Way II maybe the thing to do is use large advertisements and lengthier commercials in the introductory four months to convey the uniqueness of the brand and follow this period with smaller ads and shorter commercials in order to increase frequency so as to get prospects to purchase Milky Way II. Thus, this latter consideration brings in the issue of the timing pattern and how this strategy is executed through a media schedule.

Contingencies and Alternative Plans

Some media plans include a separate section that specifies some of the unexpected conditions, or contingencies, that may occur during the life of the campaign and propose alternative plans to go into effect under such conditions.[23] Problems that often are considered in delineating contingencies include:

☐ *Changing economic conditions.* For certain products, the general economic condition affects sales. If we based our media plan on a particular forecast, what changes should we make if the economy turns downward (or upward)? Also to be considered is that economic changes usually affect different parts of the country and different cities in varying ways. A national plan may have to switch to a more localized one under unanticipated changes.

☐ *Changing sales results.* Regardless of how general economic conditions affect a product class, individual brands can go through sales changes that were not expected when the media plan was finalized. Sales expectations could decrease or increase. The key is to know how best to change a media plan if this occurs.

☐ *Changing competitive activity.* It usually is difficult to predict how competitors will behave in the future. Thus, the media activity of competitors may be a contingency area. For example, you might have planned a four-month introduction of Milky Way II on the premise that major competitors do not have similar brands. But, if Hershey Foods introduced a similar brand a month before your introduction, your timing pattern, among other things, would likely be affected. In turn, media objectives probably would need revision.

The logical follow-through to the consideration of contingencies is to formulate alternative plans. If a particular contingency occurs, there will be a specific alternative plan ready to go on short notice. The whole process of formulating contingencies and alternative plans is like a "what if?" game. "What if predicted economic conditions—estimated at a modest 2 percent growth next year—turn downward? What would our alternative plan be under these circumstances?"

Taking into account contingencies and alternatives, of course, complicates the entire planning process. If it is difficult to develop a single plan—and it usually is—what about having three or four alternatives? Yet, many media people believe that having other options available if something unforeseen occurs is worth the added effort.

Rationale for Decisions

A *rationale* for media decisions is essential because justification and analysis must be provided abundantly within the plan. The writer of the plan can either develop an overall defense of the strategy and tactics or, as is more typical, provide the rationale for each of the major areas of the plan.

For example, once you state the target audiences for the media portion of the campaign, the next logical thing would be to provide an argument—whether you call it a rationale, justification, or analysis—for that strategy. Wherever possible, include the most objective criteria and support possible for the decisions. With the identification of a target audience, for example, you might want to provide supporting data from an MRI or SMRB report. Regardless of the objective data available for supporting decisions, though, much of the rationale for media effort is based on judgment. Nevertheless, the judgment provided should be intrinsically logical and based on careful analysis.

Integration of Plan Elements

Closely related to the rationale for decisions is the need to be sure that all of the plan elements work together as a whole. That is, the plan must be fully and totally integrated. Think of integration as what you say in the plan about how it pulls together in a synergistic way and how the various elements of the plan are linked together in a logical and systematic manner.

For example, if your media objectives during a particular period of time emphasize reach—and to accomplish this you call for an assorted media mix—your plan should explicitly state this set of relationships or linkages. Do not leave it up to the reader of your plan to discern the integration of the plan. Instead, state exactly how the plan elements work together.

More specifically, say you've decided on a media goal of 90 percent reach and 7 average frequency in January to introduce a new campaign. Prime-time network television is the sole media type you will use. (Remember, GRPs = reach × average frequency; thus, you are buying 630 GRPs in January.) Perhaps in June, when you also use prime-time network television as your only medium choice, your goal is 75 percent reach and an average frequency of 12 (GRPs = 900). Your spending levels in January and June—owing to the fact that you are using the same medium and daypart for both months—should be related to the relative level of GRPs. The ratio between spending in June and in January is about 1.5 (900 ÷ 630 = 1.43). Recognizing this relationship between a set of media goals and the manner in which you allocate your budget is what is meant by integration.

Executive Summary

Most media plans include an executive summary, usually at the front of the plan and typically limited to one or two pages. (Indeed, not just media plans but most business reports include such a summary.) The purpose of an executive summary is to provide an overview of the strategy that is being recommended.

Because a variety of executives read a campaign plan, including the media recommendations, a summary helps explain the plan to those people who are not intimately involved with the details of the strategy. For example, if an advertising agency media planner presents the recommendations to the advertising director of the brand, an executive summary might be most useful

---

EXHIBIT 7-3   MEDIA PLAN CHECKLIST

You might want to look over the following questions after completing your media plan to see if the basics are included.

Main Components of the Plan

1. Does the **Marketing Background** section provide a good foundation for the strategic decisions that follow? Is the marketing analysis complete?
2. Are the **Media Objectives** stated clearly and precisely, in terms of reach, frequency, and continuity? Are the media objectives specific? Are the media objectives defended and integrated (coordinated) with other strategic decisions?
3. Is there a clear and careful identification of the **Target Audience** or audiences? If there is more than one target, is the weighting provided, along with a rationale? Is the targeting specific and based on MRI, SMRB, or similar data, and is the data correctly used? Is target-audience definition integrated and coordinated with other strategies?
4. Does the plan include a clear and careful statement of the **Media Mix** recommended? Is there good rationale for the Media Mix, and does it integrate and coordinate with all other strategic decisions? Are media weights provided and defended? In allocating dollars to the various media types, vehicles, and units, are correct cost figures used? Are the media vehicles and units bought adequately defended?

Mechanics of the Plan

1. Does the plan have a **Table of Contents,** including page numbers?
2. Does the plan have an **Executive Summary** that includes the specifics of
   a. Media objectives (reach and frequency levels for each time period of the plan)?
   b. Target audience or audiences, including the weighting?
   c. Media mix used, including weights?
3. Does the plan include a graph of the **Media Schedule,** with the total budget shown as well as each media type used?
4. Is the plan well written? Is it written in a clear and concise manner? Is effective use made of tables, graphs, and summaries?

---

to the marketing director. The marketing director would be able to see the overall strategies recommended, rather than have to read through everything to understand what is being proposed.

Although an executive summary varies according to the situation at hand, it should, at a minimum, include brief statements about

☐ The specific media objectives sought for the advertising
☐ The target audience, or audiences, to whom the plan is being directed
☐ The proposed media mix

An executive summary does not include the rationale and analysis that went into arriving at the recommendations. A reader of the summary who has questions about a particular part of a strategy recommendation can refer to the plan itself for the detailed rationale, justifications, and integration of plan elements.

Now that you have examined what it is that goes into the development of a media plan, you might find Exhibit 7–3 useful.

Media decisions are a critical part of every advertising effort and must be considered carefully by a campaign planner. Not only has the media function grown in importance over the past several years, but also the addition of nontraditional media has added greatly to the complexity of media selection.

The media planning task consists of examining a number of variables and deciding on a set of key strategies. The process usually begins with an assessment of the marketing background of the advertised brand or service. Available marketing research is examined, and, if information is lacking, primary research may be undertaken. Along with assessing research, the planner also will develop a clear understanding of the marketing mix variables. These mix variables constitute the strategy that has been formulated for the marketing of the brand or service.

Setting media objectives is essential to the success of any media effort as part of a campaign's plan. Without knowing exactly what you want to accomplish through your media strategy and tactics, the success or failure of the plan cannot be determined. Objectives include any number of goal-oriented activities, but the matter of a plan's reach, frequency, and continuity are universally included and must be carefully balanced.

The matter of identifying the target audience is essential if you are to match these targets with available choices. And, of course, the idea is to make the identification in the most cost-efficient way possible. Planners use different variables for the identification of audiences, including demographics, psychographics and lifestyles, product/brand usage, and geodemographics. Each approach has advantages and limitations.

Establishing a media mix involves a set of decisions about which media types to use and in what relative proportion. A host of factors are looked at in arriving at this decision, including the target audience to be reached, the geographic focus of the plan, the pattern of timing advertisements and commercials, and the assorted media types available for consideration.

Once a plan's strategies have been set, the plan must be executed through a number of tactical executions, mostly involving the buying of specific media vehicles and units. Some plans include a provision for contingencies, which in turn likely mean the development of alternatives if things do not go as planned.

ENDNOTES

[1] Arnold M. Barban, Steven M. Cristol, and Frank J. Kopec, *Essentials of Media Planning: A Marketing Viewpoint* (Chicago: Crain Books, 1976), v.

[2] Arnold M. Barban, Steven M. Cristol, and Frank J. Kopec, *Essentials of Media Planning: A Marketing Viewpoint,* 3rd ed. (Lincolnwood, Ill.: NTC Business Books, 1993), xi.

[3] Mike Drexler, "Dinosaurs Awake!" *Mediaweek* (May 9, 1994), 12.

[4] For a more extensive list of nontraditional media, see Jack Z. Sissors and Lincoln Bumba, *Advertising Media Planning,* 4th ed. (Lincolnwood, Ill.: NTC Business Books, 1993), 7.

[5] See, for example, "Setbacks on the Superhighway," *Advertising Age* (March 21, 1994): IM-2–IM-4, IM-14.

[6]For good insight into the changing world of media, see "Rethinking Media," *Advertising Age* (July 25, 1994): S-1–S-27.

[7]See, for example, Arnold M. Barban, Donald W. Jugenheimer, and Peter B. Turk, *Advertising Media Sourcebook*, 3rd ed. (Lincolnwood, Ill.: NTC Business Books, 1989); Donald W. Jugenheimer, Arnold M. Barban, and Peter B. Turk, *Advertising Media: Strategy and Tactics* (Dubuque, Iowa: WCB Brown & Benchmark, 1992), Chapter 5; Sissors and Bumba, *Advertising Media Planning*, 135–153.

[8]For a thorough review of marketing, see any principles of marketing textbook. For a view more directly related to media strategy, see, for example, Jugenheimer, Barban, and Turk, *Advertising Media*, Chapter 3, or Sissors and Bumba, *Advertising Media Planning*, Chapter 7.

[9]For a more detailed discussion, see Barban, Cristol, and Kopec, *Essentials of Media Planning*, Chapter 2. Also see Jugenheimer, Barban, and Turk, *Advertising Media*, Chapter 3.

[10]See, for example, Louis E. Boone and David L. Kurtz, *Contemporary Marketing,* 7th ed. (Fort Worth, Texas: The Dryden Press, 1992), 307–312.

[11]See Barban, Cristol, and Kopec, *Essentials of Media Planning*, 11–13.

[12]See Barban, Cristol, and Kopec, *Essentials of Media Planning*, 14–22.

[13]Dean M. Krugman, Leonard N. Reid, S. Watson Dunn, and Arnold M. Barban, *Advertising: Its Role in Modern Marketing*, 8th ed. (Fort Worth, Texas: The Dryden Press, 1994), 540. Also see this source, pages 540–544, for additional insight into public relations.

[14]See Barban, Cristol, and Kopec, *Essentials of Media Planning*, 16–20.

[15]For additional in-depth discussion of the setting of media objectives, see Barban, Cristol, and Kopec, *Essentials of Media Planning*, 58–67; Sissors and Bumba, *Advertising Media Planning*, 245–259; and Jugenheimer, Barban, and Turk, *Advertising Media*, Chapter 9.

[16]The discussion of these three terms is based on Jugenheimer, Barban, and Turk, *Advertising Media*, 186–187.

[17]Jugenheimer, Barban, and Turk, *Advertising Media*, 187.

[18]Julie Liesse, "Buying by the Numbers? Hardly," [Special Report: Rethinking Media] *Advertising Age* (July 25, 1994): S-16.

[19]Jugenheimer, Barban, and Turk, *Advertising Media*, 193.

[20]Barban, Cristol, and Kopec, *Essentials of Media Planning*, 49.

[21]Barban, Cristol, and Kopec, *Essentials of Media Planning*, 72.

[22]For additional readings about media tactics, see Jugenheimer, Barban, and Turk, *Advertising Media*, Chapter 11 (for scheduling execution), and Chapters 14–18.

[23]See Jugenheimer, Barban, and Turk, *Advertising Media*, 252–256.

Related Marketing Communications

To this point in the campaign planning process you have been building your campaign by carefully researching your target market and competition, setting marketing and advertising objectives, and developing creative and media plans that will accomplish those objectives for your client. Now we turn to those related marketing communication elements that will help you to integrate and extend your strategy. These marketing communication elements are sales promotion, public relations, and direct marketing.

DEVELOPING RELATED MARKETING COMMUNICATIONS

Your approach at this stage of campaign development should be to continue to think strategically. The success of your related marketing communications recommendations will depend on the degree to which you are able to integrate them with your advertising plan so that your target audience gets a consistent message and feel from every contact it has with your promotional activities. Consistency does not necessarily mean that all campaign materials must look alike. It does mean that the target audience members should receive messages and promotions that are consistent and carefully developed to reflect their past and present experiences with your client's product or service.

One of your key decisions will be how much emphasis to put on each element in the marketing communication mix. Although this is to a large degree a budget allocation and payout problem, there should be some good strategic rationale for how much you decide to spend in each promotional area. A place to start is to analyze your consumers in terms of where they are in the sales process or purchase cycle, what types of responses you are looking for from them, and how selective (that is, targeted) you want your strategy to be in light of the relative costs of your media and promotion alternatives.

Your analysis should begin with where your customers are in the sales process. If they are prospects who have yet to purchase your product, then you might have to improve their product knowledge through awareness-building communication such as advertising and public relations. You might also consider using sales promotion to induce them to try your product. People who have purchased your product in the past can be further analyzed according to how frequently they purchase and how much they buy each time out. They might also be good prospects for sales promotion to stimulate more frequent or larger purchases or targeted forms of direct marketing and personal selling. Direct marketing and personal selling can be more costly but might be cost-efficient in terms of the likely sales response of your prospects. For your loyal customers you might consider reinforcing types of promotion, such as public relations, to maintain your ongoing relationship with them. Figure 8–1 provides a three-axis matrix against which you can compare your marketing situation to determine the relative strategic weight to give to your marketing communication elements.

As a general rule, the more targeted your media and closer to actual sales you want the customers' responses to be, the more expensive per customer your marketing communications plan will be. The less targeted and further from sales (awareness, for example) you want the responses to be, the less expensive per customer your plan will be. However, the more expensive plan on a per prospect basis could be more cost-efficient overall if the targeted consumers are better prospects than those targeted by the other plan. Awareness is easier to achieve than sales, and exposing a large, undifferentiated audience to a message is less expensive per audience member than a more targeted effort to reach high-potential prospects. But a large proportion of the coverage of a broad-based awareness campaign can be wasted if most of the audience members are not good prospects for your product.

Your ability to develop an integrated marketing communications campaign depends on the quantity and quality of information you have about your target consumers. Let's assume for the sake of an example that you have been able to build a database of information from primary and secondary research sources, such as those covered in Chapters 2, 3, and 7. This database might include demographic, psychographic, geographic, and geodemographic characteristics about your target. Additionally, you should have information on purchase behavior and media usage. With this basic information you should be able to subdivide your market into consumer segments. At the simplest, you should be able to determine who are your best customers, who buys your product less frequently, who buys your competitors' brands, and who are the people who do not purchase the product at all.

Now your task is to determine how to employ available marketing communications elements to meet your objectives against the various identified consumer segments. Suppose you decide that to increase sales and gain market share you will have to retain current customers while influencing the less-frequent purchasers and competitors' customers to buy your brand. This strategic decision confronts you with three consumer segments, each with a different profile and purchase behavior pattern. Your potential target groups might be labeled and described as follows:

☐ **Our brand loyals.** These are our best customers who purchase a lot of our brand on a fairly regular basis. When our brand is not available, they will wait until it becomes available or go to another store to find it.

FIGURE 8-1 RESPONSE, COST, TARGET MATRIX

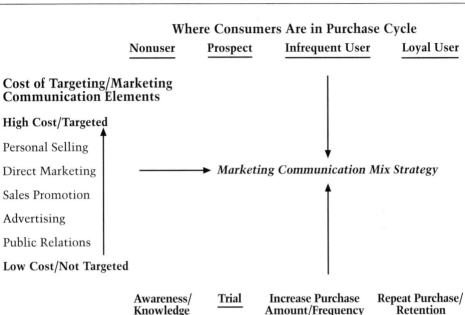

Where Consumers Are in Purchase Cycle

| Nonuser | Prospect | Infrequent User | Loyal User |

Cost of Targeting/Marketing Communication Elements

High Cost/Targeted

Personal Selling

Direct Marketing → *Marketing Communication Mix Strategy*

Sales Promotion

Advertising

Public Relations

Low Cost/Not Targeted

| Awareness/ Knowledge | Trial | Increase Purchase Amount/Frequency | Repeat Purchase/ Retention |

Response Desired to Marketing Communication Element

☐ **Brand switchers.** This is a group of less frequent purchasers of our brand who also buy our competitors' brands. They might switch brands for a change of pace or because of a promotional incentive, such as a price reduction, sweepstakes, or premium. They move around from brand to brand and are not loyal to any particular brand in the product category.

☐ **Their brand loyals.** These are also brand-loyal consumers but to our competitors' brands. They purchase a lot of our competitors' brands on a fairly regular basis. And they will shop around for those brands when they are not available in the stores where they typically shop.

This market situation can be reduced to one of retention of our brand loyals, building volume for our brand among switchers, and initiating trial and gaining some conversion among our competitors' loyals. This is a difficult marketing task that will require strategic differences in how we approach each consumer segment.

What might we do? As we look across our marketing communications options, we have to ask ourselves which combination of elements are best suited to meet our objectives for each segment. Also, we have to consider how to allocate our budget and activities against these segments. Sales-promotion incentives delivered through direct-marketing channels might be a consideration for building volume among switchers and initiating trial among their loyals. These same incentives, supported by image-oriented advertising, could also increase volume among our loyals while rewarding them for being our best customers. Special events and carefully placed public relations stories might also impress our loyals and convey the message that we really value their business (similar to Saturn's homecoming event in Spring Hill, Tennessee, to reward customer loyalty and celebrate its fifth anniversary in selling cars).

This marketing situation is probably unrealistic for most marketers because it is very difficult to dislodge your competitors' customers. It just costs too much money. However, the example demonstrates how marketing communications should be approached from a strategic perspective by considering your client's relationship with potential consumer segments as the starting point and then determining which mix of elements is most appropriate to stimulating the consumer responses desired. Tactical considerations concerning what the messages and activities will be come after the strategic integration of the marketing communications elements has been thought through.

The goal of integrating your marketing communications elements is summarized in the following American Association of Advertising Agencies' definition:

> **Integrated Marketing Communications:** *A concept of marketing communications that recognizes the added value in a program that integrates a variety of strategic disciplines, e.g., general advertising, direct response, sales promotion and public relations—and combines these disciplines to provide clarity, consistency and maximum communications impact.*[1]

The true integration of marketing communications can be compared to the work at an air traffic control tower. The elements of marketing communications are flights landing and taking off from an airport. Some jets have just completed their tasks, some need repair, and others are just starting out. Integrated marketing is accomplished by managing all of the elements so that they complement each other while allowing each to achieve its separate objectives.

Your integrated marketing communications program should be based on a clear-cut strategy for each of your target consumer segments. To help you build an integrated marketing communications campaign, we will discuss the major promotional elements advertisers and marketers consider when deciding how to approach their target audiences. The following sections focus on the use of sales promotion, public relations, and direct marketing to achieve your marketing and advertising campaign objectives. Exhibit 8–1 will give you some feel for the scope of the promotional activities available to you as you plan to extend the impact of your campaign by integrating them into your plan.

SALES PROMOTION

The rise in importance of sales promotion to marketing programs over the past 20 years highlights significant changes in the marketplace and the way marketers allocate their promotional dollars. Two decades ago it was not

---

EXHIBIT 8–1   PROMOTIONAL OPTIONS FOR EXTENDING YOUR CAMPAIGN

Sales Promotion

Consumer Promotions

Sampling, couponing, premiums, rebates and refunds, contests and sweepstakes, bonus packs, price-offs, and event sponsorships

Trade Promotions

Slotting allowances, off-invoice allowances, dating, free goods, price reductions, display and merchandising allowances, advertising allowances, count/recount allowances, point-of-purchase displays, cooperative advertising, sales contests, trade shows, and sales meetings

---

Public Relations

Product Publicity

News stories (new product introductions, dispelling misinformation, and the like), press kits, newsletters, pamphlets, brochures, press conferences, staged events such as celebrity appearances, event sponsorship and trade show support, annual reports, and information hotlines

Direct/Database Marketing

Direct mail, direct response advertising (delivered through all traditional advertising media), catalogs, infomercials, TV home shopping, telemarketing, and interactive computer services

---

unusual for the typical consumer products advertiser to spend almost 70 percent of its promotion budget on advertising. By 1981, the percentage of the promotion budget spent on advertising was down to 43 percent, and by 1992 it was down to 27 percent. In the same period of time, various types of sales promotion had grown from less than 30 percent to more than 70 percent of most consumer marketers' promotion budgets.[2] As an example, Leo Burnett USA and H. J. Heinz ended a 36-year relationship in 1994 because of Heinz's decision to reduce its advertising spending from more than $130 million to close to $40 million and putting more of its marketing budget into couponing, trade promotion, and price deals.[3] Advertising started to regain some of its lost ground in 1995 due to an improving economy. However, it is still too early to know if confidence in advertising can be restored to previous levels. The lessons learned from the period between the late 1970s to the 1990s will not soon be forgotten. The 1980s will always be the decade that saw a complete turnaround in emphasis away from advertising and toward sales promotion. What happened?

There are many possible explanations for how and why advertising gave way to sales promotion as the marketing communications element of choice. The late 1970s and early 1980s saw a tremendous increase in advertising clutter, making each ad or commercial less effective. At the same time, new technology in the form of the videocassette recorder (VCR) allowed consumers to tape their favorite shows and edit out the commercials. Television remote control devices added to the technological onslaught that gave consumers more control over TV viewing. Zapping, zipping, and channel surfing became the TV-viewing terminology to describe how viewers skipped around the TV channel landscape often avoiding TV commercials.

The price inflation of the 1970s made consumers more price sensitive. Marketers were also caught in a battle between keeping up with the inflationary rises in prices (to make a profit) while trying to offer consumers and retailers incentives for buying their products. During this decade marketers started to use trade promotions, which often came in the form of discounts to retailers, in return for extra or better shelf space or promotion support in the store's weekly advertising flyers and newspaper inserts. These promotional allowances and discounts became addicting and more entrenched as retailers gained power through size and increased technological sophistication. This newly acquired power allowed retailers to demand discounts and incentives from manufacturers who found themselves in an increasingly competitive marketplace.

Other marketplace forces were also at work during this period of time. Among them were:

1. More parity among brands in the same product category making sales promotion a point of differentiation.
2. A short-term managerial orientation that led to reliance on sales promotion to achieve short-run sales and profit objectives. Fierce competition among brand managers to get ahead created pressure to emphasize immediate rather than long-term results.
3. Consumers became more accepting of sales promotion incentives and perhaps had been taught to expect them.
4. Manufacturers became caught, to some extent, in a competitive situation where they were afraid to reduce their reliance on sales promotion while competitors continued to reap the short-term sales benefits of its use.[4]
5. The soft economic conditions of the early 1990s further reinforced a short-term outlook among manufacturers too uncertain about the future to return to a heavy reliance on advertising alone.

The main controversy surrounding the use of sales promotion has been the question of its long-term impact on brand equity. Marketers who would like to see a return to the day when advertising was king argue that promotions are simply a bribe to steal sales and market share at the expense of brand equity. The more you induce purchase through "deals," the argument goes, the less likely consumers can be persuaded of a preference for one brand over another based on tangible or intangible qualities promoted through advertising. Sales promotion experts counter with the fact that in a cluttered marketplace other aspects of the marketing program, such as shelf placement and in-store display, are important contributors to a brand's image, an important part of brand equity. Busy consumers, they add, have less time than ever to ponder and absorb the clutter of messages from typical national brand advertising.

The key argument for a primary role for sales promotion in marketing programs is that sales promotions provide companies the ability to combine short-term sales results with long-term equity building. Manufacturers are no longer in a situation where they can make a choice between the long-term equity-building strengths of advertising and the short-term sales-generating advantage of sales promotion. They simply have to be able to achieve both. Think of McDonald's as a prime example of this tug of war where hamburgers have to be sold systemwide day in and day out. And at the same time, McDonald's has to maintain its wholesome all-American family image so that the decision to eat there becomes routine for its target audience (mostly parents and their kids). One executive at McDonald's put it succinctly when he said that the company has to think like a retailer and act like a brand. The message here is that so does everybody else who wants to be successful in the changing marketplace. And the way to do this is through the successful integration of all aspects of your marketing and advertising programs.

SALES PROMOTION DEFINED

Sales promotion is the use of an incentive to buy a product that takes the form of either a price reduction or value-added offer.[5] Sales promotion activities can be divided into consumer-oriented and trade-oriented promotions.

Consumer-oriented promotions are targeted to the final consumers in the channel of distribution to induce them to buy your brand. Consumer-oriented promotions include product samples, coupons, premiums, rebates, contests and sweepstakes, bonus packs, price-offs, and event sponsorship. The goal of these promotions is to stimulate demand, usually at the retail level.[6]

Trade-oriented promotions, usually shortened to trade promotions, are aimed at distributors and retailers to influence them to carry a product and give it added emphasis in their effort to sell it to their customers. Trade promotions account for almost two-thirds of all sales promotions and half of the dollars spent on promotions and advertising combined.[7] The dollars taken away from advertising over the past 15 years have gone primarily to trade promotions. There is some evidence that trade promotions' share of marketing budgets is declining slightly in favor of consumer promotions and advertising. However, it is not clear if this is a trend or temporary blip in the cycle.

Manufacturers can choose from a number of trade promotion alternatives to try to induce distributors and retailers to push their products. Typically, they employ some combination of trade allowances, dealer contests, point-of-purchase displays, cooperative advertising, trade shows, and other incentive programs. The trade allowance is money given to distributors and retailers in return for preferential treatment. It has been the most widely used promotion and the most controversial. It is perceived by some as merely a payoff or bribe to the distributor for special consideration. And because the allowance often is taken from the advertising budget, this special treatment is sometimes used at the expense of equity-building consumer messages. The goal of a balanced campaign should be to incorporate the advantages of both trade promotions and advertising in gaining trade acceptance and stimulating consumer purchases. Exhibit 8–2 presents some of the more common types of trade spending.

To successfully incorporate promotions into a marketing communications campaign plan, it is important to know what type of objectives can reasonably be set for the sales promotion component of your marketing and advertising program.

SALES PROMOTION OBJECTIVES

Sales promotion objectives are always set with the bigger picture of the marketing plan in mind. As it is with all of the promotional elements of the marketing plan, the objectives for sales promotion are much more specific and focused than are the marketing objectives. Good sales promotion objectives are targeted and measurable as are all marketing, advertising, and promotion objectives. However, sales promotion objectives have the added characteristic of being directed specifically toward increasing the speed or frequency (sometimes referred to as sales velocity) with which consumers buy your brand. They are, among all of the marketing and promotion objectives that you set, the most focused on achieving a sales response.

As you think about where sales promotion fits into your campaign plan, here are some of the general types of goals you might have in mind for its use:

☐ *You can induce new customers to try your brand.* Samples, coupons, or refund offers can help move consumers toward consideration and eventual trial of your brand.

☐ *You can retain your current loyal customers and perhaps influence them to buy more of your brand.* Premiums such as recipes and calendars that provide ideas for new product uses can help to reinforce and increase usage of your brand.

☐ *You can increase the overall sales of your brand.* Special sizes, multiunit packaging, and premiums can be used as incentives to induce consumers to buy and use more of your product.

☐ *You can reinforce your advertising efforts by incorporating sales promotion into your campaign.* Contests and sweepstakes, for example, can generate consumer and trade involvement and excitement in a campaign.

☐ *Sales promotion activity can help to build trade support for a campaign.* The goal is to demonstrate to the trade your effort to stimulate sales, which is the retailers' primary motivation for considering carrying your brand.

☐ *Sales promotion support for a campaign can breathe excitement into the sales force for the brand at all levels of the distribution channel.* Contests, special displays, premiums, and price-off incentives can all provide a salesperson with an extra edge.

From this general sense of what sales promotion can do, you can start to think about the specific sales promotion objectives of your campaign. Sales promotion should be integrated into your campaign so that it reinforces and

---

EXHIBIT 8–2   A GLOSSARY OF WIDELY USED TRADE PROMOTION TERMS

A trade-speak-to-English glossary of some of the most common types of trade spending, translated by A.T. Kearney consultant Burt Flickinger III.

Off-invoice allowance: A per-case rebate paid to retailers when order is placed.

Billback: Additional money paid for retailers' display, ad or price cut.

Market development funds (MDFs): Money spent via a retailer to expand category sales; used to develop share in markets where category growth is high and a brand's share is embarrassingly low.

Brand development funds (BDFs): Similar to MDFs, this money pinpoints problems by brand rather than geography.

Category development funds (CDFs): Specifically drives a given category, supporting all brands at once.

Street money: Cash spent in the field, i.e., "at street level," to get more display.

Spiff money: Rewards brokers and buyers with everything from thermoses to TVs to Hawaiian vacations for "assist" in hitting case sales objectives.

Cooperative merchandising agreement (CMA): Annual incentive contract to get retailer to commit to ad, display or price feature for a brand for a time period.

Corporate sales program (CSP): An umbrella promotion across a marketer's total brand portfolio. Products often are shipped directly from the factory in ready-to-display pallets.

Producing plant allowance (PPAs): An incentive to retailers to buy full or half-truckloads direct from the factory. Saves manufacturers distribution costs.

Back haul allowances (BHAs): Money manufacturers pay retailers who'll send trucks to pick up shipments at manufacturer's own plant or distribution center.

Drop ship allowances (DSAs): Money to retailers who bypass the grocer's distribution center for preplanned orders or customized pallets.

Cross-dock or pedal runs: Cash incentives for placing full-pallet orders for four or five stores, distributed by a single truck. Marketer saves distribution costs.

Display-ready cases and pallets: Marketers pay retailers for using these cost-efficient shipments ready for immediate display.

Source: *Brandweek* (March 13, 1995): 32.

---

extends your advertising and other promotional efforts. As such, sales promotion not only adds an action-oriented component to your consumer campaign, but also provides a vehicle for reaching the trade and sales force. Trade objectives for sales promotion often include obtaining or improving shelf space and position, building inventories for your brand, gaining trade support in terms of display and advertising help, and generating enthusiasm for a new product introduction. A distributor's salespeople can be influenced to give your brand a higher selling priority and put more effort and enthusiasm behind selling it when they know that it is supported by a good promotional program.

Sales promotion objectives should be stated in the same concise terms as all the objectives that you write for your marketing communications plan (see Chapter 4 for more on writing objectives). They should be short and action-oriented. The results you expect in terms of sales, product trial, multiple purchases, or improving product display should be stated clearly and specifically. Sales promotion results, like all marketing communication elements, are expected to occur within a specific time frame that should be included in the objective. Your promotional programs and objectives should be single-minded and targeted to one market segment at a time. Do not ask too much from your sales promotion effort. It is unusual for one program to accomplish multiple objectives against different target audiences.

SALES PROMOTION TECHNIQUES

After you have set your objectives for sales promotion, you can start to think about specific techniques to use in implementing your plan. The simplest way to think of the options available is to divide them into consumer and trade promotions. Consumer promotions can then be grouped into the major types used by marketers, including sampling, couponing, premiums, contests and sweepstakes, refunds, bonus packs, price-off deals, and event sponsorship. Trade promotions take the form of different purchase and performance incentives and allowances that encourage the members of the distribution channel to carry, store, and promote your brand. Together, consumer and trade promotions become part of a push-pull strategy to move your brand through its channel of distribution to the final consumer. Consumer promotions pull the ultimate consumer into the store to buy your brand, and trade promotions push your product through the distribution channel to the retail outlet.

Consumer Promotions

Sampling is a highly effective but relatively expensive way to achieve a trial of a product. The expense comes from having to manufacture, inventory, and distribute special trial sizes of your product. However, it is a sound way to get your product in the consumers' hands at no charge and no risk to them. Sampling has gained favor with marketers because the amount of time in which a product has to succeed has dwindled, in some instances, from a year down to three months. Product trial, therefore, has become a more urgent objective to new product introductions than ever before. If you cannot get people to try your product, you can never achieve repeat purchase behavior, which is the lifeblood of business success.

Sampling can be accomplished through a number of different delivery systems. The most common distribution systems are placement in the store, delivery by mail or door-to-door placement, and inclusion with the package. In-store sampling can be done by placing the trial-size products in special point-of-purchase bins or displays. Sometimes a demonstrator is hired who can help customers to sample products such as new food items, cosmetics, or home appliances. This person can also provide additional product information and help deliver other promotional items, such as coupons.

Samples can be delivered to customers' homes by mail or through the use of delivery companies. Mail delivery can be an effective way to combine sampling with direct marketing to target consumers who are most likely to use your product. Descriptions of some of the target marketing companies that can help a marketer pinpoint the delivery of samples appear in Chapters 2 and 3 and the direct marketing section of this chapter.

Samples may be attached to or included along with another of a company's products. This is a good method when the market for original purchase is also the market for the new product being sampled. Other distribution possibilities include magazine and newspaper distribution for small products and sample packs, such as those given out to college students at the beginning of a new school year. Organizations such as Welcome Wagon that greet newcomers to a neighborhood, town, or city are also potential distributors for your sampling program.

Sampling is not without its disadvantages. Remember that the same device that can speed the acceptance of a new product can also spell quick demise for an inferior product. In addition, in-store sampling (which is usually the most desired form of sampling because it is so close to the point of purchase) requires the support of the trade that can result in additional fees and allowances to keep them happy and behind your program. You have to weigh the method you select to deliver the sample against the expense of doing so. Your objectives are always your best standard for evaluating the viability of a sampling method, but so is your budget. Make sure that the payoff is worth the expense.

Couponing is a promotional practice dating from the late 1800s. A coupon is a certificate of specific value, such as a cents-off or free product offer, that is presented to a retailer along with an appropriate purchase for its stated redemption value. Coupons have a number of advantages that make them worth considering as part of a sales promotion strategy. Taken as a group these advantages might be labeled flexibility. Coupons can be used in a lot of different ways. First, coupons allow you to offer a reduced price on a product to those in your market who are price sensitive without having to do it for everybody. Second, unlike trade allowances that a retailer does not have to pass along to customers, a coupon makes sure that the savings go to consumers. Third, coupons offer a temporary price reduction that is seen as an offer and not a permanent reduction in price. When the offer is over, the product's price should return to normal without much resistance from your customers. Fourth, retailers can use coupons for their own promotional programs, by offering double or triple the face value of the coupon to consumers. This way retailers can use the coupons as a traffic-building promotional device.[8]

Couponing is not without its problems. Due to the popularity of couponing, increased clutter has led to a decline in redemption rates. Redemption rates themselves are difficult to predict and vary by product type and distribution method. It is also hard to target consumers to get the right people to use your coupons. Often it is the established consumer who uses coupons when the marketer wants new users to try the product with the incentive of a price-off or free-product deal. Coupon fraud is also a problem and can take the form of (1) coupons being redeemed for brands not purchased, (2) salesclerks giving customers cash for coupons, (3) stores collecting and redeeming coupons with the manufacturer without having sold the required product, and (4) counterfeiters printing coupons and redeeming them with unethical retail store managers.[9] The ease of implementing a coupon program can be counterbalanced by very low redemption rates among your target consumers. Successful coupon programs are a good example of the adage that things are seldom as easy as they seem.

Couponing, when carefully planned, can be used effectively to accomplish a number of different objectives for your sales promotion program. Some examples are:

☐ *Coupons can be an enticement to gain initial trial and awareness for a new product introduction.* The coupon can either be in the form of a savings on the first purchase, or it can be part of a free-sample-offer program. Both techniques reduce the risk of the trial purchase for your target market.

☐ *Couponing can be used to encourage repeat purchase by including it in or on the package as a reward for a purchase.* This methods lets you reward both new and loyal customers.

☐ *Coupons can be a method for enticing consumers to trade up to larger sizes or multiple units of a product.* This type of couponing is often done as a short-term competitive strategy to take customers out of the market for a period of time (especially when you know that competitive promotional activity is going on) by getting them to load up on a product.

☐ *Couponing can be an effective strategy for enlisting trade support.* You can gain retailers' support in a number of ways, including having the manufacturer distribute its own coupons free of charge to the retailers or by working out a cooperative arrangement so that a retailer can build its store promotions around the coupons.

☐ *Coupons can be used selectively to target different markets.* You can offer competitors' customers and nonusers a different coupon deal than the one for current users to get them to try your brand. This works best when there is little media overlap across these groups.

☐ *Coupons can also be used to cushion a price increase by offering temporary relief from that increase.*

☐ *Coupons can be a delivery system for more than just price-off deals.* They can be integrated with other promotional elements to collect consumer information for databases, used as entry forms for contests and sweepstakes, and used to add excitement to a typical advertising or marketing campaign. Exhibit 8–3 presents some of the basic types of coupon deals upon which other variations can be built.

Most coupons (upwards of 80 percent) are delivered to consumers in freestanding inserts (FSI) in their newspapers. This type of distribution system takes advantage of consumers' newspaper reading habits, which include searching for coupons in the inserts that typically arrive with the Sunday paper or on its featured food day. However, the clutter of the FSIs has cut into the redemption rates for coupons.

Coupons can also be delivered through the mail, in stores, on and in product packaging, in newspapers as part of the run-of-the-paper (ROP) advertising, and through other media such as magazines. Manufacturers and

EXHIBIT 8–3   BASIC TYPES OF COUPON DEALS

Coupon Deal	Description
Cents-off	Most common form of couponing. Deal is a certain amount off the regular price for a specified period of time.
Free	Free product offered to those redeeming coupon. Efficient method of sampling because you only give a free sample to consumers who are interested in it.
Buy one, get one free (BOGO)	Get a free product with purchase of product at regular price. Stimulates multiple purchases. Can be used to reward regular customers. Can require customers to buy more than one unit to get the free one.
Time release	Several cents-off coupons are offered at same time but with different expiration dates to encourage repeat purchase.
Multiple purchase	Coupon offer only good when more than one unit of product is bought. Can be used to increase sales and consumption in short term or to take consumers out of the market by loading them up with the product.
Self-destruct	Two or more coupons are printed to overlap each other so that when one is redeemed the other is destroyed. Can be used to create different deals for different consumers without having to print multiple coupons. Can also be used with the time-release deal to encourage customer to redeem earlier to get a better deal.
Personalized	Coupon is personalized by location or store so that it can only be redeemed at that location. Can be used to get trade support from retail outlets.
Cross-ruff	Purchaser gets a coupon for another unrelated product with the purchase of a product. Can work when users of one product overlap with those of another.
Related sale	Coupon received from the purchase of one product is for a related product. Food manufacturers that sell related products, such as condiments that might go with cold cuts or hot dogs, could place coupons for one of their related products in the package of the other product.
Sweepstakes entry	The coupon also becomes the entry form for a sweepstakes promotion. Consumer information for databases can be collected this way.

Source: Tamara Brezen Block, "Couponing," in *Sales Promotion Handbook*, 8th ed., ed. Tamara Brezen Block and William A. Robinson (Chicago, Ill.: Dartnell Press, 1994), 103–104.

retailers are constantly searching for new ways to deliver coupons. Stores have experimented with coupon dispensers attached to shelves near products, coupons on the back of receipts, and coupons handed out by product demonstrators. Many marketers predict eventual widespread use of systems that deliver coupons to customers at home through fax machines connected to home computer and entertainment systems.

FIGURE 8–2   YOPLAIT AD WITH COUPONS FROM FSI

The main problem confronting marketers considering the use of coupons is the declining or flattening of the redemption rates, which vary widely by method of distribution. For example, redemption rates for coupons from FSIs have been hovering around 2.5 percent over the past four years. Regular in- or on-pack coupons are being redeemed at 12.5 and 9.2 percent rates, respectively. Instant on-pack coupons do the best with a redemption rate of more than 30 percent.[10]

Stimulating consumers to redeem coupons is the objective of any couponing program. By following these simple design guidelines when you create your coupon, you can help achieve that goal:

1. Make the coupon instantly recognizable as a coupon.
2. Be sure that the face value and expiration date are easy to see and read on the coupon.
3. Include the UPC and manufacturer's coupon code.
4. Put a picture of the package on the coupon to help the consumer redeem the coupon for the right product.
5. Do not bury the coupon in complicated graphics in an ad or wherever it is being displayed.[11]

Figure 8–2 is an example of an ad with coupons from an FSI for Yoplait yogurt. Notice the content of the coupons. They include the standard and necessary coupon information: savings amount, expiration date, bar code, manufacturer's code, and pictures of Yoplait products.

Sampling and couponing are among the most frequently used forms of consumer promotions. Premiums, rebates, contests and sweepstakes, bonus packs, price-offs, and event sponsorship tend to be more problematic but can also be effective devices.

Premiums, or merchandise incentives, are offers of merchandise or services (such as travel) for free or at a reduced price as tangible rewards or incentives for the purchase of a product. Consumer premiums can be offered free of charge, or they can be self-liquidating. Free premiums are often small items included in, on, or near the product in the store. Cracker Jacks is one of the most recognizable brands that uses in-pack premiums in the form of small toys. Cereal companies make similar use of in-pack incentives. Consumers like in-pack or on-pack premiums because they get an immediate reward for buying the product. Mail-in premiums, on the other hand, require that consumers respond in some fashion to an offer by mailing in their request. A typical premium tries to stimulate repeat purchases by having consumers mail in proof of having made more than one purchase of a product. Response to mail-in premiums is much lower than to in- or on-pack premiums. The reward is not immediate, and the incentive may not be sufficient to interest the customer in responding.

A **self-liquidating** premium is an offer for which the consumer pays all or part of the cost of the premium (including mailing costs) before receiving it. Self-liquidating premiums are often merchandise of some value to the consumer that the manufacturer can offer at greatly reduced prices. The goal is to offer something of real value that enhances the brand's image and creates goodwill among consumers and the trade. The manufacturer's goal is only to recoup the costs of offering the premium and not to make a profit off the promotion itself. Marlboro cigarettes, for example, offers a western apparel catalog that contains clothing and outdoor items that reinforce its brand image. These items were selected to be consistent with and extend Marlboro's image and reinforce its advertising efforts.

Premiums can also be used as part of **continuity plans** to encourage consumers to use the brand on a continuous basis by saving coupons, proof of purchase, stamps, or some item that is then turned in for the premium. The purpose of a continuity plan is to bring your customers back time and time again or to establish purchase continuity for your brand. Airline frequent-flyer programs are among the most popular continuity programs. These programs encourage travelers to fly one airline to accumulate enough miles to earn free tickets and other perks. Retailers employ this type of premium-driven program when they ask customers to save their receipts (usually requiring that a minimum amount be spent over time) for a period of time and then turn them in for cash or premiums. The key to a successful continuity program is a premium or reward of enough value to keep the customer interested and involved in the program.

Premium-based promotional programs can be expensive if they require building up an inventory of merchandise. Response rates can also be problematic in cases where the customer has to take on the burden of responding and the reward is removed in time from the purchase behavior.

Rebates and **refunds** are offers by product manufacturers to reimburse some portion of the purchase price of a product upon receipt of consumer proof of purchase. To obtain a refund or rebate, consumers are typically required to send in proof of purchase to the manufacturer. The refund-and-rebate program has the advantage to the marketer of being easy to set up on short notice to combat competitive activity. The program requires no merchandise inventories or elaborate coupon redemption procedures. Computer technology allows companies to keep track of who has already received a refund and not to get caught by consumers trying to take advantage of the offer.

Rebates and refunds are used by a wide variety of companies from marketers of packaged goods to automobiles to computers. Refunds are used to stimulate product trial, move large inventories, and boost sluggish sales of durables. The delay between purchasing and receiving a refund is the main deterrent to consumers' responses to the offer. Automotive manufacturers overcame this problem by allowing consumers to use the rebate as part of their down payment on a car, which gave them an immediate reward for their purchase. Marketers have to be careful not to rely too heavily on refunds and rebates because consumers will become sensitive to the practice and only buy during the refund-and-rebate program.

Contests and **sweepstakes** have become popular with consumers and marketers, growing by 74 percent in the 1980s to a level where more than a billion dollars is spent on this form of promotion every year. A contest is a promotion that awards prizes based on a test of skill or talent. It can require the submission of recipes, photographs, slogans, an essay, or other evidence of an ability. Judges select winners among the entrants based on their skills or talents. A sweepstakes is a promotion in which prizes are awarded based on chance. Sweepstakes are closely regulated by federal and state lottery laws, which should be checked out before embarking on this type of promotional activity. One common lottery law requirement is that consumers not be obligated to purchase a product to enter a sweepstakes. Most sweepstakes do not require a purchase but do ask that an entrant do something such as write the brand name on a card.[12] A **game** is a type of sweepstakes where winning is based on chance but involves collecting game pieces or removing ink from a scratch-off card to win. A game can be extended over a period of time to encourage repeat purchases.

Consumers prefer sweepstakes and games to contests because they are easier to enter or participate in. There are some basic types of sweepstakes, games, and contests. Sweepstakes can take the form of a simple entry blank mailed to the target audience, included in an ad, or made available at the point of purchase. Consumers enter by mailing a form or dropping it into a box at the point of purchase. The drawing takes place at a specified date. Another version of the sweepstakes requires consumers to submit multiple entries to become eligible for winning different prizes. Each prize then becomes equivalent to a separate sweepstakes, which can increase consumer involvement in the game. In yet another form of sweepstakes entrants read an ad and write down the key copy points to be eligible to enter. A similar sweepstakes mechanism asks entrants to qualify by figuring out a puzzle or guess an answer to something based on clues provided. Finally, some marketers have been using coupons as entry forms. This sweepstakes requires entrants to fill out their name and address on the coupon as it is redeemed.

Games are typically used to build store traffic. They come in three varieties. The matching-instant-winner game requires customers to match something from an ad to something at the store to win. There are games in which the consumer has to collect parts to a puzzle or game pieces to be able to win. And then there are the instant-winner games often requiring consumers to peel off or scratch off the surface of a card to see if they have won.

Contests have not changed much over time.[13] However, if you stretch your imagination, you can create unique ways to use this old promotion standard. Rolling Rock beer turned a company mystery into a contest by asking customers for their theories on what the number "33" on their bottles means. There is no answer, so the prize goes to the best theory. The prizes are running the theory as a caption with a cartoon on the subject of the mysterious 33 and payment of $3,300, to tie in with the number.[14]

Contests and sweepstakes can add obvious excitement to an advertising campaign, but they should be planned very carefully. When you consider using these forms of promotion, you should think about the potential for these activities to detract from the brand image of your product and become the entire focus of your campaign. You should also beware of professional contest and sweepstakes participants who do not enter your contest or sweepstakes for product-related reasons but to beat the odds of winning.

Bonus packs add value to a purchase by giving customers an added amount of the product for the regular price. Compared to coupons, refunds, and rebates, bonus packs provide consumers with more immediate value. However, if the bonus pack increases the size of the product, shelf space could become a problem with the trade because retailers will have to provide this extra space. Bonus packs can also be a good competitive maneuver to counter promotional activity by other brands because they load up consumers with your product.

Price-off promotions are reduced-price deals that are indicated right on the package. The consumer knows immediately that this is a deal and may use the price reduction to save money or buy more of the product. The price-off promotion can be popular with both consumers and the trade when the manufacturer allows the retailer to maintain margins. The marketer incurs the reduction as a promotional cost and passes the savings directly along to the customer.

Event sponsorship has become one of the most popular types of promotions over the past several years. Some estimates put event-marketing expenditures above the $5 billion mark. The idea behind event sponsorship is that a marketer associates its product or company with entertainers, athletic events, or other notable people or occasions for the purpose of trading off on their

---

FIGURE 8–3   CHAMPION SPORTSWEAR PROMOTES ITS SPONSORSHIP OF THE WINTER OLYMPICS

---

popularity to achieve its marketing objectives. Sponsorship of an event can be an important focal point to an integrated marketing communications campaign. First, the event can support and be supported by advertising and public relations. Second, the event can involve all important targets of a campaign from consumers to the trade to the sales force. The event not only builds enthusiasm, but also invites participation by members of the trade and sales force.

Marketers' logic behind event sponsorship is that some of the enthusiasm the highly involved and loyal audience members or fans feel for the event will rub off on the brand. Also, the assumption is that fans of an entertainer or sporting event have something in common that has brought them to the event.

The event transcends differences and allows the sponsor to associate its brand with this commonness. Most important is that event sponsors believe that the association with the event translates into sales for their brands.[15]

Notice in Figure 8–3 how Champion sportswear ties in its advertising with its sponsorship and participation in the 1994 Winter Olympics. The statistics on the value of the Olympics are staggering and reinforce its value as an event to sponsor. More than 60 percent of all American families watch the Olympics, and 94 percent of these families see sponsors as successful companies. Just over 80 percent believe that Olympic sponsors are dedicated to excellence, are vital and energetic, and are industry leaders.[16]

Sporting events receive most of the event sponsorship money (more than two-thirds). Golf, tennis, auto racing, volleyball, college basketball and football, and skiing are among the events marketers like to sponsor. Although beer, cigarette, and car companies have been the big sponsors in the past, the appeal of these events is broadening to other marketers. For example, Lever 2000 soap won *BrandWeek's* sports event award in 1993 for its sponsorship of the Atlantic Coast Conference's basketball season. Included in Lever's sponsorship package were a three-point shoot-out contest, a premium offer of an ACC Dream Team video, and an outreach program to schoolchildren.[17]

Trade Promotions

One of the important goals of any sales promotion program is to gain the support of the retail trade and distributors as well as to elicit the desired consumer response. Certain techniques are geared specifically toward the trade.[18]

We described earlier in the chapter the reasons for the rather massive shift in marketing dollars from consumer advertising to trade promotions. Almost 45 percent of all marketing expenditures go toward trade promotions. You will recall that the purpose of trade promotions is to obtain distribution and support for new products, maintain support for established products, and gain a priority for certain brands in terms of display support, shelf position, and advertising and other promotional support. (Note that different industries use different trade promotions. You should research the industry you are working in for the acceptability of these practices.) Trade promotions can be divided into those that are primarily purchase incentives and those that are performance allowances. Additional trade support is often provided through point-of-purchase display items provided by the manufacturer, sales contests, cooperative advertising money to support local promotion of the brand, and participation in industry trade shows and sales meetings to get distributors and retailers behind an advertising campaign.

Purchase incentives are payments made primarily in the packaged goods business to distributors and retailers to encourage them to purchase your product if they have not done so before, restock it if they do carry it, and increase their inventory of the product. Purchase incentives can be offered in four basic ways: (1) as a slotting allowance, (2) as an off-invoice purchase allowance, (3) as dating, or the extension of payment terms, and (4) in the form of free goods.

A **slotting allowance** is a payment to distributors and retailers to gain distribution, warehouse space, computer space, and shelf space. It is typically 5 percent to 15 percent of the nonpromotional cost of the product being sold and comes directly out of the marketing budget. Although slotting fees help to gain distribution, they are problematic for new products because they take significant amounts of money away from introductory advertising efforts.

Off-invoice purchase allowances are reductions in the price of your product to the trade, usually in the range of 5 percent to 25 percent of the regular invoice price. These allowances are limited to a certain period of time and number of orders. The objective of using this type of trade promotion is to obtain higher-than-normal inventories. This deal makes the most sense when integrated with consumer advertising and promotions that are aimed at increasing the sales of your product. Otherwise, it does not make sense to have the additional inventory on hand. Distributors and retailers will simply follow a period of large purchases with smaller purchases to even out their inventories if the larger inventories are not sold to consumers.

Dating, or the extension of payment terms, is a trade promotion that gives the distributor a discount if payment is made within a specific period of time, such as 10 days, but allows a longer period of time, such as 60 days, before full payment is required. This incentive lets the trade buy inventory early or use the savings to purchase more of your product, or both.

Marketers can also use purchase incentives to offer free goods. **Free goods** are provided to the distributor at no cost based on a predetermined ratio to cases or amount of product purchased (for example, 10 percent to be added to amount purchased). Free goods are an effective way to build inventories of your product and tend to be more effective than invoice allowances.

Marketers offer **performance allowances** to distributors and retailers as incentives to get them to increase their products' rate of sale to the consumer. The marketers' aim is for distributors and retailers to push the product through the channel of distribution by (1) price reductions to consumers, (2) advertising your product in store advertising, (3) point-of-purchase and other display support, (4) expanded shelf space, and (5) in-store demonstrations.

Distributors and retailers are not going to participate in these activities of their own volition. Performance allowances in the form of price reductions to the trade, display allowances, advertising allowances, and count/recount allowances can be effective in obtaining trade support for your product.

Price reductions to retailers so that they can then reduce the price of a brand to the consumer have become the largest category of marketing and promotional spending for many brands. It is an effective technique for gaining retailer support for your brand because it has a direct effect on sales. However, price reductions have also become the primary reason for declining support for brand advertising. The problem has become that consumers have become price sensitive and buy more often when something is cheaper rather than because it is better. This is the brand equity question concerning the role for sales promotion in your campaign. It is also the reason for careful integration of your promotional elements so that sales can be achieved but not at the expense of the brand's image.

Display and merchandising allowances are paid to retailers to obtain extra in-store effort to make a product more visible to consumers. This extra effort may include better display of your product by improving its location, providing a second location, or expanding existing shelf space. Allowances may also be used to encourage other forms of merchandising, such as product sampling, in-store demonstrations, and support for special celebrity appearances. The difficulty for marketers is in monitoring retailer compliance with this type of deal, but in-store support from the retailer can have a significant effect on the sale of your product.

Price reductions and in-store merchandising support work best when supported by store advertising that includes the brand. Thus, **advertising allowances** are normally part of a marketer's performance-based trade promotion package. This allowance is paid to the retailer in return for advertising the product in the retailer's store ads. Normally the marketer provides an illustration of the product for the retailer to use in the ad. Some allowances carry stricter creative requirements, but most give the retailer a fair amount of leeway in developing the advertising.

A **count/recount allowance** is given to distributors in addition to other purchase incentives to provide an impetus to move inventory on to retailers. The allowance is based on the distributor's inventory level at the beginning and end of the promotional time period plus the product amount being shipped.

Point-of-purchase display items that manufacturers provide to retailers can add to brands' visibility in stores. These items can vary from something as simple as a shelf-talker (a small sign on the front edge of the shelf) or poster to elaborate bins that add shelf space to a retailer's store. The primary disadvantage of point-of-purchase materials is that retailers do not use a lot of the items manufacturers provide. To prevent this type of waste and ensure retailer support, it is important for manufacturers to support these activities with other forms of trade promotion.

Cooperative advertising is an agreement between the manufacturer and retailer to share the cost of promoting the brand at the local level. The agreements can vary, but a 50-50 split of the cost is common. Most cooperative advertising is placed in newspapers but radio, television, and other media can be used. Although advertising allowances can be provided for the inclusion of a brand in a store's advertising, most cooperative advertising is designed to feature the manufacturer's brand and provide a smaller space for listing a retailer's name and location.

Contests can provide special incentives to distributors' or retailers' sales forces as well as to managers to support an advertiser's brand. Advertiser-sponsored contests often provide opportunities to win expensive prizes or trips for achieving specific sales goals for a brand. Automotive and other durable-goods manufacturers that rely heavily on personal selling as part of the marketing of their products spend a significant part of their budgets on sales incentives such as contests.

Trade shows and sales meetings are two promotional channels that should be considered in the marketing communications campaign for a brand. **Trade shows** exist in almost any industry and provide an important opportunity to showcase and demonstrate new products to members of the trade. Distributors as well as retailers attend their industry's key trade shows to identify new products to stock and sell. The trade show is also an important social occasion for manufacturers to meet with and entertain their best trade customers.

Sales meetings are promotional opportunities for kicking off an advertising campaign or introducing a new product to distributors' sales forces. Automotive manufacturers, for example, conduct annual sales meetings for dealers to introduce new models of their cars. Special meetings are held when an entirely new nameplate is being introduced to build enthusiasm for its launch. Sales meetings can be very simple or very elaborate. A big sales meeting in an enticing travel destination can be an added incentive to the trade to get behind a manufacturer's brand.

Trade promotion has become an important part of the promotional program for the typical consumer-goods marketer. However, marketers should make a careful assessment of trade receptivity and competitive activity within a given industry before blindly recommending trade promotions as part of an integrated marketing communications campaign. Also, there are often state and federal regulations governing the use of trade promotions. The most important federal regulation is the Robinson-Patman Act that requires marketers to offer all trade promotions to all retailers in a market on a proportionate basis. This regulation prevents marketers from only supporting their best volume retailers and ignoring smaller stores. Before you implement any form of sales promotion activity, check with the attorneys general offices and the Better Business Bureaus in the states in which you are selling your product for local regulations.

PUBLIC RELATIONS

The strategic use of public relations to achieve the objectives of a marketing communications campaign requires the understanding of public relations at two levels. First, we will have to distinguish between **corporate public relations** and **marketing public relations.** And second, we must have a clear sense of public relations and its relationship to the other primary marketing communications elements: advertising, sales promotion, and direct marketing.

The role of public relations in a corporation also defines its place among advertising, sales promotion, and direct marketing in the marketing communications plan. The role for public relations varies by industry and company. But in a more general sense, regardless of the emphasis given to public relations, its role is to bring about public understanding and acceptance of an organization's relevant policies and procedures.[19] In some businesses, such as health-care providers, public relations takes on a dominant role in the achievement of their marketing communication objectives. The typical large consumer-goods firm places more importance on marketing and the other marketing communication elements. Smaller firms in the industrial and business-to-business arena might see the potential for public relations in a less integrated fashion and as separate but equal in value to that of marketing. The approach in this book is to view public relations from the perspective of the large consumer-goods firm, where it has taken on a new role as **marketing public relations.**

Marketing public relations is differentiated from corporate public relations in terms of the scope of planning and activities that are involved as well as its function in a firm. Corporate public relations activities are focused on the nonmarketing communication goals of a company, which might fall broadly under the corporate image umbrella. This is a long-term mission of any company to maintain open lines of communication with its various constituencies or publics to ensure that they understand and accept its policies, procedures and activities. It is easy to see that some relationships a firm might have with its publics are nonmarketing ones, but the selling function can fall under the broad mission of public relations. Public relations can be employed to support the purchase process and maintain long-term consumer satisfaction with your company. This is the role for marketing public relations in the marketing communications campaign.

MARKETING PUBLIC RELATIONS

Marketing public relations brings some advantages to the marketing communications program that are distinct disadvantages of advertising, sales promotion, and direct marketing. Consumers understand that the intent of advertising, sales promotion, and direct marketing is to sell them something. Thus they approach these types of promotion with a fair degree of skepticism. Public relations in the form of news stories prepared by a company can be more credible to your customers because it is not overtly identified with your company but with the medium (such as a newspaper, magazine, or TV station) that carries it. Because the media tend to have more credibility with your customers, awards and recommendations from them (such as the *Good Housekeeping* seal of approval or *Motor Trend* car of the year) can be used to add believability and trust to your campaign. The downside of this advantage is that you forgo control over message content and timing, and that control is the main advantage of advertising.

Public relations activities in general are less expensive than other kinds of promotion. Refer to Figure 8–1 to see that cost is a major consideration in deciding how to integrate the marketing communication elements of your campaign. Public relations efforts often require more sweat and tears than they do money. One public relations professional advised students interested in a career in PR not to be afraid of staplers, scissors, tape, and rubber cement. The tradeoff, once again, is that the precision and control you pay for in advertising, sales promotion, and direct marketing has to be achieved through hard work and the powers of personal persuasion with the media (contacts) when you add public relations to your plan.

Public relations can easily be integrated into a campaign to support other marketing efforts. For example, event sponsorships and trade shows certainly suggest a primary role for public relations. News stories in key media vehicles can provide information about the events or shows to gain initial awareness and interest among consumers and the trade. Interviews, press conferences, social events, and press releases can all be used to achieve this type of exposure. Likewise, new product introductions can be supported with public relations activities that will extend the exposure offered by advertising. PR's use with new product introduction is unusually effective when the product is a technological advance that creates natural interest in the media.

Hard-to-reach audiences can make public relations a welcome option for your campaign. Some audiences might be too hard or expensive to communicate with using traditional promotional devices. Suppose your campaign requires the support of your employees, government officials, stockholders, or the local community. Public relations professionals call these people publics or stakeholders in your business. Activities such as meetings, workshops, annual reports, company newsletters, executive speeches, and information hot lines can reach these groups when advertising cannot.

Marketing public relations offers a great deal of flexibility that can help you to fill in the communication gaps in your marketing plan. This advantage should be counterbalanced against the reality that public relations activities take more coordination ability than most other forms of promotion. One of the most important marketing publications-relations activities in this regard is the generation of positive publicity for your brand and company.

PRODUCT PUBLICITY

The effective use of public relations in marketing often comes down to getting good **publicity** for a brand. To get that kind of publicity, it is necessary to provide interesting and newsworthy information to the media. Positive publicity can contribute to your ability to achieve your marketing objectives by:

☐ *Informing your customers about how to select, buy, and use your product.* Informational brochures and product literature can be useful in helping consumers learn to use complex or risky products. News stories and pamphlets might inform people about the broader issue of knowing how to select a car, computer, insurance carrier, or legal service, for example.

☐ *Persuading your target audience to purchase your brand.* Well-placed and -timed stories can carry more persuasive power than advertising and might be the extra nudge consumers need to buy your brand.

☐ *Dispelling negative opinions or information about your brand.* Consider what you might do if someone found a syringe in a can of your product, or you had to recall several hundred thousand cars or trucks. Publicity can help to counteract misunderstandings that people have formed about your brand. The next time you watch the evening news, consider how much of a story about a company might have been generated by well-placed publicity.

☐ *Building store traffic.* The appearance of celebrities in a store, for example, can get customers to come out when otherwise they would not. These types of events are more successful when supported by publicity.

☐ *Supporting event sponsorships, trade shows, and other promotional activities.* Good publicity can persuade your key publics or audiences to turn out

for company-sponsored activities. Advertising can only go so far in building awareness. Sometimes good publicity and associated word-of-mouth
communication can be the missing ingredient to the achievement of your
objectives. Something as simple as a news story on the business page of a
local newspaper can turn out hundreds of people to the opening of a new
McDonald's restaurant or Barnes & Noble bookstore.[20]

Publicity and public relations can play supportive roles for a large marketer
with the resources to spend on advertising, sales promotion, and direct
marketing. However, public relations can be an important promotional
element for the small regional or local company. With your small clients,
public relations is an important strategic and practical consideration.

DIRECT MARKETING

When you integrate direct marketing into your advertising campaign, you
combine the typical image-oriented qualities of advertising with the opportunity
for the consumer to respond directly to your offer. This type of strategy could
be used to maintain the image and equity in the brand while also achieving
short-term sales goals. In some cases, the direct-marketing activities will
complement your advertising, and in others the qualities of both will be
combined into the same message. The use and integration of direct marketing
should always be considered with your marketing objectives and consumer
market in mind.

The simplest definition of **direct marketing** is attributed to direct-
marketing pioneer and expert Drayton Bird. He says that it is "any activity
whereby you communicate directly with your prospect or customer and he or
she responds directly to you."[21] This definition takes into account the
tremendous changes in direct-marketing technology to include the growing
importance of database marketing. Database marketing has made any channel
of communication a potential vehicle for direct marketing. One only has to
watch the infomercials, television commercials with 800 telephone numbers,
and home-shopping channels to see that direct marketing has grown beyond
the U.S. mail as its only distribution channel.

Direct marketing has grown in importance for a number of reasons, which
together have changed the marketplace and influenced campaign planning
immeasurably. Those changes most closely associated with the new and
growing importance of direct marketing to the campaign planner are:

- ☐ **The credit card.** The convenience and widespread use of credit cards have
  made it easy for consumers to purchase products through direct response
  channels. Credit cards have also reduced the financial risk for the direct marketer because payment is immediate and automatic.
- ☐ **The 800 telephone number.** The 800 telephone number has added to credit
  cards' practicality and convenience. Purchase and payment are easy, quick,

and practical. Together with credit cards, the 800 number has allowed direct marketers to sell both low-cost and high-cost merchandise with the ease of picking up the telephone.

☐ **Computer technology.** The advances in computer technology have made it possible for direct marketers to gather, store, and analyze enormous amounts of consumer information. This information is used to segment and target consumer audiences and to customize offerings. Marketers and advertisers can develop computer databases, or they can buy them from direct-marketing and other commercial cluster-segmentation firms that have built large databases of consumer information. Some of the larger firms that have developed databases have been described in Chapters 2 and 3 and will be mentioned briefly in the next section.

☐ **Accountability.** Advertising has one major weakness that happens to be the key strength of direct marketing—accountability. When you use direct marketing, you know whether or not it is working right away. You can gauge the response and tell how effective your offer has been. The past 10 years or so have seen a large proportion of marketers' promotional budgets shift from advertising to the related marketing communications activities. Part of the reason for this movement away from advertising has been because it is difficult to establish a causal link between advertising and sales. And, as the media clutter has become more severe (making advertising less effective), marketers have put their promotional dollars into areas where accountability is easier to measure.

These reasons for the growth of direct marketing highlight an ever-increasing sophistication by advertisers and marketers to identify and reach their target audiences with as little waste in coverage as possible. This ability has been enhanced because direct marketing has become database-driven to the point that some marketers have suggested changing the name *direct marketing* to *database marketing.*

DATABASE MARKETING

Database marketing starts with either the existence or development of a database of information on customers and prospective customers electronically stored on a computer. Most databases are built around the names, addresses, and purchase histories of customers. The more purchase-relevant information that can be added to this basic data, the better an advertiser or marketer will be able to establish an ongoing relationship with his or her customers.

Databases vary widely by product categories and company needs. However, the following basic customer information is a typical starting place for company databases:

1. Accurate names and addresses of individuals or organizations, including ZIP Codes
2. Telephone number

3. Source of inquiry or order
4. Date and purchase details of first inquiry or order
5. Recency/frequency/monetary purchase history by date, dollar amounts of purchases, and product or product lines purchased
6. Credit history and rating
7. Demographic data for individual consumers, such as age, gender, marital status, family data, education, income, and occupation
8. Organizational data for industrial buyers, such as Standard Industrial Classification (SIC) code, size of firm, revenue, and number of employees.[22]

The effectiveness of database marketing depends on keeping the database up-to-date, qualifying customers, segmenting the market, and being able to predict who your best prospects are. Database information can quickly become out-of-date. People move, companies move, preferences and attitudes change, and purchase behavior changes. Because most of your strategic and tactical decision making will be based on database information, the currency and accuracy of the data are crucial. Keeping the database current should become part of a firm's normal direct-marketing activities. Information-gathering techniques can be built right into a direct-marketing program. For example, Exhibit 8–4 illustrates how some companies have collected their data as part of promotional programs.

Marketers can choose among a variety of processes to decide whether to qualify a customer in a database. The process helps you decide which of your customers is most likely to be a repeat purchaser. One common approach used to qualify customers is called the R-F-M formula. Simply stated it says that your best future prospects are those people who bought most *recently* (R), those who bought most *frequently* (F) within a specified period, and those who spent specified amounts of *money* (M). The R-F-M formula can be customized to fit a specific company's customer base by applying a point system to the recency, frequency, and money amount variables. For example, recency of purchase can be divided into past 3 months (24 points), 6 months (12 points), 9 months (6 points), and 12 months (3 points). Frequency of purchase can be quantified by multiplying purchases by 4 points each. Finally, dollar purchases can be converted to a point system by taking a percentage of each amount up to a ceiling of, say, 9 or 10 points (a ceiling avoids distortion by large purchases). The total points can be used in various ways, including ranking the value of your customers and deciding where and how to spend your promotional budget.[23]

Various strategic and tactical programs can be tested using a database because you will know exactly how your customers are responding to different approaches and appeals. The measure of the effectiveness of your direct-marketing efforts is built into your direct-marketing items because you are always asking for some type of response. The response to different creative executions, for example, can be tracked using database marketing. Database marketing offers the best way to test your advertising. Advertising pioneer Claude Hopkins believed in the value of testing in direct marketing and advertising in general. He gave this example to explain why:

EXHIBIT 8–4   DATABASE USERS AND HOW THEY COLLECT THEIR DATA

Company	Brands	Data-Collection Program
Procter & Gamble	Cheer Free, Cascade Liqui-Gel, NyQuil LiquiCaps	Collects data through reply cards in freestanding inserts offering free product samples by mail. P&G can recontact consumers about future line extensions or related new products.
MCI Communications	Long-distance service	Friends & Family program offers 20 percent discount to customers who identify people called regularly. MCI then targets those names with mail and phone solicitations.
AT&T/Walt Disney World		Callers enter joint sweepstakes using interactive phone program and are asked about Disney product and resort usage for future contacts by company.
Kimberly-Clark	Huggies diapers	Buys lists of new mothers and sends coupons, brochures, and new-product information during babies' diaper-wearing stage.
Pepsi-Cola	Pepsi	"Summer Chill Out" promotion developed mailing list with discount offer to kids.
Hallmark Cards	Greeting cards	Envelope glued to magazine so when filled out with buyer demographics and where buyer shops can be redeemed for free greeting card.
Coca-Cola	Coke Classic	"Pop Music" promotion provides CD buyers' names to partner, SONY.
Philip Morris	Merit cigarettes	"Blind" freestanding insert mail-in coupon offered unidentified product sample as part of contest promotion.

Source: "Data Collection Activity by Major Marketers," *Advertising Age* (October 21, 1991): 22.

An advertiser of many years' standing... told the writer he did not know whether his advertising was worth anything or not. Sometimes he thought that his business would be just as large without it.

The writer replied, "I do know. Your advertising is utterly unprofitable, and I could prove it to you in one week. End an ad with an offer to pay five dollars to anyone who writes to you that he read the ad through. The scarcity of replies will amaze you."[24]

A database is a powerful tool for profiling your customers and organizing them into meaningful consumer segments from which you can select your target markets and audiences. After your target prospects are identified, you can turn to strategic decisions involving the positioning of your product or service offering. Databases can help you in combining demographic, geographic, lifestyle, purchase, and ZIP Code information to target your customer. Most advertisers and marketers do not have access to this much information on their customers, but syndicated cluster-segmentation services based on geodemographic data exist for the marketer who can afford them. The better-known segmentation systems have been described in Chapter 3. They are (1) Claritas' PRIZM system, which classifies the U.S. population into 62 lifestyles segments and then locates the ZIP Code neighborhoods that fall into each of these groups, (2) Donnelly Marketing Information Services ClusterPlus system, (3) Equifax/National Decision Systems' MicroVision, and (4) CACI Marketing Systems' ACORN. These companies use similar methods. Lifestyle, socioeconomic status, demographics, ZIP Code location, purchase data, media usage, census data, and other data collected by questionnaire are combined to create meaningful consumer segments that can be located by the use of ZIP Code maps. (See Chapter 3 for a detailed description of the PRIZM system.)

Database marketing offers marketers the potential to more precisely identify their target prospect and that prospect's likely response to the message. Of course, this should be the goal of all your advertising and marketing planning. Database marketing provides the technology to achieve these results. However, even if you find yourself in a position where database marketing is not affordable, you can use its strategic principles to improve the sophistication of your campaign planning.

DIRECT MARKETING OBJECTIVES AND STRATEGY

Your direct-marketing objectives and strategy should be developed with the overall advertising and marketing communications campaign's objectives and strategies in mind. Your direct-marketing plan should evolve from your total plan and identify those direct-marketing actions and activities that must be accomplished for the overall plan to be successful. To be a vital component of the overall marketing communications effort, the direct-marketing part of the plan should have its own objectives and strategies.

Your direct-marketing objectives are statements that accurately describe what is to be accomplished over a specified period of time. The objectives are the results that must be achieved for the direct-marketing effort to be successful. Direct-marketing strategies are the methods, activities, and events that will be employed to reach the objectives. The list of strategies should include who in the organization is responsible for what and when.

The objectives for direct marketing will flow from the problems and opportunities that have been identified during the early stages of campaign planning. Some of the problems and opportunities will suggest the use of direct marketing if it is to become part of the overall campaign. For example, IBM just recently decided to get into the direct-marketing business by publishing its own personal and small-business computer catalogs. Dell, Gateway 2000, and others were pioneers in this kind of direct marketing. However, IBM (as well as Apple and Compaq) believed that it was time to use the advantages of direct-response technology, such as 800 numbers, together with the ability to build relationships (and gather database information) with its smaller customers. IBM's direct-marketing effort was launched around a 38-page catalog listing 400 products of which some are not IBM brands. In the first two waves of this effort, 1.3 million catalogs were sent out to prospective customers. IBM's decision to compete in this marketing communications channel was a result of not being competitive in the personal-computer market and allowing clones to monopolize this end of the computer business.[25]

Direct-marketing objectives (along with sales promotion) are among the most action oriented of the marketing communications objectives you will be setting for your campaign. Typical objectives will include consumer responses such as (1) generating inquiries about a product or service, (2) purchasing the product or service, (3) gaining trial, (4) increasing usage, (5) enhancing a product's image among a very well-defined target audience, (6) gathering information, and (7) building an ongoing relationship with your customers. The ultimate reason for including direct marketing in your plan is to stimulate action on the part of the consumer and build a relationship that leads to repeat purchases. Direct marketing is a long-term commitment to information gathering, storage, organization, management, and its effective use. It is not a one-shot tactic in one campaign.

Your direct-marketing strategies will be influenced by your ability to develop a well-defined target audience that can be reached with direct-marketing channels. Also, your strategy must be built around a well-conceived offer that will get consumers to respond. Here are 10 factors to think about in creating your offer:

1. **Price.** The price you offer something at should be competitive and enticing and allow you to make a profit. Over time, you should test this element of your direct-marketing strategy.
2. **Shipping and handling.** Shipping and handling charges might have to be included in the price. Most direct marketers do not charge more than 10 percent of the base price for shipping and handling.
3. **Unit of sale.** Your direct-marketing objectives will help guide you in the selection of how to offer your product. If you want to gather information, you will get more responses by offering smaller units (one or two). If you want to increase the number of units sold, then multiple units such as sets might make better sense.
4. **Optional features.** Some offers lend themselves to the addition of optional features. Colors, sizes, personalization, and unusual options that cannot be

found in stores can add value to the offer. You will have to include an extra charge for the option, but good options pull in more sales revenue.

5. **Future obligation.** One common way of keeping a customer over the long term is to make the initial offer unbelievably good (10 records for $5) in return for membership that requires buying future products at a higher price. Record and book clubs offer these "continuity" programs. However, both the initial and future offer have to be of value to the customer.

6. **Credit options.** Credit cards have been a primary reason for the growth in direct marketing. When customers can charge their purchases, sales increase. Other possible credit options are paying on installment and delaying the first payment for a specified period of time.

7. **Incentives.** Including incentives in direct-marketing offerings carry the same risks as integrating sales promotion into the overall campaign carries. You want your customers to buy your product for its value and not because of the incentive. Therefore, incentives should be tested when and where possible. Free gifts, coupons, and sweepstakes are among the more common incentives. Incentives such as toll-free ordering can add to the ease of purchasing a product and do increase sales.

8. **Time limits.** All direct-marketing programs should push the customer to take action as soon as possible. One way to create this sense of urgency is to add a time limit to the offer.

9. **Quantity limits.** A limited supply of an item can add value to the product in the customers' minds. Watch the home-shopping channels on your TV. Notice that quantity limits are displayed on the screen for some items, especially for collectibles. The notion of a limited supply makes the item more enticing.

10. **Guarantees.** Guarantees are essential to direct marketing because they reduce the risk associated with buying items that cannot be inspected first-hand. You must guarantee customers' satisfaction up front by allowing them to cancel and receive a refund. This assurance gives customers confidence in what they are going to buy.[26]

After you have considered these factors in building your direct-marketing offer, you can engage the creative process to make the offer as enticing as possible. Additionally, the offer must fit (be integrated) with the rest of your marketing communications plan. Take a look at the Kenneth Cole shoe catalog in Figure 8–4 if you do not think creativity, style, and humor are as important to direct marketing as they are to general advertising. Also, notice the toll-free 800 number at the lower left of the second page in the example.

The creative principles covered in Chapter 6 apply to direct marketing as well as general advertising—only more so. Because the main task of direct marketing is to elicit an immediate response, all copy and design work must work together toward that end. The wide range of media channels available will alter the actual execution of a direct-marketing item, so let's use the classic direct-mail piece to illustrate the types of copy and design considerations that come into play in creating effective direct-marketing programs.

FIGURE 8-4   KENNETH COLE SHOE CATALOG

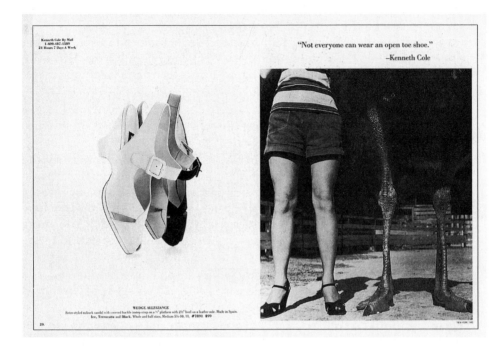

Copy Guidelines

The first and perhaps most important thing a copywriter can bring to a direct-marketing task is the attitude that the job at hand is to sell the product or service, not to write copy. Direct-marketing expert Don Kanter has said that writing is to copywriting what talking is to a salesperson. In both cases, the job is not to write or talk but to sell persuasively.[27]

Direct marketing differs from other forms of selling in that consumers cannot inspect the product. Therefore, the customer must rely on the content of your copy. The most important things to sell are (1) the value of the benefit to be derived from the product or service, and (2) confidence in the company. All advertising and marketing communications should be benefit oriented. The value of a product to a consumer is the perceived benefit divided by the price. Confidence in the company can be enhanced through the use of testimonials from satisfied customers, experts, or celebrities. Guarantees, free-trial offers, right of cancellation, and the company's reputation can all help to reduce the risk of purchasing through direct marketing.[28]

All effective advertising and marketing communications writing relies on appealing to basic human nature in a way that is relevant to the product or service benefit being offered. Products or services can either help you to gain something or do it better, or avoid some pain or loss. Most people like to make

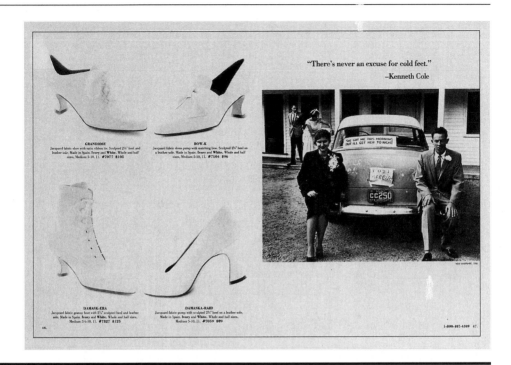

money, save time, avoid extra effort, and be praised and popular with others. Likewise, they would like to avoid the opposite of these situations. In copywriting, the link between the product benefit and the human want or desire is called the "big idea" or "position." Figure 8–5 provides an example of direct-marketing writing that achieves this link between the product's benefit and the human desire it fulfills. Notice the simple appeal to owning something that reflects the readers' desires for harmony, simplicity, and beauty (also a hallmark of the Lenox line). The copy follows through on the headline and illustration with warm, folksy copy that brings the scenes on the plates to life. Also notice that this series of plates is not available in stores, which makes the offering exclusive. The last line of the copy builds up the readers' confidence by allowing cancellation at any time.

Chapter 6 has covered the key principles of good copy. Here we will provide only a checklist of pitfalls for the copywriter to avoid in creating good direct-marketing items from ads to brochures and beyond. Carol Nelson offers the following advice in her book *The New Road to Successful Advertising: How to Integrate Image and Response*:

☐ **On Headlines**
   1. Avoid headlines that fail to involve your readers (appeal to their basic human nature and self-interest).

FIGURE 8–5   LENOX DIRECT-RESPONSE AD

2. Never assume your reader knows as much as you do (provide information).

3. Stifle the urge to be subtle or obscure (the appeal and offer should be obvious).

☐ **On Visuals**

1. Get rid of visuals that do not reinforce the written message.

2. Eliminate visuals that overpower the message and therefore create confusion.
3. Do not use clever visuals as an excuse for not being able to create a genuine message.

☐ **On Consumer Motivation**

1. Do not confuse your enthusiasm and knowledge of your product with the fact that others will not know how good it is unless you tell and show them.
2. Do not assume that simply showing your product will make people run out to buy it or order it from you. Sometimes they need an extra incentive, time limit, or promise of exclusivity to get them moving.

☐ **On the Offer**

1. Fine print, tiny type, asterisks in your copy, and mini-supers on TV put your customers on guard and work against their confidence in your offer.
2. Offers with strings attached or hidden disclaimers will hurt your image and future sales.

☐ **On Your Ego**

1. The reader does not care about you but about what you can do for him or her. This is a business transaction.
2. Make your reader feel special even when you are claiming that he or she is one of a large group of people who have bought your product or service.[29]

Media Alternatives

One of direct marketing's main advantages is in the flexibility it offers because of the variety of media, both conventional and unconventional, that can be used to deliver a message and product or service offering. This versatility translates into more room for creativity and more strategic alternatives to be considered as you integrate direct marketing into your overall campaign strategy.

Direct-marketing media are used to achieve better selectivity and segmentation of the target audience than we usually strive for with our general advertising buys. In addition, the goal of most direct-marketing campaigns is to emphasize frequency of exposure over reach. Because we are using direct marketing to narrow in on people who have potential to buy our product, we would like to establish an ongoing relationship with them. This type of strategy requires frequent contacts with our target audience. As we shall see in our discussion of individual direct-marketing media vehicles, some of these media also offer flexibility in terms of timing and ability to personalize the message.

For years, most consumers thought of direct marketing as the "junk mail" that accumulated in their mailboxes. Although direct marketing has grown beyond its emphasis on the mail, **direct mail** is still among the top advertising media categories in terms of advertising expenditures. Only newspapers garner a larger share of the total advertising expenditure pie. More than $24 billion was spent on direct mail in 1992, or approximately 19 percent of all advertising expenditures.[30] Figures 8–6A and B illustrate direct-mail pieces that appeal to an upscale audience demonstrating that the old image of direct mail has given way to more targeted efforts that include consumer groups with higher income levels.

The mailing list is the most important element in a direct-marketing effort that uses the U.S. Postal Service. Keeping the list up-to-date is very important, as we have already mentioned, but acquiring and building a good list are the foundation for a successful direct-mail program. There are two basic types of mailing lists: internal and external. The internal list of past customers that many companies keep is a place to start. This internal database can save you a lot of money because external lists that you buy from a list service or another company, which has compiled lists from its customer base, can be expensive. Typically, you will want to start with the company's internal customer list, assess its value as a mailing list, and then decide what type of external list to buy.[31]

If you are building a mailing list for the first time, you have to consider its cost in relation to your long-term commitment to direct marketing and the value of your customers as repeat purchasers. Seldom is the commitment to direct mail a one-shot proposition. Direct mail, as we will now see, has been the primary medium of the catalog business.

Catalogs have become the primary medium used to sell merchandise to highly segmented and target audiences on a national scale. The major reasons for the growth and success of the catalog business have been the decline in the quality of service at the retail level and shrinking leisure time for most consumers. The catalog business has expanded at the same time other time-saving devices have appeared, including the automatic teller machine, toll-free numbers, credit cards, overnight mail delivery, computer online inventory confirmation, and improved service from the catalog companies themselves. All of these developments allow us to control "when we do things, where we do things, how fast we do things, and...how much hassle we're willing to put up with."[32]

With the technological and consumer trends that made catalogs popular likely to continue, the future-oriented strategists should expect a time when the telephone wire connected to a computer and fax machine will become the primary device for delivering catalogs to our homes. This eventuality will also make purchasing and data collection more convenient. Every consumer purchase will represent an opportunity to improve a company's database and relationship with that customer. In a sense, the catalog business will merge with the new interactive computer technology and become part of the information and shopping superhighway.

In fact, a company known as 2Market is already offering catalogs through America Online and on CD-ROM. Among the catalogers participating are Lands' End, Spiegel, and Sony Music. The service is supported by advertisers such as Visa USA, whose business is highly relevant to the catalog business.[33]

Companies such as Sears have decided to leave the catalog business in favor of focusing on its retail business. However, successful catalogers have done just the opposite and have expanded into the retail store business. Eddie Bauer, Banana Republic, and Lands' End are among the group that now have stores in many shopping malls nationwide. Figure 8–7 demonstrates L.L. Bean's use of direct-response advertising to promote its catalog business. Also, notice

FIGURE 8–6A   BLOOMINGDALE'S DIRECT MAILER

that the company offers a toll-free number, coupon, and overnight delivery. Figure 8–8 (p. 262) illustrates how targeting a special consumer group can be combined with the power of a relevant celebrity personality to sell collectibles through a catalog.

Direct marketing has made some of its most dramatic inroads into the **electronic media,** where the applications run from direct-response TV spots to infomercials to home-shopping networks to direct marketing on computer online services and beyond. Once the domain of companies selling books, tapes, records, and magazines, direct-response advertisers on TV have expanded

---
FIGURE 8–6B   BLOOMINGDALE'S DIRECT MAILER

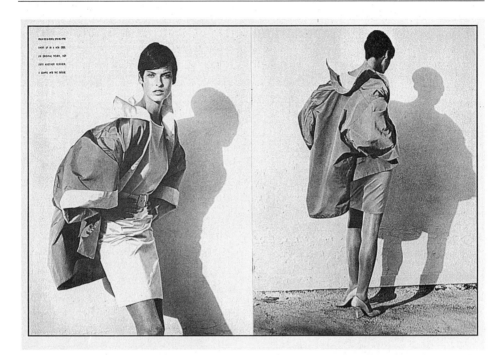

to include American Express, Time-Life, Nordic Track, Soloflex, and other formidable marketers.

Part of the attraction of direct-response TV advertising has come from the growth of cable TV. The audiences are better defined on cable TV so that advertisers and marketers can reach audiences with specialized interests such as sports, news, business and finance, movies, music, and even legal cases.

The relative low cost of time on cable TV and the availability of nonprogrammed time has spawned a long-form direct-response spot called the **infomercial.** Expenditures on these program-length ads have grown from just around $160 million in 1989 to more than $288 million in 1992.[34] The decision to use infomercials or not is different from buying traditional TV advertising time. Infomercials are judged by the amount of business or sales they bring in and not by the TV rating for the time purchased. Thus, infomercials are created, used, and evaluated in the same manner as any other direct-marketing effort.

One of the most interesting phenomena of the last five years or so has been the success of home-shopping networks on TV. **Home-shopping shows** such as QVC broadcast 24 hours a day, seven days a week. They provide prescheduled programs often based around specific product categories, such as jewelry, clothing, or electronics. QVC takes viewers' phone calls on the air to

FIGURE 8–7   L.L. BEAN'S AD FOR ITS CATALOGS

increase their involvement with the programming. It also uses traditional direct-marketing techniques, such as limiting quantities and time to order. The toll-free phone number flashing on the screen and credit-card payment make shopping on QVC easy.

Computer online services are in their infancy but no doubt are the wave of the future for direct marketing. These **interactive services** are already attracting the first round of marketers who see early entry into this medium as an opportunity to learn and grow in the new interactive environment. Catalogs are becoming available on CD-ROM, as previously mentioned. Consumers use computer technology to shop the catalogs by specifying price

FIGURE 8–8   UPPER DECK SPORTS COLLECTORS' CATALOG

ranges, subject interests, age groups, and gift occasions, for example. The interactive nature of the experience and power to use computer technology to make shopping easy and efficient will make the computer a major competitor in the media landscape of the very near future.[35]

The print media provide traditional delivery systems for direct marketing in the form of **direct-response advertising. Magazines** provide both mass audience and highly selective vehicles to choose from. The added high production quality can help to increase response rates to an offer. **Newspapers** have the value of natural timeliness and immediacy, so important to achieving consumer response. Direct marketers can consider run-of-the-paper placement, freestanding inserts, or the magazine sections that come with the Sunday paper as possible outlets. Because many of these media are also used for advertising and sales promotion delivery, they can be combined in these vehicles.

Radio is a little more difficult than other media to use in a direct-marketing program because of the lack of a visual component and the fleeting nature of radio spots. This difficulty can be offset by high levels of repetition of product

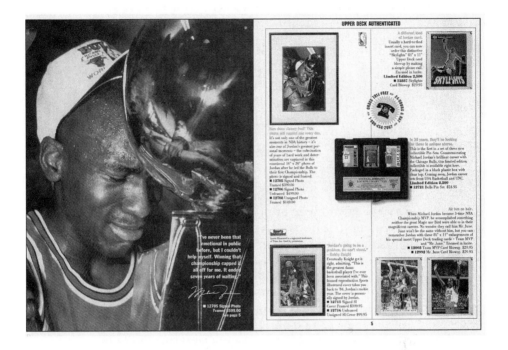

information and telephone numbers within the spot. The use of radio also requires that you run your spot frequently to get listeners to remember it. However, local radio is very selective in its ability to reach narrowly targeted audiences and relatively inexpensive compared to other media.

Telemarketing or selling over the telephone is a rapidly growing form of direct marketing. There is some consumer resistance to telemarketing as an intrusion on privacy resulting in rather low response rates. Yet, the use of 900 and 800 numbers has created the voice information-service phenomenon through which a company can provide information, entertain, and market its products. These services have a somewhat sleazy image because many consumers associate them with "sex talk" promotions and phone lines.

The future for direct marketing looks bright because it relies so heavily on the improving media and computer technology. The options for its use appear to be limited only by marketers' imaginations. It is likely that many student projects will involve small companies without the resources and knowledge to become serious users of direct marketing. However, the targeting-and-response emphasis of direct marketing should be carried forth into your campaign in principle as you develop your other promotional areas.

FINISHING THE RELATED MARKETING COMMUNICATION PLAN

The integration of the marketing communication elements of advertising, sales promotion, public relations, and direct marketing is a process of evaluating each element's strengths and weaknesses in being able (1) to reach your target audience with a minimum of waste and (2) to elicit the responses that will result in the accomplishment of your marketing objectives. You will not always have the luxury of unlimited resources with which to make these decisions. Therefore, you have to learn to live with trade-offs and still meet the requirements of your marketing communications program.

As this chapter has illustrated, the four major marketing communication elements have tremendous complementary value. Sales promotion and direct marketing push the hardest for an immediate response, often in terms of product sales. Advertising and public relations are aimed more at communication objectives, such as awareness and acceptance. However, it is when you bring the four qualities together that you realize a strong campaign can strive for both communication and sales objectives.

You should always be aware of where your target consumers are in the purchase-and-response cycle in relation to your brand. You want to reach your customers with the right combination of promotional messages that will take them to the next desired step in the purchase process. This level can be awareness and trial for an introductory campaign or a higher velocity of purchase for established products.

Stay on top of the emerging new technology. An interest in sales promotion and direct marketing will assure you that you will be where the latest technology is being applied to marketing. Computer technology will soon change the way we deliver messages and offers to consumers in their homes. The technological advances in interactive media will demand full integration of image-oriented promotions with response-based promotions. They will become one and the same, which will improve accountability for all forms of promotion.

Remember that you have to strive for both short-term and long-term results in today's marketplace. You have to be able to think like the trade and push for sales results while striving to maintain the valuable equity in your brand. Marketing and advertising have become more competitive and more results oriented. The campaign that wins the day is the one that reflects this reality and takes advantage of the new opportunities to create the many brand contacts that form the consumers' reality of your integrated marketing communications campaign.

Endnotes

[1]Bob Stone, *Successful Direct Marketing Methods*, 5th ed. (Lincolnwood, Ill.: NTC Business Books, 1994), 7.

[2]*Media Trends 1994* (New York: DDB Needham Worldwide, 1994), 9.

[3]"Burnett, Heinz Split Up," *Advertising Age Daily Fax* (November 23, 1994): 1.

[4]Robert C. Blattberg and Scott A. Nelson, *Sales Promotion: Concepts, Methods, and Strategies* (Englewood Cliffs, N.J.: Prentice Hall, 1990), 15–16.

[5]Kerry Smith, "Introduction and Overview," in *Sales Promotion Handbook*, 8th ed., ed. Tamara Brezen Block and William A. Robinson (Chicago, Ill.: Dartnell Press, 1994), 5.

[6]George E. Belch and Michael A. Belch, *Introduction to Advertising and Promotion: An Integrated Marketing Communications Perspective,* 3rd ed. (Chicago, Ill.: Irwin, 1995), 476–477.

[7]Belch and Belch, *Introduction to Advertising and Promotion,* 477.

[8]Tamara Brezen Block, "Couponing," in *Sales Promotion Handbook*, 8th ed., ed. Tamara Brezen Block and William A. Robinson (Chicago, Ill.: Dartnell Press, 1994), 99–100.

[9]Belch and Belch, *Introduction to Advertising and Promotion,* 491.

[10]Block, "Couponing," 108.

[11]Block, "Couponing," 111.

[12]Don Jagoda, "Sweepstakes, Games, Contests," in *Sales Promotion Handbook*, 8th ed., ed. Tamara Brezen Block and William A. Robinson (Chicago, Ill.: Dartnell Press, 1994), 129.

[13]Jagoda, "Sweepstakes, Games, Contests," 133–143.

[14]"Rolling Rock Asks What '33' Means," *Promo* (September 1994): 22.

[15]Kevin Wulff, "How To Compete At Sports Marketing," *The Advertiser* (Spring 1992): 73–76.

[16]David D'Alessandro, "Event Marketing Winners: Olympics, Local, Causes," *BrandWeek* (July 1993): 16.

[17]"*BrandWeek* Presents the 7th Annual Event Marketing Awards," *BrandWeek* (September 27, 1993): 48.

[18]This section is based in part on James Kunz, "Trade Promotion," in *Sales Promotion Handbook*, 8th ed., ed. Tamara Brezen Block and William A. Robinson (Chicago, Ill.: Dartnell Press, 1994), 320–334.

[19]Belch and Belch, *Introduction to Advertising and Promotion,* 518.

[20]David R. Yale, *The Publicity Handbook* (Lincolnwood, Ill.: NTC Business Books, 1995), 3.

[21]Kenneth Roman and Jane Maas, *The New How to Advertise* (New York: St. Martin's Press, 1992), 59.

[22]Stone, *Successful Direct Marketing Methods,* 38.

[23]Stone, *Successful Direct Marketing Methods,* 41.

[24]Claude C. Hopkins, *Scientific Advertising* (Lincolnwood, Ill.: NTC Business Books, 1987), 316.

[25]Gerry Khermouch, "Lands' End Does It. Dell Does It? Why Not Big Blue?" *BrandWeek* (July 12, 1993), 22–24.

[26]Stone, *Successful Direct Marketing Methods,* 79–81.

[27]Stone, *Successful Direct Marketing Methods,* 376–377.

[28]Stone, *Successful Direct Marketing Methods,* 377.

[29]Carol Nelson, *The New Road to Successful Advertising: How to Integrate Image and Response* (Chicago, Ill.: Bonus Books, 1991), 195.

[30]*Media Trends 1994,* 8.

[31]Stone, *Successful Direct Marketing Methods,* 212–215.

[32]Jay Walker, "Catalogers, There May Be a Fax in Your Future," *DM News* (December 31, 1990): 23.

[33]Kevin Goldman, "Holiday Shopping Comes to Cyberspace," *The Wall Street Journal* (November 18, 1994), sec. B, 5.

[34]"Annual Infomercial Media Dollar Expenditures," *The Infomercial Special Sourcebook Issue* (BrandWeek Supplement, 1993): 15.

[35]Gary Levin, "Catalogers Take Wares 2 Market," *Advertising Age* (November 21, 1994): 15.

Evaluating the Effectiveness of the Campaign*

It has been said that the search for a good measure of advertising effectiveness is like the search for the Holy Grail—it goes on and on and on. The search is and will remain endless for two basic reasons. First, the evaluation of advertising is often a critical factor in marketing success. A slight change in an advertising campaign brought about through some form of evaluation can lead to significant increases in sales and profits. In an aggressively competitive market, an insightful evaluation can provide a company with an edge over its rivals. When other types of marketing communication tools, such as sales promotion and public relations, are included in the promotional mix, it further underscores the importance of a good measure of effectiveness.

Evaluation also gives businesses some means of control over the tremendous sums of money spent on marketing communications. Many companies, including RJR Nabisco, Campbell Soup Company, Hershey Foods, and Nestlé Enterprises, tie their advertising agency compensation to performance evaluations.[1] Evaluations that are thorough and accurate not only enhance the success of the marketing communication program but also strengthen the morale of the people working on the campaign, both internally and externally.

Second, the search continues because it remains difficult to isolate the effects of a marketing communication campaign on sales. The measurement task is not impossible, but the large number of controllable and uncontrollable

*This chapter has been developed and written in part by Michael P. Kalasunas, senior vice-president and director of Planning at J. Walter Thompson in Chicago. Mike has been at JWT for more than 20 years and directs all advertising research for the agency. Increasingly, he spends a good measure of his time on strategic planning.

factors can turn even a simple market test into a meaningless exercise. A simple market test can easily get complicated. In the pizza delivery business, companies often use a direct-mail firm like Advo Inc., the largest direct-mail services company in the United States, to deliver coupons to households in their market areas.

Normally, the effects are fairly easy to measure. Sales typically go up dramatically the day coupons are delivered, and they continue high for the remainder of the week. If it rains, sales spike upward even higher. But if the competition is also running coupons the same day—a common situation—it is nearly impossible to determine the effect of each variable on sales. The situation is complicated even further if you consider that there are variations in the intensity of rain and differences in the degree to which a rival company is a direct competitor of the product being evaluated. Traditional researchers might describe this situation as confounding the effects of the variable you are interested in (that is, direct-mail-delivered coupons) with extraneous variables (that is, rain and competitive promotions) so that their effect on the variable you are measuring is all mixed up. A typical manager is likely to ponder these questions and simply conclude that measuring these relationships is scarcely better than judgment.

EVALUATION AS A STRATEGIC CONCERN

Managers, of course, realize that evaluation is vital to all aspects of the campaign. In today's intensely competitive marketplace, enlightened management understands that the older style of marketing practices that were often based on experience and even hunches are not likely to be as effective in the future as they were in the past. As Phillip Kotler of Northwestern University observed, "Companies find themselves competing in a race where the road signs and rules keep changing, where there is no finish line, no permanent 'win.'"[2] Smart companies integrate evaluative procedures into all areas of their decision making, including marketing communications. These procedures are often part of a system rather than project or task oriented.

Evaluation has been an important part of each chapter in this book. Chapters 2 and 3 examined many of the tests, techniques, procedures, and sources of information that are part of the research that is used to develop the strategic foundation of the campaign. This aspect of research is sometimes referred to as **developmental research.** Chapters 4 through 8 integrated the concept of evaluation as part of the method to develop the objectives, strategy, and tactics of the campaign.

The primary focus of this chapter is on measuring the effectiveness of advertising and secondarily on evaluating related marketing communications. This focus is less a comment on the relative importance of advertising and more a function of the scantiness of methodologies known for measuring the effectiveness of other types of marketing communication. The measurement for advertising and related marketing communications is sometimes referred to as **evaluative research.**

Planners tend to ask three basic questions before measuring the effectiveness of a campaign:

☐ Whether to measure or not?
☐ When to measure?
☐ What to measure?

Each of these questions is fundamentally connected to the other, so much so that a reasonable argument could be made that each of the above questions should be considered first. The second question, when to measure, is probably the most logical place to start, but usually the decision to use or not use measurement is decided first. The first two questions, whether to measure and when to measure, have an obvious effect on what to measure, but, in many ways, the last question is the most important of the three. Because of the problems associated with measurement, what to measure frequently gets translated as what you *can* measure, either because of the cost of a measurement or because planners do not feel they can measure what they would really like to evaluate, as we will later discuss. These feelings no doubt cause some planners to question whether it is worth it to measure anything.

WHETHER TO MEASURE EFFECTIVENESS

In their book *Advertising and Promotion*, George and Michael Belch point out that to ensure success in a marketing communication program, it is important to determine how well the program is working by measuring its performance against some standards. They offer the following reasons why companies do or do not use measurement:[3]

Reasons for Measuring Effectiveness

1. **Avoiding costly mistakes** In 1993, according to *Competitive Media Reporting*, more than $48 billion was spent on advertising in measured media in the United States.[4] This amount probably constitutes less than one-third of all the money spent on marketing communication.[5] If measurement could potentially increase a campaign's efficiency or effectiveness as little as 1 percent, then it would amount to savings of more than $6 million for Kellogg Co. (based on total advertising expenditures of $627.1 million) and more than $1.5 million for Gillette Co. (based on total advertising expenditures of $167.2 million).[6]

2. **Evaluating alternative strategies** Human behavior can rarely be predicted with an absolute degree of certainty. Advertising is still very much an art. Companies often have more than one strategy under consideration, each of which seems promising and each of which may have its own supporters within a company. The right kind of test can reduce the uncertainty in decision making. For example, Coors is a heavy user of spot television. Frequently, the company will test alternate versions of its advertising to determine which strategy or execution is most effective.[7]

3. **Increasing the efficiency of advertising in general** The advertising business is filled with many highly competent and creative individuals. These people often have so much of their spirit and individuality invested in an assignment that it is difficult for them to be completely objective in evaluating their own work. The instincts of even the most successful and talented people can sometimes be wrong. When millions or tens of millions of dollars are on the line, measuring effectiveness as an aid to judgment often helps decision makers tell a near mess from a big success.

Not Measuring Effectiveness

1. **Cost** Research can be expensive. As companies strive to keep their costs down, research is one of the first areas cut. Measures to evaluate advertising after it is run are particularly vulnerable. In the 1970s, when many agencies were able to retain a full 15 percent commission on advertising they placed for their clients, advertisers often requested their agencies to do special studies as part of the compensation agreement. In the 1980s, when companies began to negotiate reductions in the commissions agencies were allowed to keep, agencies increasingly turned over the job of measuring the effectiveness of advertising to the companies. Many companies found it difficult to fit the cost of testing into their budgets. Companies, and especially advertising agencies, often rationalize that if they put more effort and expense into the developmental phase of the campaign, it will be less important to measure effectiveness later.

2. **Research problems** Advertising people are uncertain about the methodologies that research organizations use and the criteria they test for. Many researchers also agree that a good test for copy should measure multiple criteria, although there is not much satisfaction with the ones that do. There is frequent disappointment with the limitations of research. Planners are often disenchanted with tests that only measure communication effects, such as awareness and recall. They want tests that isolate and reveal a direct causal relationship between advertising and sales. Few tests achieve these ends.

3. **Disagreement over what to test** Along with the debate over the value of measuring communication effects, there may be a disagreement over what aspect of the campaign to test. A sales manager may want to assess the impact of promotions on sales, whereas the corporate hierarchy may be more concerned about the company's image. Disputes over what to test can sometimes lead to no testing.

4. **The objections of creativity** Many creative people do not like copy testing. They say it inhibits their creativity. Because many tests are inexact and measure only one aspect of communication, such as awareness, copywriters sometimes protest that they do not measure the full impact of an ad, especially television commercials. Moreover, pretesting finished advertising limits creativity. Television commercials, in particular, are expensive to produce. If they do not score well in a test, a lot of money has been wasted. Wasting money is especially irksome if there is not general agreement about

the value of the test in the first place. Advertising can be tested in rough form with storyboards, "animatics," or "photomatics," but since these are not the actual commercial, some may argue that it limits the ability of the researcher to generalize the results from the test situation to the real world.

5. **Time**   Copy testing and other effectiveness measures take time; executive judgment and creative decisions can be made quickly. Many planners are concerned that with the passage of time they may lose a window of opportunity.

Resolving the Debate over Measurement

Measurement is used to add greater precision to marketing decisions. Despite the problems associated with measurement and the need to make decisions in the face of insufficient information, it does not mean there is a good argument for intuitive decision making. Rather, as Kotler says, "it is an argument for improved marketing theory and tools of analysis."[8] Progressive companies should strive to be on the cutting edge of how they evaluate campaigns in the same way that they compete to produce better products.

Developing a Research System

To foster a corporate environment that encourages innovation, it is important to view evaluative measures as part of a system. This approach tends to offer a firm some of the following advantages over evaluating a campaign on an ad hoc basis:[9]

☐ *Systems tend to evolve.* Once a system is built, it can be fine-tuned and refined to improve its efficiency and effectiveness. Ad hoc studies tend to be viewed as more discrete projects. They start, are executed, and end.

☐ *Systems provide benchmarks for learning over time.* After a system is established, it is easier to measure performance against results because the data tend to be collected and analyzed using common terms, standards, and databases. In a world where we rarely measure absolute things, measuring relative change is important.

☐ *Systems promote a holistic approach rather than a functional approach to solving marketing communication problems.* Ad hoc studies often begin with a single aspect, or part, of the campaign (such as specific ads), which an analyst then strives to understand. The analyst then pieces together all the parts in an attempt to understand the complete impact of a campaign. In contrast, systems foster a mind-set that encourages planners to begin with a concept, such as integrated marketing communications, and follow through with measures or procedures that are designed to evaluate both the effects of various aspects of the campaign and the way in which they interact. In other words, systems help predispose the planner to evaluate the impact of the entire campaign.

☐ *Research systems reside in the company (or its agency).* Many ad hoc studies are produced by outside suppliers. Often data that are used to create a report exist outside the company in the supplier's database. Storing them with the supplier makes it difficult for companies to access them should a need arise. Having a system does not preclude the use of outside suppliers, but a company with a system usually integrates data collected by others into its database—or at least makes provisions to access the information on-line.

Evaluation Is Not Getting Easier

Even as the systems and techniques to evaluate campaigns get more sophisticated, and presumably better, the task appears to get more difficult. The very companies that are likely to use the most advanced systems—the large consumer-goods companies—are the same companies that often employ the strategy of surrounding the consumer with myriad points of contact. Not surprisingly, many of these points of contact include nontraditional media that often do not lend themselves to measurement. Advertising, along with other communication tools, such as sales promotion and public relations, is only one of a number of factors that can influence sales.

Companies such as Procter & Gamble, Quaker Oats, and Kraft General Foods have fairly sophisticated and *proprietary* systems to evaluate their campaigns. However, it is doubtful that even these companies have obtained the holy grail of campaign measurement—a true measure tracing a direct causal relationship between the campaign and sales.

TOWARD A SYSTEM FOR EVALUATING A CAMPAIGN'S EFFECTIVENESS

A comprehensive, detailed system to evaluate the effectiveness of a campaign is beyond the scope of this book, but we can outline some of the fundamental elements in a system. Assuming a decision is made to proceed with the development of a system, one can be organized along the lines of the questions **when to measure** and **what to measure.** We suspect many, if not most, companies organize their systems on the basis of what they want to measure. These systems focus directly on what the research is supposed to accomplish and are *objective oriented.* Although this is a sensible approach, many companies, and especially students working on class projects, may find a *task-oriented* approach to be more practical. This approach organizes evaluative measures chronologically, according to when the need typically arises to evaluate some aspect of the campaign. We will now look at the various stages in a marketing communication campaign and examine some of the more common evaluative measures companies use, including *what* typically gets measured.

WHEN AND WHAT TO MEASURE

There are at least four stages of a campaign during which it is common to use some type of evaluative testing. They are as follows:

☐ At the beginning of the creative process—concept testing

☐ In the middle and at the end of the creative process—copy testing

☐ While the advertising is appearing in the media—concurrent testing
☐ After the advertising has appeared in the media—posttesting

Concept Testing

Following the situation analysis and until just before the actual ads are completed, planners often use some type of evaluative testing to get a feel for whether their ideas and strategy are likely to be on target, or on strategy. The purpose of this type of testing is to get feedback from the consumers before a lot of time, money, and effort are spent on producing expensive ads.

What to Test Concept testing is as much a check on the strategic development of the campaign as it is on specific executions. The testing tends to be somewhat exploratory in nature, although tentative ideas and concepts have been developed. Among the concepts typically evaluated are product names, slogans, campaign themes, advertising claims or promises, and the basic product positioning, sometimes called the product concept definition. Later during the copy testing phase, specific variables that affect the execution of an ad can be tested, such as the selection of music, choice of words, use of art or humor, and the arrangement of these elements. This is also a good stage to evaluate campaign spokespeople. Celebrity endorsers often command substantial sums of money; it is imperative to get some feedback on them before contracts are signed.

How to Test Because concept testing tends to be exploratory in nature, the research techniques tend to be more qualitative than other types of testing. Among the more common ways of gathering information are the following:

☐ **Focus groups** (for more information, see page 53)
☐ **Mall intercepts** (for more information, see page 54)
☐ **One-on-one interviews** (for more information, see page 52)

One of the keys to getting information that is meaningful is be sure that the subjects in the test groups are representative of the target audience. Although widely used, focus groups are not generally good for checking communications or getting evaluative feedback. The interaction that takes place among respondents in developmental research (see Chapters 2 and 3) is desirable. In evaluative research, it is better to measure the effects of an ad on a consumer without the potential biases that sometimes result from one member of a group influencing another. Because of potential problems with interaction effects, mall intercepts and one-on-one interviews are generally more appropriate for concept testing.

Within the various testing situations there are a wide variety of techniques and tests to elicit information. Some tests and techniques, such as projective tests and laddering techniques, are more commonly used in developmental research, although they are occasionally used for concept testing. Some of the more common tests and techniques are as follows:

☐ **Projective tests** (for more information, see pages 54, 73, 76, and 77)
☐ **Laddering techniques** (for more information, see pages 48–52)

□ **Structured and semistructured questionnaires** (for more information, see pages 72–76)

□ **Attitude and opinion scales** (for more information, see pages 73–74)

□ **Paired comparison tests** (for more information, see page 73)

The information obtained from concept testing is generally used to firm up message strategy as well as to evaluate key elements within the strategy. The next step in the campaign is to execute the strategy by developing individual ads or promotional pieces.

Copy Testing

Most of the evaluative testing done by companies and their agencies falls into this category. It can range from consumer feedback to rough ads obtained from informal interviews to the quantitative measurement of consumer responses to finished commercials. Because the testing takes place before the ads are run in the media, it is often referred to as *pretesting.*

Purpose The basic purpose of copy testing is to predict the effectiveness of an ad or a campaign. A secondary objective is to help understand the ad so it can be developed further. Over the years, many people have questioned the efficacy of copy testing, challenging either specific tests or the concept in general. To assess the value of these tests, the American Research Foundation sponsored a massive project in which it conducted between 12,000 and 15,000 interviews. Called the ARF Copy Research Validity Project, it was completed in 1990, after nearly eight years of struggling with the formidable problems involved in such an ambitious project. Although the project limited itself to television commercials, the general conclusion was that copy testing works. The study confirmed what many copy researchers had felt—copy testing is helpful in identifying television commercials that generate sales.[10] Although this is helpful information to know, the typical copy test is not able to establish a causal link between an ad and sales.

Value The value in most copy tests comes from the ability of the test to evaluate the effectiveness of an ad defined in terms of some criterion such as awareness, persuasion, or likeability (also referred to as liking). After a system is used repeatedly, average scores, or norms, are quickly developed by product type. Frequently, the research company supplying the service provides these norms. Each ad is tested against a norm to assess its effectiveness. As planners become familiar and comfortable with a technique, the results may be used to help make decisions. However, smart managers know that a copy test should only be used as a guide to decision making and not as a substitute for executive and creative judgment.

What to Test There are two types of copy tests: **diagnostics,** to help planners understand the strengths and weaknesses of an ad, and **evaluative tests,** which commonly focus on one of three criteria: communication playback, likeability, and persuasion.

Although many copy tests have diagnostic value, there is a particular type of copy test that is referred to as diagnostics. We'll look at an example of a general diagnostic test and then consider two more specialized tests: **frame-by-frame diagnostics** and **picture sort techniques.**

Diagnostics are a *type* of testing that is designed to improve ads. It is rare, however, that a diagnostic test tells a creative person how to make a commercial better. This test may suggest what is wrong with an ad, but it is unlikely to suggest what to do about it. These tests are frequently used to pretest television commercials at the rough stage. In a typical 30-second commercial there are numerous scenes, and within each scene there is a variety of elements that can be manipulated. Tests that are designed to improve specific elements within a commercial are sometimes referred to as **executional diagnostics.** In a general diagnostics test, viewers are exposed to a television commercial and then given a series of open-end questions about reactions to specific elements as well as structural statements to which they indicate their agreement or disagreement.

Following is an example of a typical diagnostic test.

Please answer the following questions:

1. What were your overall feelings as you were watching the commercial?
2. Can you describe what happened in the commercial from beginning to end?
3. What things did you learn or find out?
4. What did you like or dislike about the commercial?
5. How do you feel about specific elements in the commercial?

Please indicate how much each statement describes how you feel.[11]

1. This ad told me something new about the product that I didn't know before.
2. This ad helps me find the product that I want.
3. This ad is funny or clever.
4. I learned a lot from this advertising.
5. I find this advertising artistic.

Following each statement is an agree/disagree scale similar to the following:

Agree completely   _____
Agree somewhat   _____
Disagree somewhat   _____
Disagree completely   _____

Although companies generally use diagnostics to help them understand and improve ads, the ARF Copy Research Validity Project found that the responses to some of the statements in a diagnostics test helped companies to predict fairly well which commercials would be most successful in generating sales. The most useful questions were those that dealt with the information content of the ads, such as questions 1, 2, and 4.

Frame-by-frame diagnostics are frequently used to help marketers understand why a television commercial has not tested very well on some other type of test, such as one dealing with recall or persuasion. Even simple commercials are often made up of separate parts. These tests can provide clues as to which parts of a commercial are connecting with viewers and which parts of a commercial have dead spots. Before rejecting a commercial, managers will sometimes see if there are any parts of the commercial worth salvaging. Frame-by-frame tests evaluate consumers' reactions to the individual scenes in a television commercial. In a typical test, a copy testing organization, such as VIEWFACTS, invites consumers to a minitheater to view a series of commercials. The respondents are directed to press buttons to indicate how much they like or dislike what they are seeing. Later an interviewer will query audience members for the reasons for their reactions to specific scenes. Frame-by-frame tests provide the researcher with clues as to the parts within a commercial that work well and those that do not. These clues can be used to provide guidance to creative personnel for further copy development.[12]

Picture sort techniques is another diagnostic tool that can be used to understand the inner workings of a television commercial. One of the most widely known techniques, developed by Tatham Euro RSCG, uses a deck of still photographs taken from the television commercial being tested. Respondents are recruited and screened for target audience membership at mall intercept locations. Respondents are given a randomized deck of photographs and are asked to sort them into two piles—the pictures they remember seeing and the pictures they do not. Researchers then assign a value to each scene in the commercial according to the extent to which respondents indicate they saw it in the ad. A high score indicates that a high percentage of respondents remember seeing the particular scene. An analyst can then plot these scores from the beginning of a commercial to its end to provide insight about the attention value of each scene as the commercial unfolds.[13]

An effective commercial is one in which each scene has a consistently high level of recognition. It yields a line on a graph that is smooth rather than choppy or disjointed. The researchers at Tatham call the smooth transition from one image to another "visual connectedness." Charles Young and Michael Robinson, researchers at Tatham, supported the validity of this approach by establishing a positive relationship between visually connected ads and ads that were independently judged to be persuasive by American Research System, one of the most respected copy testing services in the United States.[14]

Communication playback is a type of test that can be used for both diagnostic and *evaluative* purposes. The intent of these tests is to evaluate whether the essential points within an ad have been communicated. The ability of respondents to recall specific information about an ad is an important measure of effectiveness. Communication playback tests can also be used as a diagnostic tool. Viewers are often asked to re-create visual and verbal elements of an ad in their own words.[15] Researchers usually pay special attention to the consumers' recall of the brand name, specific attributes or qualities of the product, the main selling message and reactions to music, special effects, main characters, key phrases, and story lines. In the ARF Copy Research Validity Project, the researchers used the following question on a paper and pencil test:

"Of course the purpose of the commercial was to get you to buy the product. Other than that what was the main selling point of the commercial?"[16]

Communication playback information can be obtained from a variety of methods, including focus group discussion (although as previously stated, it is a misuse of focus groups), one-on-one interviews, mall intercepts, and **dummy advertising vehicles.** In the latter method, a dummy vehicle can be made to look like an actual magazine, complete with editorial matter and advertisements. Subjects are asked to read the vehicle as they normally would read a magazine. The interviewer can then question the respondent on a number of criteria, including recall, main selling message, and general opinions and attitudes. Dummy vehicles are widely used because they present a fairly realistic situation to subjects.

A related type of measure can also be obtained by physiological methods. A mechanical device known as a **tachistoscope,** or t-scope, measures respondents' perceptions of various elements in print ads. This instrument is like a slide projector with a shutter attached to it that is able to vary the amount of time a picture is shown on a screen. In the beginning of the test, the image of the ad will appear on the screen so briefly that it will be beneath a respondent's level of awareness (that is, subliminal). Gradually, as the researcher increases the amount of time the image is on the screen, viewers are increasingly able to perceive various elements or messages in the ad, including the brand name, product attributes, and the main selling message. Interviewers then question respondents, as they do with dummy vehicles. The t-scope does not appear to be used as much today as it has been in the past.

The **eye-movement camera** is another mechanical device that can provide an analyst with some insight into how consumers perceive elements within a print ad. There are a couple of variations of the basic methodology. Usually viewers are seated in front of a large desk with a large mechanical device placed on top. While they are viewing test ads, a sensor directs an almost invisible beam of infrared light at one of the viewers' eyes. The beam then follows the viewer's eye and superimposes the path the eyes follow on a layout of the ad. An analyst is then able to determine which element in the ad first received the viewer's attention (that is, the dominant point of entry), which path the viewer followed next within the ad, and finally how much time each element was viewed.

If an analyst wanted to know whether a sexy-looking model attracted attention to the product (rather than detracted from it), the eye-movement camera could provide an objective measurement that might differ from a viewer's verbal reconstruction of viewing patterns. The chief objection to the use of the camera is that viewers are tested under highly artificial conditions rather than as they would normally react. Recent technological developments enable the camera to be concealed within a reading lamp so that unobtrusive measurements can be made. It remains to be seen if this development will overcome researchers' resistance to its use.

Likeability measures appear to be increasing in usage. If this is true, it is unclear whether it is because of a trend in some areas toward more entertainment-oriented ads or because of evidence that suggests that likeability measures do a good job of measuring advertising effectiveness. In the ARF Copy Research Validity project, "the most surprising finding in the study was the strong relationship found to exist between the likeability of the copy and its effects on sales." As the researchers pointed out, it was generally believed that the function of copy was to sell, and whether the copy was likeable was unimportant. The "ARF study strongly suggests that ads that are liked outsell those that are not."[17]

Likeability measures are very similar to attitudinal measures in that both types of measurement probe the evaluative dimension of what an ad means to a consumer. There are many direct and indirect questions that can be used to probe likeability. In the ARF study, the question that was successful at predicting sales was fairly straightforward and is as follows:[18]

Thinking about the commercial you just saw, please tell me which of the statements on this card best describes your feelings about the commercial.

I liked it very much.   _____

I liked it.   _____

I neither liked it nor disliked it.   _____

I disliked it.   _____

I disliked it very much.   _____

Of all the pretest measures, **persuasion measures** are probably the ones most respected by people in the advertising business. To be persuaded is to be won over to another point of view. The viewpoint of interest to people in advertising is consumers' interest in obtaining or purchasing a particular brand. Although there are numerous variations of a persuasion test, the basic design is used typically to evaluate television commercials and is fairly simple. Subjects are asked to indicate their brand preference or usage prior to exposure to a series of television commercials. After exposure, they are retested and asked to indicate their brand preferences should they win a drawing giving them a market basket full of various products, including brands appearing in the tested commercials. Any shift in brand preference is assumed to be a function of exposure to the viewed ads. There are at least several companies that offer this service: Mapes and Ross, which offers a parallel system for evaluating magazine ads; ASI Market Research Inc., which conducts tests with viewers in their own homes via cable channels; McCollum/Spielman, which also offers a parallel system for testing magazines; and American Research Systems (ARS), the successor to Schwerin Research, the company that pioneered the basic system now widely in use.

Television Tests

Testing television commercials can be very expensive. So researchers test them in a wide range of forms. The closer a commercial looks to its finished form, the more realistic the test is likely to be. However, relatively unfinished commercials do a surprisingly good job of serving as a surrogate for the final ad, especially in view of the amount of money spent in producing them. The following are among the most common stages of unfinished television commercials used in tests:[19]

story boards — a series of visual frames and script of key audio used to represent a proposed commercial.

animatic — film or videotape of a series of drawings with audio used to represent a proposed commercial.

photomatic — film or videotape of a series of photographs with audio used to represent a proposed commercial.

ripamatic — footage taken from other existing commercials and spliced together. Also called stealamatics.

liveamatic — rough film or videotape of live talent shot for a proposed commercial. Can be close to a finished commercial but does not necessarily use actual sets or talent who will be used in the finished commercial.

Methodology and Practices

There is a highly competitive business in the field of advertising providing copy testing services to advertisers and their agencies. Not surprisingly, there are disputes and controversy over techniques, methodology, and standards—in effect, over which supplier has the better service. In an effort to resolve some common concerns about copy testing, a coalition of 21 major advertising agencies got together and reached "a high degree of consensus" on nine fundamental principles underlying a good copy testing system. The coalition was called PACT, an acronym for Positioning Advertising Copy Testing.[20] The PACT principles appear in boldface:

1. **A good copy testing system provides measurements that are relevant to the objectives of the advertising.** This principle underscores the importance of evaluating a test on the basis of its potential to assess an ad's potential to achieve stated objectives.

2. **A good copy testing system is one that requires agreement about how the results will be used in advance of each specific test.** This principle emphasizes the importance of specifying how the test will be used in advance of the results.

3. **A good copy testing system provides multiple measurements because single measurements are generally inadequate to assess the performance of an ad.** This principle calls attention to the difficulty of separating out the effects of advertising from the many other factors influencing sales. Because there is no universally accepted single measurement that can serve as a surrogate for sales, multiple measures are necessary.

4. **A good copy testing system is based on a model of human response to communication—the reception of a stimulus, the comprehension of a**

stimulus, and the response to the stimulus. This principle recognizes that ads usually function on several levels:

☐ On the "eyes" and "ears—it must be received (reception)
☐ On the "mind"—it must be understood (comprehension)
☐ On the "heart"—it must make an impression (response)

Therefore, a testing system should strive to answer questions on more than one level.

5. **A good copy testing system allows for consideration of whether the advertising stimulus should be exposed more than once.** This principle endorses the idea that in some test situations the learning of test material is much higher after two exposures than it is for one, indicating that there are situations where a single exposure test could be inadequate.

6. **A good copy testing system recognizes that the more finished a piece of copy is, the more soundly it can be evaluated and requires, as a minimum, that alternative executions be tested in the same degree of finish.** This principle is concerned about the biases that can creep into a test when alternative executions are tested in different stages of finish.

7. **A good copy testing system provides controls to avoid the biasing effects of the exposure context.** This principle points out the potential biasing effects of the context in which a program is viewed, such as an off-air test versus an on-air test, a clutter reel of commercials versus a program context, and one specific program context versus another specific program context.

8. **A good copy testing system is one that takes into account basic considerations of sample definition.** This principle emphasizes the importance of proper sampling procedures, especially ones dealing with the size and representativeness of the sample.

9. **A good copy testing system demonstrates reliability and validity empirically.** This principle underscores the importance of testing systems that yield the same results each time the advertising is tested (that is, reliability). For validity, this principle encourages users to provide results or evidence about validity "which are relevant to marketplace performance." The PACT agencies were concerned that there were many systems in use for which no evidence of validity was provided.

Concurrent Testing

This type of testing refers to research that takes place while the campaign is running in the marketplace. There are two basic types: tracking studies and coincidental studies. Of the two, tracking studies are far more important.

   Tracking studies are often a major part of the management of a marketing communication campaign. According to a 1988 study by the Association of National Advertisers, more than 85 percent of the respondents to its survey indicated that they track advertising results.[21] Although the most important tracking a company can do is to monitor sales, a tracking study usually refers to some type of consumer survey. Tracking studies are a way to monitor the pulse of a campaign. If there is some aspect of the plan or some area within the marketplace that is doing particularly well, an alert, well-informed company can often increase its marketing advantage. On the other hand, the marketplace can be brutal to companies that fail to respond quickly to their problems.

Tracking studies work best when they are part of an ongoing system of obtaining information. The basic idea in tracking is to keep in close contact with what consumers are thinking, feeling, and doing. Companies are interested in information like the following:

☐ **Awareness** Companies want to know about brand awareness and top-of-mind awareness as well as consumers' awareness of new information on the product, such as new features or a change in the positioning of a brand.

☐ **Attitude** Companies like to know a consumer's attitude toward the product because of the widespread belief that attitudes strongly affect the consumer's predisposition to buy a product. The nature of the relationship between an attitude and purchase behavior can vary considerably.

☐ **Communication playback** Basically, companies want to know if they are getting the right message across. As companies employ new and different strategies, tracking studies enable them to closely monitor whether they are achieving their objectives. Traditionally, very simple recall measures were used, but in recent years there has been diminished interest in recall.

☐ **Reported product usage** Companies regularly monitor sales on a daily, weekly, monthly, and yearly basis. Some of this information comes from within the organization. Large consumer-goods companies also supplement their databases with information from syndicated research services. Tracking studies are used to understand the nature of the sales taking place. For new products, consumers are asked whether their purchases are new (or trial) or repeat. For existing products, consumers are asked about their frequency of use.

☐ **Product satisfaction** With the increased emphasis on relationship marketing, many companies are sensitive about satisfying consumers and want to know if consumers like their products and their advertising. Among the important measures of consumer satisfactions are questions focusing on the consumers' intent to repurchase a product.

To get the above information, companies usually conduct their testing in-house or use an outside supplier. Agencies typically do not provide this type of research. A company will usually set up a system to gather information on a regular and periodic basis. The system can function on an ongoing basis (weekly, even daily), or it can gather data in large blocs of interviews at a time, called waves.

Companies usually set up their own panels or use ones set up by research firms. A problem with panels occurs when consumers become overly sensitized to participating in the study, or have reactive effects, and respond in ways that differ from the consumers they are supposed to represent. Some of the more popular tracking methods companies use to gather the information include:

☐ **Telephone interviews** This method is probably the most popular one because it is quick, easy, and inexpensive. Consumers can be asked a full range of questions, from those dealing with awareness to questions on product satisfaction.

☐ **Diaries** Consumers are requested to keep a record of various activities such as brands purchased, brand switches, use of coupons, and exposure to competitive promotions.

☐ **Pantry checks** This method provides much the same kind of brand usage information as diaries. This method is more expensive to use, but the information obtained is more reliable.

☐ **Mall intercepts** Although this method is widely used for other types of consumer research, it is used only occasionally for tracking studies. Its chief advantage is that it is one of the easiest and quickest ways to get large quantities of information.

☐ **Product audits and scanner data** Traditionally, companies have supplemented internally generated sales data with marketplace product-movement data from research firms such as A.C. Nielsen. These firms were able to estimate product movement by monitoring the flow of goods in and out of retail locations and area warehouses. Estimates were based on location visits as well as store and warehouse records. Today, the information is based largely on scanner data. The two dominant firms in the field are Nielsen North America and Information Resources, Inc. The two firms offer much of the same type of information. In the interest of brevity, we will look at Nielsen, the largest of the two companies.

Nielsen North America is the largest marketing research company in the world. Although most people are familiar with the Nielsen name from its media research unit, it gets most of its revenue from marketing research services. Nielsen is a true information conglomerate in that it offers services too numerous to explain in one chapter (let alone in a small section). The major users of its syndicated measurements are large companies, such as food manufacturers and those producing health and beauty aids. By the early 1990s, approximately three-fourths of all the companies purchasing scanner data accounted for nearly $300 million in business annually, with the average firm spending more than $1 million.[22]

Nielsen monitors retail activity at the store level through the electronic capture of all UPC bar-coded transactions recorded via scanning technology. Some stores are also measured with physical audits. The basic system is called SCANTRACK, and a related system is called PROCISION. Generally speaking, SCANTRACK is the service that provides information for food, grocery, and general-merchandise manufacturers, and PROCISION is the service for health- and beauty-aids manufacturers. Companies buy information on the United States as a whole or any of 50 major markets. The heart of the SCANTRACK system is a sample of 3,000 supermarkets with more than $2 million in all-commodity volume (ACV, or the total amount of sales in a given category).[23]

Nielsen strives to be a full-service market research company providing information on all the major elements in the marketing mix. Some of the information Nielsen provides can be summarized as follows:

- **Product** Provides sales figures for specific categories for the total U.S. market, each of the 50 major markets, and customized geographic trading areas. Sales figures include those for all significant brands in the ACV.
- **Pricing** Provides information on the prices retailers charge for the brands in an ACV. This information can be broken down into types of retailers, such as supermarkets, mass merchandisers, drugstores, warehouse clubs, convenience stores, and independent drug or grocery stores.
- **Distribution** Provides information on how a category is performing within a specific retail account or type of store versus the market. Also, provides information on which key items are handled in the market but not in certain retail accounts. ACV is generally expressed as a percentage of the sales volume in a product category that can be accounted for by stores that distribute the product. If a particular store or chain has an ACV of 50 percent in a market, it sells 50 percent of all the products in its category in that particular market. ACV indicates the extent to which your product is available to consumers.
- **Promotion** Provides information on the amount of merchandising support (for example, features and displays) to brands and categories. The media research unit provides information on ratings, and Nielsen Monitor Plus provides information on media occurrence (also called incidence), expenditures, and ad descriptions for network television. Nielsen Monitor Plus also provides occurrence data for national and local newspapers (top 50), outdoor, freestanding inserts, and magazines (national, Sunday, and top 50 local).

Coincidental studies, another form of concurrent testing, are designed primarily to evaluate or measure advertising and media usage while consumers are exposed to the media. The telephone interview is the principal means by which information is obtained. This method used to be called the telephone coincidental method. Interviewers usually ask respondents questions pertaining to what they were doing just before they answered the phone. Its chief advantage is the reduction in measurement error due to memory loss. The use of this technique in recent years has diminished considerably.

Posttesting

The distinction between posttesting and concurrent testing is mostly semantic, but it is also traditional. Essentially, they refer to the same thing. Both types of testing refer to testing for the effects of an ad after it has appeared in the media. Posttesting usually refers to testing at the end of a campaign, whereas concurrent testing generally refers to testing that takes place in an ongoing campaign. Posttesting is done for two basic reasons. First, measuring the effects of a campaign provides a rigorous, objective way to assess the performance of the individuals, including agencies, who have worked on the campaign; and second, a well-conceived testing program can provide benchmarks against which future campaigns can be developed.

From an operational point of view, it is important for management to have a thorough understanding of which aspects of the campaign have gone well, which should be replaced or improved, and which should be avoided in the future. This understanding extends to the people working on the campaign, including those at the advertising agency. By establishing benchmarks based on past performances, management can use the information to fine-tune day-to-day operations as well as integrate the information into the strategic foundation for the planning of the next campaign.

Posttesting can be divided into two types: tests measuring communication effects and those measuring behavioral effects. The following criteria are among the most popular ones used for posttesting:

- **Recognition** (a communication effect)
- **Recall** (a communication effect)
- **Attitudes, awareness, and likeability** (communication effects)
- **Sales** (behavioral effects)
- **Inquiries** (behavioral effects)

Recognition tests are some of the most widely used forms of posttesting, especially for print ads. The Starch Readership Report, offered by Starch INRA Hooper, is a popular test of this type. The basic technique involves sending out a battery of interviewers the day after an issue of a magazine has hit the newsstand. A minimum of 100 readers of each sex, who indicated that they have read the publication, are interviewed. The interviewer goes through the issue page by page and asks the interviewee to respond to certain questions about each ad as a whole and various elements within the ad such as the headline, illustration, copy blocks, and logo. The test produces the following scores for each ad in the issue:

> *noted* — the percentage of issue readers who remembered having previously seen the ad.
>
> *seen associated* — the percentage who remembered seeing some part of the ad that clearly indicated the brand name or advertiser.
>
> *read most* — The percentage who read half or more of the copy in the ad.
>
> *signature* — the percentage who remembered seeing the brand name or logo.

A recognition test is a memory test. As Fletcher and Bowers point out, it is based on the assumption that an ad cannot affect a purchase decision if consumers cannot remember the advertising, and inability to remember may be the most serious shortcoming of memory tests.[24] Even though consumers may not remember a specific ad, they may have internalized its message. So an ad with a low recognition score does not necessarily mean the ad failed. Another limitation of the Starch service is that their study is not conducted on targeted consumers. Companies generally want information on their target audience. Unless the readership of the magazine closely approximates the company's target audience, the information may not be usable.

For all its limitations, the Starch service is still widely used, partly because it is relatively inexpensive and partly because Starch is the grandfather of all advertising research companies and many people are familiar with it.

Recall tests are a form of posttesting that appears to be on the decline. There are two basic types: unaided recall, which is similar to fill-in-the-blank tests, and aided recall, in which a respondent is asked to recall an ad as an interviewer provides subtle cues to aid the respondent's memory.

Gallup and Robinson is a company that offers posttesting services for both magazines and television. Its In-View service is a test based in part on recall that is designed to provide at least three measures of the impact of a television commercial:

☐ **Intrusiveness** This measure is an indicator of the commercial's ability to get the viewer's attention. It is defined as the percent of respondents who can accurately describe the commercial the day after exposure.

☐ **Idea communication** This measure is defined as the percent of respondents who can recall the commercial, including specific sales points.

☐ **Persuasion** This measure is determined by a pretest and posttest measurement of respondents' "favorable buying attitude." The pretest questions about attitude and awareness are administered to respondents during a telephone call inviting them to be in the test. The following day, the respondent is given the same set of questions, and any change in attitude represents a measure of persuasion.[25]

The Gallup and Robinson Magazine Impact Research Service (MIRS) is one of the best known of the aided recall tests. The MIRS produces measurement scores similar to those obtained for the company's In-View television service: proven name registration, idea communication, and favorable buying attitude.[26]

Over the years, recall tests have been one of the most widely used forms of posttesting. There are indications that recall will not be as popular in the future. One of the more widely used recall measures of the 1980s, the DAR (day-after-recall) measure, offered by Burke Marketing Research, is no longer in use. Burke sold its commercial evaluation business to ASI, which incorporated it into its Apex system, which measures persuasion. The separate services are now called Recall Plus and Persuasion Plus.

There have been numerous articles questioning the value of recall testing, especially compared with persuasion measures. One of the strongest articles was by Gibson, who summed up his analysis and review of the literature on the recall/persuasion controversy as follows:

> Our summary can be brief because the record on recall is so clear. We know that recall data are inherently weak. We know that the theory on which recall data are based is empirically shaky. We know that the evidence for the validity of recall is—to be charitable—"checkered." This "checkered" validity of recall is in striking contrast to the evidence for the validity of persuasion.
>
> We may not know the answer to the longest playing controversy in all of marketing research, but we do know what the answer is not—and it's not recall.[27]

In 1990, King, Pehrson, and Reid surveyed research directors with the largest agencies and advertising executives with the largest 200 advertisers.[28] Their findings revealed that recall measures were still widely in use, although used less frequently than a similar study reported in the late 1970s.[29] They hypothesize that this decline may in part be due to a shift in emphasis from quantitative techniques to more qualitative ones. Perhaps because some of the negative publicity against the measure focused on the word *recall*, some systems may use the words *communication playback* to refer to measures that traditionally have been called recall. Still, there is a long tradition of using recall measures. Researchers are familiar with its use and have developed norms for its usage. Although recall testing may not be as popular in the future as it has been in the past, it will likely remain widely in use for some time.

Attitude, awareness, and **likeability tests** appear to be used more at the pretesting and tracking stages than as posttest measurements. This timing is at least in part because of the widespread availability of syndicated services that measure other posttesting criteria, such as recall and persuasion. Syndicated studies are usually cheaper than customized testing, although the latter can be conducted with a minimum of ease and expense, depending on the extensiveness of the sample. Syndicated sources usually provide ad norms as part of the service so that advertisers can compare the relative effectiveness of their advertising against their competition's.

Attitude testing is conducted because many advertisers believe that favorable attitudes are a necessary precondition to purchasing. Although this point is widely questioned, many companies try to effect attitude change as part of their marketing communication strategy, and testing for this effect can be viewed as part of their evaluative program. Companies can use a wide variety of tests to measure for attitudes, awareness and likeability, including the ones discussed earlier in the chapter and in Chapter 3.

Many advertisers simply believe that measuring communication effects is not a valid indicator of advertising effectiveness. They may believe, as does Josh McQueen, director of research of Leo Burnett U.S.A., that testing recall and persuasion is not relevant to what advertisers want to accomplish. McQueen argues for measuring clear **behavioral objectives.**[30] For most advertisers, this means drawing a causal relationship between advertising and *sales* or *inquiries*, the two most common behavioral measures. For many companies, the task is not as difficult to accomplish as one might assume, judging from what is written about this problem in textbooks and journals.

One reason so little is written about successful measurement systems is that they are proprietary, and they are likely to work only in very specific situations. Thus, even if they were published, the applicability of the techniques employed would be limited. Moreover, a test's usefulness or value to a company may be more as a partial indicator of a campaign's success rather than as *the one indicator* of an ad's or a campaign's ability to stimulate sales. Commercial testing organizations face a near impossible task of developing systems that can be of value to a wide variety of companies and still be without some methodological flaw. Almost every technique or test that has been described in the literature about testing has some limitation.

Using **sales** as a criterion for the posttest measurement of an ad or a campaign's effectiveness is widely done. Most of this evaluation, however, is informal. For example, McDonald's is able to monitor the sales of its stores on a daily basis. The day after a new ad or campaign breaks in the media, the company can "feel" and measure the impact in the marketplace. From a methodological point of view, there could be all kinds of factors that could be responsible for the ad's success or lack thereof, but, from McDonald's perspective, its experience enables the company to feel confident about separating the winning ads from the also-rans.

Companies do use more sophisticated techniques. Typically, these are quantitative models that include gross rating points and persuasion measures as key variables influencing sales. The companies may develop these advertising/sales models internally, or they may rely on a supplier such as Nielsen North America, especially since Nielsen collects most of the data needed as input for these models. Nielsen has a special unit in its company to offer customized models to clients. This unit largely replaced one of the most talked-about testing procedures in recent years: single source data measurement.

Single source measurement uses scanner technology and media exposure data to monitor product movement (that is, sales), sales promotions, and advertising exposure from the same panel of respondents. Because all of the information is obtained from the same set of respondents, an analyst can evaluate which ads and promotions appear to have the strongest effect on sales. In the late 1980s and early 1990s, single source data analysis was widely lauded as the closest technique yet to a holy grail of advertising measurement. By 1993, interest had diminished considerably, and the largest of the systems, based upon Nielsen's SCANTRACK data, was officially discontinued.

What happened? Within a span of about seven years, there were three systems from which companies could choose: InfoScan by Information Resources, Inc., a variation of Behavior Scan, the first service offered by IRI or any company; SCANTRACK by A.C. Nielsen; and SAMSCAN, which was the last system in and the first system out of the marketplace, offered by an alliance between the SAMI Corporation and Arbitron.[31] These systems were able to do a sophisticated job of isolating the effects of advertising and other promotional tools on sales. Because of these systems, many large companies, such as Procter & Gamble, Helene Curtis, and Campbell Soup, were able to evaluate their promotional campaigns in terms of behavioral criteria, such as sales and market share. However, the single source research systems that were able to produce these results did not offer bulletproof evaluations.

Although these systems did a fine job of tracing the short-term effect of a particular ad, promotion, or campaign on sales, they were unable to assess the longer-term effects on brand equity. Moreover, for many companies, the quality of the information was less important than the cost and time it took to complete a market test. Although it has been reported that market tests cost between $200,000 to $300,000, and usually took more than six months to produce usable results, Nielsen North America indicated in retrospect that in 1992 an average test cost about $50,000 to $100,000 and took between four and six weeks to complete.[32]

Along with a number of concerns about methodology, there were some practical concerns that probably led to the downfall of single source systems. In the 1990s, companies were desperately trying to cut costs because of a sluggish economy. Nielsen's system was not only expensive to buy, but also it was apparently prohibitive to maintain. The expense of installing and maintaining people meters in particular was too costly in view of declining sales. Moreover, some of the clients that were using the SCANTRACK system contracted with Nielsen for other services, such as customized modeling systems from their Advanced Analytics unit. Media buyers also failed to embrace Nielsen's system because the SCANTRACK system provided target-audience information on a household level, and buyers preferred the information on a person or individual level. Finally, even though a company might receive usable information about what had occurred, there was no guarantee that what had worked in the past would operate the same way in the future. In the end, the Nielsen system that had shown so much promise ended without any fanfare. By 1995 IRI, which pioneered single source measurement in the late 1970s, was the only company to offer a service. Their system is again called BehaviorScan and consists of eight geographically dispersed markets where retail and consumer purchasing behavior is electronically monitored from a panel group of 3,000 households in each market. BehaviorScan combines data obtained from UPC scanners (bar-code scanners) with information about television advertising copy obtained by monitoring the broadcast of alternate commercials to targeted households through a special device attached to the panelists' television. In addition, information about sales promotions, packaging variations, pricing mix, and in-store locations is also included in the service along with media exposure data to newspapers and some national magazines.[33]

Although BehaviorScan is less ambitious than earlier single source systems, it does offer advertisers an opportunity to experiment with different promotional variables, even if it is not the all-encompassing system that some people once thought it might become.

Using **inquiries** as a behavioral measure is one of the oldest and easiest ways to evaluate advertising. Adding a coupon to an ad or using 800 numbers are two methods of inviting inquiries and providing an easy way of comparing one ad to another, especially through the use of split-run techniques. In a typical example, alternate copies of a single issue of a newspaper or magazine will carry one ad or another that is being tested. The ad that produces the most coupons returned or 800 calls is judged to be the most effective. Companies may also track which inquiries were later converted into sales.

The major disadvantage of inquiry testing is the difficulty in relating inquiries to sales or communication objectives, particularly when it is uncertain if the coupon clipper or an 800 caller is a typical consumer. Inquiry tests are a popular method with industrial advertisers who use the inquiries as a prospect list for their sales forces.

Evaluating Other Marketing Communication Tools

The evaluation of other promotional tools, such as sales promotion, public relations, and direct mail, is a complex but often neglected part of a marketing communication campaign. Measuring the effects of sales promotion should be more than counting coupon redemptions, measuring the value of the public relations program should be more than keeping track of exposures in the media, and evaluating direct mail should be more than checking sales figures. Many of the techniques discussed earlier in this chapter with sometimes only slight modification can be used to evaluate the complete marketing communication plan. Indeed, many of the research companies mentioned in this chapter routinely test many elements of the promotional mix besides advertising. Readers are encouraged to consult publications in the marketing area for more details.

A FINAL NOTE ON EVALUATION

Throughout this book we have stressed the importance of looking ahead and thinking strategically. We recognize that most of the people who read this book will not be using the principles, procedures, and sources discussed in this chapter, at least in the near future. This information will have applicability in the years ahead. We also believe that a sound system of evaluation should be built into all strategic plans. Such a system should improve efficiency and effectiveness so that a firm can fully take advantage of its marketing opportunity in the short run and develop new, market-winning strategies for the future.

ENDNOTES

[1]John J. Burnett, *Promotion Management* (Boston: Houghton Mifflin, 1993), 603.

[2]Phillip Kotler, *Marketing Management* (Englewood Cliffs, N.J.: Prentice Hall, 1994), xxiv.

[3]George E. Belch and Michael A. Belch, *Advertising and Promotion* (Homewood, Ill.: Irwin, 1993), 681–683.

[4]"Total Measured U.S. Ad Spending by Category and Media," *Advertising Age* (September 28, 1994): 8.

[5]Jeffrey L. Seglin, "The New Era of Ad Measurement," *Adweek's Marketing Week* (January 23, 1988). The conclusion in the text is based on a 1987 report indicating a steady increase in the amount of money allocated to consumer and trade promotion over the previous 10 years. These estimates, based on Nielsen data, were for the packaged goods business. At the time, "advertising" accounted for 33 percent of the amount spent; consumer promotion, 28 percent; and trade promotion, 39 percent. Although these figures might not be the same for other product categories, the report did indicate that the figures were trending upward, so that an estimate of less than one-third of all money spent on marketing communication is spent on consumer advertising is probably conservative.

[6]Total advertising expenditures are based on measured media estimates from *Competitive Media Reporting* and unmeasured media estimates from *Advertising Age.* "100 Leading National Advertisers," *Advertising Age* (September 28, 1994): 4.

[7]Belch and Belch, *Advertising and Promotion*, 681.

[8]Kotler, *Marketing Management*, xxvi.

[9]Some of this material has been adapted from David J. Curry, *The New Marketing Research Systems* (New York: John Wiley & Sons, 1993), 19.

[10]Russell I. Haley and Allan L. Baldinger, "The ARF Copy Research Validity Project," *Journal of Advertising Research* (April/May 1991): 27–28.

[11]The directions and the statements that follow were adapted slightly from the ones used in the *ARF Copy Research Validity Project.*

[12]For more information, see William Wells, John Burnett, and Sandra Moriarity, *Advertising: Principles and Practice* (Englewood Cliffs, N.J.: Prentice Hall, 1995), 690–693.

[13]Charles E. Young and Michael Robinson, "GuideLine[sm]:Tracking the Commercial Viewer's Wandering Attention," *Journal of Advertising Research* 27 (June/July 1987): 15–16.

[14]Charles E. Young and Michael Robinson, "Visual Connectedness and Persuasion," *Journal of Advertising Research* 32 (March/April 1992): 51–59.

[15]Jack Haskins and Alice Kendrick, *Successful Advertising Research Methods* (Lincolnwood, Ill.: NTC Business Books , 1993), 313.

[16]Haley and Baldinger, "ARF Copy Research," 18.

[17]Haley and Baldinger, "ARF Copy Research," 29.

[18]Haley and Balinger, "ARF Copy Research," 18.

[19] These forms are adapted only slightly from the classification in the survey reported in Karen Whitehall King, John D. Pehrson, and Leonard N. Reid, "Pretesting TV Commercials: Method, Measures, and Changing Agency Roles," *Journal of Advertising* 22 (September 1993): 91.

[20]*PACT—Positioning Advertising Copy Testing* (The PACT Agencies Report, 1982), 10–27. Also reprinted in the *Journal of Advertising.*

[21]Haskins and Kendrick, *Successful Advertising Research Methods*, 298.

[22]A. B. Blankenship and George Edward Green, *State of the Art Marketing Research* (Lincolnwood, Ill.: NTC Business Books, 1992), 301.

[23]*Nielsen Select* (Nielsen North America publication, 1994), 3.

[24]Alan D. Fletcher and Thomas A. Bowers, *Fundamentals of Advertising Research* (Belmont, Calif.: Wadsworth, 1991), 176.

[25]For more information, see Fletcher and Bowers, *Fundamentals of Advertising Research*, 200–202.

[26]For more information, see Fletcher and Bowers, *Fundamentals of Advertising Research*, 206–207.

[27]Lawrence D. Gibson, "Not Recall," *Journal of Advertising Research* 23 (February/March 1983): 45. For other criticism, see Hubert A. Zielske, "Does Day-After-Recall Penalize 'Feeling' Ads?" *Journal of Advertising Research* 22 (February/March 1982): 19–22.

[28]King, Pehrson, and Reid, "Pretesting TV Commercials," 85–97.

[29]See also Lyman E. Ostlund and Kevin J. Clancy, "Copy Testing Methods and Measures Favored by Top Ad Agency and Advertising Executives," *Journal of the Academy of Marketing Science* 10 (Winter 1982): 72–89.

[30]Josh McQueen, "The Different Ways Ads Work," *Journal of Advertising Research* 30 (August/September 1990): 15–16

[31]For more information on the early development of these systems, see Curry, *The New Marketing Research Systems*, 66–74.

[32]Wells, Burnett, and Moriarity, *Advertising*, 694.

[33]Information Resources Inc., *The Difference in Decision Making* (Chicago, Ill.: IRI publication, 1993), 9.

Preparing the Plans Book

APPROACHING THE PLANS BOOK

One of the most important things you will do in putting together your advertising/marketing communications plan will be to put your recommendations down in writing. Your written recommendations will take the form of a **plans book.** Although your first questions might be about the mechanics of writing the plans book—How long should the plans book be? How many graphs should it contain? Where does the copy and graphics (creative) go? How slick should it be? Is there an outline to follow?—you should begin by thinking about just what it is your plans book is supposed to accomplish. We ask you to start by thinking about what it should accomplish because no two advertising situations are exactly alike, and, therefore, no two plans books will be exactly the same. Your plans book should reflect who your client is, what the client's problem is, how you are going to solve your client's problems, and why your recommendations are superior to other possibilities. You will want to demonstrate to your client that you have a firm understanding of his or her current situation and the expertise and experience to achieve the objectives set for the recommended campaign effort.

This is not to say that there is not a general form that the plans book will take. There is such a form, and we will include it in this chapter. The point is that you will be confronted with a lot of different advertising and marketing situations during your career, and each of them will demand a somewhat different approach to writing the plans book. Some of your assignments might call for writing a full-blown plans book for a total marketing communications campaign that will run a year or more. Other assignments might require that you write only a fragment of a plan for a special project that has come up. Clients will vary, situations will vary, and the people you will be working with will change over time. Knowing the general form of a plans book will allow you to make the adjustments to the different situations that you will come across. Following are some situations for which you could be asked to write marketing communication recommendations:

☐ *A special project that involves a small client with a limited budget.* Here your plans book might be shorter and focused on a smaller number of media and promotional opportunities. You might not be able to afford a research or evaluation plan, and the budget could be limited or dictated to you. Do not write a big cumbersome plan for a client that requires a more limited effort. Follow the steps of the campaign planning process, but omit the areas that are not required.

□ *The National Student Advertising Competition sponsored by the American Advertising Federation (AAF's NSAC).* The competitive factor and competition guidelines will dictate a particular type of plans book. This is a textbook situation in which you are expected to demonstrate that you can develop a complete marketing communication program. However, given the potential to write long plans for the competition, the AAF has come up with page limitations and format requirements that you must follow. There is still room for creativity within the AAF guidelines. Plus, this competition provides a good opportunity to learn how to balance comprehensiveness with conciseness in writing your plans book.

□ *A new product introduction for which most of the marketing and advertising information and recommendations are entirely new.* You are likely to be required to follow most if not all the stages of campaign planning. In fact, the campaign planning process is designed for situations in which you have to build a campaign from the ground up. You might find that little planning has been done, so you will have to develop the foundation for the campaign from primary research through strategic planning and tactical recommendations. Your written recommendations are likely to be quite comprehensive for a new product introduction. You will likely find yourself thinking of ways to write a good, concise plan while still providing the research and marketing foundation to the client. Consider separating your plan from the homework you did to arrive at it. Appendices or optional fact books can supplement your written plan.

□ *A small campaign that is narrowly focused in terms of the target audience, limited in the time it will be running, and for which there is no research budget.* A lot of the assignments you will be asked to work on will be for products in the marketplace that have campaigns or some type of marketing communication effort in place. It is more likely in this situation that you will be asked to write a plan for a small part of this continuing activity. Advertising agencies have preprinted covers ready to go for the plans that are written for clients as part of a longer-running business relationship (as opposed to a new business presentation). Here, stick to the assignment and do not write more than you are asked to write.

□ *A marketing communications campaign that requires knowledge and use of sales promotion, public relations, or direct marketing, or more than one of these skills, in addition to advertising.* The AAF competition, a new product plan, and a more comprehensive plan for an existing client require that you be able to write a complete marketing and communication plan. These are the situations for which this text is written because they require the broadest set of planning abilities.

□ *A local or regional campaign or test market effort.* These situations have distinct limits, so you have to be sure not to extend a test market or more limited campaign plan into a national campaign. Recognize the part of the total effort you are being asked to work on.

☐ *A trade campaign aimed at building support among distributors and retailers.* This is another specialized situation. Know your client's needs. Your recommendations should be in the planning areas appropriate to your assignment. This is not a consumer situation. Chapter 9 on related marketing communications provides a discussion of trade considerations and how marketing communications are used to build trade support. Make sure your plans book reflects these differences.

These are but a few possibilities. The bottom line is that your plans book is the product of your thinking. It is what you say and why you say it that will make the difference. In fact, that has been the point of all the chapters in this text to this point. These chapters have provided you with the tools for arriving at your recommendations and developing the reasoning behind them.

PERSPECTIVE ON THE PLANS BOOK

Before we get into the nitty-gritty of writing the advertising or marketing communication plans book, consider what a plans book can do and what its limitations are. First, there is no sure-fire formula for writing the plans book. There are guidelines, yes, but no formula that will result in a plans book that will win a competition or get you a client. The prospect of putting your recommendations down in writing should not throttle your analysis, solutions, and creativity. However, a good plans book can go a long way toward selling your client on your recommendations. Just as an ad should not overshadow a product, a plans book is a vehicle that should present your campaign thinking as clearly as possible and with the proper support.

Second, when you are writing a plans book, you are asking your client to spend a considerable amount of money on your recommendations. So, writing a plans book is not a literary exercise. The plans book should reflect your ability to decide about the highest priorities in solving your client's problems. Your thinking and presentation must be well organized and flow logically from problem analysis through strategic and tactical recommendations. Your reasoning should be apparent and well supported. Remember, you are asking for business. You have to establish confidence in your plan.

Third, once you get the business you are pitching, the plans book becomes the key document through which you will implement and control the advertising and marketing communication campaign. You ultimately will be working with a team of people from creative, media, research, and production departments who will have to understand the details of the campaign plan and the objectives that have to be achieved. The plans book will provide the appropriate direction and standards for what is a collaborative effort to achieve real results. Otherwise, the client will take his or her business elsewhere.

Fourth, the basic thinking behind a plans book is to present to the client what you have found that is right and wrong with the current market situation, what should be done to solve the problems, and the strategy you recommend for correcting the situation. This approach is analogous to what you want from your doctor when you are sick. You want to know what's wrong and what to do about it. That's what your client wants too.[1]

PREPARATION FOR PUTTING YOUR PLAN IN WRITING

You will find it much easier to write your plans book if you stay organized and keep good records during the development of your campaign. This discipline will pay dividends in the end. In an academic setting some instructors help you to do this by requiring interim, or mini, presentations and reports. These interim activities should help you to stay organized and on track during the work-in-progress stages of the campaign-building process. The writing of the plans book then becomes a task of reducing all of your work to a clear presentation of your analysis and recommendations (easier said than done). Another reason for staying organized is that plans books are often written under deadline pressure. The easier the access to what has been done to this point, the easier the writing process will be. Good organization will also lead to a clearer and more concise plans book. Put in the time up front, and you will not fall victim to wordiness, as this famous apology makes plain: "I have made this letter longer than usual, because I lack the time to make it short."[2]

Many of you will be working in an account group or client team. The members of these groups typically carry titles that give them specific responsibilities for the work done by the group (although the final product is the responsibility of all group members). Common job responsibilities in an agency team are those of the account executive, creative director, media director, research director (or account planner), and sales promotion/direct marketing director. It is the job of the account executive to organize the work of the team and keep it organized and on track. This responsibility means that there will be materials gathered, meetings to attend, records to keep, correspondence and reports written, and individual work to be accomplished. Some clerical support is required to maintain an orderly record of the development of your campaign. This support is typically available in an advertising agency. Student teams will have to assign this responsibility to someone in the group.

A project schedule along with periodic status reports should be prepared by the account executive of each campaign team. The schedule upon which the status reports are based should be developed by starting with the dates when the plans book should be completed and the presentation made. Then work backwards from these dates and set deadlines for all the other areas of the campaign development process. The account executive should issue periodic progress reports so that all team members can see how the work of the group is proceeding. These reports can be prepared quite easily on a computer, where the status of work can be indicated in a column designated for that purpose. Also indicate who is responsible, what the deadline is, and the nature of the task to be accomplished.

If your class or project is not organized exactly as described, do not despair. There are wide variations in how campaign projects are organized. This section is based on how a campaign project might be set up. The primary lesson to remember is that staying organized and moving your efforts along at a fairly consistent pace are better than leaving everything to the last minute. You can follow the conventions recommended here or come up with an approach that fits the situation you are working in.

Having sold you on the value of staying organized, do not let organization become an end in itself. Allow some flexibility and room for adjustments. Advertising and marketing communication campaign planning is a dynamic process. You will find that some things will get done on time, others will not, changes will have to be made, refinements and adjustments will have to be incorporated into the plan, and people will have to be able to work together. Be organized but flexible enough to handle the unexpected. Remember that the quality of the work you do during a term or semester or two-week period in an agency provides the building blocks for a good campaign and plans book. If you leave everything to the last minute, your plans book will reflect it.

LOGIC AND FLOW OF THE PLANS BOOK

An outline of the advertising and marketing communication campaign planning process has been presented at the end of Chapter 1. This is a step-by-step outline presented in a fair amount of detail. To understand the logic of that outline, you have to divide it into four distinct sections. The first section, which is labeled the "situation analysis," is the analytical part of your plan. This is the section in which you demonstrate your understanding of the client's advertising and marketing problems. Here is where you identify what problems must be solved for your client to be successful. This section will include your *analysis* of the company, consumer, market, product, and competition. This analysis is then reduced to a set of advertising or marketing communication problems to be solved by your plan. The better you are able to zero in on the essential problems your client faces, the more successful you will be at solving them. A laundry list of problems is very hard to solve with one advertising or marketing communication campaign. If you can determine the client's key problems and state them simply and clearly, your opportunity to use advertising and other marketing communication elements to solve these problems should be enhanced.

A good example of a marketing communication problem is the one that was faced by the Saturn Corporation when it started to advertise its cars in 1990. Saturn wanted to accomplish some conventional objectives for a new product introduction (namely, awareness, favorable image, and purchase consideration), but one of its key problems was to avoid an association with General Motors in the minds of its target audience. Why? Because Saturn's target was (and continues to be) consumers that normally purchase Japanese cars and have a negative image of the quality of American-made cars. The company wanted to set Saturn apart from the stigma of American cars in the eyes of its target audience.[3]

The second major section of your plans book will provide *direction* for your recommendations. This section includes your target audience profile as well as the marketing, advertising, and communication *objectives* that are appropriate to the scope of your client's problem. This section tells your client what you expect the target audience to do as a result of being exposed to your campaign. Once again, clarity and focus are important. This section should flow logically from the previous section. If you have done a good job in determining why the client's problem exists, then you should be able to decide what has to be accomplished for the problem to be solved. If you are lucky, you will be setting objectives to take advantage of an opportunity rather than a problem. But, more often than not, you will be solving problems.

Returning to the Saturn example, the company was able to identify its target audience as young adults who had bought Japanese cars in the past or intended to buy one in the future. Furthermore, Saturn was able to identify some attitudinal differences between this target audience and General Motors' typical consumers. Based on these differences, Saturn was confident in describing its target audience as exhibiting the following characteristics:

- ☐ Quality, reliability, and durability were important purchase considerations.
- ☐ They were import buyers but leading-edge consumers who would take a chance on a new American corporation.
- ☐ They were motivated by value.
- ☐ They were intelligent, well educated, and well informed.
- ☐ They were always looking for something better.
- ☐ They were young at heart, but this characteristic was spread across many life stages.[4]

Notice that the target-audience information is more than a listing of demographic characteristics. It demonstrates that Saturn understands the consumers' purchase process. This insight will provide direction to the team of people who will ultimately have to develop the marketing communication programs to sell Saturn's image and brand attributes.

Saturn's objectives for the introductory phase of its campaign were (1) to create high levels of awareness about both the company and its products, (2) to develop a favorable image around the company, its products, and service, and (3) to create high levels of purchase consideration.[5] These are Saturn's goals that will come to life in its strategy and tactical recommendations.

The third primary division of your plans book will be your recommendations or programs that you have developed to achieve the objectives set in the section above. Advertising, sales promotion, public relations, and direct marketing are all possible areas in which you will be offering solutions to your client's problem. This is the section in which you unfold your marketing communication *strategy* and the substrategies in the creative, media, sales promotion, public relations, and direct-marketing areas. You will also be presenting speculative examples of the elements that will *execute* your campaign.

Saturn's objectives are fairly hollow without an accompanying marketing communication strategy that includes what messages consumers will be

FIGURE 10-1   SATURN MAGAZINE ADVERTISEMENT

Like some kind of comic book superhero, Suzanne seems to lead two lives. During the week, she's a mild-mannered property tax analyst for a large corporation. Come the weekend, though, you could say it's a different story.

This is Suzanne at her current favorite, skydiving, but it might have been something else. She scuba dives. She skis. She'd like to go sailing, but she gets seasick. Oh, and she owns two Rottweilers, and a cockatiel that can whistle half of the Flintstones' theme.

Anyway, she'd been driving a humdrum sort of econobox, and she came to feel she needed something else. Something more like her weekend, less like her week.

The Saturn SC2

Why is our SC2 so fun to drive? For some, it's the 124-horsepower engine. For others, it's the sport-tuned suspension. But for you, all we can say is "Here's the key."

What Suzanne bought was a Saturn coupe. She says it was like finding the shoe that fits—it has the styling, the handling, the performance and all the other fun-to-drive stuff her freefall/underwater/cartoon self wants.

And, funny thing, the price didn't bother her property tax analyst side one bit.

A DIFFERENT KIND *of* COMPANY. A DIFFERENT KIND *of* CAR.

SUZANNE STEHLIK bought a Saturn coupe because she didn't have enough excitement in her life.

---

expected to be aware of and favorable toward. To achieve its objectives, Saturn wanted its target audience to acquire both knowledge of the product and a specific image of the Saturn brand and company. This strategy becomes Saturn's positioning in the market against its competition.

The product knowledge Saturn wanted to convey was

- ☐ Saturn cars were outstanding in terms of quality, reliability, and durability.
- ☐ Saturn cars were high in overall value.
- ☐ Saturn cars were contemporary in design.
- ☐ Saturn cars delivered excellent fuel economy.
- ☐ The ride and handling of Saturn cars were impressive.
- ☐ Saturn was aggressive in its pricing relative to the competition.
- ☐ Saturn cars exhibited noteworthy acceleration performance.

The brand personality that Saturn wanted to communicate concerning the car and the company included four characteristics that reinforced the overall theme, "A Different Kind of Company. A Different Kind of Car." Saturn wanted consumers to believe and feel that Saturn was friendly, creative, precise, and international.[6]

The advertisement shown in Figure 10–1 demonstrates how Saturn's advertising agency, Riney & Partners, executed its strategy. Look closely at this print ad for the elements (both visual and verbal) that have been created to bring the key communication ideas home to the target consumer.

The last section of your plans book should include a research plan for monitoring and *evaluating* the results of your recommendations. This plan should be based on the objectives set for the campaign but might also include some diagnostic research to probe how various elements of the campaign are performing. The specificity with which Saturn was able to express its strategy makes it easy to measure whether or not its programs are achieving the desired results through survey research methods.

The J. Walter Thompson advertising company has reduced the logic of the plans book to a set of five questions. The situation analysis should answer the first two questions: Where are we? and Why are we there? The objectives that you set answer the third question: Where could we be? Your strategies provide the answers to question four: How could we get there? And your evaluation plan will provide the final answer to the question: Are we getting there? This is a dynamic cycle in which the information gathered from your evaluation plan will feed back into the five stages and update the answers to where and why we find ourselves in the current situation.[7]

A PLANS BOOK OUTLINE

The following outline of an advertising and marketing communication plans book includes many of the elements that could appear in the book you prepare for the problem that is confronting you. Some plans books will not contain all of these elements. Some plans books will present some of the elements in a slightly different order. However, this outline is a place to start. It is the conventional manner in which most plans books are organized.

THE COVER

The cover of your plans book should include the client's name and your agency's name (in a student competition this should be your school's name). Other information is optional in a university setting, such as the course name and competition name. The cover is the first place that you can start to sell your campaign. Consider how you want it to appear, so it will stand out among the competition. Do not leave your creativity behind after you have completed your campaign work. Extend colors, design approaches, and themes to your plans book cover. Most cover designs incorporate the client's colors and logo at a minimum.

You might want to consider going beyond this minimum standard for the cover in special situations such as the AAF/NSAC competition or new business pitch. However, ask your instructor or supervisor if putting more effort into the design of the cover is appropriate. In any competitive activity it is better to put in a little extra effort, but the cost of doing so might outweigh the benefits. Your instructor (or supervisor) is the best person to guide you in this regard. If you decide to put a little more into your plans book cover, the next three paragraphs are for you.

The plans book is considered a companion piece to the campaign presentation. It should be designed to look like the presentation. Use similar graphics on the cover and section dividers to establish a team identity. This shared look will help campaign judges and clients to make a quick association between your team and the plans book once the presentation is over.

Computer technology and the availability of color laser printers and photocopiers have added a great deal of flexibility in designing and printing full-color covers for plans books. This type of design might not be necessary for most class or routine agency projects but has become close to a necessity for the AAF National Student Advertising Competition.

Take into consideration how many copies of your plans book you will have to produce. If you have to make a lot of copies, color graphics and other fancy technological frills will become expensive to reproduce. You might decide to make full-color and comprehensive plans books for judges, instructors, and clients while providing black-and-white copies for others. Once again, you will have to assess your situation and the importance of the use of color in your plans book.

THE TITLE PAGE

The first page inside your plans book should be a title page. Once again, the content of the title page has some optional elements. The title page can include more information than the cover because cover design considerations typically do not have to be considered. Most title pages include (1) the client's name, (2) the agency's name, (3) agency team members' names and titles, (4) advisor or instructor's name, (5) course title, (6) school name, (7) appropriate dates, and (8) acknowledgments. There is a lot of discretion in how to set up your title page. The best advice is to keep it simple and clean.

You can carry some of the content from the cover on to the title page. Campaign themes, slogans, and logos can add to the continuity of the plans book as you move the reader from the cover to the inside.

TABLE OF CONTENTS

After you have completed writing your plans book, you should go back and create a table of contents, which should be the second page of your book. List the major headings in your plans book in chronological order, and then indicate the page location of each along the right-hand margin of the page. Do this last because you will not know the page numbers of your sections before you finish writing the plans book. A typical table of contents is illustrated in Exhibit 10–1.

The general form for a table of contents reflects the outline for a marketing communication plan, as shown in Chapter 1. These are the basic elements of a plans book. These headings will be given different emphasis as the marketing and advertising problems you are confronted with change from project to project. Your instructor might ask for a slightly different order, or the client's problem could require some different areas to be included. For example, the outline in Exhibit 10–1 does not include a section for a test market. If your

---

EXHIBIT 10–1   PLANS BOOK TABLE OF CONTENTS

---

*The primary research section may not be an official section, but a description of the methods you used to gather data should be included in the plans book. This section will appear in different places in different plans books depending on where the findings fit best. Primary research as an official section should be placed either before the consumer analysis or within this section as illustrated in this exhibit.

client's problem requires a test market, then you will include it in a section in your plans book (and in the table of contents).

THE INTRODUCTION OR EXECUTIVE SUMMARY

The first one to three pages of your plans book should include a brief version of the entire marketing communication plan, called the introduction or executive summary. This summary should hit the highlights of your campaign recommendations. Your client is most interested in knowing what you plan to do and what it is going to cost. The key elements of an executive summary should include (1) the central thrust of your campaign, (2) whom you are targeting, (3) how much it will cost, or the total budget, (4) the creative strategy, (5) any key elements that will encapsulate the campaign, such as the theme, product position, or slogan, (6) what media you are recommending, and (7) the scheduled time period in which it is going to run. It is often best to write the introduction or executive summary after the rest of the plans book has been completed. This will help you know your recommendations in detail and be better prepared to write a summary highlighting what you have actually put in the plans book.

The introduction or executive summary should be clearly written and organized so that the client's management team can understand the recommendations without having to distill them from the detailed presentation inside the plans book. They can and will look inside the plans book for verification and details to support the recommendations, but they typically do not want to read it in depth from cover to cover.

THE SITUATION ANALYSIS

The situation analysis actually consists of analyses of each of five subparts: a company, consumer (to include primary research), market, product, and competition analysis. The *company analysis* section should be kept relatively brief because the client already knows this information. Include enough information to demonstrate that you know the company and its product's sales history. Focus more on the company's marketing and advertising history and not on other nonrelevant historical facts. You will have to gather and understand more about your client than is necessary to put in the plans book. Do not confuse what you have to know to develop your campaign recommendations with what you have to tell the client. The emphasis should be more on problems that have historical significance for your plan than on a descriptive historical profile of the company.

An example of a historical problem for a company was the perception of most consumers (during the 1980s) that General Motors cars were of poor quality. This problem was the primary reason GM decided to create the new Saturn company. GM wanted to provide Saturn with a fresh start unencumbered by GM's poor quality image.

The consumer, market, product, and competitive analyses are the heart of the situation analysis. The *consumer analysis* section should provide the foundation for the eventual selection of your target audience. This should be an insightful analysis of the buyer behavior of the key consumer segments that have the potential to become your target audience. An important foundation for this analysis is the report of relevant findings from your primary research.

Your analysis should provide a precise description of the important consumer segments in terms of demographic factors such as age, gender, income, education, marital status, and occupation. Because demographic profiles only provide part of the picture of a prospective target audience, you should also include any psychographic, lifestyle, and geodemographic data that are available to give a richer picture of how your brand fits into the audience's lives. These factors are compared to product-usage and media-usage patterns to determine the characteristics of the prospective consumer targets for your campaign. You are looking for some insight about prospective buyers' behavior that you can use effectively as part of your strategy. You want to know how consumers use your product and what their motivations are for buying it. Saturn's comparison of the attitudinal differences between its target audience and the typical General Motors customer is a good example of how a profile can be brought to life by going beyond demographic data and discovering why people buy particular brands and products.

The *market analysis* section takes the broadest view of the market for a brand by including sales trends and geographical patterns, technological trends, economic trends and influences, regulatory considerations, changes in the structure of the market, changes in competitive activity, and changes in attitudes and lifestyles among consumers. These are essentially broad-based factors that can influence your strategy in some way. Some instructors or companies call this the marketing environment. Sometimes these broad-based factors can be an advantage. For example, attitudes toward health and physical fitness have changed enormously over the past 30 years. The result has been a boom in exercise equipment, health foods, athletic clubs, and athletic clothing. This same trend has resulted in a serious decline in smoking, beef consumption, and beer and wine sales. Do not overlook these market factors because they can constrain what you might be able to accomplish as well as provide real opportunities.

Along with these broad environmental factors, the market analysis focuses on geographic and seasonal sales patterns. The geography of sales can be broken down on a regional basis, by major metropolitan markets, and by comparing rural, urban, and suburban purchase patterns. The market analysis should provide a clear picture of where your brand does best and its market potential in areas where it may not be doing as well as expected. Market potential is evaluated by calculating and reporting the product category development index (CDI) and brand development index (BDI) for the markets your brand competes in.

The market analysis section should also include pertinent data on the size of the market in terms of sales, seasonal sales trends, market share, and structural aspects of the market, such as distribution and your client's relationship with the trade. This section should provide an overall sense of market potential, what the viable market segments might be, and where and when you should focus your marketing communication efforts.

The *product analysis* section is more than a descriptive presentation of the physical attributes of a product or products. Your client is more concerned with how consumers rate or evaluate and perceive a product than what its tangible characteristics are. The outcome of your product analysis should be problems and opportunities in the areas of brand image and potential for product positioning.

Your primary research is a potential source for information on how consumers evaluate your client's product versus those offered by competition. You will want to be able to report findings on consumers' preferences regarding the client's product as well as their perceived image of the brand. Saturn's findings concerning its target audience's attitudes toward buying General Motors' products and Japanese cars were critical in how it decided to communicate about its cars. Positioning itself as a "different kind of car company" was a direct result of Saturn's ability to analyze consumers' attitudes about its and other manufacturers' cars.

Your *competitive analysis* is an assessment of who your competitors are, what they have been doing, and what they might do while you are trying to promote your brand. If you are going to compete successfully, you have to have a good understanding of your competitors' capabilities. Analyze their advertising and marketing communication spending levels and their actual activities. Be able to predict if they are likely to respond to your campaign and how they might react. Be alert to what your competition is likely to do because it will influence your results. Remember that your marketing communication strategy is developed specifically to compete against other brands in your category. Know them well.

The situation analysis section of your plans book should not be lengthy. There are several ways to make it concise. First, use graphs, charts, and tables to present important data. The many available and easy-to-use graphics software packages should make this task much easier than it has been in the past. Try to turn your data into pictures to make it easier to digest. This will allow you to make reference to the data without having to describe it at great length in writing. Pie charts work well for illustrating market share, competitive media spending, product usage segments, and budgets. Bar graphs work well for comparing data as well as indicating trends. Line graphs also work well for illustrating expenditure and sales trends. Second, use bulleted lists to highlight or summarize key information. For example, the following bulleted list summarizes key findings on pet ownership in the United States:

- More households own dogs than cats.
- Cat owners are more likely than dog owners to have more than one pet.
- Working couples are more likely to own a cat than a dog.
- Cat ownership is on the rise, and dog ownership levels remain constant.

This is an outline form of writing that helps you to give emphasis to important information while presenting it as concisely as possible. Third, make good use of subheadings to organize your information. Your major subheads will label the primary sections of your plans book and will appear flush left in your table of contents. The next heading will indicate subsections of each major part. For example, your creative strategy is typically a subheading under your advertising strategy section. Notice that it is indented on the table of contents in the figure. You can indicate the different levels of importance of your subheads through the use of capitalization, bold lettering, and underlining. Always give more emphasis to the major sections and successively less to each subsection in a hierarchical fashion. A quick perusal of this text will illustrate how subheads are used to organize the book's content.

It is not wise to overuse subheads. Overuse of subheads can impede the flow of your writing by making it appear choppy. Too many subheads can make the organization of your chapters appear unnecessarily complicated. Also, to be consistent with this type of organization pattern of outlines, we recommend that you not use more than two hierarchical subdivisions of each major section of your book. If you do not have two or more subsections that make up a larger section, do not move to the next level of subheads. This is the same rule in outlining that guides you not to subdivide section *I*, for example, if you do not have at least an *A* and *B* subsection under it.

PRIMARY RESEARCH

Primary research is often called for in planning a campaign to collect more information on the target audience than is available from secondary sources. A lot of the consumer information you will be able to gather from existing sources will be helpful but is usually too general to guide you with specific decisions. When you are working for a local or regional client in particular, you will find that most information from syndicated sources is national in nature.

You will have some discretion about where to place your primary research in the plans book. Put your findings in the sections where they best belong. Include consumer research findings in the consumer analysis section and perhaps in the product analysis section. The description of the methods you used to gather your data should be placed immediately in front of the report of your findings regardless of where in the plans book you include your research results. If you choose to divide up your findings by placing them in more than one of the situation analysis sections, be sure to describe your research methods before the first discussion of the primary research. Another approach is to present your research in a special section called Primary Research and place it either before the consumer analysis or within this section.

Describe your research plan, to include its objectives and methodology, as precisely as possible. Tell the client what information you wanted to know but did not have. Describe the type of research you decided to execute, the sampling scheme, the questions asked, and how the data were analyzed. Then, provide a summary of your findings as a foundation for your target audience selection, objectives, and subsequent strategy recommendations.

Typical information that you will want to provide is how and why consumers buy your product, how they use it, what they like and dislike about your brand and competitors' brands, and their media habits. Research should be performed with a purpose in mind. Do not get caught up in doing research for the sake of presenting it. Make sure your research is well conceived and clearly presented. Interpret the results for the client. Do not merely present data without telling the client what they mean.

Make judicious use of tables and graphs to present your research findings, as recommended for the situation analysis. Also, place your questionnaire and any detailed analysis of your data in an appendix. You do not want to interrupt the flow of your plans book with your research materials. However, you do want these items to be available in your plans book should someone want to refer to them.

PROBLEMS AND OPPORTUNITIES

Inclusion of this section is up to the discretion of your group or instructor, but it is highly recommended because it provides a bridge from your situation analysis to your objectives and strategies. Your objectives and strategies will be based on problems and opportunities that you have uncovered in the situation analysis. This is a necessary part of your thinking whether or not you formally state your problems and opportunities. Stating your problems and opportunities is a good exercise in digging for that insight that will catapult your recommendations forward. Likewise, a good set of problems and opportunities demonstrates to the client how you got from your analysis to the objectives and strategies.

Problems are drawn from weaknesses that you found in your situation analysis. These problems can be derived from a particular piece of information or a set of findings. You may find them in any one section of your situation analysis or in all of the sections. Exhibit 10–2 illustrates how problems were deduced from various sections of the situation analysis.

Notice that the problem statements in the exhibit are conclusions drawn from the situation analysis. They state what the weakness is in the situation without offering a solution. Do not steal the thunder from the rest of your plan by presenting what you are going to do about the problems in this section. Leave your solutions to your strategy section.

As you analyze your marketing situation, your aim should be to find some opportunities in addition to problems. An *opportunity* is something that you find in the situation analysis that you can take advantage of in your plan. The opportunity may be the result of a particular company or product strength or a weakness exhibited by the competition. It could be an opportunity to take advantage of a trend or change in government regulations. Your client might be the first to incorporate something new into a product. There are a lot of places to look for opportunities. The important thing to remember is that in analyzing your situation, you should look for opportunities as well as problems. Exhibit 10–3 (p. 310) illustrates how opportunities might be derived from the situation analysis.

You will run into situations where it is not clear whether you have found a problem or an opportunity. Many situations are actually hybrid cases where a problem can be turned into an opportunity. However, the relationship between your problems and opportunities is not necessarily to restate your problems as opportunities. Look for genuine opportunities that the situation analysis presents apart from the problems you have found.

Your list of problems and opportunities should include only those areas that are relevant to the marketing communication plan. A client may have problems, such as store location, that cannot be solved by marketing communications. Leave these problems out of your plans book.

TARGET-MARKET PROFILE

This section of the plans book tells your client to whom your marketing communication campaign is going to be directed. It sets up the marketing, communication, and advertising objectives, in that the underlying assumption is that the objectives will be achieved against this group.

The target market profile also tells your client where the resources and efforts of the company are going to be focused. The consumer and market analysis

---

EXHIBIT 10–2   DERIVING PROBLEMS FROM THE SITUATION ANALYSIS

Company Analysis

Company X has been changing advertising agencies at a rather frequent rate resulting in inconsistent advertising messages with no recurring and unifying theme. A real-life example of this type of problem might be the advertising campaign for Burger King, which does not have the same consistency as the campaigns run by McDonald's and Wendy's.

Problem

Company X's advertising messages are inconsistent with no recurring and unifying theme.

Consumer Analysis

Consumers in the product category perceive all the major brands to be relatively alike. They tend to buy when a brand is on sale and then repurchase whatever other brand is on sale the next time they buy. Category usage is high but brand repurchase is low. The soft-drink category might exhibit these characteristics for many brands.

Problem

Consumers in category are not brand loyal.

Combined Market, Product, and Competitive Analysis

The company's current models are lagging the competition in technological sophistication. The company is presently working on new models but has to sell its existing inventory. Automotive and computer companies often have to work within the constraints of this type of problem.

Problem

Company X's models do not offer the most current technology available in the market.

---

sections of your plans book set up the selection of the target market by analyzing the various potential market segments that might become the focus of your campaign. Therefore, the profile of the target market should come as no surprise.

The target market for a given brand or product is the segment whose needs and wants are best met by the product. This means that the target market for a brand may not always be the heavy-user segment in the category. Different brands in many consumer product categories meet different needs. Your situation analysis should provide you with the appropriate insight with which to select a target that will best respond to your product and marketing communication campaign.

A typical target-market profile for a manufacturer of canned vegetables might look like this:

Primary Market

☐ Heavy users (35 percent of the users and 65 percent of the total consumption) who need on hand large quantities of inexpensive food for their families

Market Analysis

Economic and social trends indicate consumers are moving away from more formal clothing for both work and leisure, and your client sells men's and women's suits. Any industry that is sensitive to fashion trends has to be concerned about this problem.

Problem
The market for company X's product is relatively limited.

Product Analysis

The client is operating in a parity product category where there are differences between brands, but these differences are not known to consumers. Furthermore, it is not clear whether or not these differences would be important criteria to the purchase decision. Over-the-counter drugs and personal-hygiene-products marketers have to be concerned about consumer understanding of brand differences in their categories.

Problem
Consumers perceive company X's brand to be the same as the competitors' brands.

Competitive Analysis

Company X was the first to enter the growing health-food market and established itself as the category leader. Since then, new competitors have made inroads, and this has altered company X's brand position in the market. These new competitors have also been successful in influencing consumer preferences for the types of foods offered in the category. As new categories grow and mature, consumer preferences for certain attributes and types of products often change. This can be a natural result of new competitors entering the category and offering new benefits to the consumer market.

Problem
Company X's brand has lost its position and image in the category due to changes in consumer preferences and new competition.

- ☐ Female homemakers
- ☐ Age 25 to 49
- ☐ Blue-collar occupation
- ☐ Household income $15,000 to $30,000
- ☐ Resides in size B and C counties
- ☐ High school education
- ☐ Family size 3+ skewing to 5+
- ☐ Eastern and Midwest regions

Secondary Market
- ☐ Trade
- ☐ Buyers for chain supermarkets and independent grocers that cumulatively represent a minimum of 65 percent of total canned vegetable sales
- ☐ Current brokers/wholesalers[8]

EXHIBIT 10–3   DERIVING OPPORTUNITIES FROM THE SITUATION ANALYSIS

Company Analysis

Company X has established a strong distribution system and has good trade relationships with its retailers. It would like to use this experience and positive image with the trade to support a new product introduction. This could be a fairly common advantage to a company wishing to extend its product line around an existing brand name.

Opportunity

Company X already has a strong distribution system and good trade relations.

Combined Consumer and Product Analysis

Company X has found out that consumers want a particular product attribute that company X's brand has but that has never been advertised. Consumers do not associate company X's brand with this attribute. This may appear to be too good to be true, but 7-Up found itself in this exact position regarding the caffeine in soft drinks. It never had caffeine in 7-Up and was able to take advantage of the fact that consumers were unaware of this.

Opportunity

Company X's brand contains a highly desired attribute that consumers are unaware of.

Combined Market and Consumer Analysis

The increase in two-wage-earner families and the aging of the population have made company X's experience in the service area the foundation for expansion of its business. Lawn and garden services, house painters, snow removal companies, and house cleaning firms are all benefiting from this current trend.

Opportunity

Company X's services are in more demand due to reduced leisure time for people to do chores and the inability of older consumers to do these household jobs.

Product Analysis

Company X had been focusing on one particular use of its brand and in doing so had marketed to one market segment. Analysis of the product found that it offered other uses that appealed to different market segments. Some readers will recognize this as the classic Arm & Hammer baking soda case where they advertised the product for use as a deodorizer in kitty litter and the refrigerator among other things. The reality is that some companies miss opportunities because they only see their products from one perspective.

Opportunity

Company X's brand has multiple uses, most of which have yet to be marketed to the appropriate market segments.

Competitive Analysis

The analysis uncovered that existing competitors were upgrading their models and by doing so making them more expensive. Their move upward was leaving the lower end of the market open and ripe for entry by a new company willing to sell cheaper models. This has happened in the automobile industry, where companies that entered the market with cheap subcompact cars could not resist the temptation to build bigger and more expensive cars. Often the low end of the market has been abandoned, thus providing an opportunity for another manufacturer to enter the market.

Opportunity

There is no competition for company X in the lower end of the product category.

Notice that in this example there is a secondary target market, the trade, which will have to be sold on carrying the product. These two targets complement each other. Usually there will not be two or more consumer markets because it is difficult to design a marketing communication campaign that can communicate with equal effectiveness to more than one consumer target. However, as we saw in Chapter 8 on marketing communication, the trade is an important target if an advertiser hopes to gain distribution for the product advertised to the ultimate consumer.

Although it might be simplest to identify one target audience, there will be situations in which you will have to combine several submarkets into a group that is large enough to warrant your marketing communication effort. Or you might be asked to develop a campaign for a large client that sells to more than one market segment. In these cases, you will find yourself defining more than one market as the target of your campaign. When this occurs, it makes sense to determine which markets are primary and which secondary.

A short rationale should be provided for the selection of your target markets. Notice that in the example some of this rationale concerning the size of the target markets has been built into the profiles. The rationale should be brief because you have spent some time and space in your consumer analysis supporting this choice.

MARKETING, COMMUNICATION, AND ADVERTISING OBJECTIVES

Usually it is not the job of the advertising or marketing communication team to develop the marketing objectives. These should be provided by the client. However, the marketing objectives are often restated here to demonstrate to your client how the proposed marketing communication campaign supports its total marketing effort. Additionally, smaller clients may not have the sophistication to provide marketing objectives to you. In this case, you will have to make some estimate of your sales, share of market, or profit objectives. Estimating may not be as difficult as it sounds because smaller clients are likely to be retailers or local businesses for whom there is a much more direct link between marketing communication activities and sales.

Chapter 4 has presented a detailed discussion of how to set objectives. Your job in your plans book is to present a set of objectives that provides clear direction to your campaign. You should also demonstrate that you understand the interrelationship between the sales goals of marketing and the communication goals of advertising and the other marketing communication elements. You might find that you can skip setting communication and advertising objectives at this stage in favor of presenting them with the appropriate marketing communication elements. This decision depends on how extensive your advertising, sales promotion, public relations, and direct-marketing recommendations will be.

Setting communication and advertising objectives at this stage assumes that your marketing communication recommendations are simply the execution part of the plan. However, if you intend to give each marketing communication element a major strategic emphasis, then you should defer your communication, advertising, and other objectives for the appropriate section.

Budget

There is some discretion as to where the campaign budget should be included in the plans book. Some clients and agencies like to put the budget right after the marketing objectives so that expenditures can easily be compared to what they are going to achieve. Others (usually agency presenters) do not like to tell the client what a campaign is going to cost until after they have convinced the client's management team that the recommendations are really worth the costs involved. You will have to assess each situation to determine where it makes the most sense to present the budget.

Another way to look at the budget is in terms of presenting the total figure broken down by major marketing communication elements to illustrate the relative strategic emphasis given to each early in the plans book. Then, each marketing communication element's budget can be further broken down in its section.

The other approach is to build toward the total budget by placing it at the end of the book. This approach does make it difficult for the client to remember how the budget relates to objectives and the elements of the campaign. But it places the budget closer to the recommendations that are the items the client is really paying for in the final analysis.

List all expenditures that will be incurred in the implementation of your campaign, including not only media but also research, production, and contingencies. The budget presentation should not be more than a page or two and can be presented in both tabular and graphic forms. Tables can be used to break down the budget into all its important items, and pie graphs can be used to illustrate just the major allocations.

Marketing Communication Strategy

Your marketing communication strategy is your plan for how you are going to achieve the marketing and communication objectives that have been set. Make sure that your strategies cover all of your objectives and at the same time establish the direction for how you are going to use your marketing communication elements. Your strategic statements should make it apparent how the marketing communication recommendations will fit together to accomplish your objectives.

Each strategy statement should have only one focus. It should state how you are going to employ some promotional element or combination of elements to achieve the campaign's objectives. Keep your strategies broad and directional. Do not let them become tactical. For example, state if you are going to use advertising to maintain the brand's image during peak sales cycles. But do not state what the ads will look or sound like or what the slogan will be. These explanations are reserved for the actual advertising part of your plan.

A short rationale should be provided for each strategy that links it back to your problems and opportunities, objectives, and key information that have been gleaned from the situation analysis. For example, if you found that there are certain times during the year when sales really dip and you have set an objective to achieve better sales during these periods, you should have a strategy that addresses that problem. And your short rationale should be able to provide the link between the strategy and objectives.[9] Here is an example of this relationship:

Promotion Strategy

Emphasize sales promotions during slow sales periods in July and August to build product categories in which company X is not realizing its full potential.

Rationale

The strategy is based on the realization that sales promotion is required to bolster sales during slow periods and for products that are not reaching their sales potential. Company X should continue to use advertising during peak sales seasons to maximize margins and profit when consumers are buying at higher rates.[10]

ADVERTISING STRATEGY

Your advertising strategy consists of two substrategies that address what will be said in the recommended advertising messages and how media will be used to deliver these messages with the greatest impact. These substrategies are the creative and media strategies that make up the heart of most of the marketing communication campaigns that you will be working on.

Creative Strategy

The creative strategy section of your plans book will tell the client how advertising messages are going to be used to achieve the campaign's objectives. This section and the appendix will also include examples of how the creative strategy will be implemented. The organization of the creative section is a mirror of the organization of the entire marketing communications plan. You know who your target audience is and should restate it in this section. You know what the problems and opportunities are and will be translating them into problems and opportunities that advertising can respond to. You know what the marketing objectives are and will be writing objectives for your creative strategy that reflect what your creative recommendations can contribute to the achievement of those objectives. Your creative strategy will tell the client how your creative product will achieve the creative objectives, and then you will present example ads that you believe will do the job.

The elements of a creative strategy vary from advertising agency to advertising agency, but most include the following items in what is called the *creative platform.* All creative platforms include a restatement of the target audience. Throughout the development of the creative strategy, it is imperative to keep the target audience in your mind's eye. Know to whom you are talking and what has to be communicated to them.

Next you will want to present the objectives of your creative strategy. This is what you want the strategy to accomplish. Remember that these will be couched in communication terms, such as *to convince, to establish in teenagers' minds, to make aware, to remind, to educate, to persuade, to counter the impression,* and *to demonstrate how to use.* Think in terms of what you want the target audience's response to be. What do you want your target audience to think, feel, or do after seeing or hearing your ad? Also be ever mindful of what advertising can accomplish by itself. Do not set marketing or sales-oriented objectives here unless direct marketing is a key element and you expect to generate sales.

Your strategy is a statement of *what* you are going to say or offer in your ads to get the response you have set for your objectives. This is the reward or benefit that the target audience is going to receive for having done what your ad has asked it to do. This can be an emotional or tangible benefit. The target may feel better, know more, be more successful, solve a problem, or be given an opportunity. This is the essential promise of your advertising.

Your strategy will also include support or selling points that should convince the target audience that it will receive the benefit or reward promised. These are the reasons the target audience should believe your advertising. And, finally, your strategy should set down what will be the tone, style, or personality of the advertising. The style or tone should reflect the nature of the target audience as well as be consistent with your product's or brand's image.

The most concise way to present the creative strategy is in the form of a creative platform. Clients, instructors, and agencies vary to some degree on what they want to see in the creative platform. Be flexible enough to adjust to these differing requirements while maintaining in your mind the purpose of the creative strategy. Chapter 6 provides you with some alternative versions of creative platforms that you should refer to before you write one for your campaign.

Examples or prototypes of your *creative execution* of the creative strategy should be included in the plans book. If these examples are numerous, you might consider including representative examples here and placing the rest in an appendix. Print ads should be in a semicomprehensive layout form with illustrations and display copy sketched in. Body copy can be ruled in and provided on a separate copy sheet.

Television spots are best presented in storyboard form and radio commercials as scripts. Large-scale ads, such as outdoor and transit ads, should be scaled down but still maintain the life-size proportions of the posters. All executions should be copied so that they can fit into the plans book. Sometimes photographs of the ads in their media context can aid a client in seeing how they will look in their real environment. For example, a photograph of an outdoor board in place or transit card on a bus can supplement the scaled-down example of the ad.

The *media strategy* part of your plans book can be divided into five subsections: (1) a statement of key media implications to be drawn from the situation analysis and marketing communication strategy, (2) media objectives, (3) media mix strategy, (4) the media plan and schedule, and (5) media budget summary. Your media strategy recommendations are based on a thorough understanding of how media can be used to help achieve the campaign objectives. This requires a review of the situation analysis and marketing strategy with an eye toward identifying those problem areas that are really the concern of the media planner. The media planner should be looking most closely at data and information concerning the target audience, geographic markets, possible seasonal sales patterns, competitive spending levels, and the nature of the marketing communication and advertising objectives. Here we are looking down the road a bit to get a sense of how difficult (or easy) it is going to be to put enough media weight against the target audience at the right times and in the right places to meet our objectives.

Suppose as you review the client's situation, you notice that it is easy to identify geographic and seasonal sales patterns. Add to this the lucky fact that product distribution is sufficient in these areas to meet demand. However, you also notice that media availability is sparse in some of these markets. One of your main problems becomes how you are going to reach your market given the problem of media availability. This is a media problem that your plan will have to address.

Very often the media implications concern how to achieve the advertising objectives. Advertising objectives stated in communication terms all carry with them media implications. For example, awareness might be easy to achieve and not tax the media planner. But more difficult objectives, such as changing images or attitudes, require media plans that can reach an audience with sufficient weight and on a particular type of schedule if they are going to have any chance of success. If your audience never sees or hears your ad or sees or hears it too infrequently, it probably does not matter how good it is. Here advertising exposure patterns are everything.

The marketing communication budget also has major implications for the media strategy. Upward of 80 percent of the money spent on a campaign is spent on media. This means that the media planner must not only ascertain how to solve specific problems, but he or she must also do it on a budget or efficiently.

Media objectives are set to provide standards to be met and direction for the media strategy. The criteria for media objectives are well established in the advertising business and reflect the availability of audience data with which they can be measured. The minimum requirements for media objectives are that they state how much reach, frequency, and gross impressions or rating points a plan is expected to achieve. These are measures of potential exposure of your message. They are discussed in detail in Chapter 7. Campaign continuity is also an important media consideration. Continuity is concerned with how constant your message exposure will be. Media planning is a game of trade-offs. On a given budget, you can expose your message to a lot of different people (reach) or expose it to fewer people more often (frequency). Likewise you can limit your media weight to short periods of time (flights) for impact, spread it out for continuity (but lose some impact), or combine some of each by varying media weight from one time period to the next (pulsing). You determine which of these patterns is best by comparing the alternatives to what the entire campaign has to achieve.

Setting media objectives is no different from setting objectives for other parts of your campaign. They should always include a target audience, criterion to measure, and time limit in which they will be achieved.

There is a tendency in planning the *media mix strategy* to jump right in and start buying specific media vehicles, such as *Time, Newsweek,* and *Sports Illustrated.* Resist this temptation. Before you think about specific vehicles, you should analyze and evaluate how each media type will help fulfill your media objectives. Here you are concerned with the strengths and weaknesses of the major media alternatives and what mix of these media will work best in your campaign. Your evaluation of media alternatives should include both quantitative and qualitative factors.

The two primary quantitative criteria that you will want to look closely at are the relative cost-efficiency of each medium and its ability to deliver your message to the target audience. Some of these data are available in syndicated media-audience reference sources, some will have to be calculated, and some come from experience. For example, if you are involved in a new product introduction on a nationwide basis, you will be looking carefully at national media, such as television and magazines. You probably will eliminate local radio, direct mail, and perhaps outdoor ads because they cannot deliver your target audience in an efficient manner. Likewise, if you are working for a local retailer with one store, you would eliminate the media you would use for a national brand. You might instead consider radio, newspaper, direct mail, and outdoor ad possibilities.

It is a good idea to rank your media alternatives from best to worst in terms of their ability to deliver your audience in a cost-efficient manner. To rank the choices, you will have to calculate cost-per-thousand or cost-per-rating-point figures, or both, as the basis for your comparisons. Also consider where your competition is spending its media dollars. You will have to evaluate whether you want to go head-to-head with the competition or diverge and select media that you can dominate without worrying about competitive activity.

Qualitative factors include creative message requirements, such as the use of sound, motion, product demonstrations, coupon offers, or color. The media environment should be evaluated in terms of its news value, entertainment value, and quality. You are trying to ascertain what the media environment might add or take away from the effectiveness of your ad. Controversial topics, for example, tend to scare advertisers because they do not know how the controversy will rub off on their advertising. Some media, such as television and newspapers, have a built-in risk in this regard. Media that carry only advertising messages, such as outdoor ads and direct mail, do not have this characteristic. A lot of these qualitative considerations can be very important and come from experience with the media.

After you have evaluated the media alternatives, you should decide on the relative weight that is going to be given to each medium in the mix. Some of your media choices should be identified as primary because they are going to carry the major responsibility of delivering your audience, and others will be support media. Support media typically add something special to the campaign, such as reaching more of the audience, adding synergy in terms of a different way to execute the creative message, providing a vehicle for delivering samples or coupons, or providing a special timing or placement advantage. For example, an owner of a local, upscale specialty shop might put most of the money into local media. But the owner might add a small-space ad in *The New Yorker* for image and status reasons because many of the customers read that magazine.

For each media type selected, you should be able to describe how it is going to be used. For example, what dayparts are you going to use for television and radio? Are there special programming considerations? What types of magazines have you selected? What types of ads are you recommending? What types of newspapers will you use? Are you recommending particular days of the week and sections of the newspapers in the plan? What size showing is being recommended for outdoor ads and why? If direct mail is recommended, how many pages will the mailing be? What about color? How many pieces will you be printing?

After you have made these decisions, you can present the specific media vehicles that you are recommending. Obviously, vehicle selection should fit the strategy and rationale that have preceded these choices. You will want to describe which TV programs, radio stations, magazines, newspapers, and other media you are including in your schedule.

Your *media plan and schedule* is easiest to visualize in the form of a media calendar or flowchart. The media calendar will illustrate how you have scheduled your media over time and what weight you have given to your selections. Your scheduling and media mix strategies will be obvious from one look at this calendar. Figure 10–2 provides an example of a media schedule calendar. Notice that each medium has its own symbolic code so that you can tell from a glance how each is scheduled.

The last item that you will want to include in your media strategy section is a *media budget summary.* Media budget summaries can take a number of different forms depending on those factors that are most important to your plan. If market coverage is important, then you might present how much money you spent in each medium by market. Perhaps scheduling is the most important consideration, in which case you can present the budget by each quarter of the campaign year. If product support is important, you can show how much money you have spent in support of each product in a product line. If more than one factor is important, do not be afraid to provide more than one table to illustrate how the media budget has been allocated.

SALES PROMOTION, PUBLIC RELATIONS, AND DIRECT-MARKETING STRATEGIES

The sales promotion, public relations, and direct-marketing sections of your plans book should follow the general form of the media section. You should be able to state specific objectives appropriate to what you want these marketing communication elements to accomplish. Likewise, describe the strategies recommended and include the actual activities or techniques you have selected to implement these strategies. Include examples of your tactics, as you did in your creative strategy section. To illustrate how your entire plan fits together, you may provide a schedule of these activities in each section to demonstrate how they dovetail with your advertising media recommendations. Finally, a brief budget summary should demonstrate how you have

FIGURE 10-2   MEDIA SCHEDULE CALENDAR

MEDIA CALENDAR

EXAMPLE
GENERAL HOSPITAL
MADISON DMA
OCTOBER 7, 1990

1991 Monday (Sales) Dates	January	February	March	April	May	June	July	August	September	October	November	December	TOTAL TARGET RATING POINTS (TRP'S)
Media	31 7 14 21 28	4 11 18 25	4 11 18 25	1 8 15 22 29	6 13 20 27	3 10 17 24	1 8 15 22 29	5 12 19 26	2 9 16 23 30	7 14 21 28	4 11 18 25	2 9 16 23	
ADVERTISING PROGRAM	SUSTAINING			EMERGENCY AND OBSTETRICS					NEW SERVICE INTRODUCTION		SUSTAINING		
ADULTS 24-54													
TELEVISION: 30'S MADISON DMA					200 TRP'S PER WEEK				300 TRP'S PER WEEK		200/WEEK		5300
20% DAY, 50% FRINGE, 30% PRIME													
13 WEEKS AT 200 TRP'S PER WEEK													
9 WEEKS AT 300 TRP'S PER WEEK													
RADIO: 60'S, MADISON METRO									200 TRP'S PER WEEK				1200
1/3 AM, 1/3 DAY, 1/3 PM													
6 WEEKS AT 200 TRP'S PER WEEK													
4 STATIONS													
20 SPOTS PER STATION PER WEEK													
NEWSPAPER—JOURNAL AND TIMES									1 INSERTION PER WEEK				554
1/4 PAGE WEEKDAY (B/W)													
8 INSERTIONS													
NEWSPAPER—JOURNAL AND TIMES									1 INSERTION PER WEEK				346
1/2 PAGE SUNDAY (B/W)													
5 INSERTIONS													
OUTDOOR: #100 SHOWING		600-625 TRP'S PER WEEK								600-625 TRP'S PER WEEK			15332
25 LOCATIONS PER #100 SHOWING													

TOTAL RATING POINTS: 22712

Source: Roman G. Hiebing, Jr., and Scott W. Cooper, *The Successful Marketing Plan: A Disciplined and Comprehensive Approach* (Lincolnwood, Ill.: NTC Business Books, 1991), 216.

allocated your marketing communication dollars to the recommended activities in each area.

Not every plans book has a complete set (sales promotion, public relations, and direct marketing) of marketing communication recommendations. How extensive these sections are will depend on the scope of the marketing communication problem you have been asked to solve.

CAMPAIGN EVALUATION

The purpose of a campaign evaluation plan is to provide a methodology for determining whether or not you are achieving your stated objectives. Because you have set objectives for your overall campaign and each substrategy, you will have to decide how you want to measure your campaign results. You can follow sales results on a trend basis and evaluate how effective the campaign has been in terms of sales. You and your client can decide if it is wise and necessary to be more diagnostic by testing the effectiveness of your creative messages, media mix, sales promotion activities, or media spending levels.

The nature of your evaluation plan will be influenced by how much money your client wants to put into monitoring and evaluating your campaign. This plan can run from a simple before-and-after survey of communication objectives, such as awareness, knowledge, image, and preference, to an expensive and elaborate controlled experiment (test market) in the marketplace. This plan should answer the question, Are we getting there?

You have at your disposal methodologies ranging from focus groups (with all their inherent external validity problems) to surveys to field experiments (which are very expensive). Many clients are taking the responsibility for evaluative research away from their agencies. Nonetheless, you should be able to demonstrate to your client how you will judge whether or not the recommended campaign is being successful.

APPENDICES

You will want your plans book to be a clear presentation of your analysis and recommendations unencumbered by unnecessary items. Yet, you also want your client to see that you have done your homework. The appendices of a plans book are good places to include research findings, media calculations, extra ad examples, and alternative strategies.

Do not allow your appendices to become catchall sections in which you indiscriminately deposit material. Make sure that the appendices genuinely add something to the impression you want to make. They should serve a purpose.

KEY POINTS TO WRITING THE PLANS BOOK SUMMARIZED

Exhibit 10–4 lists 16 points to remember while writing your plans book. These tips also follow the general logic of campaign planning from your situation

---

EXHIBIT 10–4   16 KEY POINTS FOR WRITING MARKETING COMMUNICATION RECOMMENDATIONS

☐ Develop an outline before writing.

☐ Develop tables, graphs, and visual support before writing.

☐ Make your situation analysis as concise and factual as possible.

☐ Use primary research to support your consumer and product analyses.

☐ Make sure your problems and opportunities reflect each section of your situation analysis.

☐ Resist turning your problems and opportunities into objective and strategy statements.

☐ Keep all objectives to one sentence.

☐ Write objectives that are specific, measurable, to be achieved within an established time frame, and aimed at a specific target audience.

☐ Make sure strategies describe how objectives will be achieved.

☐ Make sure your advertising and other marketing communication recommendations are on target and on strategy.

☐ Be creative.

☐ Show your ads.

☐ Make sure your media plan will deliver the reach, frequency, and media weight necessary for your campaign to achieve its objectives.

☐ Integrate all promotional recommendations into a unified campaign.

☐ Propose how you plan to measure your results.

☐ Be clear and concise but not brief.

---

analysis through your plans for executing the substrategies of marketing communication. The arrangement of the plans book follows a logical flow. Within this framework you can adjust and adapt to the specific marketing communication problem confronting you.

Advertising and marketing communication demand creative and innovative solutions formed within the discipline demanded by carefully set objectives and strategic thinking. Art for art's sake will not help you to achieve your objectives because often it is created without regard for the target audience or an understanding of what has to be communicated to them for a campaign to succeed.

The plans book should be a clear presentation of your analysis of the marketing situation, problems and opportunities, objectives, strategies, recommended tactical executions, and evaluation of results. The marketing communication plan should be effective and efficient. Although the process you undertake to put this plan together is dynamic, the final plan should be a carefully crafted set of recommendations that are easy to understand and that push for closure in terms of solving the client's problem.

ENDNOTES

[1]Robert L. Baumgardner, "Writing Plans and Recommendations," in *What Every Account Executive Should Know about Writing Plans and Recommendations*, ed. American Association of Advertising Agency Committee on Client Service (New York: American Association of Advertising Agencies, 1988), 7–8.

[2]Blaise Pascal as quoted in John Bartlett and Justin Kaplan, eds., *Bartlett's Familiar Quotations*, 16th ed. (Boston: Little, Brown, 1992), 270.

[3]Raymond Serafin, "The Saturn Story: How Saturn Became One of the Most Successful New Brands in Marketing History," *Advertising Age* (November 16, 1992): 1, 13, 16.

[4]*Saturn Communication Strategy 1992* (Spring Hill, Tenn.: Saturn Corporation, 1992), 8.

[5]*Saturn Strategy*, 3.

[6]*Saturn Strategy*, 7, 9, 10.

[7]*Advertising Planning Methods* (New York: J. Walter Thompson, 1987), 1.

[8]Roman G. Hiebing, Jr., and Scott W. Cooper, *The Successful Marketing Plan: A Disciplined and Comprehensive Approach* (Lincolnwood, Ill.: NTC Business Books, 1991), 100.

[9]Hiebing and Cooper, *The Successful Marketing Plan*, 114–115.

[10]Hiebing and Cooper, *The Successful Marketing Plan*, 115.

Presentations:
Selling Face to Face

The best-laid plans, the painstaking research, the precise and accurate strategy, the sharpened proposal—all can amount to nothing if your presentation to win an account falls on its face. And everyone in the agency or on the team is sure to hear the thud.

One way to guard against such failure is to think about your presentation from the client's point of view, not your own. Given the pressure of an upcoming presentation, the inclination is to think of your own goals and needs during the presentation planning stage. But thinking that way pushes the client into the background. Instead, you should push the client into the foreground by empathizing with the client's wants and needs.

ROLE PLAYING AS THE CLIENT

One of the main goals of your presentation is to build your prospective client's confidence in you and your agency. With that goal foremost in your mind, you need to immerse yourself in that client's wants and needs. They are not a mystery to be unraveled. In fact, often they are the commonsense aspects of selling. If you think back to your own selling experiences, you're sure to find a variety of tips, those important dos and don'ts, to help make your presentation a winning one. And if you think like the client—actually role play as the client—then you're sure to find concerns that your presentation should address.

Prior to creating a plan for the presentation, ask yourself this question: *If I were the client, what would it take to convince me that I should choose this agency and not one of the others?*

To answer that question, you will need to role play as the client. You will need to empathize by getting outside of your mind and into the mind of the client.

What follows is an exercise in role playing as the client. It includes some possible questions from the client and prospective answers that could lead to considerations of what to include in your presentation. Don't restrict yourself to these questions and answers but create your own as well. And create them before you actually begin planning your presentation.

Client:	I want my company to make money, and I wonder if this agency knows how to do that.
Possibilities:	Show evidence of your agency's success and the success of its clients. Draw similarities between the work you've done for those clients and the work you'll do for the client.
Client:	How well do they know my business?
Possibilities:	Prove you do. Show and tell what you know about the client's business. Assume your competitors will do the same, especially with obvious information. So, show and tell the not-so-obvious information. Talk the client's talk. And walk the walk.
Client:	How well do they know my competition?
Possibilities:	Show and tell what you know about the competition. Make it inclusive. Relate the competition to the client. Give historical, present, and future trends describing that relationship. Point out the differences between the competition and the client, emphasizing the advantages, certainly, but not excluding the disadvantages altogether.
Client:	Can I get along with these people?
Possibilities:	Greet the client before the presentation. Smile. Be friendly. Make eye contact. Admit it when you don't know or are unsure about something. Stress the longevity in your business relationships.
Client:	Do I think these people work well together? Does one hand know what the other one is doing?
Possibilities:	Show how well you get along. Lighten up the passing of the baton from one presenter to another. Play off of one another. Talk together, but without excluding the client. Give evidence of coordination and organization within the agency. Reveal the hierarchy of who will handle what for the client.
Client:	I have my agenda for this meeting, so let's see if they address and meet it.
Possibilities:	Never lose sight of the original task or assignment. Refer to your task and goal. Remind the client how focused you are on that task and goal. Show and tell how various parts of the presentation address and meet the client's agenda for the meeting.
Client:	I hope I'm not bombarded with a lot of gory details and complex information.
Possibilities:	Keep it simple. Keep it focused. Or, as the old adage goes, "Tell 'em what you're going to tell 'em. Tell 'em.

Tell 'em what you told 'em." Prioritize what you say and show. Emphasize some things over others. Repeat key themes and concepts.

Notice how your pointed consideration of these questions raised new questions or even possibilities for presentation material in your mind. But this wouldn't have been the case if you hadn't considered the client's point of view. All of the questions and concerns were client based, and all of the possibilities offered were in response to the client. This is what is meant by empathy and role playing.

PLANNING THE PRESENTATION

With the client foremost in your mind, you will need a plan for your presentation, one that guides the coordination of activities ranging from the dynamic interplay of presenter and audio/visual aids to thematic focus in the script. This plan serves as your map as you wind your way through the presentation process. It tells you what to do when and with whom. And it all starts with deciding on a presentation strategy.

THE STRATEGY

Think of planning your presentation in the same way you would plan an ad. You know it will represent the image of your company, and the presentation message will link your company to the customer or client. You also know that the message should be clear, succinct, and, in most cases, singular. Beyond that you know that the message will come to nothing if you don't have the customer or client's attention. That's always the first job of any ad or presentation. Think back to the chapter on the creative part of the campaign, for instance, where you tried to link the rightness of the message with the uniqueness of the idea so that one complemented the other, and they both served to grab audience attention.

Each of these considerations at the creative level concerned your creative strategy or guide for what to include in an ad and how to include it. The same type of strategic thinking goes into your presentation planning. And as with an ad, your tasks begin with deciding on goals and a message. From there, you need to decide on the best means to achieve those goals and to convey the message.

Goals

The formal presentation plan starts with your consideration of goals. Goals address what you want to achieve. After you've determined what those goals are, it will be much easier to design the presentation. In Exhibit 11–1, you'll see a list of four basic presentation goals. These goals are explained later.

Identify the Objective The question to be answered here is, Why are we doing the presentation? The answer is not as easy as it may seem. Certainly you're

---

EXHIBIT 11–1   PRESENTATION GOALS

☐ Identify the Objective
☐ Get and Keep Attention
☐ Bond with the Audience
☐ Establish Credibility
☐ Be Persuasive

---

doing the presentation to win the account. That's the easy answer. But the more difficult and more important answer, the one that will lead to winning the account, centers on the client, particularly what you want to achieve in the client's mind.

Obviously, your determination of the presentation's objective guides your planning. So, the first thing you need to do is write a concise and pointed objective for the presentation, one that includes the communications effect you hope to achieve, just as in strategic thinking for an ad. Some possibilities include building understanding, convincing, motivating to action, or changing opinions, attitudes, or beliefs, with the last clearly the most difficult of all.

Get and Keep Attention Whatever you say or show in the presentation will be meaningless unless those you want to reach are paying attention. To keep them involved, you should consider a few surprises at the outset and along the way, the kind that raise eyebrows and pique one's attention. You should also give long and hard consideration to the beginning and end of your presentation. A presentation is like a horse race; it's the beginning and end that count. Possible openings for the beginning of your presentation are featured later in this chapter.

Bond with the Audience You need to find common ground with the client. In this way, you will be perceived as on the client's side, with the client's best interests at heart. Part of that common ground relates as well to the personal connection you make with the client. There's nothing wrong with friendliness throughout the presentation, but it's especially important at the beginning.

Establish Credibility The client has doubts. Much is at stake for the client, and so the doubts surface. One key doubt relates to your credibility. Your presentation plan should include pointed strategies for eliminating that doubt.

Be Persuasive Plan your presentation so it makes the most of important character traits, such as sincerity and trustworthiness. Project those traits. With your presentation content, hook into the prospective client's wish list of needs and wants. What you say and show requires alignment with those needs and wants.

Overall, these five goals—identify the objective, get and keep attention, bond with the audience, establish credibility, and be persuasive—should guide your presentation plan. As you consider them, you are sure to generate a variety of tactical possibilities that you could use in your presentation. Through your analysis, you'll be able to create a blueprint, a guide for making the hard decisions centered on what to say and show.

DECIDING WHAT TO PRESENT

Once you've determined your strategy, including important goals, you will need to determine the tactical approaches for reaching those goals. For instance, assuming the beginning and end of the presentation are the most important parts, then you will need to design both according to the goals you've outlined. What follows is a list of primary tactical considerations, complete with suggestions about how to craft or structure certain parts of the presentation.

SCRIPT TREATMENT

As an overarching term, the script treatment embraces both the storyboard and actual script for the presentation. The storyboard is a visual representation suggesting the flow of time and components in the presentation. It is similar to a storyboard for a television commercial. The script is the actual words spoken by the presenters. Obviously, it should coordinate tightly with the storyboard.

Storyboarding

Just as you begin a television commercial with a storyboard, you also begin the tactical plan for your presentation with a storyboard. This plan requires imagination and a solid grip on key messages, themes, and your strategic considerations, such as your objective or the need to establish your credibility. In a large sense, the storyboard represents a visual walk through the presentation or a form of blocking used in dramatic play production. The storyboard suggests the sequences of what happens next. It includes rough designations of time and shifts of presenters. It also includes visual cues, such as slides, boards, or flip charts.

Block Out the Presentation on Cards or Paper Because your presentation is much longer than a typical commercial in which you might show 10 frames to suggest the flow through 30 or 60 seconds, you will need to begin creating the storyboard for your presentation on large-sized paper or note cards, with each note card representing each sequence or shift in message or presenter.

In their important book *How to Create and Deliver Winning Advertising Presentations*, Sandra Moriarity and Tom Duncan suggest a technique of using planning cards (note cards, actually).[1] On each card you write a key word or phrase suggesting a key message or part of the presentation. You then go through a process of sorting and reshuffling the cards until you arrive at what seems a workable order of presentation messages.

Another possibility is to begin with large-sized, unlined paper, the kind found in big layout pads. Simply block out spaces as junctures in time. To accommodate visual aids such as slides or flip charts, you may want to devote two blocks or spaces, side by side or one on top of the other. You will also need a small amount of space to indicate time passing.

Block Out the Main Presentation Parts Do not write on the storyboard absolutely everything that will be said or shown. Rather, begin coordinating the presentation's main structural parts, namely the beginning, middle, and end. The time devoted to each part is a strong consideration at this storyboarding stage. For example, based on your strategic overview of the presentation situation (that is, client's needs, importance of creative versus promotion versus media, and the like), you may decide to block out more time for creative than promotion or vice versa. Or you may decide to frontload the creative—that is, put it up front or close to the beginning. In this respect, the amount of time given to each of the main structural parts and what takes place inside those parts suggest what goes on your storyboarding note cards or paper.

In an important way, too, the storyboard should not be seen as a fixed and finite blueprint for your presentation. It should always remain flexible, allowing you to add or delete as new insights emerge over time. It should also be rough, much like an "idea page" when you begin thinking creatively about what you should say and show in an ad.

With storyboarding the idea is to put your vision of the presentation down on paper. How will the presentation begin? How will it proceed? And how will it end? What will be the main thrust or message of these three main parts of the presentation? Each of these major parts (beginning, middle, end) needs to be blocked out, spurring you on to imaginative and strategic insights regarding what to say and show. Further, they need to be blocked out so that you can make assessments about the presentation's flow from one part to another. Ultimately, as you view the storyboard as a whole, you will gain a sense and understanding of the presentation's organizational and motivational strengths and weaknesses.

Scripting

Simultaneously with storyboarding, you should produce a rough script to coordinate with the storyboard's blocking and proposed flow. In some cases the script will be written by the individual presenters. In other cases, key people will be designated as scriptwriters, ideally working in close cooperation with the presenters, who, after all, must feel comfortable with the script. To put unnatural or foreign words in a presenter's mouth may create an artificial or insincere presentation, definitely something to be avoided at all costs.

Scripting captures the flow of messages. It also narrows its focus to the beginning, middle, and end of the presentation, eventually working its way into the various sections within each of those three major parts. Important to scripting, though, is the need for a message platform, the governing themes or anchors for your messages.

Overall, the script should reflect your presentation goals, including your objective, and it should be appropriate to your audience. It should also contain repeated references to the main messages, which are the governing ideas or themes of the presentation. Such references act as transitions or bridges, linking the presentation's main parts and sections to one another and, at the same time, creating a solid foundation of meaning for the prospective client.

Exhibit 11–2 highlights four script tips, which are elaborated on in the text that follows.

EXHIBIT 11–2   SCRIPT TIPS

☐ Decide on Governing Messages or Themes
☐ Unify and Coordinate Sections
☐ Think Beginning, Middle, and End
☐ Improve Writing Style

Decide on Governing Messages or Themes A 30-, 60-, or 90-minute presentation cannot contain only one message. There will be a range of information provided, and often it will span topics, such as creative and media. At the same time, you should strive to link the diverse topics or information to a few governing themes threaded throughout the presentation. The themes unify all that you say and show, and they serve to anchor the client's internal responses in a meaningful, easily understood context. The messages presented through the script attach themselves to that theme.

Unify and Coordinate Sections Your governing themes will help unify and coordinate the diverse sections of the presentation, but you will need to do more to achieve that result. Within each section, such as creative, media, and promotion, you should strive for consistency of format and structure.

☐ *Be consistent with the use of words and terms.* Consistency is an important goal of your storyboard as well, but consistency in the script means tightening the language so that you cut down on the amount of material the client is expected to decode or remember. For example, if your creative is introduced through objectives and strategies, then you may be inclined to introduce all of your media and promotion the same way. This consistency provides symmetry between the sections and makes it easier for the client to follow your presentation, even though you may be moving quickly from one part to another. By placing the objectives and strategies in a consistent order from section to section, you wouldn't use objectives to introduce the creative through objectives and then wait until the end of the media section to announce the media objectives.

In a similar way, you would keep your wording of terms consistent from one part to another. For example, if you use the word *objectives* in the creative part of the presentation, you wouldn't change it to *goals* in the media and promotion parts. All language would be consistent.

As you plan visuals, such as slides and charts, in the script, you should keep what is said about them consistent with what is portrayed on them. There is nothing wrong with saying aloud what is also shown on a slide. Indeed, repeating key words or terms from slide to slide or presentation section to section serves to unify and coordinate your presentation even more.

☐ *Use transitions.* Along with the consistency of wording and language within the different presentation sections, you should also use transitions to link the sections. For example, if your creative section emphasizes target market involvement in the ads through the use of pointed consumer benefits, then the bridge or transition to the next section may include a similar focus on involvement and benefits. You might say, for instance, "As involved as the audience will be with the creative appeals in our ads, they will be equally involved with the media we selected. Here's how."

As you can tell from this example, the wording has redirected the focus from creative to media, presumably the next section to be presented. As such, the wording acts as a bridge, linking one section to the next. And as you advance section to section, you would continue to use the same tactic. In this case, the use of involvement as a transition might even be considered the governing theme, once again threaded throughout the entire presentation. And it's important to note that its use helps the client more easily understand and grasp the main ideas or meanings of the presentation. In this respect, notice how your use of transitions, combined with your concentration on unifying and coordinating all the sections internally and within the presentation as a whole, serve to put the client first, with a genuine appreciation for what it is the client needs to know.

Think Beginning, Middle, and End On a larger plane than the individual sections, think of your presentation as having three distinct parts: a beginning, middle, and end. Obviously, each of these parts should be tied together, in much the same way that you would tie the sections of the presentation together. But here, you're dealing with larger blocks of the presentation, and each one should be controlled by different priorities.

☐ *The beginning.* The beginning and end are considered the most important parts of your presentation. Some professional presenters believe you should design the end of your presentation first, before the beginning. Others believe you should design the beginning first, before the end. Either way, you should know that these two parts represent the key to your presentation's overall success.

We will start with a look at your presentation's beginning, though, again, you could easily start by designing the end first. It is with your beginning that you either rivet the audience's attention on your presentation or you don't. If your beginning is slow, ponderous, self-consumed, uninvolving, uninviting, or unexciting, your presentation is in serious trouble. That's why you need to take pains to avoid these problems.

At the same time, given the importance of the beginning, you should consider how it relates and coordinates with your presentation goals, such as bonding with your audience or prospective client. From its beginning a good presentation accomplishes the following four results:

1. It grabs attention.
2. It previews the subject by introducing the main messages or themes.
3. It clarifies and emphasizes what's in it (the benefit) for the prospective client.
4. It establishes you as a credible source.

EXHIBIT 11–3   HOW TO THINK ABOUT THE BEGINNING

☐ Ask a Question
☐ State an Unusual Fact
☐ Give an Illustration, an Example, or a Story
☐ Give a Quote
☐ Tell What's Common between You and the Client
☐ Use Humor
☐ Tell Why You're Credible

By considering these results, you should have an idea about what to say or even what to show at the presentation's beginning. You know, for instance, that before the beginning blends into the presentation's middle or body, the audience should be riveted, clear about the presentation's focus and benefit, and confident in your credibility. The question is, How do you do achieve these desired results? The following techniques, highlighted in Exhibit 11–3, are some of the tried-and-true methods:

1. *Ask a question.* This rivets and focuses audience attention.
2. *State an unusual fact.* This raises eyebrows, especially when the fact is central in some way to the client's needs, wants, or problems.
3. *Give an illustration, an example, or a story.* This pulls your audience into the presentation.
4. *Give a quote.* And why not a quote directly from the prospective client or someone the client knows or respects?
5. *Tell what's common between you and the client.* If, for example, both your agency and the client were central to furthering a certain business practice or perspective, make that known.
6. *Use humor.* But be careful, because what's funny to one person is not necessarily funny to another. And especially be careful not to offend someone. For instance, you wouldn't be inclined to tell an ethnic joke as part of your beginning. Finally, make certain your humor relates to the client's general business or the situation at hand. There are books in local libraries that contain humorous anecdotes for all occasions and situations. They may be helpful to you.
7. *Tell why you're credible.* The key here is understatement and subtlety, not overstatement and boldness.

In conjunction with the words that address all or part of these seven possibilities, you should also consider the need for visual or mnemonic support in the introduction. It is well known that visual aids stimulate interest, provoke thought, and clarify main points. In addition, studies suggest that visual aids produce at least three times more learning than words alone. Generally our own inventory of knowledge increases dramatically when we see something rather than hear something. That's why strong consideration and solid strategic choice of visual aids are so important, especially given the crucial nature of your introduction.

☐ *The end.* Like your beginning, your presentation's end, or close, looms as significant, simply because it will be the last thing the prospective client will remember about you and your agency. This is why care needs to be taken with the ending. Overall, you should seek to reinforce the presentation's goals and to consolidate the main points around the governing themes that have acted as glue for your presentation. Exhibit 11–4 lists the following possible presentation endings:

1. *The happy ending.* End on a positive note. Be upbeat and optimistic.

2. *The funnel ending.* Here, you distill numerous points made in the presentation down to a few main points, often centered on the governing themes.

3. *The "we're here to help" ending.* Position yourself as a genuine, sincere, and constructive solution to the client's problem.

4. *The predict-the-future ending.* Make projections of how your proposal will have an impact on the client's future, obviously in a positive way.

5. *The quote ending.* Possibly picking up on a quote from your beginning, circle back to that quote at the end. You may expand on it, or you may introduce a new quote, but one that fits with the governing themes of your presentation or the original quote.

6. *The emotional ending.* You may want to emphasize the enthusiasm of your agency for the account.

Of course, you can adapt one or more of these types of endings to your particular purpose, but you should remember to consolidate ideas and reinforce presentation goals. Beyond that there is one other thing to remember, and it's extremely important: **Ask for the business!**

☐ *The middle.* The middle, or body, of your presentation is where your campaign proposal is fleshed out, clarified, and supported. To be effective this section requires data and information—sometimes a lot of it, which means that you run the risk of tedium in your presentation. It is here, in the middle, that the client is most likely to be distracted, bored, or otherwise disinterested, unless you make provisions otherwise. You can keep the client interested by embedding the script with elements to alleviate these potential problems. These elements are often meant to ease the flow of data or information, but they are also often meant to pique client interest and regain what may be flagging attention from the client. Considerations for your presentation's middle can be seen in Exhibit 11–5.

1. *Keep words and terms alike or similar.* Whether said or shown on slides or charts, the words should be consistent section to section.

2. *Tie concepts to the main messages or themes.* Tighten your script to make certain that diversions don't occur and that the messages or themes act as the anchors for the bulk of data and information.

3. *Embed minor diversions for strategic purposes.* For example, if you have flooded the client with a wealth of data or information, as may happen

---

EXHIBIT 11–4   HOW TO THINK ABOUT THE END

☐ The Happy Ending
☐ The Funnel Ending
☐ The "We're Here to Help" Ending
☐ The Predict-the-Future Ending
☐ The Quote Ending
☐ The Emotional Ending

---

in the media section of your presentation, take a breather and inject some humor or a brief anecdote. However, always make certain the humor or anecdote relates to the topic at hand.

4. *Get personal.* Again by way of a brief diversion when the data or information is potentially overwhelming, find choice spots to link yourself and your agency with the client's business. For instance, relate some personal information that may be of interest to the client, perhaps your own experiences in working on a similar account and how you learned the importance of a particular strategy or tactic.

5. *Simplify complex data or information.* Boil things down. Distill the complexity out of what you say so that you're able to say and show a few main points to be remembered, particularly as they reflect the consequences of the data or information.

6. *Summarize frequently.* Even though you're complementing the script with visuals and thus reinforcing memorability and learning, you will still need to summarize along the way. Be judicious about which points you summarize, giving preference to those points preceded by lengthy or complex data, information, or explanations.

7. *Use transitions.* Given that your presentation's middle represents the bulk of time and the diversity of sections, you should remember to use transitions to keep the presentation smooth and maintain the client's interest. Link sections by repeating key words or terms, whether you say them or they are shown as slides, transparencies, or boards. And make certain to tie the wording of the scripts for each section to your primary presentation goals.

Improve Writing Style Once you've made determinations about the structural integrity and content of the presentation's main parts and sections, you should concentrate on stylistic improvements in the script. Again, ideally the presenters should be actively involved in the writing, whether writing their parts themselves or overseeing someone else's writing. In either case, attention needs to be paid to the script's style. When two or several presenters write their own scripts, it is especially important to consider style because it should be consistent from section to section.

The following stylistic tips can be applied during the original script writing or later during revision and editing. They are shown in Exhibit 11–6.

EXHIBIT 11–5   HOW TO THINK ABOUT THE MIDDLE

☐ Keep Words and Terms Alike or Similar
☐ Tie Concepts to the Main Messages or Themes
☐ Embed Minor Diversions for Strategic Purposes
☐ Get Personal
☐ Simplify Complex Data or Information
☐ Summarize Frequently
☐ Use Transitions

---

1. *Write in a conversational tone.* Write like you talk, but with some elaborations at key points. This doesn't mean you should glut your script with jargon, but it does mean you should strive for a conversational realism and warmth in the style. For example, use contractions (it's, we're, you're, and the like) whenever possible, or tailor the script to the speaking style of the individual presenter, both in respect to word choice and sentence pacing. And avoid tongue-twisting language or hard-to-pronounce words.

2. *Use action verbs.* As most writers know, the action verb is a great friend. The quiet, helping verbs (is, was, am, were, and the like) are enemies. Action verbs breathe life into the writing and speaking. They stimulate the listener to imagine and construct scenes, emotions, and meanings. Because they suggest action, such verbs activate the listener's mind, urging the listener to participate and become involved. For example, consider the impact if you begin part of your script with action verbs, such as *imagine, think, remember, recall,* or *visualize.* Consider, as well, how your presentation will impact results when you use action verbs such as *propel, surge, advance,* or *stimulate.*

3. *Use transitions at points of potential dislocation in the script.* Transitions make the listening life easier for your prospective client. In using transitions, you guide and direct the client from old to new topics or slants in your presentation. In essence, transitions help the listener connect the diverse parts of your presentation. Common transitions include the following:

   ☐ To add something, use *also, in addition, moreover, furthermore,* or *similarly.*

   ☐ To support a preceding idea, use *for example, for instance,* or *to illustrate.*

   ☐ To inject contrast, use *however, nevertheless, despite,* or *on the contrary.*

   ☐ To summarize, use *in conclusion, therefore, consequently, in summary,* or *as a result.*

   Such transitions are commonly used as introductory words or phrases, but the best transitions, and those that assure your script of a tighter and more unified organization, make use of key terms and concepts repeated from one sentence or paragraph to another. For example, if the word *benefit* is central to the client's understanding of your creative proposal, then you

---

EXHIBIT 11–6   TIPS TO IMPROVE THE SCRIPT WRITING

☐ Write in a Conversational Tone
☐ Use Action Verbs
☐ Use Transitions at Key Points
☐ Vary the Sentence Pacing
☐ Write Short Paragraphs
☐ Explain and Repeat Difficult or Knotty Concepts

---

should repeat that word at key points in the creative section of the presentation.

4. *Vary the sentence pacing.* Sound out your script either by reading it aloud, humming it with breaks when sentences end, or both. If the reading aloud or humming results in a singular rhythmic drone of words, then changes are needed. To add variety to the rhythm, vary sentence lengths. If you have two long sentences together, for example, then think about following them with a short sentence or phrase, especially one that's loaded with meaning because it will be the one that will stand out for the listener. The key is not to write a script in which all of the sentences are of approximately equal length but to add variety of pacing to the sentences by varying their length.

5. Write *short paragraphs.* The presenter finds short paragraphs easier to remember and less intimidating. Short paragraphs also force the scriptwriter to focus on organization and embed more transitions.

6. *Explain and repeat difficult or knotty concepts.* Remember how your consideration of the presentation began, with the client foremost in your mind. The same is true as you think from the client's point of view when deciding what to explain or elaborate and what to repeat. If a certain concept seems particularly difficult or knotty for the client, elaborate it, perhaps by use of analogy or example. Repeat it as well, although you may want to consider repeating it in a different context, such as using a new or different analogy or example. Overall, when certain concepts are especially vital to the presentation's success, give strong consideration to their elaboration and repetition, both within their appropriate sections and within the beginning and end of the presentation.

You will hear and read different opinions about whether you should write every word of the script and whether you should memorize it word for word. A common suggestion is that you memorize only the beginning and end. Then rely on key words or concepts to guide you through the presentation's middle. Obviously, the choice is yours, depending on how you feel the most comfortable and confident. But be aware that complete memorization can break down and leave you speechless. Often it's better to have a firm grip on the flow of the presentation rather than every presentation word, with key terms and concepts memorized.

Structural Integrity

Your considerations of storyboard and script demand attention to the structural integrity of your presentation. You only have a certain amount of time to persuade your prospective client that your agency should be the agency of choice, so considerable pressure is on you to make the presentation a winning one. Consequently, you should view your presentation both as a whole and as parts and sections within the whole. The structural integrity of the presentation means you give the parts and sections strategic and pointed emphases, certain not to give all of them equal weight.

Think of your presentation time as valuable real estate. You must decide how to divide that real estate, knowing your success will rise or fall depending on your decisions. For example, how much time should you devote to the beginning? The middle? The end? To the research? The creative? The media? The promotion? The budget? In each of the national winning American Advertising Federation (AAF) student team presentations between the years 1990 and 1993, the creative section received the most time and was generally placed closer to the beginning of the presentation than to the end.

Tight organization in the presentation suggests your dedication, thoroughness, and desire to the prospective client. Although your presentation will no doubt contain light moments (and it should), make no mistake about the fact that this is serious business for the client. Large amounts of monies are at stake. And the client's reputation is on the line.

As you consider the steps and tips in planning out your presentation, you should be aware that your initial script treatment, including the storyboard and script, is ultimately refined over time. By revising both the storyboard and script to accommodate the needs and wants of the client and your presentation goals, you will find yourself deleting some ideas and including new ones. Eventually, you should merge the storyboard (the choreography and orchestration of the presentation) with the script, so that they are combined and reflect the precise flow of the presentation.

DESIGNING AND USING VISUALS

Several important studies suggest the importance of visual aids in persuading someone to act on something in a business presentation. A UCLA study, for instance, found that 90 percent of what an audience believes and trusts comes from visual and vocal signals, and only 7 percent comes from actual content. A study at the Wharton School of the University of Pennsylvania found that people were more likely to act on a recommendation when visual aids were involved than when they were not. And a University of Minnesota study found that 43 percent more persuasion occurs when visual aids are used than when they are not. Such studies legitimize for us what we may already know: Visual aids play an important role in presentations meant to persuade.

Of course, those involved in the AAF competition know the restrictions placed on use of visual aids. For the 1995 competition, for instance, teams were only allowed two carousel projectors and two front projection screens. The possibilities of a full multimedia presentation are limited as a result. Still, there is certainly ample opportunity for putting together a first-rate visual presentation. But to do so requires insight on your part about basic principles governing specific types of visuals. Suggestions for use of visuals follows.

PRINCIPLES FOR DESIGNING VISUALS

Principles of design governing visual aids are often consistent with principles of design governing other forms of visual expression, such as ads, poster art, or photography. Though certain principles might change as you move from boards to slides to transparencies, for instance, essentially the foundation of basic principles remains the same. You should become familiar with those principles, which are shown in Exhibit 11–7.

1. *Put words near the top.* Words near the top of the enclosure or page lift the viewers' eyes and are easier to read. So, with flip charts as well as slides or transparencies, place words or images in the top two-thirds of a page.

2. *Limit the number of words.* Don't expect the audience to read too much. Use only key words, especially when the visual field is crowded, as with lists or a number of items.

3. *Use uppercase and lowercase letters.* We're accustomed to reading words in uppercase and lowercase letters. To use both plays into our reading habits and makes the reading easier.

4. *Use large letters.* Don't be misled by how easy something is to read when you're right on top of it. Assume a safe distance from the visual field, and then judge how large the letters should be.

5. *Use sans serif fonts.* As with all parts of your presentation, your inclination should be to maintain consistency throughout, and this applies as well to your choice of typeface and size of lettering. Try to keep the lettering consistent with that used in your plans book. But remember, too, to display words without serifs in your visuals to make reading easier and reduce eye strain.

6. *Use a single orientation.* Choose either a landscape (horizontal) or portrait (vertical) format for your visuals, not both. As much as possible, you should stick with one orientation or format. Only when you cannot apply that orientation should you change.

7. *Use borders.* Borders frame the words or image and direct the eye to what you want seen or read. Often presentations include the name of the agency subtly within the border or as a break in the border, usually in the lower left of the visual field. The border used within slides or other visuals should be consistent and continuous throughout.

8. *Add color.* As with advertising generally, color adds considerable attention-grabbing potential to your visuals. Particularly with slides, color can be used to lead the viewer from one line of words down or up to another. One of the most common of all slide treatments is to highlight in color the item or line of words the presenter is addressing. A rule of thumb is not to use

---

EXHIBIT 11–7   PRINCIPLES FOR DESIGNING VISUALS

☐ Put Words near the Top
☐ Limit the Number of Words
☐ Use Uppercase and Lowercase Letters
☐ Use Large Letters
☐ Use Sans Serif Fonts
☐ Use a Single Orientation
☐ Use Borders
☐ Add Color
☐ Keep Visuals Simple and Singular
☐ Condense Sentences and Paragraphs to a Few Words
☐ Use Bullets and Graphic Flourishes
☐ Condense Complex Numbers into Pie Charts and Bar Graphs
☐ Reduce the Number of Curves on a Graph to No More than Three
☐ Use Charts, Graphs, and Diagrams Appropriately

---

more than three colors. You need to make strategic decisions about the actual choices of color. Contrast works best here, with an understanding that black type or images on a yellow ground shows up well for reading, although the yellow can be a visually nervous color. You may want to consider a cool-color background, such as blue, which tends to recede and not advance. Then your words or images would be a hot color, such as yellow, which tends to advance and not recede. And color choice like your other choices should be consistent and continuous throughout.

9. *Keep visuals simple and singular.* Don't be tempted to cram as much as humanly possible on one slide or flip chart. Instead, be tempted to limit what you include, trying to keep each visual enclosure limited to one core idea or concept, even though it may be elaborated with separate items beneath.

10. *Condense sentences and paragraphs to a few words.* Condensation is important in your visuals. Again, highlight key words or terms and don't feel obliged to abide by rules of grammar, particularly in respect to complete sentences.

11. *Use bullets and graphic flourishes.* Of course, consistency remains important here, so that a governing graphic, such as bullets or checkmarks, are used page to page or enclosure to enclosure.

12. *Condense complex numbers into pie charts and bar graphs.* Don't expect your audience to wrestle with numbers on a screen or page. Simplify those numbers so that they can be understood in a glance. And avoid pages or visual fields full of numbers.

13. *Reduce the number of curves on a graph to no more than three.* As with condensing numbers generally, you should limit the curves you show on each graph. Again, simplicity leads to clarity and comprehension here.

14. *Use charts, graphs, and diagrams appropriately.* Charts, graphs, and diagrams serve various functions. You should know them. Use bar charts to show comparisons. Use pie charts to show relationships of parts to a whole. Use graphs to show changes and trends. And use diagrams to show complex ideas or concepts.

These 14 principles for designing your visuals apply for most visual formats you'll use, whether they are boards, slides, flip charts, or transparencies. In essence, they're good basic rules of visual design. As you begin to consider the visual formats themselves, you may select them on the basis of other benefits or principles that follow. First, however, review some of the previous principles by looking at Figure 11–1. The exhibits are rough layouts reflecting certain key principles.

Selecting Visual Formats

The basic design principles previously listed apply with some minor variations to all formats of visuals. These visual formats offer you a good selection from which to choose. Each format has advantages and disadvantages. Some of the advantages are highlighted in Exhibit 11–8. The information that follows on the advantages of various formats is adapted from the Moriarity and Duncan book on advertising presentations.[2]

Comprehensives (comps) Create comps of actual ads and sales promotion materials. Despite the visual power of slides or transparencies, nothing quite beats comps where clients can lay their hands on the real thing. Comps can also be brought closer for inspection, creating involvement on the part of clients.

☐ Use acetate overlays for a glossy finish.
☐ Letter in headlines and subheads but not body copy, which should be neatly ruled.
☐ Present comps on boards, using an easel or wall background.
☐ If the viewing distance is 12 feet, the board size should be 18 inches and the type size approximately 60 points. If the viewing distance is 14 feet, the board size should be 24 inches and the type size approximately 72 points. If the viewing distance is 16 feet, the board size should be 36 inches and the type size 120 points.

Props Props can mean animate and inanimate objects, including people. Props convey a sense of real world and real life to the clients. They can be valuable for breaking down the walls between you and the client and for creating involvement. Your choice of props depends on your presentation goals and messages but might include the following:

☐ Member(s) of your target audience
☐ Miniversions of your client's product
☐ Technological additions, such as computers or telephones

FIGURE 11–1 KEY DESIGN PRINCIPLES

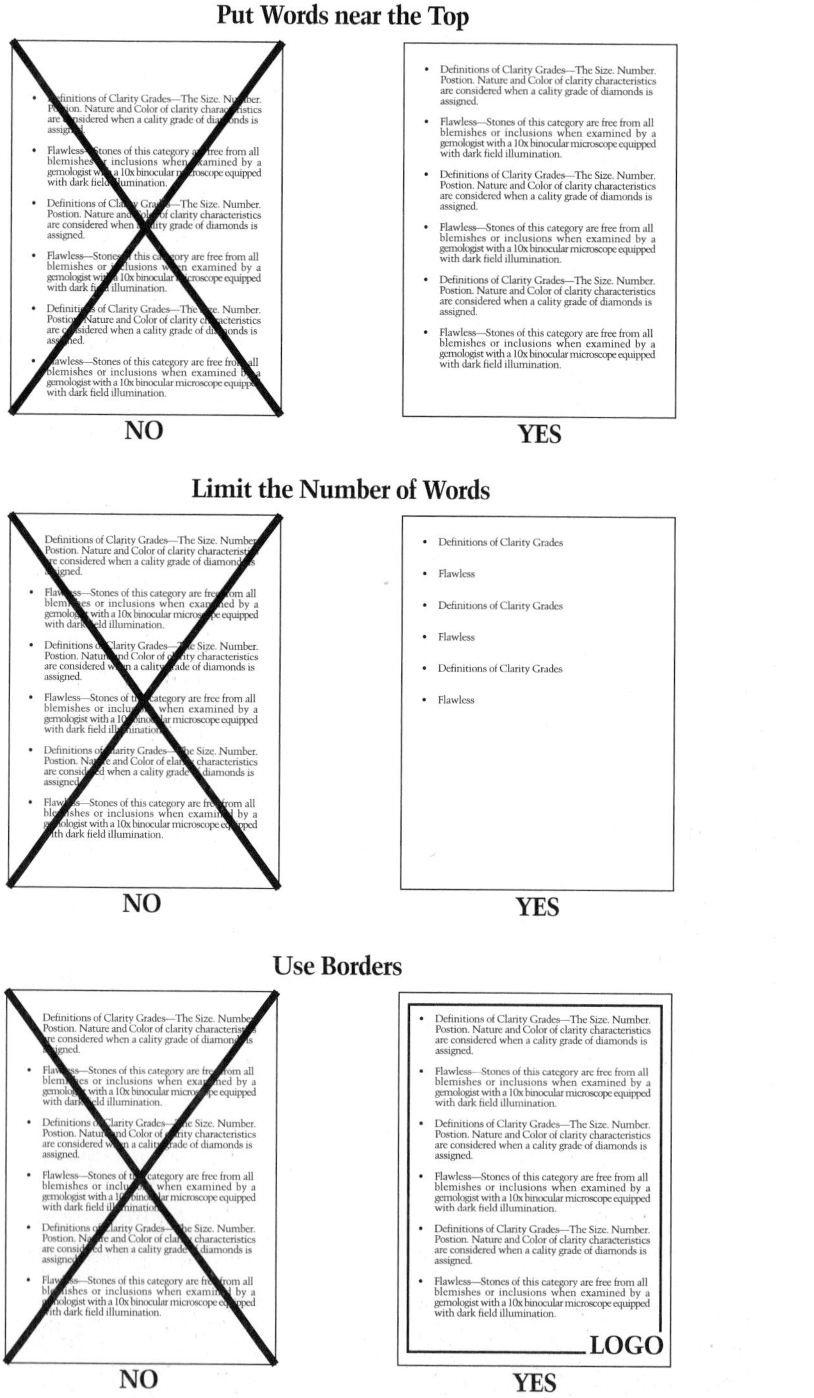

Put Words near the Top

NO

YES

Limit the Number of Words

NO

YES

Use Borders

NO

YES

EXHIBIT 11–8   FORMATS FOR VISUALS

☐ Comprehensives (comps)—Involving, Shorten the Psychological Distance, Personable
☐ Props—Real, Personable, Flexible, Eye-catching
☐ Layout Pads and Flip Charts—Flexible, Involving, Cost-efficient
☐ Slides—Slick, Sophisticated, Dramatic
☐ Transparencies—Portable, Flexible, Inexpensive

☐ Print or broadcast media samples
☐ Ad samples

Layout Pads and Flip Charts Layout pads and flip charts shorten the psychological distance between you and the client. You can write on them, handle them, and move them closer. They seem more real and exciting to the client, and they can be safe because they don't break down as some machinery tends to do at the most inopportune times.

☐ Use bold magic markers to write. Create contrast with the background.
☐ Don't be afraid to add or delete on the pads and charts as you present them.
☐ Lightly pencil in cues for yourself on the back of the pad or chart.
☐ Follow the size and lettering guidelines noted previously for comps.
☐ Staple a blank sheet behind each page so that bleeding or fuzzy lettering doesn't occur.
☐ If you're concerned about the quality of lettering or art, go to the Yellow Pages or other sources, such as children's coloring books, for traceable images. Clip-art books and rub-on letters are also helpful.

Slides Slides are the visual bread and butter of special presentations, such as the competitive student presentations sponsored by the American Advertising Federation. They, however, often make for somewhat stiff and formal presentations. So they're not always appropriate for professional or student class presentations. And they can be costly, even though they are becoming increasingly sophisticated and easy to do as the years advance. Computer software is commonly available to produce slides.

☐ Storyboard the slide presentation before presenting, using cards or layout paper.
☐ Be concerned about the film you use. It should match the lighting.
☐ Try to use a copy stand for shooting word or visual image slides.
☐ If your word slides are shot from 11-by-8½-inch paper mounted, make certain the type size is at least 24 points.

Transparencies Although often slighted, transparencies or overheads are easy to make, inexpensive, portable, flexible, and malleable, in that you can write on them while they're being shown. They also command audience attention.

EXHIBIT 11–9   SHOWING DATA

☐ Tables
☐ Line Graphs
☐ Bar Graphs
☐ Flowcharts
☐ Pie Charts
☐ Diagrams
☐ Pictographs

☐ Use frames for holding the transparencies in place.
☐ If you need to use tape, don't make it masking tape; instead use drafting tape.
☐ Make certain to label each of your transparencies.
☐ Lightly pencil in cues or tips for your presentation on the frame borders of each transparency. Such tips could remind you of script points or wording, or even remind you of your physical presence, such as remembering to smile or to hold your hands at your sides.

Remember that your visuals should complement your script. There should be tight syncopation between one and the other. Anything less signals unpreparedness and a loose organization of the presentation.

Visuals for Data and Numbers

A variety of visuals can help you convey data and numbers quickly to the client. All of them can be created on computer, then enlarged for display or photographed for slides. Moriarity and Duncan are the vital resources for information on the following types of depictions, which are noted in Exhibit 11–9 and then illustrated in Figure 11–2.[3]

1. *Tables.* Tables are good for showing extensive data and numbers, but those kinds of detail can be bad for your presentation. However, tables may serve your purpose if you intend to linger over the data and want to dwell on some of the subtleties within them. You can always highlight some of the data by using boldface, color, or some other technique.
2. *Line graphs.* Line graphs work on two dimensions, showing time horizontally and volume or amounts vertically. According to Moriarity and Duncan, line graphs are effective for showing trends or changes over time.[4]
3. *Bar graphs.* Bar graphs show units and are effective for making comparisons. They can also be shown three-dimensional, creating depth in the visual image and thus highlighting key comparisons.
4. *Flowcharts.* One of the most popular uses for a flowchart is to show media uses over time. But Moriarity and Duncan say other uses may include showing a decision-making process or the progress of a creative idea from inception to execution.[5]

FIGURE 11-2   DISPLAYS OF DATA

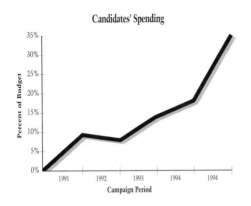

Line Graph

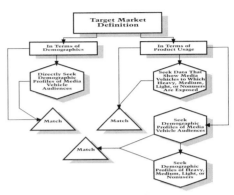

Flowchart

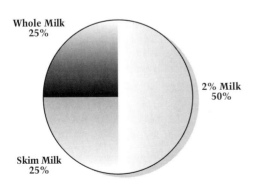

Bar Graph

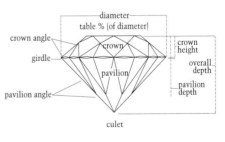

Pictograph

Pie Chart

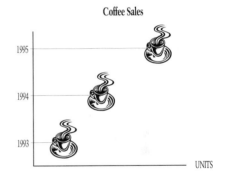

Diagram

CHAPTER 11 PRESENTATIONS: SELLING FACE TO FACE

5. *Pie charts.* Pie charts show the relationship of parts to a whole and are generally appropriate for showing percentages. Moriarity and Duncan advise not having more than six pieces in a pie chart.[6] An interesting and arresting visual adaptation of pie charts is to have them explode, separating one wedge or piece from the others.

6. *Diagrams.* Diagrams, often considered charts, are effective for showing how something works. They can also be used to show cross sections or even the flow of one element to another.

7. *Pictographs.* Pictographs lend visual excitement to data because the data are captured in an arresting visual field. For example, if you were pitching an automobile manufacturer, you might be inclined to show data inside the outline of a particular car model. Or if you were pitching a travel agency, you might be inclined to show data inside the hull of an airplane.

You can view the various representations of these methods for showing data in Figure 11–2. All of them can be generated by computer. And all simplify within a glance what could be complex data to explain in words.

MAKING THE PRESENTATION

A lot can go wrong with your presentation. Machinery can break down. The lighting may not be right. Heads can get in the way. All sorts of disastrous and sometimes unimaginable things can happen. It's your job to make sure they don't. The following tips are organized according to two primary concerns, your visual aids and you as a presenter. These tips should guide you in making certain everything goes according to plan. (See also Exhibit 11–10.)

PRESENTING VISUALS

1. *Don't block the audience's view.* Take pains to clear the viewing area before starting. Make certain about audience placement so that heads and arms don't obstruct the view.

2. *Direct audience attention.* The audience is watching you. If you cast your eyes to the visual, the audience's eyes will follow. At key words use a pointer, especially for emphasis.

3. *Round off big numbers.* Though you may be speaking of millions of dollars, don't be tempted to show the entire figure. Abbreviate and round off big numbers so that they are easily read and understood.

4. *Use circles, arrows, and other directional devices.* Help your audience direct its attention by use of such devices.

5. *Keep transparencies in a binder and slides in a carousel.* Avoid shuffling your visuals about or keeping them loose.

6. *Tape all cords to the floor.* No mystery lies here. The last thing you want is to fall flat on your face, literally.

EXHIBIT 11–10   CHECKLIST FOR PRESENTING VISUALS

☐ Don't Block the Audience's View
☐ Direct Audience Attention
☐ Round Off Big Numbers
☐ Use Circles, Arrows, and Other Directional Devices
☐ Keep Transparencies in a Binder and Slides in a Carousel
☐ Tape All Cords to the Floor
☐ Project Images Straight on the Screen
☐ Show and Remove Visuals at the Right Time
☐ Cover Parts of Some Visuals at Times
☐ Begin and End with Lights Full Bright
☐ Use Visuals to Help Other Parts of the Presentation
☐ Make Certain the First of Everything Is Ready
☐ Bring Spare Everything

---

7. *Project images straight on the screen.* Before you begin the presentation, make certain slides and transparencies are aligned properly on your screen.

8. *Show and remove visuals at the right time.* The general formula is to introduce, show, and comment. For example, introduce the slide, show it, and then comment on it. Don't be afraid to read word slides, transparencies, or flip charts verbatim, emphasizing or highlighting key words.

9. *Cover parts of some visuals at times.* You can cover all but one line on a flip chart or transparency, then show each of the next lines one at a time. You can highlight certain lines on slides with color. You can shoot slides so that one shot has one line on it, then the next has two lines on it, and so on, primarily for use with two or more projectors.

10. *Begin and end with lights full bright.* Don't upstage yourself with a visual. You take the lead and direct the audience, and when your use of a visual is over, take the lead again.

11. *Use visuals to help other parts of the presentation.* As mentioned previously, keep cues or notes on transparency frames or on flip charts (front or back). Write key words from the script lightly on the palm of your hand.

12. *Make certain the first of everything is in place and in working order.* Put an opaque slide as the first slide and make certain the carousel tray is ready at slide one. Stretch a rubber band around the flip-chart pad. Check the sound level if you're using audio. Clean fingerprints from overheads. Make certain of the focus on slide and overhead projectors.

13. *Bring spare everything.* Bring as much as you can to the presentation—not that you'll use it—that can bail you out of a jam: spare bulbs, binders, an extra carousel, extra flip-chart paper, magic markers, pens, a screwdriver or good Swiss army knife, and an extension cord. Make a checklist before

leaving for the presentation, and then check off the items as they're readied for transport.

Final Checking at the Site

Along with the previous checklist for presenting your visuals, you should also give consideration to the room where they will be presented. Consider all the room necessities for making a presentation: lights, temperature, chairs, and tables. You should make certain they are ready to operate for your benefit. (See Exhibit 11–11.)

1. K*now whom to call for help.* Wherever you are presenting, the owners or managers are certain to have staff people to help. Know who they are and how you can reach them in a hurry.
2. K*now the building's facilities and equipment.* Your presentation room will be in a building. You should know where certain facilities and operations are in that building. For example, know where the fire alarms are, where the restroom is, where the stairs and elevators are, and where the copy machine is.
3. *Check the equipment.* Do tests on slide projectors, easels, and overhead projectors.
4. *Check the room temperature.* Make sure it's not too hot and not too cold.
5. *Check chairs and tables for positioning and stability.* If allowed, arrange the chairs and tables to suit your presentation's purposes. For informality, avoid lecterns or tables separating you from the client. Leave room to stroll. Also check for broken or weakened chair and table legs.
6. *Check lighting and light switches.* Know how to work the dimmers, for instance.

You as Presenter

Many items on the previous two lists go beyond the use of your visuals. They begin to move into another sensitive area in your presentation's success: you. All the best visuals will come to nothing if you don't present well. The following tips can help you personally as a presenter. They are highlighted in Exhibit 11–12.

1. *Rehearse. Rehearse. Rehearse—as a team and alone.* Nothing will stop your jitters more than your own confidence that you know what to say and do during the presentation. And nothing builds that confidence like rehearsals. Organize dress rehearsals, the kind that simulate as closely as possible the environmental conditions of the presentation. As we discussed previously, some professionals advise not memorizing the script, others advise memorizing the first and last few minutes, and still others advise memorizing the opening lines to each section or part of the presentation.

EXHIBIT 11–11   FINAL CHECKING AT THE SITE

☐ Know Whom to Call for Help
☐ Know the Building's Facilities and Equipment
☐ Check the Equipment
☐ Check the Room Temperature
☐ Check Chairs and Tables
☐ Check Lighting and Light Switches

Remember, you can also help yourself by leaving cues in handy places around your presentation area and on your own hand.

By the time the presentation begins, you should be prepared to present it without note cards or sheets of paper. That's the ideal. Strive for it.

2. *Make eye contact.* This is one of the most important considerations in nonverbal communication. Look for one person first, then make eye contact every three to five seconds with different people. Or, make eye contact in a *Z* direction around the room.

3. *Smile.* A smile helps put your audience at ease. Draw happy faces on your notes or in secret places to remind you to smile.

4. *Don't drink before a presentation.* Drinking liquids may make things more difficult for you. If you need to refresh yourself and moisten your mouth or lips, use Vaseline or bite your tongue.

5. *Use talcum powder.* Talcum powder will help keep you dry. As the saying goes, "Never let them see you sweat."

6. *Face your audience head on.* This will suggest your confidence and sincerity.

7. *Practice gestures beforehand.* Make pointed gestures during highlights in the presentation. Don't cross your arms. Keep your arms and hands at your side, but use them for emphasis when the time is right.

8. *Vary the distance and movement in relationship to the audience.* Don't just stand in one place. Move around. Be comfortable. At key points shorten the distance, literally and figuratively, between you and the audience.

9. *Practice vocal tone, pitch, and pace variations.* Use pauses to emphasize key points. Deepen your pitch by speaking from the diaphragm. Punch certain words or concepts. Vary your volume and rate of speaking, so you speed up in some places and slow down in other places.

10. *Lean forward, not backward, and hold yourself erect.* By leaning forward you'll seem eager and enthusiastic. By holding yourself erect you'll seem confident and sure.

11. *Dress for the occasion.* Look professional.

EXHIBIT 11–12   TIPS FOR YOU AS THE PRESENTER

☐ Rehearse. Rehearse. Rehearse.
☐ Make Eye Contact
☐ Smile
☐ Don't Drink before Presentation
☐ Use Talcum Powder
☐ Face Your Audience Head On
☐ Practice Gestures Beforehand
☐ Vary Your Movement
☐ Practice Vocal Tone, Pitch, and Pace
☐ Lean Forward
☐ Dress for the Occasion

AAF PRESENTATIONS

The AAF sponsors more than 200 student chapters, which include more than 6,000 student members from across the United States. The National Student Advertising Competition (NSAC) is the cornerstone of AAF's involvement in higher education. Held annually, the AAF competition includes teams of students from 15 districts nationwide. The teams compete at district levels first, with the winners of each district then moving on to the national finals.

For decades AAF's NSAC has been the national testing ground for advertising student knowledge, insight, and creative problem solving applied in a real-world, corporate environment. Arguably the most prestigious, difficult, and comprehensive of all student advertising competitions, the NSAC features a different corporate sponsor each year. The sponsor presents competing teams with a case study, which acts as the foundation for the advertising and communications problem to be solved by the student teams.

Each team produces a 50-page plans book, creative and promotion exhibits, and a 20-minute presentation. The presentations are given before panels of distinguished judges from the sponsoring company and advertising and media firms. Counting for one-half of the total scoring from the judges, the presentation part of the competition takes on significant importance.

Over the years the presentations of the national winning teams have been videotaped by AAF and are available for review. Many professionals consider these winning presentations top drawer, reflecting the highest standards of advertising education professionalism. Over the years, too, certain schools have developed a legacy of successful participation in the competition. Although some schools come and go, others successfully participate year in and year out. Similarly, while some faculty advisors for the school teams come and go, others have developed their own legacy of advising teams.

We the authors asked four faculty members, with many years of experience advising successful AAF teams, to inform others about what makes a winning AAF presentation. The faculty members—Howard Cogan of Ithaca College (the

1993 national winner), John Murphy of the University of Texas at Austin, James Terhune of the University of Florida, and Jon Wardrip of the University of South Carolina—have advised a cumulative total of 40 teams. Their views, which follow, are in response to questions on planning, preparation, and production.

PLANNING

1. *What are the most important characteristics of a quality presentation and quality presenters?*

    According to Jon Wardrip, clarity, simplicity, and surprise are the three key characteristics of a quality presentation. Howard Cogan would agree, especially in respect to surprise. For Cogan, Ithaca teams try to "break the mold." A firm believer in presenting as an ad agency would present, Cogan advises his teams to depart from the traditional two-lectern/slide presentation. The 1993 national winning team from Ithaca, for example, used a truncated circle as a table directly in front of the judges. The presenters sat around the table, at times rising when they spoke and relying, for the most part, on an extensive look at and analysis of the creative and promotional executions.

    When it comes to the actual presenters, all of the advisors believe that those students who are quick on their feet, professional in appearance and manner, devoted throughout the teams' plans book and presentation efforts, and able to project enthusiasm stand a good chance of being selected as presenters.

2. *How many presenters are used, and how are they selected?*

    Generally, there were four to five presenters on each team, with alternates serving as understudies. John Murphy arranged auditions for any student in the advertising campaigns class who was interested in becoming a presenter. Class members judged the auditioning students by their auditions, factoring in their devotion and work effort on the team, and voted for them by rank. For James Terhune, a faculty panel helped evaluate those auditioning.

    The auditions generally included reading or memorization of part of the plans book. Each audition lasted three to five minutes. Clearly, the advisors involved students fully in the selection process.

3. *How is the order of presenters arranged?*

    The order of presenters varied, ranging from having the strongest presenter open and close the presentation to having the various sections of the presentation (creative, media, and the like) dictate who will present when.

4. *When do teams begin planning the presentation?*

    The timeline for the competition allows little time for presentation preparation overall. Generally, the presentation is made approximately two weeks after the plans book is completed and sent in, a formidable task that chews up a great deal of time during the spring semester of each year. However, the advisors typically make certain that photos and slides for possible use during the presentation are taken during the entire duration of work on the plans book. Photos and slides of people, media, and research activities serve as examples. For all the advisors, the presentation planning began in earnest the very next day after the plans book was sent in.

PREPARATION

1. *What are the stages of preparation?*

The stages of preparation varied for each of the teams, but a common denominator to all was the storyboarding or scripting of basic concepts and presentation sections. South Carolina has scripted the presentation on a blackboard, indicating the sequencing of information to be told and shown. For Texas, the presentation has been an extraction of the plans book. Following decisions about how much time to devote to each section, decisions are then made about slide content, props, and staging (choreography).

In some cases the presenters have written their own scripts, in keeping with the need for a presenter to feel comfortable with his or her own words. At South Carolina, for example, the presenters have written their own scripts and then been critiqued by other team members based on an outline of script content derived from the collective wisdom of the team members. In this way, the presenter's style is his or her own, but the content is certain to be precise and reflective of the entire team's focus. This approach also keeps all team members involved and gives them a sense of importance. For all teams, the production of slides and photos took place from the beginning to the end of the teams' involvement in the competition.

At the rehearsal stage, the advisors sought to have students memorize their scripts. At Ithaca, the presenters were encouraged not to use note cards. At Florida, the students gave up to 20 mock presentations prior to the final presentation at the competition because they believed repetition keyed memorization. Florida faculty also offered suggestions by observing at least one of the presentations. At Texas, the teams presented to other classes as well as team members. At South Carolina, the teams presented to nonpresenters who acted as the agency review board.

In overview, the preparation process included the following: scripting, script revision and editing (often many times in a kind of narrowing or funneling process), simultaneous slide content and other audiovisual decisions, rehearsals (again, many times), and final presentation. The advisors tried to involve as many students as possible in both the presentation planning and preparation.

2. *Within the presentation, how much time and emphasis are devoted to the various sections?*

At Texas and Ithaca, the presentation's structure has been heavily influenced by the judges' score sheet. At the same time, the general rule of thumb was that the creative part of the presentation carried the sales load. For example, a review of the national winning team presentations from 1990 through 1993, show that each of the presentations devoted significantly more time to creative than to any other section of the presentation. Often other primary considerations, such as media or promotion, were embedded into the creative sections of the presentations, which seemed in most instances to dominate the presentations.

PRODUCTION

1. *How do the teams produce audiovisual materials?*

   With AAF restrictions on the production of audiovisual components of the presentation, the teams tended to "stay in house," often relying on team members or students with special expertise in the production area. For example, at Florida, photojournalism students have been instrumental in producing slides and commercials. At Ithaca, corporate communications and photography students serve the same function.

2. *What is done to unify the presentation?*

   Besides precise coordination of script and slides or other audiovisual aids, always the result of constant practice and rehearsal, the teams made certain the presentations reflected the plans books. Throughout presentation planning and preparation, the plans book stayed front and center as a resource and guide. Additionally, the teams tended to stay focused on the assignment as thoroughly outlined and described in the case studies. Remember that as time passes and the work on the plans book and presentation gets fast paced and frenzied, it's easy to lose sight of the original task or assignment. Always that task or assignment should remain front and center.

   The teams tightened their presentations by using common graphics and graphic flourishes on slides. For example, team (agency) logos were consistent and continuous on all slides. Similarly, identifiable themes and patterns of expression threaded their way throughout the presentations.

3. *What needs to be done just prior to arrival at the competition site?*

   Often, the presentation teams brought their own equipment (such as slide projectors) to the competition site in order to rehearse before the presentation. They also tended to make advance arrangements before their arrival with the host hotel for conference rooms and equipment.

   The teams arrived a day early in order to orient themselves to the area, the hotel, and the competition environment. The practice at South Carolina, for instance, has been that the students relaxed, toured, and viewed the competition site two days before the presentation. The day before the presentation, they rehearsed. On the day of the presentation, team members enjoyed breakfast together. For Jon Wardrip, the advisor, this is similar to having them survey the playing field two days before the competition and then scrimmage the day before so that there are no surprises on competition or game day.

   This type of tradition tends to pervade the teams from the four schools. For example, at Ithaca on the day of the presentation the nonpresenters are not allowed to talk to the presenters about how other teams are doing. Howard Cogan and his wife, Helen, also take the students out to dinner as a matter of tradition. At Florida, every attempt has been made to have all team members travel to the district competition. According to the Florida advisor, James Terhune, this allowed "everybody to share in the experience."

EXHIBIT 11–13   **TIPS FROM AAF ADVISORS**

☐ Begin Immediately after Plans Book Is Completed
☐ Consider "Breaking the Mold"
☐ Take Slides and Photos throughout Work on Plans Book and Presentation
☐ Involve Students with Special Expertise (Slides, Photography)
☐ Involve All Team Members at All Stages of Planning and Preparation
☐ Strive for Unity in the Presentation through Consistent Graphics and Words
☐ Script or Storyboard Basic Concepts and Sections
☐ Involve Presenters in the Writing of the Script
☐ Put on Rehearsal Presentations to Other Groups (Classes, Faculty)
☐ Plan a Strategy for What Happens at the Competition Site
☐ Rehearse. Rehearse. Rehearse.

For all the teams, rehearsal at the competition site was a must, whether it was in a hotel room or a separate conference room. And though the traditions may change from one school to another, they exist in full force.

Each AAF competition team develops its own routines about how best to meet the rigorous demands of putting a presentation together. For these four successful advisors, the competition represents a highlight for advertising students. With many years of team competition experience, the advisors' main insights on primary concerns and practices for successful teams tend to cluster together, regardless of the year, the team composite, or the sponsoring company. Those insights in the form of tips are shown in Exhibit 11–13.

The authors of this book thank the advisors for their time in sharing their competition team experiences. Each advisor seemed genuinely committed to the students and their academic, personal, and professional growth through the competition. And each advisor was more than willing to share "war stories" of the competition experience. One story, from Professor Howard Cogan of Ithaca, stands out as symbolic of the commitment, intensity, and purpose of the competition.

After a national competition when the Ithaca team did not win the first-place award, Professor Cogan walked through the hotel lobby and saw one of his prize students sobbing uncontrollably off to the side. The student was slumped on a bench and hid his face in his hands. Feeling the student's pain and sadness himself, Professor Cogan walked to the student (we'll call him John) and put a sympathetic hand on his shoulder.

"John," he said. "Don't be so sad. We're fourth in the whole country. That's great. That's terrific. The best programs are here, and we finished close to the top. Don't feel bad about that."

John turned, gathered himself, and said, "That's not what I'm feeling bad about."

"What then?" Professor Cogan asked.

"I'm feeling bad that we just lost a multimillion dollar account," John said without hesitating.

In a nutshell of a story and for many who know of the AAF competition, that's what it's all about.

ENDNOTES

[1] Tom Duncan and Sandra Moriarity, *How to Create and Deliver Winning Advertising Presentations* (Lincolnwood, Ill.: NTC Business Books, 1989), 45–48.

[2] Duncan and Moriarity, 57–60.

[3] Duncan and Moriarity, 61–73.

[4] Duncan and Moriarity, 68.

[5] Duncan and Moriarity, 64–65.

[6] Duncan and Moriarity, 67.

Howard Cogan and the 1993
National Champion Ithaca
College Team

Jon Wardrip and the
University of South
Carolina team

James Terhune and the
1991 Universtiy of
Florida team

John Murphy and the 10th
District winner from the
University of Texas at Austin

INDEX